——— THE PENGUIN ———
HISTORY OF AUSTRALIA

John Molony has written a history for the people which is an enticing and comprehensive blend of social, political, cultural, economic and environmental history. He includes those so often neglected by historians, the 'ordinary' Australians whose class, race, age or gender rendered them 'unimportant'.

Here is the story of the making of a nation, the slow and painful process by which a people have come to identify with each other and with the land they inhabit. It tells of strangers and of the strange land which they encountered, confronted and, ultimately, came to understand and respect.

While Molony deals with the strength of the British heritage, he is keenly aware of the richness resulting from its blending with other cultures. Although Molony is not blind to the failures and follies which followed the white peopling of Australia his thoughtful and timely history is an acknowledgement of the considerable achievements of 200 years.

John Molony was born in Melbourne in 1927. Married, with four children, he now lives in Canberra where he is Manning Clark Professor of Australian History at the Australian National University. Among his interests is assisting in the resettlement of Asian refugees. His great love is Australian football.

For my pioneering grandparents
Thomas Molony and Catherine Melican
Michael McInerney and Mary Neylon

By the same author

The Roman Mould of the Australian Catholic Church (1969)
An Architect of Freedom (1973)
The Emergence of Political Catholicism in Italy (1977)
I Am Ned Kelly (1980)
Eureka (1984)

THE PENGUIN
HISTORY OF AUSTRALIA
JOHN MOLONY

PENGUIN BOOKS

Penguin Books Australia Ltd
487 Maroondah Highway, PO Box 257
Ringwood, Victoria 3134, Australia
Penguin Books Ltd
Harmondsworth, Middlesex, England
Viking Penguin Inc.
40 West 23rd Street, New York, N.Y. 10010, U.S.A.
Penguin Books Canada Limited
2801 John Street, Markham, Ontario, Canada L3R 1B4
Penguin Books (N.Z.) Ltd
182–190 Wairau Road, Auckland 10, New Zealand

First published by Viking 1987
as *The Penguin Bicentennial History of Australia*
Reprinted 1988
First published in paperback by Penguin Books Australia Ltd 1988
Copyright © John Molony, 1987

Produced by Viking O'Neil
56 Claremont Street, South Yarra, Victoria 3141, Australia
A division of Penguin Books Australia Ltd

Typeset in Baskerville by Abb-typesetting Pty Ltd, Collingwood, Victoria
Printed by Australian Print Group, Maryborough, Victoria

National Library of Australia
Cataloguing-in-Publication data

Molony, John N. (John Neylon), 1927–   .
   The Penguin history of Australia.

   Bibliography.
   Includes index.
   ISBN 0 14 009739 2.

   1. Australia — History. 2. Australia — Social
   conditions. I. Title. II. Title : The Penguin
   bicentennial history of Australia. III. Title :
   History of Australia.

994

 This publication has been partially funded by
The Australian Bicentennial Authority to celebrate
Australia's Bicentenary in 1988.

Title page illustration: 'View of the settlement on
Sydney Cove', from Hunter's *Historical Journal*.
(Courtesy of Hordern House, Sydney)

Acknowledgements

The Australian Bicentennial Authority invited me to write this general history of Australia. I am grateful to it for this opportunity and also to the Australian National University, which released me from teaching during the writing, and to the staff of the Chifley Library at the University, who made me welcome in their midst.

Given the eighteen months I had to write the manuscript, it was rarely possible for me to turn to primary sources in libraries and archives. In most cases, I had to rely on the work of other historians of the Australian past, and it is on their work that this book is mainly based. Their imprint is stamped on its every page and in those instances where I have departed from their interpretations I have done so with respect. I salute and thank my profession.

My academic home, the History Department of the Faculties at the Australian National University, welcomed me almost daily and its members encouraged and assisted me in every possible way. I hope that this book will worthily take its place in the long list of publications that has come from that department.

Many people helped me in ways that mere thanks cannot repay. My gratitude goes to David Bennett, Maurice Cowan, Phillip Crotty, Frank Dogan, James Gibbney, Ian Hancock, John Merritt, Damien Molony, Kevin Peoples and Douglas Webster. I claim all of them as friends.

Justice demands that I add the name of Gerry Walsh who has inspired me for over twenty years by his love for and profound knowledge of Australian history. This book is only a token repayment of my debt to him.

Contents

All historical references to weights and measures are given in the way they were originally expressed, in imperial. General references and references to weights and measures made after the change-over to a metric system in 1966 are in metric.

inch	=	25.4 millimetres
foot	=	30.5 centimetres
yard	=	0.914 metres
mile	=	1.61 kilometres
ounce	=	28.3 grams
pound	=	454 grams
ton	=	1.02 tonnes
acre	=	0.405 hectares
square mile	=	2.59 square kilometres
gallon	=	4.55 litres

Introduction

The making of a nation is a slow and painful process. It needs a people who identify with each other and with the land they inhabit. Australia began that process on 26 January 1788. The beginning was an unhappy one for all who took part in it whether free or felon. Those who landed at Sydney Cove on that first day of white settlement knew nothing of the future. For the majority, because of their pasts, the future would always bear a convict taint. The wardens of the open-air prison expected to do their task and go home. None could have foreseen the pull the land would exert.

Vast in its spaces, forbidding in its wilderness, inviting in its coastal beauty, the land lay before the newcomers. They had to grapple with it and come to terms with its harshness because it gave no quarter. In time their flocks, herds and crops spread across the land until it gave way to desert. In time the strange became the familiar and ultimately the loved. The prisoners, who came with thought only of escape, remained to become one with the land. Many of those who came to do their job and leave, stayed because the land had also claimed them as her own.

Two hundred years have passed since that first day of arrival. This book attempts to tell the story of those years. My brief was to write of the land and its white peopling. So few of those who came or were born here, who lived here, loved here and rested their bones in the soil of the land are named in these pages. So little of what they did is spoken of but all of it, and all of them, is here. Australia today bears them in herself.

Another people are glimpsed fleetingly in these pages. It was not my privilege to write their history, because I am not one of them. My people have taken enough from them. It is not for me or any new Australian to beg those who were here, who were at one with their land for so long before us, to join now in being one people. That gift lies in their keeping. It is not enough but it is something to say to each of them, the living and the dead, 'Sorry mate'. Reconciliation must be our first aspiration as we celebrate the Bicentenary.

CHAPTER ONE

Sydney Cove

High summer saw a fleet of eleven ships take up moorings at a small cove in a noble and extensive harbour on the eastern coastline of the southern continent. A few, dark-skinned people of the Cadigal band, whose ancestral home that place had been for age upon age, watched closely from nearby scrub. The date was 26 January 1788 and the newcomers called the cove after an English public servant named Sydney. To the Cadigal people such things meant nothing. Their reaction to these monstrous, white-winged vessels with their unknown cargo was to stay quietly in the bush. The modern history of the world's oldest continent had commenced with the coming of a new people. The Aborigines and the land with which they formed a unity were, for good and for ill, the setting of one of the last significant developments of human expansion on earth.

The British decision to send Governor Arthur Phillip to found a penal settlement at Botany Bay, a few miles south of Sydney Cove, was made with breathtaking nonchalance and almost criminal negligence. The ancient European dream of a great southland and the later voyages of Spaniards, Dutch and Portuguese to its coasts was of small moment to the men in the British government. What counted to them was that their own James Cook had claimed possession of its eastern portion in 1770 and named it New South Wales. Cook had done so aware that between 1606 and 1619 the Dutch had charted the north-east and west of the continent and that Abel Tasman had touched the south-east portion in 1642. He named it Van Diemen's Land, but he was unaware that it was cut off from the mainland by a strait. In 1644 Tasman went down part of the west coast and called that portion of the continent New Holland. Later, in

1699, an English adventurer, William Dampier had landed on the north-west coast and found it arid and barren with native inhabitants who seemed to him the most miserable beings on earth.

Cook did not know that eighty years before the Dutch voyages the west coast had been visited by Portuguese and that between 1521 and 1528 the east coast had probably also been charted by the Portuguese and Spaniards. Before that time there had been constant contact between the people of Cape York Peninsula and Papua through the islands of Torres Strait and the arrival of the native dog, the dingo, about 4,000 years ago clearly indicated outside contacts. There were cultural and trading links across Torres Strait and some genetic mixing so that Papuan cults, ideas and customs stretched right down the coast of Cape York Peninsula.

Furthermore, since the early 1700s, sailors from Macassar in the Celebes had come annually to collect and preserve seaslugs, called tre-pang, along the Arnhem Land, Carpentaria and Kimberley coasts. Theirs was an established industry, the produce of which they sold to the Chinese. During their visits they were in regular contact with the local people and passed some customs and words into the language of the natives. At times many Aborigines accompanied the Macassans on their praus to their homeland, and there were relations between the Macassan visitors and Aboriginal women. The annual contact influenced Arnhem Land society in the same way, but to a lesser degree, than that between the people of Cape York and Papua had done.

Cook was thus doing nothing new in sighting the continent which was certainly not unknown. The importance of his voyage lay in the fact that he had named and claimed it for his king. It was of consequence too that he had done so without 'the Consent of the Natives' which he had been expressly ordered to obtain. He had not judged this formality necessary, as it seemed to him that those he encountered made no use of the land and therefore did not own it. He and his party had been impressed with the novel flora and fauna, the apparent fertility of the soil and the healthi-ness of the climate, although they never moved far from Botany Bay itself and saw little else of the continent, except during the seven weeks spent repairing the *Endeavour* after it ran onto coral in the Great Barrier Reef. It was of some importance that Cook was able to state that Norfolk Island, a thousand miles away in the Pacific, possessed pines and flax both of which the English, as a naval power, always needed.

In London, after 1771, it was well known that land in vast abundance and seemingly lying idle was available in New South Wales. Furthermore it was sufficiently remote from England to be a suitable location for an open-air prison. The problem of what to do with English prisoners demanded action because the growth in the number of persons being sentenced had resulted in crowded and unhealthy gaols, particularly those in the old hulks of vessels moored on the Thames. As well as being expensive to maintain, these prisons posed serious consequences in the form of moral and physical contagion to the London populace. Moreover, since the American War of Independence in 1776, it was no longer possible to cast off the unwanted refuse of British society by sending convicts to America, and an experiment in 1775 in West Africa had resulted in the death or desertion of eighty percent of the 746 sent there. Another destination to which convicts could be transported had to be found.

In 1779 Joseph Banks, who had been the botanist on Cook's expedition, suggested Botany Bay as a suitable site for a settlement, and in 1783 James Matra, also a member of the expedition, recommended it as a colony for those Americans who had remained loyal to Britain in the War of Independence. Matra stressed that the flax plant, used for making sails, could be grown at Botany Bay, that a trading post with China, Russia and Japan could be established there and that in time it could become a site for a naval base, while its very occupation would be of strategic use in keeping the French and Dutch at bay. The idea of settling American royalists was rejected, but the Pitt government chose Botany Bay as a site for a penal colony. The choice was made even though no one had visited the place for sixteen years and, on his return to England in 1771, Banks had admitted that it was the barrenest region he had ever seen, despite its botanical attractions.

Suggestions were put forward that Botany Bay be further investigated before committing a large group of men and women to exile there, but to no avail. The lack of seriousness about the whole affair was further illustrated by the choice of Phillip as commander. Part-sailor, part-farmer, Phillip, though in the long term an admirable choice, was given a job no one else sought nor those in control considered of any real significance. Indeed, the lack of planning was finally illustrated by Lord Sydney's wish that the First Fleet sail in December 1786. This would have allowed only a few months to prepare for the voyage and the later settlement, but ample time it seemed to dispose of a body of troublesome wretches. If good came of the venture, so much the better.

Largely due to Phillip's initiative in making as thorough preparations as possible, the Fleet did not sail from Portsmouth till 13 May 1787. It left with scarcely a mention of its departure in the newspapers and to the undoubted relief of the scheme's initiators. The two naval vessels, *Sirius* and *Supply*, and the nine merchantmen converted to carry the convicts

On 6 May 1770, Cook gave the name Sting-Ray Harbour to a bay on the south-east coast of Australia where two large sting-rays were caught. His Journal records that he changed it to Botany Bay given the 'great quantity' of botanical specimens collected there by Banks and Solander.

called at Rio de Janiero in August and Cape Town in October, procuring fresh supplies at both and, at the latter, 500 animals of various kinds were taken aboard. It was some comfort for all to know that, given the vast distance of about fifteen thousand miles between Botany Bay and home, some form of relief in necessity would be available from the Dutch at Batavia or at the Cape. The passage of 252 days was remarkably successful with only forty-eight deaths since embarkation and the vessels of the Fleet were never separated by accident from each other for even a single hour. From the quarterdeck of the armed sloop *Supply* Phillip led his fleet with 1030 people aboard, of whom 736 were convicts, into Botany Bay on 18 January 1788. As they had less than two years of basic supplies, the need to settle quickly and begin the cultivation of the land was apparent to the Governor and his subordinates.

The earlier, favourable opinions given on Botany Bay seemed fantastic to Phillip and his officers in the light of the reality they encountered. Apart from the apparent infertility of the soil, the most compelling negative aspect of the location for a settlement was the lack of fresh water, which indicated the need to move elsewhere. A few miles to the north of Botany Bay lay Port Jackson which Cook had named but not entered in 1770. Phillip investigated its possibilities as a site and returned with the good news that it had the 'finest Harbour in the world' and that a stream provided fresh water at a cove so deep that the fleet could easily and safely unload its cargo.

Botany Bay was quickly discarded as the site for the settlement but its name became part of the historical legend. Botany Bay was the chosen place for the felon, the outcast, the offscourings of British society. To Phillip it had no value as a site, although he regularly sent detachments back there in the following months as if he were afraid to accept that Cook and Banks had been so mistaken in their judgement of the place. Meanwhile, men, women and children, the convicts and the free, depended upon Phillip for their lives. Their confidence in the Governor was not misplaced.

As preparations were being made to leave Botany Bay on 26 January, everyone's attention was diverted to the arrival of two frigates flying the golden lilies on a white field of the flag of France. Under the command of Jean-François de Galaup, Comte de la Pérouse, they carried a French exploratory and scientific expedition. The subsequent, fleeting contact between the English and French was harmonious. Both bore with them the long traditions of their past, and in the case of the English some vestiges of those traditions remained intact despite the fact that they had come to found a penal colony. The idea of parliamentary democracy, the role of the monarchy and traces of experiments in republicanism arrived together with the Authorized Version of the Bible, the Book of Common Prayer, philosophical and political theories and the thought of Hobbes, Locke, Hume and Berkeley. Shakespeare and Milton were there with them, as were Francis Bacon and Isaac Newton, with the first steps of modern science and technology, and the high standards of the Royal Society.

In the persons of those British officers, as well as in the sailors and convicts, some of this past was subsumed and in various ways it was to pass on, filtered through the strands of a penal society, to the generations of the future. At this lonely outpost in the Pacific all rivalries between the French and English, whether economic or military, were set aside as was the division between Protestant and Catholic. The Protestant religion was represented in the person of Reverend Richard Johnson, Anglican chaplain to the First Fleet, while Father Louis le Receveur, Franciscan friar, man of letters and scientist with the French, personified the Catholic. Le Receveur died and was buried at Botany Bay three weeks later — almost symbolic of the early fragility of the Catholic faith in the new land. Johnson lived on to help affirm the predominance, by convention at least, of his own.

On the evening of 26 January, musket volleys were fired and toasts to the success of the new colony drunk as the Fleet settled in at Sydney Cove. Those first weeks saw feverish activity, highlighted by festivities approaching a sexual orgy when the 548 male convicts welcomed the 188 women convicts ashore during a violent thunderstorm on the evening of 6 February. Other celebrations took place when the British form of government in the shape of a military despotism was officially set up on the following day. All white persons, of whom more than two-thirds were in bondage, were assembled. The youngest convict was John Hudson, aged nine, who had been given seven years' transportation for stealing, and the oldest, a woman of eighty-two, Dorothy Handland, who had been convicted of housebreaking. She hanged herself from a gum tree a year later. Two-thirds of the convicts had been sentenced for minor theft and their average age was under thirty. Apart from the English and Scottish the main nationalities were black and white Americans, Germans and Norwegians, while the Jews were a significant religious group.

By unfamiliar sounds and sights, birds, trees and the clear blue of the sky, all were reminded that they were far from home — a home which most could never hope to see again. The Act of Parliament founding the colony together with Phillip's commission as Governor was read, and Phillip made a speech exhorting the convicts to industry, decency and righteousness. In the following week fourteen marriages were solemnized amongst the convicts, thus planting the seeds of a new, white society in assuredly unpromising soil as the motives of many of the contracting parties were based on the false notion that marriage would ensure better rations and other favours from Phillip.

Shelter was a paramount necessity, as well as fresh water although fine weather was an advantage. There was the occasional torrential downpour but, as it was summer, the sun soon shone again and spirits lifted. Only a small group of carpenters could be found amongst the sailors and convicts, and Phillip himself had to lodge in a canvas structure which let in rain and wind. Most of the cattle which survived the voyage soon disappeared into the bush and, in September, the last remaining cow was slaughtered for food. The sheep, pigs and poultry fared better as they stayed about the settlement, but six months later none remained except for one sheep. No plough was available to till the soil and no one possessed satisfactory expertise for cultivating a place where even the seasons were unfamiliar.

Above all it was the land itself that daunted them for its soils were thin, sandy or rocky, which bent their picks and hoes, its vegetation strange, and its trees generally resistant to carpentry except for the abundance of cabbage-tree palms that were growing near the small creek upon which everyone depended for water. It became known as the Tank Stream after a large tank was cut out of sandstone in its centre to hold the water. There about the Cove, the little settlement could only achieve its primary objective of existing, with the occasional bird or fish to vary the diet of salt meat, while bread became so scarce that guests brought their own supply when they dined at an officer's table, including Phillip's. In July all but two of the convict ships sailed for home, and in November everyone watched with heavy hearts as the others, the *Golden Grove* and the *Fishburn*, slipped out of sight through the Heads. By the end of the year, most of the officials were convinced that the whole experiment had been a disaster and were hoping that common sense would prevail in London and that Sydney Cove would be closed and an end put to the settlement in New South Wales.

In those very early days, Phillip, acting according to his instructions and his own benevolent disposition, had insisted upon cordial relations being established with the Aboriginal inhabitants, commonly called natives or Indians, who numbered about 2,500 in the Sydney region and who spoke three major languages. The Governor had been impressed by their behaviour. Indeed, the upright bearing of a group of them at a cove on the harbour had led him to give it the name 'Manly' and he took no

Arthur Phillip Esq.
Captain General & Commander in Chief in & over
the Territory of New South Wales.

Arthur Phillip was forty-nine when he arrived in Australia as the first Governor. Serious of mien and character, he was in ill-health when he left for home in 1792 and took four years to recover. He married twice but had no children.

retribution when he was later speared at the same spot by an Aborigine. As time went by, two things became apparent to the Aborigines. First their visitors were clearly bent upon permanent residence and secondly there were those amongst the whites who did not scruple to take, by stealth or force, any of the natives' possessions which took their fancy including canoes, spears, shields and fishing lines.

The fact that these objects were essential to the survival of the Aborigines was accepted by Phillip, who issued fruitless instructions forbidding the whites to appropriate them. The Aborigines themselves retaliated by killing several convicts and stealing their shovels, spades and pick-axes. Finally the arrival of the whites was followed within a year by a virulent outbreak of smallpox which decimated and eventually killed at least half of the local blacks. Such a coincidence could scarcely escape the notice of the Aborigines, whom most observers credited with considerable intelligence.

Phillip had been told that his role was to govern the whole eastern portion of New Holland. No one knew for certain whether the east formed a whole with the west, because there was still the possibility that a sea divided the continent. It was nevertheless taken for granted that a vast tract of land was open and free for the taking, because the Aborigines did not seem to possess it. To the whites, possession meant personal ownership and consequent use, normally by agriculture. Furthermore in those first encounters the Aborigines did not appear to dispute possession of the land except during one episode in which a party of convicts was driven away from a cove where they had attempted to land. In short the very nature of those initial, generally amiable encounters tended to make concrete in the white mentality the erroneous notion that the blackman's relationship with the land was a matter of no importance to him. This happened despite the fact that several whites perished when, unarmed and singly or in pairs, they encountered Aborigines in the bush. Such reprisals surely indicated that, despite the apparent passivity of the Aborigines, their true appreciation of the white presence was given expression when possible.

Ages before the first foundations of the Greco-Judaic world were laid, the Aborigines had lived on this continent, if indeed they had ever lived elsewhere. At least 50,000 years before the birth of Moses, civilization existed here. The legends told by the blacks of Baiami, the creator, and of Kunapipi, called the Mother, went back before Celt, Pict or Saxon, before Alfred, the Magna Carta or the Druids and kings of the Irish. In all of that time the Aborigines had loved, married, mourned their dead and passed on their knowledge from generation to generation. With their elaborate rituals of dance, music and song, their cave and bark paintings, their rock engravings, their carefully woven stories of the past, the Aborigines had preserved their history back to the very dawning of the Dreamtime when all things had their origins. To them the land had no existence separate from their own being, with which shore and river, tree and shrub, rock and mountain, bird and mammal were entwined.

The Aborigines had social and economic systems — based on extended family groupings, and hunting and gathering grounds — which were neither primitive nor rudimentary. Over 200 distinct languages and four times that many dialects were spoken amongst 500 groups who all had the ability to communicate with each other. Barter and interchange along regular trade routes traced an intricate and highly complex system of human and material contacts throughout the entire continent. The old men were preservers of tradition rather than developers of a legal system, while medicine men and warriors held a place of importance but not superiority. The groups were not nomadic in the sense of being aimless wanderers but their movement was a carefully planned act, within the territory accepted as their individual reserve and its purpose was for gathering food and water. To them water was especially important because over half of the continent was arid or semi-arid and rainfall was low in most other regions. Many of the names they gave to places were understandably connected with the availability of water.

The Aborigines were not totemic because to them all reality was sacred, nor were they pantheistic because their concept of the sacred extended beyond the material world. Their lives were neither haphazard nor disordered, but all work was directed to daily sustenance. Times of great scarcity could cause abortion, infanticide, the neglect of the old and infirm, while blood was sometimes shed over territorial disputes. In short the Aborigines were neither savages nor primitive nobles but a people who had developed a degree of civilization which, except for the subjugation of the women by the men, impressed many white observers and in Cook's eyes gave them a happiness and tranquillity unknown to Europeans.

In material terms Aboriginal civilization was based more on an understanding and use of the environment than on technological developments. Nevertheless, the blacks were capable of making highly refined tools from stone at least 20,000 years ago in a manner which was then more advanced than any other known civilization and they shaped the land itself to their own purposes by controlled burning-off. They thereby created vast pastures which were of importance to later European expansion and had a profound ecological impact over many centuries.

By the use of burning-off, the Aborigines moulded a suitable environment for the animals they hunted, especially the kangaroo. They also used water management systems in dry areas, and fishtraps, some of them very elaborate and extensive, in rivers, as well as huge nets to trap ducks and other bird life. At Port Jackson and other places on the coast their principal food was fish which they caught from canoes with great skill. Consequently with their knowledge of animal and plant species they were able to live in moderate comfort from the land and their numbers, probably about 750,000 in 1788, were balanced to the land's capacity to produce. The Aborigines were predominantly pastoralists rather than cultivators of the soil. They had understood the best use to which they could put the land long before European settlement.

Phillip, and some few of his officers, realized that they had come amongst a people possessing their own unique civilization. But, like the blacks, the most pressing concern of the whites was to survive and long-term reliance on the supplies brought with the Fleet was not possible. A little agriculture was begun on small plots around the settlement, but stealing became so widespread that Phillip resorted to the use of the death penalty for the worst cases and flogging, sometimes up to 2,000 lashes, for the lesser. Scurvy soon became prevalent, and Phillip reported to the home authorities that it was raging 'in a most extraordinary manner'. The Aborigines did not suffer from it because of their abundant supply of fresh and green food taken from the land, which the whites soon began to seek with some small measure of success.

When the French were at Botany Bay, La Pérouse had said that, from his observations, Norfolk Island was a place fit only for angels and eagles to inhabit, but Phillip, obedient to his orders before leaving England, sent Lieutenant King there in February 1788 with a party of twenty-three, including fifteen convicts. His task was to found a settlement, obtain timber from the pines, cultivate the flax plant and forestall occupation by any other nation and, given the recent presence of the French, the Governor's alacrity in the matter was understandable. The actual settlement was moderately successful, although the timber proved to be unsuitable for ship building while the flax was diseased.

By 1790, want, loneliness and general unhappiness at Sydney Cove caused many to despair so, in an attempt to alleviate the situation on the mainland, Phillip sent 183 convicts, twenty-eight children and eighty-one marines to Norfolk Island where there was a better chance of survival. Despite the fewer numbers, by April the residents at Sydney were down to the meagrest possible rations and in May an elderly convict, Joseph Owen, died of starvation. Some asked why they had been abandoned by

The tiny settlement of Sydney Cove in 1788. Bennelong Point, where the first sheep grazed, is on the left and the Tank Stream entered the cove at the top. The present Cahill Expressway runs across the cove through the hut with the flagpole.

England complaining that 'the mother country has entirely forsaken us' in 'the worst country' in the world but no one dared to conclude that neglect was part of the pattern of improvidence in which the origins of the settlement lay.

It was becoming increasingly clear that mere existence itself was at stake, especially when Phillip's flagship, the *Sirius*, was wrecked at Norfolk Island. She had already returned successfully with provisions from the Cape after circumnavigating the globe under Captain Hunter's command and on this occasion she was on her way to Canton for more supplies. A relief ship, the *Guardian*, sent out from England, was also lost after striking an iceberg near the Cape of Good Hope and the situation worsened at Sydney with consequent dismay and misery. By mid-1790 New South Wales was entirely cut off from any means of contact with the outside world except through the small vessel, *Supply*, which no one, including Phillip, wanted to risk losing on a further, and perhaps, final voyage.

Despite the difficulties, Phillip tried to buoy up hopes by keeping an air of optimism about him. The marines who had accompanied the First Fleet were disinclined to attend to other than military duties, which in effect were non-existent so the Governor had to turn to selected convicts as overseers and even as police. This step caused much resentment amongst the marines and especially from their commandant Major Robert Ross, who, chagrined at being forced to live at a place where 'Nature is reversed', became a constant thorn in Phillip's side. Phillip solved the problem of his irritating subordinate by sending him to take charge on Norfolk Island in March 1790; there he was at least out of sight.

A civil and a criminal court had been set up on 7 February 1788, and floggings and hangings became regular occurrences thereafter. The first person executed in the colony was Thomas Barrett, aged seventeen, for stealing, and on 26 March 1789 six marines were hanged for robbing the stores. Anne Davis was hanged on 23 November 1789 for theft and was the first woman to be executed in the colony. The convicts attempted to add another facet of civilization in 1789 by performing a comedy, 'The Recruiting Officer', which was well received. Sydney itself was laid out about the Cove, the first streets of 200 feet in width were planned, orange trees planted, bricks made at Brickfield Hill and a bridge built across the Tank Stream, while Phillip himself issued strict orders forbidding the pollution of its water. Exploration took place and the Hawkesbury and Nepean rivers were discovered and partially mapped although it had been possible to penetrate only to within some twelve miles of the Blue Mountains to the west.

Sydney remained little more than an infant town situated on a splendid harbour where the soil was unsuitable for cultivation. The gradual realization of this fact had caused Phillip to make the most important decision of his governorship. About sixteen miles from Sydney there was a place which the Aborigines called Parramatta. Surrounding it, the land seemed fertile and by November 1788 it was settled. Phillip had a town laid out there with a mile long main street, a residence for himself, a barracks and houses for the inhabitants. The town was set on country which, with its trees and general lushness gave 'a very park-like and beautiful appearance'. The settlement was originally called Rose Hill and nearby some beautiful birds were noticed which, after the place of their discovery, were given the name 'rosella'.

Near Rose Hill, cultivation of the land by the white settlers began. Phillip's instructions were to try to persuade former convicts to remain in the colony and farm it rather than go home. He was empowered to grant them thirty acres of land with twenty more if married and ten for each child. In 1791 an ex-convict James Ruse, who began life as a Cornwall farmer, received at Rose Hill the first land grant of thirty acres in New South Wales upon which he grew wheat and other crops and from which he proved to Phillip's satisfaction he could support himself and his convict wife, Elizabeth.

The first sign of relief for the colony was seen on 3 June 1790 when the transport *Lady Juliana* with a cargo of 222 female convicts, provisions for those on board, mail and news from home sailed up the harbour. Men wept, women with babes in arms were distracted with joy and the settlement seemed saved at last. A fortnight later the store ship *Justinian* berthed with supplies of food followed by the 'sick ships' of the Second Fleet with their cargo of ill and dying. Even though a dreadful toll had already been taken on the voyage out when a quarter of the 1,000 convicts had perished, another 150 died soon after landing. The Second Fleet was the most cruel and most inhumane espisode of the whole epoch of transportation, and its origins lay in the utter neglect of the English authorities.

Despite all these new arrivals, who by their presence gave the clearest possible proof that the home authorities had remained mindful of the purpose for which the colony had been founded, it was not until December, when a ship arrived laden with provisions which Phillip had procured from Batavia, that the crisis was over. The point had been well, if unintentionally, made that in an emergency white civilization on the southern continent would have to make shift for itself.

In 1792, weakened in health, Phillip prepared to leave New South Wales for ever. He looked back on five years of stoically borne hardship, criticism from subordinates both convict and free, much opposition, frustration and human misery all around him. Nevertheless, his purpose had been achieved for the settlements around Sydney and on Norfolk Island had survived with their populations of over 3,000 and 1,100 respectively. The convicts were in the proportion of five males to one female yet the birth rate was rising, 1,700 acres of land were under cultivation, 3,500 acres had been granted to seventy-three persons on the mainland, live stock were increasing in numbers and general hopes were buoyant. Before leaving England, Phillip had stated that he did not intend to lay the foundations of an Empire using convicts; but by 1793 only a handful of free settlers had arrived. This meant that the pattern was already shaped of a society dependent upon convict labour employed and fed by the government. Moreover, it was a workforce markedly ill-fitted and ill-disposed to work as has always been the case with forced labour.

Phillip sailed for home on 11 December 1792 with a few dingoes, four

Some idea of pronunciation in the 1830s can be gained from this inscription erected over the grave of the colony's first farmer. Axcelsis (excelsis), houre (our), forst (first), natef (native), and tock (took) are examples.

kangaroos and two favourite Aborigines, one of whom, called Bennelong, was commemorated by the naming of Bennelong Point on Sydney Cove because he had lived in a hut built there for him. Bennelong was presented to the King and returned later to the colony with a weakness for alcohol. In subsequent years Phillip, now ageing but formerly absolute ruler of half a continent, became an admiral. He died in 1814 perhaps secure in knowing that he had served humanity well in his total devotion to the founding of the colony, although at times he acted harshly especially in his use of the lash as the main form of deterrent.

As time passed and memories were muted, a mythology grew up around the First Fleet with its cargo of human jetsam washed up at Sydney Cove. Because they were the pioneers and in some measure the cornerstone of the new society, it was considered necessary to distort the reality of their origins and of those who followed them. The stain of the convict origins was another powerful factor which led to either forgetting or whitewashing the past. Poverty, land enclosures and a brutal system of legal enactments in England tended to obscure the truth that a sizeable proportion of the convicts were professional thieves hardened by repeated criminality. In the main they were working class, unskilled, town dwellers to whom law breaking had become a way of life (a law breaking, though, that was engendered by environmental factors consequent upon the dislocation caused by the Napoleonic wars and the rapid growth in population).

Nevertheless, it became part of mythology to see the convicts as sturdy agricultural labourers or downtrodden city people who had poached a hare or stolen a handkerchief to buy bread for their suffering families. Unquestionably there were some such amongst the convicts but in too small a minority to matter; poachers, for example, made up less than one percent. Crimes against property predominated making up over eighty percent of the convictions, while crimes against persons were less than three percent. At the time of their transportation the majority were unmarried, aged fifteen to twenty-five and had been sentenced to seven years' transportation which, for most, effectively was a sentence of permanent colonial residence in the same way as a fourteen-year or life sentence was. The females were almost all former domestics except for the thirteen percent of them who had been prostitutes.

In September 1791 the first convict ship from Ireland, the *Queen*, arrived with 133 men, twenty-two women and a Dublin boy, David Fay, aged eleven aboard. From that day the Irish became another source for myths. No one could question the effect upon Ireland's population of England's long occupation, the subjugation of its people and the suppression of its dominant religion. Similarly, the centuries-old struggle, political and often violent, of the Irish for their freedom, was part of history immortalized in symbol, song and memory. It was easy to see the Irish transportees as political prisoners tinged with the nobility of rebellion.

Yet of the 50,000 Irish transported up to 1852, at least two-thirds were convicted for theft. There was a higher proportion of them drawn from rural areas than was the case with the British convicts and the religion of ninety percent of them was Catholic. The small but constant trickle of political prisoners amongst them, to whom thievery was repugnant, made up about a fifth of the Irish convicts, although in the first fifteen years the proportion reached a third. While that minority were unquestionably men of high principle and integrity, the majority of the Irish did not vary significantly from the English in their background of criminality.

Other mythologies grew up around the convicts centered on the ideal of mateship with which they were said to be endowed in abundance. There is little evidence that they shared such virtuous necessity more than others who formed bonds to protect life or property. Certainly they were mates in their hatred of law enforcers, their distaste for work, their use of rhyming slang and flash language to disguise the meaning of their conversation and in their feeling of being the dregs of society. But several factors combined to produce the one significant result of transportation, despite all its indignity and misery — a turning away from criminal activity by most convicts to a life based on economic independence. Better food, a healthier climate, a sense of freedom rather than incarceration in a dingy prison, all helped to transform and reform the convicts. Above all there was the chance to make a living by other than criminal means. Upwards of ninety percent of the convicts eventually turned to respectable ways of life because they were given the opportunity to become independent in a land where abundance was the norm.

A partial explanation for this reformation also lay in the methods of deterrence. Phillip established the pattern in the earliest days when the lash and the gallows became the way of punishing wrongdoers and of terrifying those so inclined. Broken skin and exposed rib-cages were common and 100 lashes by an experienced flogger became a normal penalty for even minor transgressions. Deterrence was accompanied by the constant hope that a noticeable practice of good behaviour would result in rewards, and freedom from servitude was the one goal to which all strove. Gradually a system was established based on a 'ticket of leave' granted by the Governor. Although freedom of movement was restricted

AUSTRALIA'S FIRST CHURCH

Erected, June 10ᵗʰ 1793. Destroyed by Fire, Oct 1ˢᵗ 1798.

Ground Plan

Locality of Church

Richard Johnson, Anglican chaplain to the First Fleet, was represented by Grose as a 'Methodist' and a 'troublesome, discontented character'. Many convicts loved him for his kindness although others, perhaps resenting being forced to attend services, were probably responsible for the destruction of his church.

the 'ticket of leave' permitted the convict to become self-employed and to hold property rights. A conditional pardon gave freedom and all rights provided one did not return to the United Kingdom. A full pardon or the expiration of a sentence meant a convict became fully emancipated. An emancipist, whether by pardon or completion of servitude, was rarely permitted to forget that his or her original condition was that of a convict or 'a Government man or woman' as the local saying put it. The old stain of convict origins died slowly, whether for individuals or for society itself.

A more subtle attempt at reformation was the manner in which the authorities, closely allied by the law and the Anglican Church, sought to inculcate submission, repentance, obedience and the desire to conform. The Reverend Richard Johnson on 3 February 1788 chose as the basis of his first sermon to the original community the words of the Psalmist 'What shall I render unto the Lord for all His benefits towards me?' To the preacher it was ordained by God that some should be in an exalted state and others subject to them. About him stood the upholders of good order, resplendent and sweating in uniform; above him flew the flag of Great Britain, while the tones of 'God Save the King' had scarcely died away.

The convicts who stood about listening to Johnson did not know that their sovereign, George III, was spasmodically insane nor that across the English Channel the stirrings of a revolution of such magnitude were afoot in France that, given time, would cause the values their rulers held sacred to be questioned. They did know that their one chance of earthly redemption lay in conformity and, given the incentives, it is scarcely surprising that so many of them took it. Others, however, chose another path, and as early as July 1788 eleven men and one woman had absconded. Attempting to escape became a regular practice amongst the homesick and the desperate and the Irish in particular were prone to bolt into the bush. In November 1791 one group of them, made up of twenty men and one woman set out for China, which they believed to be within six weeks walking time. Eighteen survived and some of them tried it a second time, but gradually the conviction was borne in upon all that New South Wales was a place from which escape was well-nigh impossible. A woman convict gave part of the reason for unrest when she wrote home in 1788 and complained of their 'disconsolate situation in this solitary waste of creation' where distress, especially amongst the women, was 'past description'.

Five years after settlement there was still much distress but the sense of isolation was breaking down. There were ships lying at anchor in the harbour. Trading vessels from India, the United States, China, Batavia and England, and whalers and sealers, were calling at Sydney regularly. Nevertheless, the colony was to continue as a gaol, because in London the authorities remained convinced that the cheapest way to solve the problem of crime and its effects was transportation. Over 4,000 convicts had arrived in five years and the pattern for the next fifty years of white settlement of the continent was set with a penal colony as its essential basis.

CHAPTER TWO

Traces of Permanency

Forlorn, tiny, uncertain of its future, the settlement held a precarious foothold about Port Jackson in 1792. Thinking inhabitants, whether convict or free, realized their insignificance in the eyes of those who had sent them there. The sender of a letter, whether private or official, could not expect a reply within a year so that problems, sorrows, joys and plans all took on the face of the unreal as they faded into the past. New South Wales was another world, washed by seas of silence stretching endlessly from one end of the globe to the other. Between the settlement and home there were lands peopled by strange and nameless races, while inland from Sydney Cove lay the vast, mysterious continent locked behind the mountains to the west. Life went on with new arrivals and departures, births and deaths, primitive manufacturing, commerce and social relationships as for the majority of the white inhabitants there could be no turning back and home was forever New South Wales.

The colony was rapidly becoming a virtual slave farm as the government increased the use of assignment of convicts to land owners to decrease costs on the public purse and increase profits to private individuals. With considerable justification a convict wrote to Governor King in 1805, 'By what authority do those in power at Home — by what right do you — make slaves of Britons in this distant quarter of the globe?' Maurice Margarot, one of the 'Scottish Martyrs' transported in 1794 for fourteen years on charges of sedition refused to work, claiming that transportation, not slavery, was his sentence. Margarot was able to avoid forced labour but most convicts had no choice either in their masters or in the mode of their employment.

With their fishing grounds and hunting lands increasingly invaded the

Aborigines were rarely seen except for those few who came about the town. They had learnt a lesson from the fire power of the whites even though they could throw several spears while the others had to reload their firearms. Though to go alone into solitary places was imprudent, the whites, when armed and together, normally went about without fear. A little knowledge was gathered of the local languages and even of the beliefs of the Aborigines, but they had become mere objects of curiosity to whom food and other items were sometimes dispensed as to a lower order of humanity. Unlike the settlers at the Cape of Good Hope, white society in New South Wales, given the supply of convicts, did not have to rely on black labour, which further lessened the white estimate of the Aborigines.

Although the Aborigines played no role in the economy of the whites, other relations, at times, took place and it was soon noticed that venereal disease had spread amongst them which they quickly named Goobah-rong as if to imply its dreadful effects. The erroneous notion began to take hold that, because some black women seemed free in sexual rela-tions, marriage and fidelity were of no consequence amongst the Abori-gines. All that logic could imply was that a proud people reduced to bewilderment and even starvation would barter for survival. As for the convicts, the gross imbalance of the sexes meant that they knew necessity of another kind and they took every opportunity to satisfy it.

In England some critics thought that the settlement in New South Wales was absurd, impractical and grossly expensive. Half a million pounds had been spent up until the end of 1792, but Pitt was convinced that no cheaper method could be devised of disposing of the Kingdom's worst criminals who, at home, would help to corrupt others. It was, of course, a simple matter to set up the convict establishment but it was another to police it, and something was clearly required as the marines had refused to undertake the task. The answer, devised in England in 1789, was to send out a special New South Wales Corps which some newspapers called 'The Botany Bay Rangers'. The Corps arrived in 1790 and its commander Major Francis Grose, who had been appointed Lieutenant-Governor, assumed control when Phillip departed in 1792. From the moment of its arrival, the Corps became a decisive force in shaping the future of the colony.

The Corps consisted of about 500 officers and men and, as a garrison, it had little to do except look after its own needs which Grose was quick to foster. He gave land grants and the use of up to ten male and three female convicts to the officers. The combination of free land and free labour was a particularly useful device. The convicts remained depen-

Sydney in the early 1800s had begun to take on many aspects of a settled community. From the Rocks area, the hospital buildings are on the right and, above them, a row of convict houses and the tower for the new St Phillip's Church. The Government Dockyard is in the centre and, to the far left, the Governor's House is on the top of the hill. Below it is the Government Wharf and Store. The drawing was done by Edward Dayes from a picture painted in the colony and engraved in London in 1804.

dent upon the government for provisions which, as time went on, the officers sold to the government from their land holdings. As no thought had been given to the necessity of a currency, the most precious commodity, liquor, became the principal means of exchange for goods and labour. It remained such until 1813 when Spanish dollars with the centre removed, called 'holey dollars', circulated widely, together with promissory notes. The Corps assumed control of the economy, chiefly through the use of rum as the main item of barter and for paying wages and the whole of economic, legal and social life quickly took on that tenor peculiar to a despotic military regime.

With Grose in charge, all civil authority was abolished and passed into the hands of the military, where it was both used and abused for years to come. The original Corps had drawn a sizeable proportion of its numbers from criminal elements, and convicts were soon enlisted in its ranks, which did nothing to enhance its reputation. Captain Paterson, second-in-command of the Corps, succeeded Grose at the end of 1794 until the new Governor, John Hunter arrived in September 1795. Paterson merely accentuated the worst aspects of Grose's system by further land grants to the Corps, but in that respect the colony itself benefited because, with free land and convict labour readily available, economic development followed and the opening of rich land in the Hawkesbury River district continued. The Corps also made a contribution to growth in the free population as in those early days it was almost impossible to induce free persons to migrate as settlers, while, upon discharge, many of its members themselves settled in the colony.

The days of famine were at an end, livestock flourished, agriculture with the production of corn and potatoes went ahead, the first shipment of cedar logs was made to India, trading ships continued to arrive with stores, a handful of free settlers took up land, and most convicts whose terms had expired remained in New South Wales and felt that they belonged there. After a brief eight years, Sydney welcomed Hunter with the face of permanency of which the building of the first Anglican church by Johnson in 1793 was the symbol, even though it was paid for in rum bought out of his own pocket at 4s 6d per gallon and sold as wages at 10s per gallon. It seemed to be taken for granted, however, that conflict with the Aborigines was part and parcel of development, and black-white relations on the Hawkesbury had deteriorated almost to the point of open warfare.

Hunter, aged fifty-eight in 1795, had come out to Botany Bay with the First Fleet so he knew a good deal about the early days of the colony but his life had been largely spent at sea. He was quickly aware that his subordinates had a vested interest in the continuation of the rum trade, of their monopoly of commerce, of their use of convicts and of the growth of their land holdings. At the time Captain John Macarthur, aged twenty-eight in 1795, was both leader and example to his fellow officers of the Corps. He was one of its original members and he had fought a duel with a marine captain before embarking to New South Wales, then quarrelled with Phillip but prospered under Grose. Within four years from his arrival in 1790, he had extensive land under cultivation at Parramatta, selling the produce to the government, of which, as Inspector of Public Works, he was a part. Seemingly insatiable in his lust for power and wealth, he rapidly made Hunter's life miserable by resisting vigorously any step to curb his and the Corps's control of the economy.

The five years of Hunter's period in office were spent in a losing battle trying to wrest back control from the military. The good done by the Corps for the economy was in part negated by the harm it brought to small land holders, who could not compete with it when selling their produce to the government stores and who were often reduced to poverty and bankruptcy by the prices, sometimes 500 percent higher than cost, of the goods imported or bought on arrival by the Corps. To curb high profits going into private hands Hunter tried, without success, to establish a public store. He also failed in his attempt to cut back the number of convicts working for the officers and generally expenses rose on government requirements. There was a drought in 1798–99, the Hawkesbury flooded in 1800 and the Irish political prisoners proved troublesome. The Governor's period of command, if not control, was an unhappy one.

Hunter took refuge in travelling and exploring, using his considerable talents as a naturalist to good stead, while Macarthur and other detractors denounced him, unjustly, to London so that he was eventually recalled. He was not a capable administrator, but, in the main, his fault was to clash with the Corps, which brought about his downfall. He left in October 1800 pleased that his name had been given to the proud river at Newcastle and that a fine herd of sixty cattle had been discovered beyond the Nepean River on an area known subsequently as the Cow Pastures. They had thrived in the wilds since the disappearance of their ancestors, two bulls and four cows, in 1788, and grown in numbers to about 300 by 1800.

Hunter did not then realize that the most significant occurrence of his governorship was the arrival of thirty-three Spanish merino ewes from the Cape of Good Hope on 16 May 1797. They were sold to Macarthur and other officials to add to their flocks of various strains including Bengal sheep.

Hunter was mainly responsible for the discovery of the lyrebird, koala, platypus and wombat and many of his original drawings were worthy of preservation. He permitted the opening of the first brewery in Sydney by John Boston and gave licences to operate public houses in order to curb the rum trade. He also attempted to set rates of pay and made attendance at church services compulsory. The opening of a playhouse on 16 January 1796 had caused him some misgivings, but the recitation of a couplet on opening night summed up the ability of the early colonists, free or felon, to laugh at themselves. 'True patriots all, for be it understood, we left our country for our country's good.' Richard Johnson left the colony with the outgoing Governor and Samuel Marsden became senior Anglican chaplain. Johnson had served his Lord with honour and humanity, with love: the words of a grateful convict were his epitath, 'physician both of soul and body.'

The years of Governor Philip King (1800–1806) were ones of remarkable progress. King had also come as a naval officer with the First Fleet and then served as Lieutenant-Governor based at Norfolk Island until 1796. He could draw on his personal and practical knowledge of those early years with Phillip, and his attachment to the colony was shown by the names he gave to his first two sons, Norfolk and Sydney, born at Norfolk Island to a convict mother, Ann Inett, without benefit of marriage. He quickly settled to command although progress depended more on private rather than government development despite his increasing use of convict labour on government buildings.

Like Hunter, King tried to control the rum trade by reducing imports, but the widespread use of illicit stills thwarted his purpose. Goods were sold at only a fifty percent mark up through the public store and profits on imports induced private speculators into trade which broke the monopoly of the Corps to some degree. With the increasing interest shown in wool by Samuel Marsden and by John Macarthur, its quality began to improve, although sealing and whaling had already assumed the role of primary export producers. Coal was mined at Newcastle for local use but some shipments were made to India and the Cape of Good Hope while more vines and tobacco were planted in the colony. In 1803 King permitted the establishment of the first newspaper, the *Sydney Gazette* edited by the convicted shoplifter George Howe but censored by the Governor's secretary. As the founder of the press in New South Wales, Howe began a tradition of generally responsible, but often inflammatory and rowdy journalism.

King's treatment of, and dealings with, the Aborigines were humane and placatory and he considered them 'the real Proprietors of the Soil' but this did not prevent him from making land grants, including one made improperly to his successor. Despite his good intentions, he came no closer than others to an understanding of the Aborigines, whose conduct he deplored as ungrateful and treacherous, although what benefits they were alleged to have received from the coming of the whites remained unclear. The Cadigal people had been reduced from about fifty in 1788 to three in 1790 and other bands living in close proximity to settlement had so dwindled in numbers that they were little more than an irritant, but, to his credit, King tried to protect them. The vaccinations he introduced against smallpox were too late to be of any consequence to those already ravaged by it but it was a successful step for the whites.

Both Hunter and then King as naval men encouraged exploration by sea. In Hunter's time Matthew Flinders, naval lieutenant, and George Bass, sailor and surgeon, had found the strait between Van Diemen's Land and the mainland which, as Bass had already deduced its existence, was named in his honour. Its use thereafter on the passage to and from England cut two weeks from the voyage as it was no longer necessary to go south around Van Diemen's Land. Flinders returned to England, where in January 1801 he was given command of the *Investigator*. In this ship he charted the southern coast of Australia before returning to Sydney Cove in May 1802. From July 1802 to June 1803 he did a circumnavigation of the entire continent. This voyage in the leaking *Investigator* was one of the great feats of navigation and hydrography of modern times. Flinders was the first to give general use to the name Australia for the land to which he made such a great contribution. He had the misfortune whilst on a trip home to England to be detained in December 1803 by a heartless French commandant on Mauritius. Broken in health and hope during the seven long years of detention on the island, while he longed for his beloved wife Ann, he died in England on 19 July 1814, the day after his monumental *Voyage to Terra Australis* was published.

The idea still prevailed that there was probably an inland sea in the centre of the continent, but it was at least certain, due to the work of Flinders, that eastern and western New Holland were the one vast land mass, although little interest continued to be shown in its western half. Meanwhile, knowledge of the east had expanded with an exploratory voyage resulting in the finding of 'a noble sheet of water' in 1802 which was first named after Governor King and then called Port Phillip. Fears of an alleged French intention to settle on Van Diemen's Land and a desire to get rid of some of the convicts from Sydney convinced King of the need to put a settlement there. It can therefore be claimed with some accuracy that strategic motives were foremost in the founding in September 1803 of what became the worst convict hell in the world. Under Lieutenant John Bowen a party of twenty-four convicts settled near the mouth of a small stream flowing into the broad Derwent river. They called the place Risdon Cove but it was a miserable, wind-swept and infertile place.

In that same year David Collins, who had arrived originally with Phillip in 1788 as deputy Judge-Advocate, was sent out directly from England with troops, 308 male convicts, eighteen hopeful settlers, several married women and children and stores to set up a new dependency on the mainland. Collins arrived on 9 October 1803 which was the true birth date of the later colony of Victoria and settled near Sorrento on Port Phillip Bay. The chosen spot was unsatisfactory given the hostility of the Aborigines, the sandy soil and scarcity of fresh water, although the Bay teemed with crayfish which were caught and consumed in thousands. Under such circumstances, the troops proved difficult to control and everyone was miserable in such a barren place, so Collins removed to the Derwent, where he and his party arrived in early 1805. Five convicts were missing at the time of the departure from Port Phillip, and one of them, William Buckley, survived and lived with the Aborigines for the next thirty-two years.

At Risdon Cove, Collins was again dissatisfied so he moved across the river to Sullivan's Cove which became the site for Hobart Town. Founded much as Sydney Cove was, with the same hardship, uncertainty and lack of interest by the home authorities, the new settlement was sustained by Collins's cheerful and decent character although everyone was forced to live on the local game, chiefly kangaroos, for the first two years. As Lieutenant-Governor, Collins suffered loneliness of mind and heart. He was separated for many years from his wife Maria, who could not come out with him in 1788 and refused to do so in 1803, and he fathered four children in the colony, thus earning the disapprobation of some of the upright who knew little of the human spirit but much about the rules by which they judged it.

New South Wales continued to prosper, especially in children as the small number of convict women bore them in increasing numbers because of their improved health resulting from a better climate, more wholesome food and greater freedom. Many women were forced to opt for marriage, even to scarcely acceptable partners, because it was preferable to do so than become a servant which usually entailed prostitution and no permanency. King had founded an orphan school for females at Sydney in 1801 in order to remove them 'from prostitution and iniquity' which he felt prevailed to an unacceptable degree. His institution added to the handful of rudimentary establishments engaged in education and run by the Anglican Church or private entrepreneurs.

The children born in the colony had already taken on some common characteristics being generally finely-limbed, of fair complexion with light hair and dark eyes. They were also said to be of volatile dispositions and proverbial talkers. After twelve years of settlement, one in six of the white population was born in and knew no other home than New South Wales. Their parents still longed for news of other lands, but to those born here the world across the seas was already foreign. Physical reality to them was the harbour with its township around Sydney Cove, the little settlement at Parramatta and the struggling farms on the Hawkesbury, the yet unpassed mountains to the west, the heat and humidity of summer, the familiar songs of the birds, the scents of the flora and the shape of the fauna. To the native-born none of that reality was strange, and they accepted it as their own world. They were kindred to the Aborigines for their sinews were moulded from the same earth which knew neither bond nor free, black nor white.

King's greatest worry was of the time and place of an expected Irish uprising. That it would take place seemed certain and, after the unsuccessful rebellion in Ireland in 1798, the presence of about 600 'United Irishmen', who were thought to be still infected by seditious sentiments, was used to give point to the fears. Unconfirmed rumours of an insurrection caused King to have several Irish cruelly flogged in 1800. They included one lad of twenty years, Paddy Galvin, who was sentenced to 300 lashes at the behest of Samuel Marsden. As the skin and blood fell from him, Paddy was asked where the pikes were hidden. He replied that he did not know nor would he tell his tormentors if he did. He said that they could hang him before he would make music to the tune of which others would dance upon air.

Despite his unease the Governor was sufficiently liberal-minded to permit a convict priest, James Dixon, to celebrate a public Mass in Sydney on 15 May 1803 and monthly thereafter. Dixon was an innocent but convicted victim of the 1798 rebellion. That quarter of the population which was Catholic, and grieved the loss of the Mass, was delighted by the Governor's decision. The Governor's indulgence seemed to have good effects initially and yet by 4 March 1804 King regretted his decision. At Vinegar Hill, near Toongabbie, about 300 Irish and a sprinkling of English convicts, to the cry 'Death or Liberty', rose in futile insurgency against their gaolers with the intent of escaping from the colony. All hope of conciliation was lost when George Johnston, at the head of the government troops, dishonourably tricked the leaders into capture and the slaughter commenced. There were seventeen killings, nine later hangings, countless lashings, and dispersal to gaols and coal mines for many others.

This ill-conceived episode had both an immediate and a lasting outcome. Irish catholicism and insurrection were seen by some as synonymous and by none more so than by Samuel Marsden. Anxiously he foresaw the colony being lost by England unless stern measures were taken to contain the Catholics. To him the Irish were ignorant, uncivilized and savage, destitute of any true religion and without morality, while the Mass was no more than depraved superstition. He gave as his opinion that all would be well if the authorities were sensible enough to impose his own form of Christianity on everyone. Marsden's logic resulted in Catholics being compelled to attend Anglican services after the withdrawal of Dixon's permission to celebrate Mass. More importantly, it gave impetus to the opinion that the Irish were second-rate or worse. At

In a later period, Australians wanted to know what convict life was like and turned to Marcus Clarke's novel, *For the Term of His Natural Life*, for evidence of the brutalities of earlier days. The silent film version premiered at the Theatre Royal, Newcastle, in 1927 and was successful throughout Australia where some 1,250 picture theatres had been built.

the same time they were coerced to conform to Anglicanism which itself held little sway over the hearts and minds of most, whether convict or free. In the long run further point was given to the idea that Anglicanism was a mere handmaiden of the state in the preservation of good order.

A minor but more disappointing source of anxiety to King was the behaviour of John Macarthur whose inclination to rebel was no less than that of many of the turbulent Irish. The difference lay in Macarthur's background, position, persistence and artfulness. An enraged King lodged Macarthur in prison in September 1801 after Macarthur and Paterson, commanding officer of the Corps, fought a duel, because Paterson refused to join Macarthur in refusing allegiance to the Governor's authority. King decided to send Macarthur home for court martial in England, where, after being censured, he resigned from the army. He received a promise of a grant of 5,000 acres of the best land in the colony and fostered his grand scheme of providing the home market with the finest of wools by his purchase at auction of eight prime Spanish sheep from the Royal flocks. Upon Macarthur's return as a civilian in 1805, King had to admit, with some pretence at good grace, that he had been out-foxed by the cunning mischief-maker, whom he called with irony the 'hero of the fleece' but to whom he was forced to grant 5,000 acres of land at the Cow Pastures. King concluded his relations with Macarthur and the Corps with some relief knowing that his own days in the colony were at an end and that he could depart cheerfully in August 1806 leaving the 'hero' to his lands, flocks and plots.

In 1805 a census was taken in New South Wales of all the white popu-lation and its flocks and herds. In round figures there were 7,000 people of whom 4,000 were men, 1,300 women and the rest were children of whom less than 100 had received any formal education. Some 2,000 convicts were guarded by over 600 officials from the Governor down and including the Corps. The colony had at last become self-sufficient in grain and sheep numbers had risen to 20,000 of which Macarthur owned at least a quarter. King had always been determined to cut costs having learnt from Hunter's fate that the one thing which ultimately mattered in London was to reduce official expenditure. His cut-backs resulted in unsaleable imports in 1801–03 but the frontier of economic expansion had opened, although it was to the sea rather than to the land.

Further commercial contact had been established with the Pacific Islands, China, India and South America. The seal fisheries of Bass Strait seemed an endless source of riches, and they attracted vessels from all over the world. Some of their crews were villains who abducted black women, and often treated them barbarously, but their offspring had families which, in time, preserved the blood of the Aborigines of Van Diemen's Land. Sydney merchants, many of whom were emancipists, grew rich on the trade in seal oil and furs, and whaling became firmly established as the leading industry. Fleets of vessels from many nations came in and out of Sydney and Hobart as they searched for the deep sea sperm whales, which produced oil for lamps and tallow for soap and candles. Female whales were hunted when they came into bays to give birth, as whale bone was used in women's garments and umbrellas.

In 1804 King, outraged that the Americans were building vessels on the islands of the Strait 'in violation of the Law of Nations', encouraged shipbuilding, and within a year the first locally made whaling vessel, the *King George*, was launched in Sydney. The East India Company had a monopoly on trade, but Robert Campbell, a Sydney merchant, had £50,000 worth of goods in his warehouse by 1804. He decided to break the Company's monopoly in 1805 by taking a cargo of oil and fur skins to

England, which was in technical contravention of the regulations against private trading. His act of defiance opened up New South Wales as a regular trading post.

Campbell had taken an important step in the commercial history of the colony and in the following year vessels passing through Sydney left for English and Chinese ports with over 2,500 tons of sperm oil. In 1807 one vessel alone, the *Favourite*, owned in Nantucket, USA, sailed for Canton with 32,000 seal skins. Unsurprisingly, such carnage could not last and already sealing was in decline as the islands were worked out, but for thirty years, whaling, rather than wool, remained the main export earner of the colony.

The main thing the colony lacked was a free labour force. After eighteen years of settlement, only 610 free settlers were mustered and there was nowhere to turn locally for free labour given the attractions of sealing and whaling. The resumption of the Napoleonic Wars meant that fewer ships were available as transports and there was a greater need for convict labour in the British shipyards. As a result, only about 500 male convicts arrived in 1805–07 so that the cry was soon heard for more workers to make the land prosper. For the time being at least, England's seemingly inexhaustible source of criminals was the only long-term hope, and no one looked to the local Aborigines as an alternative for the black people remained disinterested in taking part in the white economy.

The waters between the mainland and Van Diemen's Land had risen to form Bass Strait about 12,000 years previously. Since that time the Aboriginal race had survived on the large island undisturbed, and probably numbered about 5,000 at the time of the coming of the white man. As early as 1804 a bloody encounter between the whites and blacks took place at Port Dalrymple, where a new settlement had briefly existed before Launceston was chosen as the permanent site. The commandant, William Paterson, rightly judged that the encounter would be productive of much mischief in the future. From such bloody clashes, and others on the mainland, some whites concluded that they were dealing with treacherous, bloodthirsty and revengeful savages, who would bide their time before retaliating for the real or imaginary wrongs done to them. The way to placate them, it was thought, was to be liberal with food and trinkets. To the blacks such things could never make up for the loss of their land which deprived them of dignity, purpose in life, the sacred places of their ancestors and the source of their food.

In and around Sydney the Aborigines had ceased to pose any threat to white settlement and other mythologies about authority and human relationships held sway. There was an air of festivity and expectation on

20 April 1806, for it was a great day in the history of the colony. On this day, King decreed that God was to be praised for the mercy which had been shown to the sovereign and his realm by the providential defeat of the Spanish and French at Trafalgar in the previous October. His words also served to remind some how far they were away from home as it took seven months to hear the news of victory. Napoleon, it was hoped, would eventually reap his doom even with Nelson gone. Furthermore, the local Irish seemed suppressed. The new Union Flag was flown to symbolize the shackling of Ireland to Britain and Freemasonry had been forbidden in New South Wales as a dangerous sect. It was reasonable to suppose that in London more thought would now be given to the future of Sydney Cove with the danger of invasion of England by the French finally over. Thus a general air of well-being prevailed in high quarters although Collins and his charges in Hobart were at risk of starving. Their main source of meat was pigs fed on whale oil, which made the pork taste like the oil used in lamps. Expectancy, however, served to heighten the hopes of all, including the convicts, for a new Governor was in the offing and who could tell what the change would bring?

The arrival of William Bligh in August 1806 should have given pause for thought to those whose disposition led them to question the orders or even the whims of higher authority. John Macarthur on behalf of the free citizens and George Johnston for the military welcomed Bligh with an address in which they expressed their confidence that the new com- mander-in-chief, 'by a just, moderate, firm and wise government', would promote the happiness of all the deserving inhabitants of New South Wales. It was a pious hope for the new man was above all his own man. Bligh had survived a mutiny on the *Bounty*, an arduous voyage calling for magnificent seamanship and courage on a small, open boat from Tahiti to Timor, two courts martial and several naval campaigns. Foul- mouthed, tyrannical, hot-tempered and impatient with incompetence, he was, nonetheless, prompt to obey orders and eager to have his own obeyed without question or hesitation . One order he had been given was to stamp out the trafficking in spirits which still prevailed in the colony. Unwisely, instead of tackling one disorder at a time, he soon issued an intemperate tirade against Macarthur, thus drawing up a battle line from which only one victor could emerge. In Macarthur's eyes, New South Wales had now become 'a perfect hell.'

The rum trade, a suspect currency based on promissory notes com- bined with a decline in the transport of supplies during the Napoleonic Wars had produced a setback in the colony's economy. A great flood of the Hawkesbury in 1806 rendered 1,200 people homeless and worsened

Dennis Dogherty was one of the 'old crawlers' who remained in penal servitude at Port Arthur where he was photographed in 1874. The convicts did not change in appearance over the years from 1788, although few carried the scars of the system of transportation as visibly as Dogherty.

the economic distress. Bligh acted humanely in organizing relief for the Hawkesbury settlers and promising that the government would buy their next crops but the Corps resented this promise as it interfered with its ability to control trade. The Governor was forthright in forbidding the use of rum as barter and outlawing private stills, and he attempted to harden up the currency by insisting that sterling be used. These initial measures would probably have proved acceptable provided he refrained from any direct attack on powerful vested interests, whether in the hands of the Corps or of private persons.

Governor Bligh's personality was such that he could not help himself. Three influential persons, Lord, Kable and Underwood were imprisoned for a month for insulting his office and its authority; Dr D'Arcy Wentworth was summarily suspended from his hospital superintendency for using the labour of convicts alleged to be patients; the Irish were outraged because he dispersed the leaders of a rumoured plot even though they had been acquitted; and moderate elements in society were disgusted at his tolerance of Richard Atkins, the Judge-Advocate. The Judge was a sensitive man broken on the wheel of a harsh society which he found unbearable and from which he fled into the solace of drink. Conscientious but incompetent, Atkins was already a shambling wreck at the time of Bligh's arrival, which deprived the Governor of the legal advice he sorely needed, and the Governor had to face his adversaries virtually alone.

With his encouragement of agriculture rather than sheep breeding, and the fact that in eighteen months he granted only 2,180 acres of land compared to King's grants amounting to 60,000 acres, Bligh further alienated the wealthy and powerful. Marsden was sufficiently perceptive to remark that any Governor who attempted to curb such elements, including himself, would be resisted implacably. The only firm support Bligh received came from the poorer farmers, especially on the Hawkes-bury, who were grateful for his attempt to break the monopolies, but they were without a voice, unorganized and at a distance. On the other hand, the Corps was closely bonded, capable of any mischief and possessed a strong and impetuous de facto leader in the person of Macarthur. By late January 1808 Macarthur had every reason to act against Bligh for he was in court properly charged with several 'misdemeanours and outrageous offences'. The six officers of the Corps who were acting as a jury in Macarthur's trial released him when he refused to be judged by Atkins. Bligh regarded the behaviour of the officers as treasonable which prompted their commanding officer, George Johnston, to demand the Governor's resignation and have him arrested on the twentieth anni-versary of the colony, 26 January 1808. Two weeks before a vessel had arrived from the Cape of Good Hope bearing 8,000 gallons of spirits destined to be used as currency by the Corps. Understandably the depo-sition of Bligh became known as the 'Rum Rebellion'.

Although not without precedent in British colonial affairs, the arrest and deposition of Bligh was caused almost entirely by his attempts at reform. Had he been permitted to continue in office there would have been a wider distribution of wealth in the colony. In the event Johnston himself, having been used as a tool by Macarthur and his friends, was left to his own fate by them and was lucky that he was merely cashiered when found guilty of mutiny by a court martial in London. He returned to the colony in 1813 to die in riches and respectability in 1823, survived by his beautiful Jewish wife, Esther, who had come to the colony as a convict aged sixteen and remained 'through evil and through good report the faithful wife and companion'.

Macarthur found it convenient to remain in exile until 1817, while his wife, Elizabeth, watched over his affairs and most notably his sheep for those nine long years, thereby laying her claim to be a true founder of the

Thomas Kelly was one of the last of the Port Arthur convicts. Another Kelly, John, unrelated to Thomas but father of Australia's most famous outlaw, Ned, arrived in Van Diemen's Land in 1840 after being sentenced to seven years' transportation on a charge of stealing two pigs. John Kelly was set free in 1848 and went across Bass Strait to settle at Port Phillip where Ned was born in 1855.

wool industry. Their marriage had been happy from its earliest days and John acknowledged that his 'best beloved Elizabeth' was a woman beyond compare to whom he felt eternal gratitude. She welcomed him home joyously after their 'cruel separation', not remarking that it was entirely his own fault that they had been so long apart but noticing that he had changed little except that gout bothered him more.

The administration of the colony understandably remained unchanged under the interregnum during which the three acting Governors were all commanders of the Corps. Bligh himself left Sydney on 12 May 1810 after a farewell fete given in his honour by his successor. He lived in obscurity as a vice-admiral, undaunted by the fact that twice in his life he had brought men to mutiny. He was a great navigator and loyal lieutenant to whom Nelson once said: 'Bligh, I thank you; you have supported me nobly!' His imprudent spirit, unbridled tongue and vile temper had ruined the substance of the good he so courageously attempted to achieve.

Recognition was readily granted in England that New South Wales had achieved its purpose and remained a fit place to which to send convicts. Any intention by the French to settle had been thwarted, Van Diemen's Land was firmly established, the population had grown to 12,000, some schools, a few churches and a post office existed and Sydney itself was beginning to look like a future city. All manner of fruit and vegetables grew profusely. Land exploration had taken place to the south-west up to a distance of over 100 miles. Horse racing, cricket, primitive football, cockfighting and sundry other English sports were engaged in and the upper orders held evenings of refined entertainment.

Trading and dealing in imports were flourishing, even if sometimes they resembled gambling rather than commerce, and local manufacturing had commenced. Woollen, linen and leather goods were made and several potteries, four breweries and eight windmills were in operation. Hops had been grown since 1806 by James Squire at Kissing Point, but scarcely any wine was produced because the vines were annually blighted. The pastoral industry was developing very slowly because there were still too few sheep in the colony growing fleeces from which coarse hair had been totally bred out. In any event, sheep sold at £2 each after the Hawkesbury floods and there were very few settlers with the capital required to put a flock together. Local publishing had begun to develop; the *Sydney Gazette* continued, and the first book, with the formidable title *New South Wales General Standing Orders*, was published in 1802 followed by the *New South Wales Pocket Almanack* in 1806 and thereafter annually from 1808 until 1835.

Some of the names of those who came in bondage were now bywords for commercial success. Mary Reiby owned vessels, shops, warehouses and farms, while Simeon Lord and Henry Kable were pillars of minor commercial empires. Those with capital and contacts in England could start a valuable enterprise with comparative ease and the Blaxland brothers were notable examples. Gregory arrived in 1806 followed later by John. They were able to buy 1,700 head of cattle from the government herds, receive in perpetuity 4,000 acres of land of their own choice and had at their disposal forty convicts who were maintained for eighteen months at government expense. It was indeed a liberal arrangement and partly explained the rapid prosperity of some free settlers to whom similar avenues would never have been opened in the old countries. Enterprise and necessity were the twins that grew to abundance and ease; decency and order were enjoined on all and observed by many, while the rights of free individuals were respected provided they did not conflict with the ambitions of the powerful.

The lot of convict women continued to be shameful and cruel. In countless instances they were forced into prostitution on the long voyage to Australia. They arrived to a brutal society and found themselves dumped on the shore as there was no shelter provided for them until 1803. Their condition was sometimes worse than that of the Aborigines, who, at least, had the consolation of their families in the process of their decimation. Admittedly some convict women were depraved by choice. For most, necessity knew no virtue when it came to obtaining the means of subsistence for themselves and their children, of whom over half were born out of wedlock as only a quarter of the women were married. For most convict women to be a domestic was virtually to become a mistress. One observer thought that the colony was a burden on the Mother Country because licentiousness prevailed everywhere due to the tolerance shown to fornication. To such observers, the fornicators, unless checked, would inherit the earth. In reality the earth seemed to be gathered into the hands of the Macarthurs, Blaxlands and others in whom the same act of procreation was seen as virtue.

Many, nameless to posterity, continued to suffer under the convict system and amongst them some were exiled to Norfolk Island. Most convicts were lonely and longed for loved ones, whose fading faces and voices were far away in England or Ireland. On the mainland the chain gang and convict garb were familiar sights, constantly reminding everyone of the purpose of the colony's foundation, and lashings and hangings were common occurrences to which even the refined became accustomed. The convicts separated themselves into their own classes and they informed on one another, creating hatred and bitterness. In prisons and lock-ups, young men grew old and worn in bondage, while the road gangs were abominations in which vice and misery abounded and on many a wrist and ankle the marks of the manacles remained for life. Although many convicts escaped the worst hardships of the system by government service in offices or in assignment to private individuals, New South Wales remained a prison for those who came there under sentence.

Close to hand there were other forgotten ones as the blacks about Sydney, reduced now to a remnant, were regarded by some whites as superior to brutes only in their use of weapons and fire. They were powerless when confronting the techniques of industrial man with their own ancient means of a paleolithic society. Some few survivors had gone back towards the mountains or to places unknown to them in previous generations. There, to the now mournful tune of their songs and the recitation of their ancient legends, they dreamt of the seasons before the days of Botany Bay and Sydney Cove. For them the future was shaped by forces beyond their control.

CHAPTER THREE

'The Land, Boys, We Live In'

The fate of New South Wales in 1810 was still in the balance. While playing a minor strategic role as an obstacle to French settlement, it could have remained useful for a time as a dumping ground for English and Irish criminals, as well as being a whaling station. There was little about it which would have ensured long-term survival, especially if the cost to the British government was not commensurate with the economic returns and prospects. To ensure permanent survival, a ruler was needed who combined commonsense with vision, a sense of humanity and the will to use authority. Economic success required a staple product which would attract capital and ensure profit. The ruler was at hand and, on the land spreading out from Sydney, sheep in increasing numbers and with ever finer wool were growing the staple product. When Lachlan Macquarie arrived in New South Wales in 1809, he found it a vast prison. He left in 1822 and it had become a colony.

Lachlan Macquarie, Scot, soldier, a man with enlarged opinions of his own capabilities, quick to be hurt under criticism but of loyal heart and considerable vision, took office as Governor of New South Wales on 1 January 1810. Essentially he was a benevolent autocrat to whom the idea of being curbed by advisors was an anathema. New South Wales to Macquarie was a 'Convict Country', which all, free or bond, had to accept as reality and he was determined to govern it as such. His powers, like those of his predecessors were immense. To let the death penalty run its course or to exercise mercy, to grant freedom or refuse it, to give land or withhold it, to assign convicts or keep them in government service — all this and much besides lay in his keeping.

The new Governor, like Phillip, had fallen almost by chance into his office when the duly nominated governor declined to accept the position. Macquarie received detailed instructions on such matters as the necessity to improve the morals of the colonists by encouraging marriage, promoting education and prohibiting the use of 'Spirituous Liquors'. He was also told to see to the increase of agriculture and stock numbers. Unlike Phillip, he was fortunate in that he arrived with his own regiment of 700 soldiers to replace the New South Wales Corps. The Corps had contributed something in progress together with a good deal in monopolistic economic activity and widespread strife, and the colony was well rid of it, while the absence of the principal actors in the Bligh affair helped also. The general population, especially those who were firmly settled, free or emancipated, saw in Macquarie's person and office the promise of stability after the turbulence of the preceding few years. Economic depression, droughts, floods and caterpillar plagues could not be avoided and occurred variously in 1814, 1817 and 1819. Yet the population, especially the number of convicts, grew rapidly with the final cessation in 1815 of the Napoleonic Wars in which Britain had been spasmodically engaged for over twenty years. Three-quarters of the convicts transported to Australia arrived after the end of the Napoleonic Wars.

Without work, especially among a large convict population, discontent and misery would soon become widespread and Macquarie, with great good sense, was always ready to embark on public projects, particularly in times when the economic situation or natural disasters combined with an abundant supply of convict labour to put at his disposal a workforce not readily employable in the private sector. He built roads, schools, barracks and general utilities, which helped compensate for the neglect of the previous decade. In this he had the support of Francis Greenway, cantankerous and querulous but an architect of some genius, who had been transported for concealing his assets in bankruptcy. Greenway was able to blend the new landscape and the lines of the classical past into buildings which reached their apogee in his masterpiece, St Matthew's Anglican church at Windsor. Greenway led a life of disorder and unhappiness and even Macquarie's patronage did not save him from a flogging by an enraged army officer who deemed himself insulted by the architect. Thus the division in society based on the refusal of many of the free to accept the human worth of the bond or former bond was already apparent.

Macquarie was determined to enhance public morality by encouraging marriages and, in cooperation with the ministers of the now several denominations, by enforcing attendance at services by the convicts. At heart he held that only the Anglicans had any legitimacy and in 1818 he

deported Jeremiah O'Flynn, the original claimant to the Catholic chap-
laincy. With some justification, the Governor considered O'Flynn lacking
in sound constitutional principles and uneducated, and he soon established a relationship of greater trust with O'Flynn's successor, Father
John Therry, and Macquarie laid the foundation stone of St Mary's
church at Hyde Park on 29 October 1821 as the last public act of his
governorship. When the priest passed him the trowel to set the first stone
Macquarie put him at ease by saying that, as an old mason, he would do
the job well.

Education for the growing population of colonial born had become a
pressing concern. The Governor decided to establish the new
'Macquarie' townships of Richmond, Windsor and Liverpool in each of
which he set up a school, and he also opened an orphan school for
females in Parramatta. His own principles did not deter him from using
flexible means to obtain his ends. A hospital was erected at no cost to the
government by giving the builders the right to import 45,000 gallons of
spirits and thus control trade, which gave rise to the name of Rum Hospital, although the gracious building deserved better. In 1817 Macquarie
showed considerable courage by helping with the establishment of the
Bank of New South Wales without authorization from London, but he
was always careful to appease the ruffled by naming towns or geographical features after English royalty or officials in those instances
when he refrained from permitting them to be named after himself.

As the first military Governor, Macquarie's interest in exploration by
land was uppermost. The land between the sea and the Blue Mountains
was rapidly filling up with settlers, and in 1813 William Wentworth,
Gregory Blaxland and William Lawson crossed the mountain barrier and
saw pastures 'sufficient to feed all the stock in the colony for thirty years'.
A road was built which opened the plains beyond the mountains to
grazing, and thus, subsequently, gave rise to the foundation of the town of
Bathurst in 1815. The fine lands of the Hunter Valley near Newcastle
were soon occupied and Port Macquarie was named by John Oxley in
1818. Macquarie visited it and decided to place a settlement for hardened
convicts there so that, with its majestic headland looking out to the Pacific
and over the mouth of the Hastings River, with long miles of glorious
beaches to north and south, it became a place of human suffering and
degradation. Norfolk Island, long since proved useless for timber and
flax, was abandoned in 1814 and its inhabitants transferred to Van
Diemen's Land, where some took up residence at New Norfolk, built inns
and churches, farmed hops and grew prosperous.

Collins of large heart and cheerful disposition had died in 1810 and

Hobart Town was named after Lord Hobart, Secretary of State for the Colonies. There were attempts to shorten it to Hobarton and, finally, in 1881, Hobart was settled on. By 1820 the town had taken on a semblance of order and was unlike the shanty town Macquarie had seen when he visited in 1811. South Sea whalers had already made it their base and by 1825 it had become the second colonial capital.

was succeeded in 1813 as Lieutenant-Governor of Van Diemen's Land by 'Mad' Tom Davey, whom Macquarie considered a low buffoon but who did all he could with the human material at his disposal. The first direct consignment of 200 male convicts arrived in Hobart in 1812 but a vessel carrying female convicts was captured by an American privateer. The women were put down on an island in the Atlantic on 17 January 1813 and never heard of again. Davey's humane disorganization gave way to a semblance of order in 1817 with the arrival of William Sorell. The new Lieutenant-Governor quickly put paid to the lawless regime of escaped convicts led by Michael Howe, who called himself 'Governor of the Woods'. Sorell gave shape to the administrative life of the island; supported the development of agriculture and pastoralism; tried, without much success, to protect the Aborigines from the worst ravages of the whites, and ruled firmly over the convict establishments.

Once elements of social harmony had been established, free settlers began to come in increasing numbers and Sorell, in recognition of their needs, started the Bank of Van Diemen's Land and imported merinos from Macarthur's Camden flock to form the base of the fine wool industry. Respected and even loved by many who saw his essential decency and sense of justice, Sorell came into disfavour because he lived with another man's wife while his own remained in England with their seven children, but Macquarie was tolerant of this situation. His career was over by 1824 and Van Diemen's Land owed much of its early development to his wise rule.

The convicts to Macquarie were children of misfortune, although he had a generally low opinion of many of the women whom he regarded as 'very depraved'. Once a convict became free the Governor held firmly that he or she stood on an equal footing with everyone else and that no obstacles ought to be put by society in their attaining such a state. In his judgement most convicts, with proper encouragement, would regain their rightful place, and he illustrated his policy by selecting those who proved their value to fulfil roles of responsibility. He mixed socially with some chosen few of them and named Michael Robinson as poet laureate despite his convict status and the generally poor quality of his verse.

There were immediate objections to this policy of social equality and Marsden refused to associate with two emancipists whom Macquarie appointed to the board of trustees of the Parramatta turnpike road to which the clergyman was also nominated. Judge Jeffrey Bent would not permit ex-convict attorneys to plead in his court, which effectively kept it closed for eighteen months, and on similar grounds, the officers of a new regiment, which arrived in 1814, refused to dine at the Governor's table. Undeterred, Macquarie made land grants to emancipists but they were small in acreage, averaging twenty to thirty acres each. The Governor always looked favourably upon those born in the colony, who, together with the emancipists, made up three-quarters of the population. They were the people whom Macquarie deemed the established inhabitants of the land which, following the lead given earlier by Flinders, he called Australia. To his London superiors, he made it plain that free settlers, including the Blaxlands, were 'by far the most discontented Persons in the Colony' as they thought that the government owed them favours because they had deigned to come to Australia. He also pointed out that it cost more to settle them in comparison to emancipists. To him the best settlers were the former convicts 'who cultivate the ground in Gratitude', while the free settlers either allowed it to lie idle or sold it as quickly as possible.

The Aborigines came early to the benevolent if paternalistic attention of the Governor, who set up a school for them. After meeting with the remains of the groupings around Sydney, he invited them to closer and more open relations. Annually, at Parramatta, he engaged in a kind of festivity, handing out medals and uniforms to the Aborigines and generally behaving as if the Indian Raj could be duplicated in Australia. It was all completely futile, not solely due to a clash of civilizations but because the Aborigines refused to relinquish their own ways and adorn themselves, corporally or spiritually, in the trappings of another's.

An old black man put in words the dilemma which the relationship between the two races now presented. In response to a remonstrance that his fire threatened to burn down a hay stack, he replied with the dignity of immemorial security, 'You know that we must have our fire; the country is *ours*, *you* must take care of your corn'. In the end it was a question of whose fire was the strongest, and in 1815, despite his good will, Macquarie sent an expedition to the Hawkesbury district to punish the Aborigines for their predatory habits, which often included killing and stealing livestock, and to offer them the chance to become settlers. The military shot fourteen of them dead and took five prisoners.

Despite Macquarie's efforts at moral reform, the estimate held by many in the British Isles and expressed by William Wilberforce in the House of Commons was of 'a nest of vipers' fast being built in New South Wales. It was therefore decided to send out a competent person with the task of ascertaining the true state of affairs. John Bigge, not yet forty but experienced as former Chief Justice of Trinidad, arrived in September 1819. He was asked to report whether transportation was sufficiently horrendous as a form of punishment or whether Macquarie with his 'ill considered compassion' was turning the place into a happy haven for criminals.

Bigge went to work with a will, ably abetted by John Blaxland and others whose antipathy to Macquarie was deep-seated. Given his advisors, it was easy for Bigge to conclude that the colony should become a vast sheep-walk, ruled by men possessing large estates and with a properly submissive convict work force at their disposal. This was a proposition Macquarie partly agreed with, but he also had another vision of a penitentiary gradually evolving into a society in which men and women, reclaimed from crime by honest toil and the chance of a stake in the land, would throw off the stains of their past and become the rulers of their own destiny. Bigge's was a realistic political judgement because it fitted closely the developing economic reality and also cut the cost to the home country of the upkeep of the convict establishment, a matter which necessity made uppermost in the minds of the British civil servants and their political masters.

Phillip erected a timber-framed, wattle-and-daub government house at Parramatta which Hunter rebuilt in brick in 1800. Macquarie extended it and Greenway supervised the building of the front portico in 1816. The elegance of old Government House delighted the visitors Macquarie liked to entertain there.

Bigge's other strictures on Macquarie's rule, accusing him of over-spending, erecting ostentatious public buildings, showing favour to emancipists and mismanaging convicts, were unjust and mainly ill-founded. The principal accusation was that the Governor had deprived free settlers of convict labour, which was wide of the mark. Macquarie had certainly turned to a renewal of public works in 1817 which necessitated the increased use of convict labour. But it was a disastrous year of floods during which the influx of convict labour could not be usefully assigned.

Bigge's accusations were fed by the exclusive element in society who wanted to keep ex-convicts on the fringe and themselves control the economy by using convict labour to that end. In the midst of all the tension caused by Bigge's visit, it was with relief that Macquarie finally heard that his third attempt to resign had been accepted. He sailed from Australia in 1822 and eked out his days at home trying to salvage his reputation from the 'false, vindictive and malicious' report of Bigge. Macquarie left his mark on the land not merely with his name, which was revered by thousands, but through a legacy worthy of every generation because he tried to judge human beings on their potential rather than their past.

The population was approaching 25,000 of whom two-thirds were convicts or ex-convicts, so it was easy to brand them all with criminality. The remarkable fact, however, was that the criminals and former criminals generally behaved in a way far removed from that which had caused them to be transported in the first instance. Even more positive was the notable manner in which the children born from them rejected a tendency to crime. They were often slighted by the local appellation 'Currency' which implied that they were of lesser value than those of sterling character born of free parents in the old countries.

The native-born tended to marry amongst themselves, to avoid the 'higher orders' in society and to work industriously. Newcomers sometimes regarded them with humour because — out of the amalgam of accents ranging from cockney to Irish, from rural English to Scottish, and from the upper classes to the dwellers on the hulks — a new idiom was emerging spoken in a new accent which, in both tonality and content, seemed inferior and slightly foreign. Finally with their quiet assumption that Australia was their home by right, their easy manner and their familiarity with each other and the land itself, they seemed to imply that theirs was a unique position. Governor Macquarie had accepted all this and indeed seemed to show pride in it while others, and notably the well-to-do, deplored it.

In London the question was finally asked whether New South Wales could continue to be ruled by an all-powerful governor in the manner of Macquarie or whether it was time to give the more respectable citizens a say in their own affairs. It was clearly inconceivable that any form of democracy based on a vote could be introduced into what was, in effect, a huge prison. Nevertheless, some of the more worthy citizens could be called upon to advise the Governor in an official way and in 1823 a Legislative Council for New South Wales was established.

Van Diemen's Land was given a Council in 1825 and it then began to enjoy a little independence from Sydney. Chief Justices were also appointed in Sydney and Hobart to preside over the courts and a legal system began to proliferate with quarter sessions, petty sessions, paid and unpaid magistrates and all the other trappings designed to ensure that law and good order prevailed, especially in the realm of the acquisition and retention of property. New South Wales was especially fortunate in that, with the appointment of Francis Forbes as first Chief Justice, it acquired a judge of probity, dignity, wisdom and honour. At the same time, the role of the Church of England was also strengthened symbolically by a regulation, which never became effective, issued in London in 1825 which set aside one-seventh of the land for the support of its clergy and schools, despite the fact that the Church was not by law established as in England.

John Macarthur was the principal representative of that portion of the community which saw itself as possessing both the right and duty to lead other less advantaged persons, and he was duly appointed to the Legislative Council. Since his return to Botany Bay in 1817, he had greatly prospered with enormous increases to his land and flocks. By 1822 he was winning gold medals for his wool from the Society of Arts in London and also receiving extraordinarily high prices for it. His days of wholeness in mind and body were drawing in, and by 1832, officially now a lunatic, he was removed from the Legislative Council to die in 1834 survived by Elizabeth, three sons and three daughters whose loyalty and hard work were much responsible for his reputation as a breeder of fine-woolled sheep. His remains were put to rest at Camden Park which had grown to over 60,000 acres of the finest land in the colony. Never one to curry favour with friends or to forgive an enemy, implacably opposed to those who wanted rights he saw as contrary to his own, he remains the unique publicist of the pastoral industry, without being its only founder.

While Macarthur was declining, others were on the rise and none more so than William Charles Wentworth. Son of D'Arcy Wentworth's union with a convict woman, Catherine Crowley, William was born at sea on

St Matthew's Church at Windsor was Greenway's masterpiece. The foundation stone was laid on 11 October 1816. The ceremony was repeated two days later when it was noticed that the silver dollar and dump Macquarie had placed beneath the stone were missing.

the voyage to Norfolk Island in 1790. Always conscious of the 'sacred claims' that Australia had upon him, he was educated in England, and went to the bar there but devoted much of his life to winning a free constitution for his country, although his own concept of freedom was limited by his developing conviction that democracy had to be reined in by men whose intelligence and position gave them an obligation to rule.

When Wentworth realized that his father had been tried four times for highway robbery and that, having quarrelled with John Macarthur, he could not marry his daughter Elizabeth upon whom he had set his heart, he became the most vigorous crusader for the Australian-born and the arch enemy of the exclusive clique who declined to mix with emancipists or to see them restored to their full civil rights. After being called to the English bar, he wrote, at Cambridge, a poem which was full of pride in his beloved Australia while still seeing her as England's 'last born infant' and therefore 'A new Britannia in another world!'

Like so many provincials since empires first founded colonies, Wentworth always suffered from not belonging in either world. His heart, his struggles and his sufferings were all Australian while his spirit, mind and final hopes rested in England. They proved to be irreconcilables that never fused. On his return to New South Wales in 1824, he spent his energies attacking the government and the landed establishment in the *Australian* newspaper which he and Robert Wardell founded. He praised Macquarie's successor Brisbane for his liberal stance and attacked Darling (Governor 1824–31), who believed that upholding the King's authority was his foremost duty even when doing so aroused widespread displeasure. Darling was openly in favour of the large landholders, but he brought some benefit to the colony by creating an effective civil service.

During his early years of struggle for popular rights, Wentworth's most notable victory, for which he had long fought, was the introduction of trial by jury into the criminal courts which was achieved by 1833. Privately, however, he was becoming a mirror image of Macarthur and those whom he most despised. He bought a stately mansion at Vaucluse and adorned it with all the trappings of another world, he multiplied his sheep runs to at least fifteen and his legal activity helped to swell his wealth. The poor, the humble, the emancipists and the native-born still looked on him as their hero, especially when he and his friends, from the beach at Vaucluse, farewelled the departing vessel of the despised Darling with a blaze of bonfires and barbecues, gin and beer. How far he would lead them if their desire was genuine equality with their betters, was another matter, but, in the meantime, lion-hearted and lion-maned, Wentworth went his way scarcely noticing that New South Wales itself was changing.

The ways of change were steady but perceptible and they included the establishment of a Chamber of Commerce in Sydney in 1825, a subscription library under the direction of Thomas de la Condamine, Darling's secretary, which was opened in the following year, and in 1827 the Colonial (later Australian) Museum was founded. Gradually Australia was developing from a much despised and maligned prison to a place suitable for British capital and British free settlers. Wentworth himself wrote a book on the colony detailing its development which had helped produce this effect. The economic advantages to be derived from wool, the opening of new lands to the pastoral industry and the ready availability of a labour force, still based on transportation but gradually including free settlers, all helped development. It was fashionable in some quarters throughout the 1820s to portray Botany Bay, with intentional use of the name, as a sink of inquity into which the scum of humanity was thrown, although by the 1830s this misrepresentation was wearing thin in the eyes of those with any real knowledge of the colony.

After the crossing of the Blue Mountains, exploration went ahead apace. In 1818 the Surveyor-General, John Oxley, pushed further west past Bathurst and then north-east, naming the rivers, the Namoi, Peel, Apsley, Macleay and Hastings. His most important discovery was that of the Liverpool Plains where settlement soon followed. Phillip Parker King, who was a legitimate son of the former Governor, was born on Norfolk Island in 1791. From 1817 to 1822 he carried out four skilful surveys of the coast of northern Australia, thereby making a significant contribution to exploration. At an early age, King was made a fellow of the Royal Society, and in 1855 he was promoted to Rear-Admiral. He was amongst the very few native-born in that period who become well known outside their own country.

For the brave, the skilled or the mere adventurous, exploration was always hazardous, and it demanded courage and perseverance. The navigators and explorers had to face uncharted seas, dense bush, flooded rivers, extensive marshes, trackless wastes, high slopes followed by deep valleys, and not infrequent attacks by Aborigines which were forcefully repulsed.

While further coastal surveying had not revealed land fit for pastoralism, the conviction was still strong that close to the coast or beyond the mountain range there would always be fertile land available. Such proved to be the case when, in the steps first of James Meehan and later Charles Throsby, settlement took place in a vast area beyond the Cow Pastures through to Bathurst in the north-west and then down through Goulburn, past Lake George, to the south-west. Throsby said with justification and foresight that he had covered ground 'where fine woolled sheep may be increased to any amount in a climate peculiarly congenial to them'.

Although the continuation of exploration south-west of Sydney was relatively simple as the terrain was not difficult, in the opening up of pastoral country, it was one of unparalleled importance. Hamilton Hume, born near Parramatta in 1797, and English-born William Hovell set out from Hume's station near Gunning in 1824 with a small party, including six convicts. They soon came to a gracious river which they left with the Aboriginal name Murrumbidgee and going further south they saw the Alps, which they named, to their east. The highest peak of the Alps was not named until 1840 when Paul Strzelecki called it Kosciusko in honour of the Polish democratic patriot.

When Hume and Hovell arrived at another imposing river, with winding billabongs and great gums hugging its banks, they called it Hume. It was changed later to Murray in honour of an English public servant of minor consequence and never went back to any of its names, such as Millewa, from the tongues of the old people who had lived from its munificence for long ages. Hume and Hovell arrived, eleven weeks after setting out, at Corio Bay and they mistook it for Westernport which was their objective.

Hume and Hovell's journey was not followed up until 1836 when Major Thomas Mitchell also went south and west. He penetrated into country which caused him to prophesy that he was 'the harbinger of mighty changes' because men and animals would trace his path into land of undreamt fertility. Unmindful of the Aborigines who had long been there, or even of the help given by them to him in his journey, Mitchell proclaimed that at length a country had been found 'ready for the immediate reception of civilized men' and he called it 'Australia Felix' to contrast it with those wastes he had seen a few weeks before as he explored the desert about the Darling River.

When searching for a suitable site for another penal outpost at an appropriate distance from settlement, Oxley discovered in 1823 a river flowing to the coast about 600 miles north of Sydney. He called the river after Governor Brisbane and a settlement was established at Moreton Bay in 1824. Convicts who had been reconvicted since their arrival in the colony were sent to Moreton Bay and Captain Patrick Logan became commandant in the following year. Logan was later remembered by some as the founding father of the north because of his drive to establish the settlement and his exploratory work in the region. By the convicts, he was regarded as a depraved beast to whom cruelty was natural. In eight months in 1827 he ordered 200 floggings totalling over 11,000 lashes in a convict population of less than 700. When he was killed by the Aborigines the convicts 'manifested insane joy at the news of his murder, and sang and hoorayed all night'.

Despite the presence of the penal settlement, pastoral expansion went ahead in the north. Allan Cunningham, botanist and explorer, made his way from the Hunter Valley onto the Darling Downs in 1827 and he described the more than 5,000 square miles of the Downs as inexhaustible in pasture with an 'extraordinary luxuriance of growth' suitable to both sheep and cattle. Cunningham then found a pass which bears his name between the Downs and the coast, thus allowing the settlement of the Downs and with easy access to a port at Brisbane.

While these exploratory expeditions had almost immediate economic significance through the expansion of the pastoral industry, another development in settlement occurred in those years which, while merely symbolic of its stated objective, had the psychological effect of making British claims to the whole of the continent a reality. Over twenty years previously, a French expedition had named the whole south-east coast-line Napoleon's Land with a gulf called after Bonaparte and another after Josephine. There were fears that the French intended to take some part of the mainland for their own, a mistaken but understandable reaction given the Napoleonic Wars. The long-term effect was a determination to get in first and in 1824 a military station was placed on Melville Island to the north-west of the continent and moved onto the mainland two years later. A settlement was also established at Westernport where Hume and Hovell thought they had been and another began at King Georges Sound in the extreme south-west of the continent. The first two were quickly relinquished but the last became Albany and, in time, flourished, especially as a whaling station and was thus the first white settlement in Australia's western half.

In this manner, the secure tenure of the whole land mass was ensured by the 1820s and the means of using those parts of it which were regarded as suitable were increasing rapidly. By a happy combination of careful breeding for the climatic conditions and the available grasses, the sheep fitted the new land as easily as the kangaroo had done. It was an ominous coincidence that, when he came to Australia, the white settler in some measure adopted the precise means of subsistence of the Aborigines. For food and eventually for profit he fished the seas and for the same purpose he used the land but the pastoral industry caused immediate and understandable conflict with the Aborigines. Where the kangaroos had grazed the sheep did likewise, yet, while the Aborigines were content with a moderate sufficiency of land, no boundary could contain the whites.

Thus, the spread of the pastoral industry was the most decisive threat to the continued existence of black civilization and, in some real measure, to the very race itself. That the Aborigines opposed white expansion with all the forces they could muster is undeniable. It is equally a fact that in the end in Australia, as elsewhere when a more technologically advanced civilization clashed with one not so advanced, the civilization of the white race triumphed. One result was that, although in 1821 a meagre 175,000 pounds of wool were exported to England, the clip increased to a million pounds in 1826 and to two million four years later, although Spain and Germany still accounted for the greater imports of wool there.

The basis of a permanent and expanding economy was thus laid, which served rather than competed with British interests, opened up possibilities for surplus capital and labour, and gave prospects of bene-ficial trade. As a consequence, Australia showed no signs of doing other than becoming a large scale consumer of British manufactured goods, and India and China played a minor role in imports. Most attention was rapidly fixed on the pastoral industry to the detriment of manufacturing, which had already shown promise. Items ranging from salt to ships, candles, leather goods, some tobacco and good quality cheese, cloth, hats, blankets and stockings were made and the wine industry was improving. There were also some developments in exports with flour to the Cape Colony in 1820, horses to Batavia and India, timber to England and wheat to the Cape and Rio de Janiero. None of this ceased, but its importance diminished as wool became the dominant staple component in the economy.

In 1828, a census was taken in New South Wales, just forty years after Phillip and his contingent had perched themselves precariously at Sydney Cove. The blacks, or what remained of them, were not counted, but the whites now numbered 36,598, of whom a third lived in Sydney. The ratio of one, who had come by their own choice, to three, who had not, still prevailed amongst the adults while only one child in four could look to parents without the convict stain. There were three males to every female so that it was a male dominated society, and 25,248 declared themselves Protestants to 11,236 Catholics, which left only 114 non-Christians. Those simple figures reveal more about New South Wales than any number of diatribes designed to denigrate it. The colony was home to the native born, to the emancipists and to those who worked its soil and minded its flock. The rest, jailers and newcomers, were transients to be tested by time. Amongst those who passed the test was John Dunmore Lang.

Lang was an indomitable Scottish Presbyterian minister, writer and historian. He was also a man of large vision, financial ineptitude, narrow prejudices and almost unrelenting bigotry. His whole life was given point by an unsurpassed love for Australia, which seemed to start from the day of his arrival in 1823 and grow in intensity thereafter. Impressed with the need to uplift educational standards, he was concerned with the founding of a school and for the general population he started a newspaper. His greatest weakness was an insatiable urge for litigation, while his quick-ness to judge his fellow man was legendary. Lang was encouraged and never criticised by his wife, Wilhelmina, whom he married when he was thirty-one and she, eighteen. The couple shared with many other Aus-tralians the tragedy of infant mortality, as five of their ten children died very young. Of Australia, Lang wrote that she could never be 'a land of slaves', and his life's work was devoted to her uplifting.

By the late 1820s, there were 13,000 convicts put out to work for masters, mostly in the pastoral industry, and their labour was the key to economic development. Bigge's recommendations had been followed about the use of convict labour, which made for a harsh system of chance in which a convict enjoyed reasonable comfort and dignity under a humane master but degradation and suffering under another. British capitalists had also listened to Bigge and New South Wales was now seen as a place where capital could be safely invested; they had turned their attention to the benefits to be gained from a colony where physical coercion was the accepted means of controlling a labour force. The lash was used vigorously throughout the whole of society, and public hangings, to the order of forty to fifty a year, provided a form of sport, as well as a warning, to the populace. When the rights of property were violated the law normally showed no mercy. William Longhurst, aged twenty-three, was hanged in 1827 at Hobart for sheep stealing, which was the only charge levelled against him since his arrival a few years previously. Port

From necessity, the dwellings of the early settlers were makeshift and rude. Local materials, bark, saplings and hewn timber were used because stones and bricks were unavailable.

Macquarie and Moreton Bay (Brisbane) had become places of exile and punishment, and then, in 1825, Norfolk Island was reopened to become a place where death was often chosen as a way of escape by those whom the system had broken beyond hope. Under the command of Lieutenant-Colonel James Thomas Morrisset and his second-in-command Foster Fyans the island of 'soft beauty' became again the 'old Hell' where men were driven to suicide by lottery. One convict, Michael Burns, was given 2,000 lashes in less than three years and one of his transgressions, for which he received a flogging was 'Singing a Song', presumably a rebel Irish song. Norfolk Island was 'a place of sorrow and wailing' into which men entered without hope but filled with horror.

While the regime, with every encouragement from London, per-petrated its brutalities on the outcasts a veil of normalcy was gradually draped over public society. Another small step towards self-government was taken in 1828 with the enlargement of the Legislative Councils to fifteen members, seven of whom were nominated by the Governor while the rest were government officials, so that authority continued to reside where it had always been, except that the Governor now ruled through legislation rather than simple fiat. In other ways, society was developing despite a severe drought in the late 1820s which was made worse by the unrestrained buying of sheep and cattle by anyone with capital. An Agri-cultural Society had been founded, of which Brisbane was the patron, with the express purpose of importing further pure merinos to improve the colony's flocks. The pastoral industry was boosted by the free grant-ing of land to settlers to the extent of three million acres on the mainland in the 1820s and a further two million in Van Diemen's Land, where settlement was necessarily much more confined.

The two most notable examples of patronage and dealing in high places of the period were the foundation of the Australian Agricultural Company in 1824 and the Van Diemen's Land Company in 1825. The former had its origins in the efforts of Macarthur and other wealthy land-owners, who formed a company in London with a capital of one million pounds and were then granted a million acres in the Newcastle-Port Stephens district of New South Wales. The Company proposed to con-centrate on fine wool and cattle, as well as to produce flax, olives and other items. It initially faltered under bad management, but, gradually, with convict servants, vast flocks and the coal leases granted at Newcastle by the government in 1828, the Company prospered and gave an example of successful expenditure of capital, which was not lost on British investors.

The Van Diemen's Land Company received 330,000 acres in the

James Oatley arrived in Sydney in 1815 to serve a life sentence for stealing two feather beds. He made this, his nineteenth grandfather clock, in 1822. The case is of Australian cedar and is typical of much high-quality Australian furniture of the period. Oatley had been conditionally pardoned in 1821 and died at Sydney in 1839.

north-west of the island at 1s 6d per acre. It suffered huge losses due to ineptitude and was detested by the locals for its demands for convict labour and claims to government favours. Gradually the Company developed an area of prosperous country which took in the whole of the north-west of the island and was based on centres at Burnie, Stanley and Woolnorth. The first manager, Edward Curr, held that a treaty ought to have been made with the Aborigines, but eventually the conflict between them and the Company's servants became so intense that the virtual extermination of the local blacks, either by killing or deportation to government reserves, became inevitable. Both companies survived, although much reduced. In its dealings with the general public, the Van Diemen's Land Company continued to act in the imperious manner it had begun to use in the 1820s.

Culture, whether popular or high, was a frail growth in a society still struggling to implant itself. Nevertheless, Sydney, with increasing numbers of fine houses, owned by officers, merchants, professional men and land-holders, with flowers, vegetables, fruit trees, English dogs, fine carriages and servants, bore testimony to stability and permanence. The twice-knighted physician and landowner John Jamison had a fine estate near Penrith where he built a famous home called Regentville. At his table it was possible to dine casually on 'mock turtle soup, boiled fowls, round of beef, delicious fish of three kinds, curried duck, goose and wildfowl' all washed down by madeira, burgundy, various liquers and English ale.

Conversation amongst the majority revolved less and less around the affairs of the mother countries, and a greater emphasis was placed on the social, political, economic and personal matters of daily life in New South Wales. Dinners and balls were held; hunting, horse and boat racing were popular; cricket, introduced in 1803, was given permanency when the military formed a club in 1826 and prize fighting was enjoyed by the 'lower orders'. The people could depend on an ample supply of food, with mutton and beef much more readily available to everyone than had been the case in England and Ireland. Fruit grew in abundance — figs, strawberries, gooseberries, oranges, apples, pears, grapes, and peaches. In fact, every common fruit known in England and most of its vegetables adorned tables which in the past had not seen other than potatoes and an odd apple.

Van Diemen's Land, so much more restricted in area and cut off by Bass Strait, took on, nevertheless, with its dominant convict sub-structure, similar characteristics to New South Wales. Indeed, its history since 1803 was that of the parent colony but written small except in violence. Half of the island's white population of 5,468 in 1820 was convict. Some of them were sent to the far west coast to Macquarie Harbour where they suffered such misery that many preferred death to life and there was one notable case of cannibalism during a failed escape bid in 1822. Commercially the island began to stand on its own feet. Wool was exported to England and soon afterwards wheat was sent to New South Wales. Van Diemen's Land was an island of huge forest areas, wild rivers and impenetrable mountains, especially in the south and south-west, but in its central parts and on the northern and eastern coasts lay fertile land, and its general beauty had taken the hearts of many who had come there.

In both places, much of life was brutal and coarse, with sports and recreation that included over-drinking and brawling, while there were the ever-present reminders that both were penal settlements still. Soldiers stood about or marched through the streets of every garrison town. A whole series of regulations governed personal movement, firearms were controlled, the laws strictly enforced, and general musters of the population and its livestock held, thereby recalling to everyone the purpose of foundation. Yet because the means of subsistence were at hand, with employment of some kind open to all except those regarded as incapable or incorrigible, hope was also present. Hope for the future spelt the difference between Australia and the Old World, although most people were conscious for several months of the year of another difference, in Sydney at least. One visitor to the city in the 1820s wrote, 'English shops — English faces — English everything — but the heat! the heat alas! that destroys the illusion.'

Some colonial children in the late 1820s were the sons and daughters of men and women born in the colony. The sons continued to show a sense of independence, while newly-arrived observers often noticed that the young women had a saucy spirit and fetching look and were not afraid of work, even of the non-genteel kind. From the very beginning the newly-opened continent had been regarded with astonishment in the scientific circles of Europe. Botanists, geologists, zoologists and geographers pored over this 'reversal of Nature', full of freakish things like egg-laying mammals and flightless birds, trees which held their leaves and shed their bark, red blackberries and black swans. The Philosophical Society of Australasia was founded to awaken a spirit of research and excite a thirst for information about all these natural wonders, but few of the native-born and old hands took any interest in its proceedings.

The first and second generation of native-born were fiercely proud of being Australians and of Australia itself, and that, for the time, seemed enough. Few of them were invited to the dinners Wentworth and his friends put on, but they could all have joined in the toast which was invariably proposed on such occasions 'The land, boys, we live in'. Had they done so, they would presumably have been unaware that the rejection of Macquarie's vision of Australia, in which they would inherit the land, had meant the acceptance of Bigge's vision, in which the wealthy would come to control it. The land in large measure was being given to those who came with wealth and patronage, and the pattern of large scale ownership was already set for the future.

CHAPTER FOUR

Pastoral Australia

The 1830s helped to establish the future shape of Australian society. They were the years of pastoral expansion, free immigration and new ways of granting land. During the decade, an economic system based on imported capital was consolidated, the struggle between the exclusives and the emancipists spent itself, the assignment of convicts in New South Wales ceased and the stage was set for the cessation of transportation itself. In the west the first settlement began to show signs of permanency, while South Australia, much vaunted child of brilliant ideas, had to tread the hard road of practicality. From Van Diemen's Land settlers came across Bass Strait to Port Phillip, and Major Mitchell's route to the south was followed by overlanders from New South Wales, who helped found Melbourne and open up Port Phillip to sheep. The progress made in democratic developments centered on trial by jury. A national ethos was in the process of being formed in the bush by convicts, ex-convicts and the native-born. Finally, the 1830s also saw a hardening of attitudes to the Aborigines, which meant their virtual extermination in Van Diemen's Land and their decimation along the eastern seaboard.

In the previous decade, public servants in London and their administrators in Australia were in charge of a prison, the regulation of which was comparatively simple, although with the coming of more free settlers the nature of the old penal society was changing. In the 1830s it became clearer to the public servants that, as well as a vast goal, Australia might be an attractive location for a greater infusion of British capital, satisfy the urge of some of the middle class to acquire land, which was no longer a possibility at home, and provide employment for deserving unfortunates from an over-supplied labour market. But a plan was needed to achieve these laudable objectives, and, at the same time, untangle the web of favouritism, speculation, absentee landlordism and sheer ineptitude which already plagued the administration of land settlement, although under Governor Darling some headway had been made in sorting out these problems. An attempt at a different method of settlement, based on British capital and without a convict workforce, was tried in Western Australia, but, by the early 1830s, it had begun to crumble and gave point to the need for an entirely new method.

Captain James Stirling explored the Swan River area of Western Australia in 1827 and was impressed with its strategic value and economic potential as a site for a new colony. A settlement there would forestall the French for good; provide a link with India, China and the islands to the north; and, eventually, become a stopping place between Britain and eastern Australia. Possessed of a fine climate, some promising soil and abundant water, it seemed ideal. Back in London, Stirling pressed the government to establish a settlement at the Swan and, although initially reluctant because of the expense, the decision was finally made to go ahead. On 2 May 1829, that area of Australia which did not make up part of New South Wales was, at the mouth of the Swan, taken possession of for Britain by Captain Fremantle. The continent was now officially

The site of Fremantle was established in 1829 and it was a well ordered town by 1832. Aborigines often assembled there to feast on whales brought to the port by American whalers, and from there the Fenian prisoners escaped in 1875. Fremantle was the site of the unsuccessful defence of the America's Cup in 1987.

British. Six weeks later the first Governor arrived, in the person of Stirling, accompanied by free settlers, public servants and soldiers, and, on 12 August, a tree was felled to mark the foundation of Perth.

A mania for the Swan River had begun in England, fostered by Thomas Peel in secret partnership with Solomon Levey, a former convict who had become a millionaire in New South Wales. Levey put up £20,000 towards the venture, all of which he finally lost. Peel was prepared to provide the settlers if the government gave the land; a million acres was promised but only 250,000 were granted in the first instance. More importantly, no convicts were to be sent out, which meant that there would be no cheap labour. Despite the presence by 1830 of over 4,000 persons on the land between the coast and the mountains and in the two towns of Perth and Fremantle and the fact that Stirling was sufficiently confident of the future as to hold a ball in Government House, the colony rapidly languished so that in 1832 only 1,500 were left.

The main reason for decline was that by this time land could only be acquired at 5s per acre instead of freely and English interest had fallen away. Furthermore, it had become apparent that sufficient suitable land, available markets and a ready supply of labour were all lacking, and, had it not been for Stirling's persistence and Peel's great fortitude, the settlement would probably have been abandoned. Stirling went to England in August 1832 to ask for further financial help but was refused. Western Australia, like Sydney Cove fifty years previously, seemed to be left to work out its own destiny. Nevertheless, because it had started on a basis of private English investment and its early men of mark were drawn from the lower gentry, Western Australia remained more heavily under English influence than the other colonies.

It was in this atmosphere of unsuccessful settlement that the ideas of a skilled propagandist and entrepreneur won favour. Although Edward Gibbon Wakefield had never visited Australia, while serving three years in Newgate Prison for the abduction of a fifteen-year-old heiress, he thought about the fact that England lacked land but possessed both capital and labour. He decided that perhaps if decent English stock could be enticed to Australia with the promise of land and labour a new age would dawn. The linchpin of the plan was to set the price of land high enough to ensure that the moderately affluent alone could buy it, while the rest would remain, at least temporarily, as a labour force. A high price per acre would also ensure the concentration of settlement, which, in Wakefield's view, would result in the growth of civilized communities, while low prices would mean the dispersal of settlers on large tracts of land without the softening effects of civilization. If necessary, the proceeds of land sales could be used by the government to bring in more and more labourers, who in turn would eventually buy land, and a chain effect would thereby be initiated, thus planting the basic elements of British civilization on the limitless wastes lying idle in Australia. One thing eluded Wakefield. How high was the price to be set? It could not be too low — perhaps 12s — perhaps £1 per acre would be enough, and later, time and experience would work it out.

Wakefield's theory ignored the possibility of ineffective administration, greed, the effect of speculation, differing soil qualities and the small size of local markets for consumable products. For New South Wales the scheme bordered on the absurd as it never addressed the problem of what to do about those who had simply gone inland and squatted. The squatters were already occupying thousands of acres of Crown land and it was unlikely that they would pay any price for it, no matter how low, while in Van Diemen's Land most of the good land had already been taken.

Nevertheless, the public servants in London were sufficiently interested to give the plan a try, and a new system for the whole of Australia came into effect in 1831. There would be no more free grants, and land was to be sold within the settled districts contained within the so-called Nineteen Counties, which included an area of about twenty million acres stretching west to the Lachlan River, north to the Manning and south to the Moruya. The price was set at a minimum of 5s per acre, which horrified Wakefield as he thought it far too low. In fact, the new arrangement of sale at 5s per acre meant very little because, before 1831, it was already difficult for a man without means to hold onto land even when he got it for nothing, as the history of failure amongst small settlers had already proved. After 1831 it became harder to get land, except beyond the boundaries of the Counties, but it was still a problem to hold it, once acquired, if further capital was lacking to improve it. Men of slender means rarely passed on land as an inheritance, and Wakefield need not have been alarmed at the low price set by the government.

It was clear that there were advantages to be gained by the use of the revenue from the sale of land being applied to forms of assisted migration. England with its unemployment problem and Australia with a shortage of labour would benefit. There was some hope also that the government may through selectivity help to redress the gross imbalance between the sexes, which by 1833 still stood at three males to one female. In the event, £125,000 was raised from the sale of 350,000 acres in New South Wales from 1832 to 1836, while 40,000 immigrants arrived as well as 35,000 convicts in the decade to 1840. Many convicts became assigned workers in the pastoral industry, but most of the immigrants preferred to remain in or close to Sydney and other centres. Rural labour consequently remained scarce and wages high, while farming, fundamental to Wakefield's scheme, did not prosper. Methods of farming were often primitive, drought and crop diseases were frequent, transport to market was costly and the alternative of pastoralism too attractive to those with capital and the desire for a quick return for farming to be successful. There was the added anomaly whereby the new regulations on land sales could only be applied in settled areas, where there was some hope of surveying the land, while the squatters out in the unsettled districts had free use of the land. As a result, an invidious distinction arose between the unlawful squatter on his broad acres out beyond control, on the Monaro, the Murrumbidgee or, on the Liverpool Plains, and the farmer eking out a less profitable existence on his narrow ones closer to Sydney, for which, moreover, he had to pay at least 5s per acre.

There was, however, one virgin territory where the ideas of Wakefield could be applied without prejudice from existing arrangements. In a voyage remarkable for courage and tenacity, Charles Sturt in 1830 traced the Murray to its mouth at Lake Alexandrina in South Australia. He proved clearly that the west flowing rivers in New South Wales flowed into the Murray and that the Murray itself emptied into the ocean rather than into an inland sea. He also opened up South Australia from the east, and the promise of a territory, both fertile and vacant, about the Murray basin seemed to invite settlement. Back in London, Wakefield felt that here was the ideal place for his schemes of colonization on a systematic basis, but the Colonial Office vacillated until 1834, when the colony of South Australia was established on paper. It would have remained no more than a scheme had not George Angas formed the South Australia Company to finance the venture, which got underway in 1836.

On 28 December 1836, Governor John Hindmarsh landed in the *Buffalo* at Holdfast Bay where Glenelg now stands. The province of South Australia was proclaimed, and several toasts were drunk to its success. A few days later, Surveyor-General William Light persuaded Hindmarsh that the perfect site for the settlement was a few miles inland across the plains. Adelaide was then laid out to a masterly plan, and the business of opening up the country began in earnest. Wakefield's scheme went astray for there was an immediate tendency to speculate in land rather than work it. By 1841, only 2,500 acres out of 299,000, sold at 12s per acre, were under cultivation; 12,000 assisted migrants, many of whom were totally unsuited to the pioneering venture, had arrived, and the total population was 15,485. Amongst the arrivals there were no convicts as the Colonial Office had decided that, like Western Australia, the new colony was to remain free of the penal taint.

Land, rather than its produce, quickly became the unique commodity

The German settlers in South Australia were notable for their industry and orderliness, both of which are evident in this scene. The buildings were strongly constructed and tidy. Clearly, women's labour was essential to the settlers' economy.

in which the colonists dealt and the South Australia Company led the field as a large-scale speculator. Under such circumstances, the labour force had to be given some purpose, so George Gawler, who succeeded Hindmarsh in 1838, decided to equip the colony with all the necessary public works generally found in a flourishing community with a solid economic base. While living in a primitive dwelling himself, Gawler saw to it that harbour works, public buildings, roads and bridges went ahead, and he even gave aid to those who remained unemployed. The question soon arose as to who would foot the bill as the local treasury was clearly incapable of so doing for any length of time. In London, the public servants refused, credit collapsed and South Australia, which had promised so much, came to a temporary halt.

There were some who were prepared to stick it out and, in doing so, they ran contrary to Wakefield's ideal of systematic colonization. Squatters, ignoring the land sales, began to settle beyond the 150 square miles of the province, thus breaking any theoretical connection between land and labour. At Klemzig and Hahndorf there were German settlers who had come to South Australia between 1838 and 1839 to practise their own kind of Lutheranism in peace. They began to flourish in their neat villages, but again, their success owed nothing directly to Wakefield because they leased the land from Angas at a nominal rent and worked it with their own labour. Their wives and daughters were soon seen in Adelaide selling dairy produce and vegetables to the townsfolk, while their men planted grains and, later, vines. Amongst the first sheep shearers in South Australia were German women and by 1843 a large proportion of flocks were shorn by them. In the late 1840s, German Catholics followed the Lutherans to South Australia and, with their Jesuit chaplain, settled near Clare at 'Sevenhill', where a college, an imposing church and a flourishing vineyard were established.

Although scant attention was paid to his ideas, Wakefield made a contribution to Australian development as lasting as that of Macarthur and the founders of the wool industry. While they wanted to cover the land with the finest of sheep, Wakefield wanted to plant it with the best of people. Not for him the convicts but the sons and daughters of England's deserving classes. In his scheme the land was to be used primarily for production and secondarily, by its sale, for settling England's surplus population. With his theory even partially accepted, immigration to Australia, free or assisted, became fundamental to its development. Like Macarthur, he was a superb publicist and during the 1830s the population of free persons in New South Wales rose four-fold, largely due to the spread and acceptability of the idea of immigration which he, Wakefield, had fostered.

Despite the unpromising beginnings of the two new colonies, in the west and at South Australia, Botany Bay wool, so fine, soft and long-stapled that English wool sorters could pick it by touch in a mixed bale, had become the major element in the economy, although fishery products still contributed heavily to export earnings. Pastoralists demanded more and more land, British manufacturers more wool, and the planners pleaded in vain for concentrated settlement, rather than haphazard dispersal into the interior. In the final analysis, the squatters had to come out victorious because capital, most of it British, talked louder than theory. Nothing, but especially not lines drawn on a map, could stop the squatters. It was futile to attempt to do so in South Australia and it had already proved futile in New South Wales where, since the declaration of the Nineteen Counties in 1829, the sheep had been expected to stop their outward movement at this boundary. Pastoralism, by its very nature, opened up vast tracts of land, even though it implied unbridled lawlessness to the authorities, who also felt that the use of Crown land without precise regulations on tenure and cost was intolerable.

The land itself posed some obstacles to the coming of the squatters but never in a permanent manner. Drought, flood and fire were brutal but passing phenomena, although the effect of a prolonged drought was drastic on wool quality as well as flock numbers. On the pastoral lands there was no prolonged cold or snow, no impassable mountain ranges or huge rivers, no dense forests or immense swamps. There were no indigenous creatures to prey on the sheep except the dingo, which could be controlled but never, it seemed, conquered. The land appeared to betray its original inhabitants, as it was a welcoming haven to the hard-hooved sheep, which adapted remarkably quickly to the new environment and the merino blended with the landscape and flourished. Pastoral expansion also turned a society previously dependent on the sea and coastal shipping into one which looked inwards to the land itself as the source of its commerce, wealth and culture. The sheep were subject to catarrh, footrot and fluke, but they quickly recovered or multiplied again because the breed was extraordinarily prolific in lambs as well as fleece. The pastoral industry appeared to require no particular initial aptitude in those who undertook it, although time would prove the contrary, and thousands who had never previously touched a sheep quickly became pastoralists. The industry did not require the same kind of concentrated workforce as did agriculture because it was not labour intensive, except for brief periods, such as shearing.

The only force perhaps capable of stemming the squatting movement was the government, but Richard Bourke, Governor of New South Wales between 1831 and 1838, was reluctant to do so. He saw the signs of prosperity, the inflow of capital, the increase in immigrants, the opening of the country, the dulling of the old animosities between emancipists and exclusives, and the general recognition given to Australia with the waning of the Botany Bay slur. For all this, he was prepared to accept the dispersion of settlement and even the effective transfer of thousands of square miles of land into the hands of a few. Bourke governed wisely and with forebearance in times of great prosperity, but his liberality left its legacy.

George Gipps, Bourke's successor, was an asthmatic who worried through sleepless nights in Sydney about the dispersion of the population into the interior but even more about the threat to the primacy of the Crown with its proclaimed right over the land. More than anything, Gipps was troubled with his vision of a future Australia where a rough, unlettered, unskilled and godless race would arise. He feared that no cleric, policeman, schoolmaster or genteel influence would penetrate those vast and almost trackless wildernesses, upon which he foresaw a civilization based on the development of a mixed race of black and white would take shape.

Gipps was not aware that the elemental force of racism was at work shaping white Australia. With the virtual rejection of the Aborigines as equals and their exclusion from an economy based on the pastoral industry — a rejection the Aborigines partially dictated because participation in a workforce that threatened to destroy the very basis of their civilization was an anathema to them — a great gulf had opened between the races. White and black went separate paths which, unlike Latin America where there was interbreeding between the races, could only lead inexorably to an exclusive and foreboding conclusion for the dominant section — white Australia.

All these worries about the future or the encroachment on Crown lands meant little to the prospective squatters — to the military and naval officers, lawyers, clergymen, merchants, government officials, sons of the English gentry, assorted immigrants and a sprinkling of the native-born who had sufficient capital or could raise a loan from one of the new banks which fed on pastoral expansion. The intending squatters then obtained a few servants, although new immigrants went reluctantly into the bush. Having purchased a flock from one of the inner properties and acquired stores for a year, they set out inland with drays, bullocks, a horse or two and a cow. They went out further and further until unoccupied country was found with suitable water and feed and there they squatted on a tract of land extensive enough to pasture the flock and they called it a run or a station.

The shepherds, mostly convicts, ex-convicts and native-born, were found to be generally faithful and efficient. They lived in huts, with two shepherds and a hut-keeper in each. The huts were rough constructions of slabs and bark, spaced a mile or more apart, and the shepherds were responsible for guarding a flock of 500 to 1,500 sheep, depending upon the feed and water available. At night the flock was enclosed within temporary fences close to the hut and a constant watch was kept for dingoes.

The lives of the squatters in the early days, with only the barest commodities available, differed little from those of the shepherds. The squatters also learnt to rough it in the bush, where many lost count of the days and recognized Sundays perhaps by having a shave, although some read the Bible or gathered the shepherds for prayer. Very little was done to erect permanent buildings, because squatting remained illegal until the end of the 1830s. Squatting was thus a life which, for both masters and servants, bred qualities of trust and dependence of man upon man for there were scarcely any women in the bush. To survive, a man had to turn to his mate and, if alone, as was often the case, to his own ingenuity and ability to improvise with whatever was at hand. Authority meant little in a society removed by weeks or even months from its source, while

Although idealized in these illustrations, some squatters had good relations with the Aborigines. The amicable method of deciding territorial boundaries did not long endure and Land Commissioners were required to settle disputes. The bottom scene notes the absence of predatory animals, whether native or imported.

the only escape from boredom was drink, when it could be had, together with reading for those who were capable of it and telling yarns by all.

In New South Wales, including the District of Port Phillip, by 1840 there were 718 squatting stations with 7,000 people, of whom 2,600 were convicts, while a million and a half sheep ran on over a million acres of Crown land. In the bush amongst the convicts, emancipists and native-born, the ethos of early Australia was given form. It was a harsh creed of mateship between men, and survival was its purpose. In time the women came, bringing with them the gentle touch of more civilized ways but always at the cost of hardship to themselves. They cooked, sewed, milked cows, planted fruit trees, vegetables and flowers to lighten the harshness, ran fowl yards, nursed the sick, read aloud to menfolk and children and often they played musical instruments. They brought their religion with them, and on many a station the Bible was read or the rosary said at night.

The bush children depended upon their mothers for their early education, which was finished at boarding schools for the successful, while those of the poorer squatters and servants remained children of the bush to repeat the ways of life of their parents. All their lives the women had to battle against the same odds as the men, with the added handicap of isolation from other women. Illness, childbirth or death emotionally drained brave spirits like Georgiana Molloy at Augusta, Western Australia. Three years after the death of her baby girl she wrote, 'language refuses to utter what I experienced when mine died in my arms in this dreary land, and no one but Molloy near me' and, later, when her little son drowned in the well by the house, her sorrow was so complete she hid it in her heart.

The main thrust of the squatting movement from New South Wales was west, until the good land was taken, and then south into Mitchell's Australia Felix, later officially called Port Phillip. The first development had been started there in 1834 by the Henty family, who, after two years of hardship at the Swan River, had moved to Van Diemen's Land in 1831. They requested but failed to obtain permission to occupy land across the Strait in Port Phillip. They came over in November 1834, nonetheless, and squatted at Portland Bay, where Mitchell, to his surprise, found them on his exploratory journey in August 1836, when they were already established. In 1835 John Batman, Sydney-born of a convict father and now a grazier in Van Diemen's Land, also came across Bass Strait. He went up a pleasant river called the Yarra and saw a spot he judged would eventually be 'fit for a village.' He also saw land of which he had not seen the equal and he was determined to obtain some of it for himself and his fellow Van Demonians.

No amount of legal argument could ever prove that the Aborigines had no right to the land and thereby that they had no right to dispose of it. Some very few observers of the relations between blacks and whites had recognized this fact, and Captain F.C. Irwin of the 63rd Regiment, after the tragic 'Battle of Pinjarra' between blacks and whites in 1834 in Western Australia, suggested that 'a formal treaty' should be entered into between the two races 'as a measure of healing and pacification'. Batman knew nothing of Irwin's suggestion and in some ways he was an untrustworthy man. Nevertheless, he had some respect for the Aborigines and he gave trinkets to those whom he called 'the real owners of the soil' in exchange for 600,000 acres of land, promising them an annual tribute as evidence of his desire to protect them. All of this was drawn up in treaty form and duly signed according to the ability of each party, but the treaty was rapidly found to be null and void because it was against the rights of the Crown. As a result, the one attempt made to give some recognition to Aboriginal rights was set aside lest it interfere with the British government's determination to dispose of the land as it saw fit.

Batman's move to Port Phillip was quickly followed by others. John Pascoe Fawkner was one of the first, and within a year a small community was flourishing. The Hentys at Portland and the other settlers from Van Diemen's Land that were grouped around Port Phillip Bay meant that the early development of what was to become the colony of Victoria was entirely done from across Bass Strait. Victoria was never the daughter of New South Wales, although it remained dependent upon it in all administrative matters until 1851, but much of the history that followed has obscured its Van Demonian origins. Batman himself became an object of ridicule by many, although he had, with some civility and no violence, tried to buy Aboriginal land which others simply took without any reference to the original owners, who had never surrendered their right to it.

In the tracks made by Mitchell, the rush to Port Phillip from New South Wales began and in late 1836 a squatter, in the space of a few weeks, saw 100,000 sheep, with their owners and shepherds, cross the Murrumbidgee at Gundagai. In September of that year, the government had been forced to acknowledge that a settlement already existed in the south. A surveyor, Robert Hoddle, arrived with Bourke in March 1837 and the Governor named Batman's site after a British Prime Minister, Melbourne, while Hoddle himself laid out the future shape of the city. He dissected a square mile with narrow, lane-like alleys and fine wide streets which, running almost south to north ensured that Melbourne and its citizens would be swept by hot or cold winds dependent upon the season. Four years later, 20,000 people lived under the generally benign and reasonable guidance of Charles La Trobe, who had been appointed as superintendent in 1839. La Trobe brought his Swiss wife, Sophie, a daughter and a prefabricated house with him. He left a legacy of upright behavior, high moral standards and devotion to culture and learning.

The squatters soon had over a million sheep and their runs stretched almost to the limit of pastoral land in Port Phillip. Some of them were women, who, after the death of their husbands, took up or were obliged to oversee a run, hoping thereby to provide for their children. Others were single women like Anne Drysdale and Caroline Newcombe who together held a successful run on the Barwon River near Geelong in the 1840s and another on Indented Head in the 1850s. The runs were relinquished with Anne's death in 1853 and Caroline's subsequent marriage in 1861. They were pioneers of a long line of women who, throughout the continent, ran properties successfully and in so doing earned the respect of their employees and the local communities.

Usury was the usual basis of the pastoral economy as no fixed interest rates were set on loans and the squatters were often in need of extra capital, particularly in times of drought. Their tendency to occupy runs much in excess of their needs caused Bourke to attempt some control over them in 1836 by appointing land commissioners to sort out the frequent disputes that arose between them and by charging £10 annually for their runs. The responsibilities of the commissioners were immense and the territory they had to cover equally so. They were often accused of bias and favouritism in their decisions, but their role was a necessary one in places where other forms of law were almost totally absent. In the settled districts and in Melbourne, Bourke priced land at a minimum of £1 per acre and in town land there was rampant speculation. In August 1840 the government received £14,220 from the sale of forty-five lots in Melbourne at an average of £316 each and within four months the same lots were sold at double to five times their original cost. The government gained nothing from those subsequent transactions, and, unless the economy prospered, only speculators reaped profits while genuine purchasers faced possible ruin.

Meanwhile, George Arthur, Lieutenant-Governor of Van Diemen's Land since 1823 and exercising full power after the island was made a colony in its own right in 1825, had set ideas on the land question as well as most other matters. He was a highly efficient administrator, determined and inflexible in his control of the convicts, whom he regarded as slaves, and constantly aware of, and vehemently opposed to, moral transgressions of any kind. His high ideals did not prevent his acquiring great wealth in land which he bought with foreknowledge of its rising value. When he became aware that the new regulations of 1831 were about to be proclaimed and that henceforth free grants would cease, he parcelled out 250,000 acres to anyone to whom even the whisper of a promise of land had been made by London.

The basis of the island's economy was the assignment system, which land sales and immigration threatened, but Arthur need not have worried. In England, Van Diemen's Land was regarded simply as a prison so that convict arrivals accounted for 20,000 new hands in the 1830s, almost twice the number of free persons settling in the same period. Arthur had closed the old penal establishment at Macquarie Harbour on the south-west of the island and set up a new one at Point Arthur in 1830. It was close to Hobart, isolated on a narrow peninsula and joined to the mainland by a thin strip, called Eaglehawk Neck, which could easily be guarded by ferocious dogs. The convicts did all they could not to be sent to Port Arthur, and those who survived a term there did their best never to return. Only about seven percent of the convicts were confined at Port Arthur. The rest were worked in chain gangs on public utilities, notably road building, but the majority were forced to take their luck with assignment.

Liberal in matters touching religion and education, both of which he fostered, Arthur gradually became hard-hearted toward the Aborigines. By late 1830, he decided that any chance of peaceful relations between

Over 12,000 convicts served their sentences at Port Arthur between 1830 and 1877. The church was completed in 1836 but reduced to a ruin by a bushfire in 1884. Port Arthur is visited by thousands of tourists annually and the site presents a vivid reminder of the harshness of the penal system.

the races was negligible. He and others, notably property owners, failed to comprehend that to the Aborigines, a people whose very existence was threatened, retaliation by taking human life or stealing animals was an act to which they could see no alternative. Arthur concluded that segregation was the only solution, so he determined to drive the remaining Aborigines, now much less than a thousand, onto the Tasman Peninsula which, with Port Arthur already nullifying its natural beauty, was to be their home. His 'Black War', in which he personally directed 5,000 men in a kind of hapless beat down through the island, bagged two Aborigines and cost £30,000. The Governor then decided on a form of conciliation which entailed removing the remaining Aborigines to Flinders Island in Bass Strait where their extinction was virtually ensured.

The Christian faith was part of the common cultural possessions of the general population, although indifference or rejection of religion was the attitude of many. Nevertheless, the churches, with their ministers, cult and structures, were regarded as a fundamental part of society, as much as the burgeoning banking system and the network of public utilities were accepted on other levels. The government was prepared to recognize this fact by granting aid to any Christian Church prepared to accept it. This decision, hailed by Bourke as the 'Magna Carta of the Religious Liberty of this Infant Empire', excluded the small community of about 1,000 Jews. In 1837 they converted a private house in Bridge Street, Sydney into a synagogue. The Jews built their first formal synagogue at Hobart in 1843, established the oldest women's organization in Australia — The Hebrew Ladies Maternity Society — at Sydney in the same year and their first newspaper, *The Voice of Jacob*, was published in 1842. Meanwhile, the Christians progressed rapidly with the benefit of state aid, which helped to build churches and maintain clergy to the number of about one to a thousand of the population.

The optimistic idea that the perfectibility of man could be achieved through the vehicle of education was widespread, particularly amongst the well-to-do. To that purpose, private schools were founded, some of them with educational standing of value while others were second rate. Throughout New South Wales, churches of all denominations attempted to support schools where, more often than not, ill-prepared masters taught ill-disposed pupils. Bourke was troubled at the proliferation of such establishments, so he suggested that the government should itself enter the field by erecting and controlling schools in which religion would be confined to scriptural readings and a weekly visit from the clergy who would instruct their own particular flock. In the beginning, the Protestants were against the proposal and the Catholics were for it, so that, in a

welter of opposition, approval and some recrimination, Bourke's proposal lapsed, leaving an enduring legacy of inter-faith bigotry.

The future of transportation itself was closely linked to the question of
responsible government and, consequently, formed a major debate of
the period. On the one side, there were those to whom the system had to
cease for strictly practical, religious or humanitarian reasons. John Dunmore Lang was adept at describing its worst characteristics and implying
that transportation was merely a method of promoting rogues, both
socially and financially, while William Ullathorne, a young and impetuous Catholic priest, was even more eloquent. He proclaimed that 'a
vast portion of God's earth' had been turned into a 'cess-pool' where
60,000 souls were 'festering in bondage' and called for 'the removal of
such a plague from the earth'. There were, however, much more
powerful economic interests whose arguments would win the day for or
against transportation.

Free immigrants, some emancipists and native-born feared that the
continuation of transportation would mean that wages would always be
depressed. The great majority of squatters and large landowners of New
South Wales and Van Diemen's Land saw the retention of assignment as
essential to their prosperity. The followers of Wakefield and the founders
of South Australia had turned their faces sternly against transportation to
their colony, but they knew that their own economy faced a threat while
their neighbouring colonies continued to receive a cheap, convict workforce. The fact was that the two systems of transportation and free
migration could not go hand in hand.

In the event, a committee of the House of Commons deliberated on the
matter. Hidden in its workings was the conviction that there were disturbing elements at large in British society, including the Chartists and
the unemployed, who would be better out of the country but who would
never go to a convict settlement. The committee recommended in 1838
that transportation to New South Wales and the settled parts of Van
Diemen's Land be abolished. In 1839 assignment ceased, and on 18
November 1840 Sydney Cove saw the last batch of convicts disembark
from the transport *Eden*. Fifty-two years of a penal society, 80,000 convicts, misery, criminality and reformation, death in bondage and success
in freedom, marriage, children and homes had all laid the foundations of
the future.

The tentative steps towards responsible government in New South
Wales began to show promise of fruitful fulfilment. In 1835 John
Jamison, 'the hospitable Knight of Regentsville', became the first Presi-
dent of the Australian Patriotic Association, which was inspired by
Wentworth and founded to secure some form of representative govern-

ment in the colony as well as trial by jury. The Association also busied itself with defending the old land system, upholding transportation and attempting to introduce Asiatic labour. It clearly expressed the new harmony of interests between the old enemies — exclusives and emancipists — who, based on their propertied and business wealth, now saw their position threatened unless they could achieve power over legislation. Wentworth's old paper, the *Australian*, began to attack him as one who had taught the people 'what liberty was' but had now betrayed them.

In South Australia freedom from transportation permitted the reality of a minor form of responsible government to be achieved. Adelaide, by 1840, was a small city of 2,000 with all the outward symbols of civic pride, together with churches belonging to almost every known sect. On 31 October 1840 the first election in Australia for positions of public responsibility was held there. It was for a mayor and town council, the ballot was not used, there were property qualifications and former paupers and criminals could not vote. The election itself went off with moderation, good order and a careful choice of candidates, which were expected qualities in a colony determined to stay free of the excesses allegedly so prevalent in places where convicts set foot. In Western Australia, itself still free of convicts, jealous eyes were cast upon their young, neighbouring, sister colony, and the *Perth Gazette* reported that runaway convicts were already infecting South Australia while the 'newfangled system of emigration, it would appear, is not working so well as anticipated.'

While some struggled to assert their rights against a distant Crown others were more anxious to uphold theirs in the society about them. Despite the increasing influx of free immigrants, archaic regulations, more consistent with a feudal society, bound servants to their masters. Regularly, magistrates who were themselves employers sentenced servants to imprisonment for disobedience, insolence and absconding although servants sometimes sued successfully for wages due or redress of wrongs done. By 1840 some slight improvement in the regulations was achieved in New South Wales. Women servants could no longer be sent to prison, while males could only be sentenced to three months for breaches of the Master and Servants Act, but to the workers the net result was still little more than virtual slavery.

In such circumstances, the embryonic beginnings of trade unions and benefit societies took place amongst skilled workers, including compositors who formed the Australian Society of Compositors. In January 1840 the compositors on the *Sydney Herald* (1831), which became the *Sydney Morning Herald* in 1842 and survives to the present, struck for an improvement in apprentice ratios. The competition for readers in New South Wales was fierce with the *Australian* (1824–48), the *Monitor* (1826–

This view of Sydney in 1824 is taken from King's Cross looking to the township across the Domain. The largest buildings, over the head of the convict on the right, are the 'Rum' Hospital, then the Convict Barracks to the left, St James's Church with the spire, Barnett Levey's Windmill atop his Theatre Royal in George Street and in front St Mary's Church with the presbytery and school to its right. On the far left the dome of the markets can be seen.

42), Lang's *Colonist* (1835–40) and the Catholic *Australasian Chronicle* (1839–48) all in the field so that no paper could fail to publish on time. The compositors were quickly reminded that any combination amongst them was illegal, any dictation to their employers was intolerable, and that British or Indian compositors could be brought in at short notice to replace the recalcitrant. In the event, convict labour was used to break the strike as was done later in the year when the Sydney bakers struck. It was already clear that the struggle between capital and labour was conducted by rules drawn up to ensure that, temporarily at least, capital retained the ascendancy.

Until 1803 no special provisions were made for female convicts, but in that year a building at Parramatta had been designated as a factory. It was little more than a refuge where conditions were so bad that the women preferred to face all manner of hardship rather than be detained there. After 1821 the Female Factory held 1,500 inmates, who broke stones, made cloth and sawed wood. The women were divided into three classes — prospective assignees, mothers of illegimate children and those undergoing punishment. There had been repeated outbreaks of violence in the Factory, but some improvement was shown after the arrival of the first nuns to come to Australia. Five Irish Sisters of Charity, including two nurses who pioneered their profession in Australia, arrived with Ullathorne in 1838, and their devotion to the women was remarkable. Nevertheless, the Factory remained a constant reminder of the degradation of being a convict, especially as its occupants were women. This was never more apparent than on those occasions when a kind of slave market took place there — the women were lined up and men took their pick of them as brides.

Amongst the convicts, one group stood out because their background was different from all the rest except for the Irish political prisoners. They were Canadian rebels to the number of 149 who were transported in 1839 and 1840 for attempting to overthrow British rule in their homeland. The rebels with an English or United States background came from Ontario and they were kept at Hobart. There they led a miserable existence, and fifteen were sent to Port Arthur for trying to escape. The French Canadians, from Lower Canada, were fifty-nine in all, and, after the death of one of their number in Van Diemen's Land, their exile was spent in Sydney where they cut stone for the new Parramatta road. They found the whole environment alien and harsh with some comfort coming from their contact with the first Catholic bishop in Australia, the English Benedictine monk John Bede Polding. The exiles left little mark of their passing, whether at Hobart or Sydney, and, unlike the English and Irish convicts, the great majority of them returned home as soon as they were pardoned.

In the larger centres of settlement — Sydney, Hobart, Melbourne, Adelaide and to a greater extent at distant Perth — life continued to reflect the parent civilization in the British Isles. The convict era for Brisbane was over by 1839, and by the next year the Darling Downs were open to settlement, and the squatters pushed to the north and west, but Brisbane remained small and struggling. Elsewhere, regattas were held, cricket played, the first steam vessel was seen on Sydney Harbour in 1831 and the Mechanics' School of Arts, founded in 1833, proposed to assist the citizens to become 'fervent worshippers at the shrine of science' with carefully fostered 'habits of intellectual intercourse'.

In Melbourne, La Trobe was happy that British 'perseverance and industry' had resulted in banks, newspapers, churches and other comfortable reminders of the home country although the sides of the streets were still lined with eucalyptus stumps and in Collins Street one was so huge that a building had to be skewed to go around it. In South Australia overlanders from New South Wales were arriving with flocks and herds, which added to the stability of the settlement and strengthened the economy of Adelaide where Colonel Light's plan for the city was taking shape. The *South Australian Gazette* had commenced printing in Adelaide in 1837. In May 1838, when the colony was only seventeen months old, the Theatre Royal was opened and the play *Mountaineers, or Love and Madness* presented to an enthusiastic audience.

All these signs of development were noted by visitors, who also expressed some criticism. In 1839 an exploratory expedition from the United States called at Sydney. The men were delighted to find themselves 'in a civilized country' and more especially to be in a place where 'their own language was spoken'. Their leader, Captain Wilkes, remarked that the inhabitants seemed intent upon making money; that the press was unruly; drunkenness abounded in a city where 250 taverns, in a ratio of one for every 100 inhabitants, catered for the thirsty; and that everywhere the cicadas were deafening — although his overall impression was favourable. Charles Darwin arrived in Australia on the *Beagle* in 1836, but he was disappointed in 'the state of society' in Sydney. He visited Bathurst and gave an incorrect explanation for the canyons in the Blue Mountains and later passed the most 'dull and uninteresting time' of his whole voyage when he called at King Georges Sound in the west. Nevertheless, the evidence he gathered from the flora and fauna, and on the Aborigines, helped with his later formulation of the theory of natural selection, and he always maintained a keen interest in Australia.

On the frontiers of expansion, in river valleys, on vast plains bounded by countless miles of bush, on the slopes of hills and mountains, civilization was being established which had many faces. Georgiana Molloy lived on through her sorrows in the west, and when she carved a garden out of the wilderness she thought that she had come to a Garden of Eden. At night she turned to prayer and to the piano and thus the bush gradually became home. Robert Campbell on the Limestone Plains, 190 miles south-west of Sydney, built a home which later became a gracious mansion, reigned over seventy workers and pastured thousands of sheep, and, on Sundays, worshipped at the nearby Anglican Church of St John. At Entally House, near Launceston, Thomas Reiby, whose mother, Mary, had made a fortune, lived until 1842 in a kind of fortress with two towers slotted with musket holes as a precaution against bushrangers. The furniture of his home was in the Regency style, while the timberwork was Australian cedar.

The white civilization taking shape, both in the towns and in the bush, was an amalgam of those which had grown in England, Scotland and, to some degree, Ireland in the preceding centuries. In the main it was solidly Protestant, virtuous, hard-working, courageous and persevering against great odds. The pioneers were prepared to suffer hardship in order to get a foothold in the Australia they were in the process of building. Many of

Once security to their runs was secured, big squatters built imposing homes. Samuel Talbot held 40,000 acres of fine land at Malahide, Van Diemen's Land, and in 1852 joined other large landholders in a petition to the Crown for the continuation of transportation.

them were pretentious and looked down on those whom they considered to be of 'the lower orders', yet everyone had to contend with physical difficulties and varying degress of loneliness, isolation and heartbreak. In their determined quest to conquer and possess the land, to wrest out a living in commerce and minor industry, to build schools, churches, roads and court houses, Australians began again the work their ancestors had taken centuries to do in their homelands. Within a half century of settlement, the foundations of a British civilization had been laid down on a continent which was months removed by sea from its cultural origins. The fact that one aspect of this civilization was that of a penal colony did not stop the determined drive of many citizens to shape a free society.

In the bush, normally far removed from the influence of either the law or religion, there were barbarous aspects to white behaviour. In 1837 and early 1838 in the Gwyder and Namoi River districts several whites were killed by Aborigines who resented their intrusion onto their traditional hunting grounds. Subsequently, on the Myall Creek, 350 miles north-west of Sydney, the convict servants of Henry Dangar murdered about thirty Aborigines — men, women and children. Their deed followed closely the slaying of ten drovers by a party of blacks on the Broken River in the Port Phillip District. Governor Gipps set up a system of protector-ates, under the direction of George Robinson as Chief Protector, who was entrusted with the task of looking after the interests of the Aborigines. However, many whites were convinced that they were the ones who needed to be protected and that it was natural for advanced civilizations to exterminate those who were seen as savages. They requested Gipps to 'levy war against the Blacks' but the Governor refused and was strongly supported in his stand by the Attorney-General, John Hubert Plunkett. As a result, some of Dangar's men were brought to trial at Sydney for murder, and seven of them were hanged. Many squatters saw Plunkett as the real murderer, and he was detested and feared thereafter.

The Aboriginal Protectorate system was well-meaning but inept and proved a costly failure. Gipps and Plunkett were helpless when the poisoning of water holes and of flour became a more favoured method of extermination than shooting. White attitudes towards the blacks were hardening and an anonymous grazier on the Murrumbidgee summed them up. To him the Aborigines were 'a scoff and a jest on humanity' and he thought that their extinction was virtually ensured. His view was one which some segments of the press, notably the *Sydney Herald*, defended and propagated, thereby heightening adverse public opinion and helping to justify murder. As for the Aborigines, death, dispersal and the loss of their hunting grounds continued to take an awful toll as the past and its Dreamtime changed to a reality with which they could not cope.

Remote from all that was happening in her distant realm, an eighteen-year-old girl was crowned as Queen Victoria in London in 1837. When they heard the news in Perth the inhabitants gathered, as they did in all the centres of her vast Empire, to pledge their loyalty to the new mon-arch. Hopes were expressed that her reign would prove fruitful and memorable, but even the optimistic little dreamt how decisive it would be in binding Australia in all its parts to the distant Crown. When she died, over sixty years later, Australia was more closely knit into the Empire than it had been when she came to her throne.

CHAPTER FIVE

New Peopling of the Land

To the Aborigines it was pointless to ask how many generations must pass before a land and its people become one. To them there had never been a time in which their unity with the land was lacking. For the whites unity grew from long residence and involvement although it differed in meaning and quality from that possessed by the Aborigines. Nevertheless, in its own way, it did come about for many, although for some it never happened.

As an old man in Melbourne in the late 1860s, John Pascoe Fawkner could look back to 1803 and remember it vividly. As a boy of eleven he had landed at Port Phillip in that year with his convict father, his mother and sister. They were on their way to Van Diemen's Land with Lieutenant-Governor Collins where, in young manhood, Fawkner saw Lachlan Macquarie on the Governor's visit to Hobart in 1811. Three years later Fawkner was given 500 strokes for aiding a party of convicts in an unsuccessful bid to escape, and he then served two years hard labour as a cedar cutter on the Hunter River in New South Wales. Having married a convict, Eliza Cobb, at Launceston in 1822, he went on to lay the foundations of a fortune at Port Phillip where he established the *Port Phillip Patriot and Melbourne Advertiser* in 1839. He later became 'the tribune of the people' during his eighteen years as a member of the Legislative Council in the place to which he had come as a boy fifty years before when no white man lived there. Although the sounds and sights of his London childhood remained with him to the end, Fawkner knew no other home than Australia.

Charles Glover, aged eighteen, was sentenced to fourteen years' transportation at Leicester for theft in 1835. Two years later he was convicted at Sydney for stealing from a dwelling and putting its occupant in fear of his life. This time he received a life sentence to Norfolk Island which, for a lad of twenty, was little short of death and probably less acceptable. Throughout the following six years, he was in constant trouble with the authorities for minor offences ranging from refusing to work, being insolent, fishing without permission and not having his shirt on at a muster. Glover was fortunate in that his years on the island mostly coincided with the five years of Alexander Maconachie's superintendency.

Maconochie was an enlightened penal reformer, who did much to mitigate the vindictive barbarisms perpetrated on convicts at Norfolk Island, but he was removed from office in 1843, when it was decided in London that his regime was too lenient. Glover certainly benefited from Maconochie's decency and humanity, and he was removed from Norfolk Island before the reigns of Joseph Childs and John Price, two succeeding monsters of cruelty who deliberately fostered hatred and fear as they flogged and tortured the prisoners. In August 1844 Glover arrived at Hobart, and for the next ten years he was an irritant to the authorities, whether as a member of a chain gang or, later, as a ticket-of-leave holder. He was given 100 lashes in 1845 for striking a watchman, was in and out of solitary confinement, doing hard labour or having his ticket revoked. After nearly twenty years of servitude and now in his late thirties, Glover was given a conditional pardon, which meant that he could not go back to Leicester. Married and settled at Sidmouth, north of Launceston, he worked as a farmer and carter, had a family of nine children and died as a respectable member of society in 1869. Penal servitude and the passing years had made Charles Glover an Australian. His story was not atypical of the convicts.

Horatio Wills also had memories, but they were entirely Australian for he was born, the son of a convict father, on the Sydney waterfront in 1811, where the nearby Rocks area was a haunt of pickpockets and whores and a scene of destitution and misery. In his youth, he went to sea as a sealer, but later settled to an apprenticeship as a printer and in 1832 published his own weekly journal, *Currency Lad*, to which he gave the motto 'Rise Australia'. Yet the old culture of lands he had never visited and people of whom he had only read remained entwined with his being although he loved the land of his birth. In 1840, on his way into the Port Phillip District with wife and child, shepherds and flocks, to find a suitable squatting run, he camped overnight near a hill to which, mindful of Noah and the patriarchs, he gave the name Ararat after the mountain on which the Ark came to rest. The native-born always carried the stories of other lands with them but coming to peace with Australia came easily. They were its sons and daughters, and keen observers noted that, in their knowledge of the bush, they were nearly the equal of the Aborigines.

A family with an indomitable mother was that of the Glasgow merchants of Huguenot descent, Forlonge. Eliza and John decided to send their two sons, William and Andrew, to Australia after the loss of several children to tuberculosis. In 1826 Eliza and the boys went to Leipzig to study the wool industry at first hand. When John joined them in 1828, Eliza set out on foot to visit the sheep studs and select ninety-eight Saxon sheep, which she and her sons drove from Leipzig to Hamburg and later from Hull to Liverpool. By 1831 Eliza and John had arrived in Van Diemen's Land in the wake of the boys and settled near Campbell Town. John died in England in 1834 on a trip with Eliza, but she returned to see her sons go insolvent in the depression of the 1840s. Andrew went to America, while William remained to become a wealthy pastoralist in Victoria and a member of Parliament.

There were some who tried to understand that Australia was not alien but only different from England. Annie Baxter arrived in Launceston as a young bride of seventeen in the early 1830s. Within a few years she was

The long voyage of the emigrants began in tearful farewells to loved ones from whom separation would last for life. The voyage itself was often one punctuated by storms and tedium, but on arrival hope of a new life in a land of plenty predominated.

lonely, unhappily married and struggling to survive on a run north-west of Port Macquarie on the Macleay River. She grew to love the bush with its huge trees that at first seemed forbidding. Its immense silence, broken only by rare bird calls and the wind rustling the bark and leaves, soothed her spirit and in spring the profusion of wild flowers enchanted her senses. Gradually the wildness of the new land seemed tamed, and often, when out riding alone, she would remember the last line of a poem of her childhood, 'Man is distant, but God is near!'

Louise Clifton came out to Western Australia with the founders of the new settlement called Australind. It was a venture in systematic colonization based on Wakefield's theories and it came to nothing within a few years. The founders laid out a town on the Leschenault Estuary, with areas set aside for fine parks and public buildings. On her arrival, Louise found the original tent settlement picturesque in its setting under spreading trees with hills as a backdrop and birds singing everywhere. Yet when a storm came in the night it terrified her; mosquito bites caused violent irritation; the family tent became a scene of watery desolation and the cry of the wild dog in the distance brought a fear of the unknown. The next day, Monday 7 June 1841, dawned fine and calm and the distant hills and valleys reminded her of the French countryside so that she felt at peace. Louise came to terms with Australia, married, bore children and lived out her life in the west. Thousands like her, who left no written record, did the same throughout the Australian continent.

The failure of Australind, the attraction of the eastern colonies, the reluctance of settlers to buy land at the now established minimum price of £1 per acre, and the consequent break in the cycle of land sales producing free immigration caused, by the late 1840s, a change of heart in Western Australia. It seemed evident that the prosperity of the east had been built on convict labour, so the westerners petitioned London for the privilege of receiving felons into their colony, although ten years earlier disgust at any such prospect had been expressed. With New South Wales now closed to convicts and the supply at home still being maintained the British government found no difficulty in agreeing. From 1850 to 1868 ten thousand male convicts were shipped to Western Australia, after which the whole system was completely abandoned.

Throughout the penal colonies, the basis of the economy had gradually shifted to free labour, while the upkeep of the convict establishment, with its military and civilian personnel, became a burden on British government coffers. A sense of moral outrage added to financial considerations so that the convict was dispensed with and his and her memory erased as quickly as possible. Yet without convicts and that haphazard but largely successful system called transportation, Australia, had it been founded at all, would have been a vastly different place by the middle of the century. Essentially, transportation gave a purpose to settlement, while convict labour made the experiment in colonization possible. In the very early days, Australia as a white civilization existed because of the convicts. Sixty years later it could do without them and, where possible, even the physical remains of their passing were abandoned and fell into ruins.

Transportation had helped solve the problem posed by the criminal element in Britain, and it was inevitable that the authorities there would turn their minds to using the new colonies as a receptacle for the poor. There were at least 100,000 on poor relief and, like the criminals, they were a seeming threat to both the economy and morality. In the twenty years from 1830 to 1850 over 200,000 immigrants arrived in Australia of whom 70,000 were assisted to come to New South Wales. Many lacked skills, but most wanted to better themselves, and the majority were under thirty, could read and write and their very presence helped change the face of convict Australia.

In the early 1840s the optimism of the pastoral industry was eroding. By 1839 George Gipps was concerned that capital was flowing in at too fast a rate for its absorption and that speculation had dulled the wits of the colonists. Imports were more than double exports in value; much of the former in luxury goods — carriages, jewellery, wines and spirits — and the anxious governor contemplated with distaste the champagne bottles with which he asserted the Melbourne countryside was littered. The banks were overflowing with cash which made loans easily obtainable at rates from ten to twenty-five percent depending upon the security offered. Land sales, both rural and urban, rose daily. The newcomers knew nothing of the lesson of hardship learnt by the old hands. Five years of severe drought from 1837 to 1841, though causing further imports including wheat for flour, mattered to few because wool prices temporarily remained high until they began to fall in 1841.

In London, word of the drought caused alarm and investors began withdrawing their colonial funds, especially as there were good profits to be made at the time in British railway development. Merchants in Australia had a glut of imports, and graziers, to whom they had made loans or given credit, were asked to pay their accounts. There was a chain reaction of increasing withdrawals of cash from the banks, and four major colonial banks including the Bank of Van Diemen's Land failed. Credit became very hard to get.

The recession coincided with a labour shortage in the pastoral industry. Convicts, in New South Wales at least, were no longer available and new immigrants stayed in Sydney, causing further competition on a shrinking labour market and resentment amongst the local labour force. Large landowners, including Wentworth, wanted to import cheap labour from China, India and the South Sea Islands, which greatly concerned Attorney-General Plunkett who thought that the labourers would be treated like slaves. At the same time several hundred colonials left for Chile, in the hope of finding better times there.

Immigrants, however, continued to pour into New South Wales, largely financed by the land sales of the late thirties. In 1841 over 20,000 assisted immigrants arrived but by 1843 the number had dropped to a mere eleven. From 1837 to 1839 almost a million acres of land were sold. In 1843 and 1845 the total scarcely reached 10,000 which, in addition to revealing the weakness in the economy, proved the absurdity of Wakefield's theory based on an artificial price for land. The great days were gone and there were bankruptcies amongst all classes. Sheep which sold at 35s a head in 1839 brought 6d a head with the station thrown in by 1843. There was widespread unemployment in Sydney, with 700 men registering at Gipps' newly opened unemployment office. Wentworth, himself a sufferer from the economic slump, told the Legislative Council that he knew a man with 10,000 sheep who could not get credit for a bag of sugar.

Gipps was unjustly blamed in London for the overuse of the land fund in bringing too many immigrants to the colony. In an attempt to remedy matters, he tried to curb interest rates, and, perhaps influenced by the fact that there was a lack of space for debtors in the prisons, he abolished imprisonment for debt and allowed Wentworth's bill of a lien on wool and stock to become law which meant that sheep owners could borrow on future wool and stock sales. Some survived on their future prospects. Others kept going by boiling down sheep carcasses for tallow, which was of considerable financial benefit and also helped to cull the flocks and thereby improve their quality.

The economy slowly recovered and by 1845, when the price of wool rose to 14d per pound in London, there were increasing demands for labour in the country districts, a slight revival in land sales and a greater air of optimism prevalent. An old resident with some insight said that 'the wool trade stopped grass growing in Sydney streets.' Despite all that had happened, there was little thought given to the main lesson: foreign capital in the Australian economy could be relied upon to the extent that profits were assured but would be quickly withdrawn if better profits were offered elsewhere. Another lesson, better learnt, was the folly of attracting immigrants without capital and then having little or no work to

The pastoral industry became labour intensive during the shearing season. This shed was well organized. In a rapid series of movements taking only a few minutes, the wool went from the sheep to the fleecing table, then to the wool press, after which the bales were sewn up for transport.

enable them to establish themselves. Assisted immigrants by their very circumstances were without the means to settle on the land, and the depression of the early 1840s meant that many joined the ranks of Sydney's unemployed.

Caroline Chisholm arrived at Sydney in 1838 from India with her husband Archibald who worked for the East India Company. She had neither means nor training but was a woman of immense courage, inflexible integrity and possessed of a great love for suffering humanity. She decided to go to the aid of the immigrants when, as depression and drought struck, she observed that single girls were being dumped on the wharves with nowhere to go. Finding a group of sixty-four girls sheltering in the Rocks area with only 14s 3d amongst them, she set up a Female Immigrants Home with the support of the clergy, the Governor's wife and, after some initial wariness, of Gipps himself. There she gave protection and shelter to hundreds of young women, some of whom she accompanied into the country districts where, having established depots at various points as far south as Gundagai and as far north as Armidale, she found employment for them, which was often followed by marriage. By 1842 she was also concerned about families who, having migrated in the hope of better things, found themselves destitute.

Caroline returned to England in 1846 and became a publicist for Australia. She formed a society to send out groups of families, which in five years despatched some 3,000 persons, and she agitated for, and achieved, better conditions on the vessels carrying the immigrants. Her plans for families to immigrate, most of whom hoped to settle on the land eventually, alarmed some squatters and landholders who feared competition from successful farmers. Her Catholic faith and the possibility that her exertions would bring a surfeit of Irish Catholics to Australia stirred John Dunmore Lang to fury as he contemplated the possibility of his beloved New South Wales becoming a province of popery. Lang, for his part, helped many Scottish Presbyterians to immigrate, who, being of high moral character and of industrious habits, contributed to the growth of the colony and helped to balance the influx of paupers. Caroline continued her work, and in six years assisted 11,000 people to settle as servants, wives and farmers in New South Wales while her criticism, energy and experience contributed to changes in the selection of migrants, their treatment on the voyage out and their reception in the colony.

In South Australia, experience was the great teacher as the dream faded of eager farmers growing miraculous crops and finding prosperity in a season. It was soon realized that only the southern portion, or about a quarter of the colony, was suitable for agriculture while the rest was practically desert. The account of Sturt's journey into the Centre in 1845, where he discovered Cooper Creek and passed over land which made man and beast quail at its barreness, had convinced the colonists that their future lay close to the coast. With increasing experience of local weather and soils, by the mid-1840s, 900 farmers had 27,000 acres under wheat, and were producing more than the colony could use. By the end of the decade there were exports to the other colonies and to ports on the Indian Ocean. In 1843 John Ridley perfected a machine that reaped, threshed and winnowed wheat, which helped reduce labour costs. Initially only the wealthy could afford it, but gradually its use became widespread throughout the colonies. Within a few years, South Australia had become the granary of the whole continent and the pastoral industry also contributed to its economy with high returns from wool sold to Britain.

The rule of George Grey (Governor 1841–46) also helped South Australia climb to prosperity. He suffered demonstrations and abuse, a good deal of it warranted, because under him the days of plenty based on government spending were over and there were retrenchments and all manner of cuts in public finance. The colony was given a nominated Legislative Council, but Grey largely ignored its requests for democratic reform and he ruled with much caprice and some wisdom. The discovery of minerals, first silver and lead, and then copper at Kapunda and Burra, meant that his governorship was marked by economic developments of great importance to the future of the colony.

At the Burra, immense deposits of copper were found and mined by Cornish and Welsh miners, who flocked to its six small towns bringing with them the techniques they had learnt at home. They lived in three-roomed, attached houses built for them by the mining companies which, lined up around a square, were perfect replicas of the villages from which they came. A hospital, churches, shops, a library and two Oddfellows Lodges were erected, and mail came five times a week from Adelaide, ninety miles away. By the late 1840s, there were 5,000 people at Burra with some 2,000 of them opting to live in dwellings excavated into the

Copper was first found at Kapunda, sixty-five miles from Adelaide, in 1842, and in forty years over 70,000 tons of the ore were produced. In the 1870s Kapunda was the second largest town in South Australia with a population of over 10,000.

sides of a creek, where they endured damp and disease. Burra produced three-fifths of the copper exported from South Australia. Thirty-seven mining companies were listed on the Adelaide Stock Exchange and the colony was the principal exporter in Australia of minerals worth over two million pounds sterling from 1845 to 1851. The mines closed in 1877 but open-cut mining started up again in 1971, and the homes of the Welsh and Cornish survived largely intact, to the benefit of those in later generations who visited there to think about the past.

At the very height of the depression, London decided to give a further measure of self-government to New South Wales, though not to Van Diemen's Land because democracy was considered incompatible with the continuation of transportation. Henceforth, the Legislative Council in New South Wales was to comprise twelve members nominated by the Crown and twenty-four elected by that one-third of the adult males who possessed sufficient means to be considered capable of voting. Six of the members were to be elected to represent Port Phillip, which had been fruitlessly petitioning for separation from New South Wales since 1840. The local press in Melbourne as well as Geelong, where the *Geelong Advertiser*, which was started in 1840 as the District's first rural and morning newspaper, supported the move for separation vociferously. Gipps reported that election day in Sydney, 15 June 1843, had gone off well although there had been mild riots amongst the contending parties with the loss of one life.

At the time, Wentworth was at daggers drawn with the Governor because Gipps was determined to regulate the extent of squatting runs and make the squatters pay higher fees for their occupancy of them. The two men were also in conflict over Wentworth's intention to extend his domain into New Zealand. Between 1839 and 1841 New Zealand had been officially an extension of New South Wales, so that Gipps had jurisdiction there. Wentworth and a few friends had attempted to acquire twenty million acres in New Zealand at a cost of a farthing per 1,000 acres but the bid was blocked by Gipps who earned the sworn enmity of Wentworth. Gipps was dismayed when William Charles was duly elected to the Council, and the fact that Wentworth wanted to be called 'Honourable' possibly indicated how far he had come from the days of his liberalism. James Macarthur, son of old John, stood for and was defeated in Cumberland, but Lang won a seat for Port Phillip, which meant that the old colonists were sure to have a voice in government.

The new Council met with neither parties nor plans but it had an opposition to the Governor, drawn largely from the squatting and business establishment. The opposition was conservative and represented those of the wealthy classes who survived the depression. The Council had no control over the land fund or other revenue or government spending, but it was in some measure a sounding board for grievances. It could pass legislation on other matters provided neither London nor the Governor rejected its bills. From a sense of frustration in the Council, a system of Select Committees arose which investigated many important facets of life in the colony and their reports eventually formed the basis of much useful legislation.

The major issue facing the government was that of the tenure of the squatters of whom fewer than 200 held seventy-three million acres of land, running 5,500,000 sheep by the end of the 1840s. Gipps was determined to make them pay some form of adequate licence fee but their resistance was such that he was anxious lest they rise in revolt and he hoped that in such an eventuality the army would be able to control them. They used their paid London agent to persuade the British government to nullify Gipps, so that, by 1847, they were given fourteen-year leases with the right to buy their land. The large squatters had thus won the battle and, secure in their tenure, they had consolidated their position once again, after the drought and depression. No amount of legislation but only bad luck, bad seasons, falling prices or ill-management could ever make them relinquish their hold on the land. Their main contribution to public life was a concerted effort to have transportation revived to New South Wales.

By 1846 there was only one remaining convict to every sixteen free persons in the colony and the majority of the population, particularly the townspeople and the workers, were implacably opposed to a revival of transportation. With good cause, they were fearful for their jobs and mindful of the animosities of the past when emancipists and exclusives struggled for position. Nevertheless, a Council committee chaired by Wentworth and made up largely of squatters recommended revival on the grounds that it would build New South Wales into 'a mighty colony'. There was sufficient agreement in London to make it possible for a transport, the *Hashemy*, to arrive in Sydney in 1849 with 236 convicts aboard. Public meetings of protest were immediately organized, and the general outcry was such as to make it plain, even to Wentworth, that the days of transportation were over for ever in New South Wales. It was also plain to the Sydney workers and their leaders that, provided they were united, they could win concessions from the government.

Port Phillip up to this time prided itself on being free from the convict taint, despite the numbers who had come across the Murray or Bass Strait with their masters and the 543 more who arrived from Van Diemen's

Land with conditional pardons. The squatters were convinced that an influx of convicts would be an economically sound move. London again acquiesced, and, starting in 1844, Port Phillip received allegedly reformed felons directly onto its own shore from the model Pentonville Prison. Many residents referred to them as Penton-villains. The British government called them exiles, to soften the criminal connotations and 1,727 of them arrived up until 1849, which made lame the later claim of freedom from convictism in Victoria's past.

The coming of the exiles, in which the generality of citizens had no voice, served to strengthen the argument by the Port Phillip District for separation from the rest of New South Wales. Separation remained a recurrent theme of the 1840s and revolved largely around the proceeds from the sale of land, most of which, though raised in Port Phillip, was used in the older parts of the colony. Separation would give the residents of Port Phillip a direct voice in their own affairs. In protest, they elected only one member to the Legislative Council in 1848 out of their available six. To make the point even more firmly, they voted in the distant Earl Grey, secretary of the Colonial Office in London, to represent them on a body which they considered to be a farce. Such buffoonery was a legitimate attempt to force the British authorities to act. When people in Melbourne heard on 11 November 1850 that separation was on the way, they lit bonfires on the hills to spread the word to the interior and the celebrations went on for a week. On 1 July 1851 Charles La Trobe became Lieutenant-Governor of the newly proclaimed Victoria, the Riverina remained part of New South Wales and the old colony asserted its superiority by claiming control of the Murray to the Victorian bank.

In Van Diemen's Land transportation remained an ever-present reality and its consequences were daily more apparent. In 1846 there were 66,000 free persons on the island of whom the majority had served time as convicts. There were also 30,000 convicts, who were thrown on the employment market after doing a period of probation in the gangs. Unemployment was widespread, even amongst the free immigrants, vice of all kinds from thievery to buggery was everywhere apparent, and Tasman's isle began to bear 'the name of Sodom'. Grey rightly affirmed in the House of Lords in 1850 that both New South Wales and Van Diemen's Land were 'completely the creation of transportation, and Port Phillip hardly less so' and that South Australia could not have survived without the sheep, cattle and other resources provided by the convict colonies. None of this was any longer to the point, and a society was formed in Sydney to agitate for the complete abolition of transportation to eastern Australia. The upshot was the founding of the Australasian

For 'home' consumption it was useful to portray conditions in the colony as ideal. Some colonial gentry observed Christmas in this way. The majority of the population celebrated in a much more modest manner but all tried to keep up some of the traditions of 'home'.

League in 1851 which bound itself to resist the setting up of European prisons on Australian soil and, as a symbol of their resolve, the founders set the Southern Cross on the same flag with the Union Jack.

While attending meetings and signing petitions proved a useful political breeding ground for a minority, the majority of the people were more interested in their day-to-day activities. Except for baptisms, marriages and funerals their lives were largely unrelieved by public ceremony, whether civil or religious, or by festivities except on occasions such as St Patrick's Day, the Queen's birthday, the opening of a public building, road or bridge and, for those with means, attendance at the theatre, where farce and imported plays were popular. Isaac Nathan, the first musician with a European reputation, had arrived in Sydney in 1841 and set up a singing school. In 1847 his *Don John of Austria*, the first opera composed, written and performed in Australia, was produced at the Victoria Theatre in Sydney.

Sunday was a day of rest, at least in the towns, but any great cycle of Christian life enshrined in liturgy was lacking. Without Lent, Easter began to lose meaning, Christmas became a day for picnics and for some it was more important to balance their books than to make peace with God. Nathaniel Pidgeon, Wesleyan lay preacher, went about the streets of Sydney singing of sin and salvation, while at New Norcia, out from Perth, Rosendo Salvado, a native of Spain, celebrated the feast of the Immaculate Conception in 1846 by opening a school for Aboriginal children. John Bede Polding, now Catholic Archbishop of Sydney but still the humble pastor to the convicts, the poor and the dispersed of the outback, dreamt of a Benedictine church in Australia which would become a beacon to beauty, truth and culture in the land. His dream was shattered on the rock of practicality, when the Irish secular clergy took over his Benedictine church. Culture, whether high or low, religious or secular, was a fragile growth insofar as it expressed a spirit purely Australian.

One third of the adult population was illiterate, and, though newspapers flourished in every major centre, they were restricted in readership by availability and cost. Mates gathered to yarn around the campfire and in shanties in the bush and their conversation was likely to differ little from that in the towns, except that, amongst the urbanites, 'home' across the seas figured more largely.

Apart from the large scone of flour and water, cooked in a camp oven and called a damper, few inventive departures were shown in cooking, except that it was common for the kitchen to be entirely removed from the actual house itself in order to minimize the danger of fire. Mutton, whether fresh or salted, was the staple meat still, although it was sometimes varied with beef and pork. Tea, being light to carry and not subject to spoiling, was drunk in prodigious quantities, with beer only gradually replacing spirits while colonial wines were drunk only by a few.

The habits of the past were retained in clothes, with the exception of stranger forms of headwear to ward off both sun and flies. Otherwise, the heat of the Australian summer was borne with serges and tweeds, petticoats, waistcoats, flannels and the assorted paraphernalia of England and Ireland, depending upon availability and means.

The last found of the continents was also the first born, and its worn hills, deserts and wild coasts, its flora and fauna seemed to bear marks from an age when the world was young. In its very vastness of three million square miles, with so much of it not yet seen by the whites, the continent posed both a problem and a threat and some wondered what was at its heart. Ludwig Leichhardt, with four white men and two Aborigines, stepped out from a station on the Darling Downs in 1848 to walk from east to west. He and those with him were never seen again, even though other parties went out to find them. It meant that the bush or the desert had added to those already claimed since those early days when a party of Irish convicts had left Sydney, vainly hoping to walk to China. There was a mystery in the land which challenged all those who tried to give it meaning in art and literature and Leichhardt's name remained in legend as one whom the vast bush had claimed.

William Wentworth was the first native-born who tried to say something of his home with the poem he submitted for a prize at Cambridge in 1822. He ran second to the pretty effusions of Winthrop Praed who, having never seen Australia, relied on his own fervent imagination. Wentworth's poem was a song full of triumph and undisguised love for the land of his birth, which he called 'Mother Earth', while England seemed foreign to him at the time. He spoke of the Aborigines as the 'lords of this old domain', but, forgetful or unmindful of their culture, he asked the goddess of the Warragamba mountains:

To wake to life my country's unknown lyre
That from creation's date has slumbering lain.

He concluded with the promise that, in her decline, Britain would be able to look 'with parent eyes' to the south where she could then relive her old glories in the new land, which possibly gave the English judges pause for thought. Unlike Praed, Wentworth did not see the Christian religion as the carrier of the culture that would make his country great, and thus he began, probably unconsciously, a tradition that endured.

Charles Harpur was born on the Hawkesbury River in 1813, received a wide but informal education, never set foot out of Australia, became a gold commissioner at Araluen in New South Wales and, though a currency lad, was determined to become the 'Muse of Australia'. Living in an age in which beauty was equated with classical forms, Harpur remained stilted and guarded in his poetry so that his cultural identification with his homeland was flawed. Yet he drew around him others, Daniel Deniehy, Henry Kendall, N.D. Stenhouse, and John Le Gay Brereton who understood and admired his work, and he made them realize that, in the shaping of an essentially Australian culture, poetry was fundamental. He loved the bush where 'a mighty stillness broods' and he cried, 'My country! I am sore at heart for thee!' as he watched the 'lawless Squatters' and their 'Hacks' claiming it for their own.

Generally, by the end of the 1840s, an air of optimism had begun to prevail with the weathering of the depression. In Western Australia, the colonists eagerly awaited the arrival of the first convicts but in the meantime they had to get by with a handful of Chinese who had arrived in

Mechanics' Institutes probably originated in Scotland and the first in Australia was opened in Sydney in 1833. This Institute at Williamstown, Victoria, dates from 1860. It has served as a library, a theatre in which Melba once sang, council chambers, primary school, temporary church and is now the site of the local Historical Society.

November 1847, while on many properties flocks were shepherded by Aborigines. However, non-white labour was regarded as a temporary expedient, and wages of £50 to £60 per year with rations were offered for white shepherds. The first batch of seventy-five convicts disembarked from the *Scindian* on the twenty-second anniversary of the foundation of the colony in June 1850 which was regarded by the *Perth Gazette* as 'a very fit day for the commencement of the new order of things'. The newspaper immediately demanded that the convicts be put to work building a prison for the local Aboriginal prisoners, who were incarcerated in such a confined space that one of them had died from suffocation.

Education and state aid to religion were still burning questions, especially in South Australia with its vaunted role as a haven for religious dissidents. Immigrants were now flocking there and, with its promise in wool, wheat, metals and commerce, the colony was determined to apply the principles of religious and civil freedom dear to many of its founders.

In 1851 state aid was abolished in South Australia, which put the churches of all varieties on an equal footing. Meanwhile, New South Wales had started to fund both public and denominational schools in the fond hope that peace would be assured between the churches and educational standards improved. Almost everyone agreed that Christianity was basic to education, but what was Christian, as distinct from purely denominational, was the issue at stake. Those few who thought that the matter was of no moment could afford to bide their time until the protagonists wearied themselves, at which juncture the secularists would have their day.

Moral enlightenment was part of the creed of the day and was expressed in savings banks, temperance societies, the building of private schools, and the setting up of charitable organizations. Sydney had a Benevolent Society; an asylum for the destitute in Pitt Street; and a number of hospitals, though they were generally of a very low standard. The Christian ethic of loving one's neighbour was evident in some aspects of public and private life, and everywhere there was a sense of striving to build the Australian colonies on the pattern of the home societies.

Secure in their own particular belief in a supreme being and convinced that it was both unique and exclusive, it was easy for the whites to conclude that the Aborigines had no such belief at all. One practical result of this arrogance was that the blacks were judged incompetent to give evidence in court under oath. The Aborigines' Protection Society stated bluntly that the rejection of black evidence, 'renders them virtually outlaws in their Native Land which they have never alienated or forfeited.' Plunkett, as Attorney-General, had long held the view that it was monstrous to deny the blacks a right to give evidence, yet he was ineffective in shaking the law makers in either Sydney or London.

Indeed, Robert Lowe, an outspoken champion of the rights of the underdog and of so much else in the slow process of democratic development in Australia, refused to support Plunkett because admitting Aboriginal evidence would put whites at the mercy 'not of man [but] of savage and blood thirsty cannibals.' The fact was that there had been instances of ritualistic cannibalism practised in New South Wales, and Aborigines sometimes told whites what they knew their interrogators wanted to hear, rather than what they themselves knew to be true.

In 1849, the matter of Aboriginal evidence came to a head after Edmund Kennedy, on an exploratory journey on the Cape York Peninsula, was speared to death in the presence of his Aboriginal companion, Jacky Jacky, who had shown great courage and loyalty throughout the whole episode. It was clear that Jacky Jacky knew the Aborigines who were responsible for the slaying, but Plunkett was powerless to act in bringing them to trial, as the only witness, Jacky Jacky, could not give evidence. Plunkett had another try at putting a bill through the Legislative Council, and he used the argument that, as the Aborigines were being poisoned and shot, the only remedy was to accept their evidence in the hope of convicting the white killers. His remarks alarmed the squatters and their allies in the Council, and Plunkett was again accused of showing favouritism to the blacks. In forlorn anger, as he saw the majority line up to defeat his bill, Plunkett said that as every Aborigine 'had stamped on him the image of his Creator, he could not but believe that the treatment that had been visited on these blacks was sufficient to call down the vengeance of Heaven'. Aboriginal evidence was finally admitted in the New South Wales courts in 1876.

CHAPTER SIX

The Golden Ground

The great southern continent and its white inhabitants lay at peace in 1851. Sixty-three years had changed much of its more verdant land where sheep now walked in millions, while the cultivation of crops and the rearing of stock for food had taken some hold on the coastal fringes. The vast heart of the continent had barely been touched by the white settlers, to whom it was a distant back country of desert dunes, forbidding heat and unknown dangers. The whites had come to terms with the ancient fauna, although the wild dog, like themselves a newcomer, remained a menace. No one realized that some of the birds, unlike the dog which had arrived in the previous 5,000 years, were so native to the land that they had no origin apart from it. Was this the cradle of all that grew and walked? What other mysteries did it hold in its keeping? These questions remained unasked because the business of the day was to acquire and retain the means of sustenance, and about that men and women, and many children also, went by force and habit.

Already Australians were showing an inclination to become urban dwellers in cities which hugged the coast and they looked back to the bush as an unknown land. The needs of administration and the facilities of ports helped the growth of the cities and created a demand for labour, but it was clear that immigrants in particular preferred to live in an urban environment. In Sydney, over a quarter of the 186,000 citizens of New South Wales lived in a city which had its gentry and its slum dwellers, its offices and factories, and banks and shops of all varieties. Melbourne held about the same proportion of the 100,000 who lived in Port Phillip as did Hobart of the 70,000 in Van Diemen's Land. The tanneries, foundries and breweries were almost all in the cities, but of the 500 industrial enterprises in operation by 1850 a half were flour mills, which were constructed where convenience dictated.

In Melbourne, the tradesmen were found about the central areas and the professional men had moved onto Eastern Hill, while some workers and others of the better-off had taken up residence in the suburban land beyond the township. Richmond and Collingwood were already dotted with villas and cottages, and Toorak and Prahran, south of the Yarra, had seen the same process. In both Sydney and Melbourne, the suburban sprawl had already begun. There seemed to be limitless land and, as yet, only the sheep were there to occupy it.

There was little variation in day-to-day life over the vast areas where pastoralists had expanded. Out beyond Bathurst in New South Wales and in that land, so often wet with creeks and swamps beyond Mount Buninyong in Victoria, little stirred except the sheep, followed by their lonely shepherds. It had frequently happened in previous years that one of their kind, idly kicking at the soil or scratching at a rocky outcrop, had seen something gleaming which had proved to be gold. Gold, however, was a treasure it was unwise to talk about in a convict colony, and silence was kept as to its whereabouts because all gold was supposed to belong to the Crown.

Other mineral deposits had already been found as well as coal. Mining

S. T. Gill is best remembered for his sketches of the goldfields but his delicate work also preserves a record of Adelaide's buildings in the 1840s.

was already fundamental to the South Australian economy and since 1848 iron ore had been smelted to pig iron near Mittagong in New South Wales. In such circumstances, it was not strange that some men should begin to think of the probable existence of gold and other precious metals in useful quantities, but an event elsewhere was needed to cause the next step to be taken. By 1849 the rich goldfields of California had drawn some Australians to go prospecting there and they learnt the prevailing methods of separating gold from mud and dirt. Amongst them was English-born Edward Hargraves, who returned to New South Wales convinced that the gold he had come across in meagre amounts in California lay in abundance under Australian soil. He was proved right in a measure that even Hargraves, much given to self-importance and exaggeration, never dreamt possible.

Hargraves taught four young Australians how to use the Californian techniques of panning and cradling, and they soon found rich deposits of gold in the Wellington district in early 1851. Hargraves publicized the finds in the press, named the area Ophir and claimed, and eventually received, £10,000 as a reward from the government. There was an immediate rush across the Blue Mountains to the fields situated beyond Bathurst, and by 15 May, 300 diggers were on the Ophir fields. Australia's first gold rush had commenced. This prompted an old soldier to ask for the importation of a regiment to keep order as he feared that 'all the horrors of California', with murders, riots, lynchings and general unrest, would follow in the wake of the diggers.

Sanity prevailed in Sydney and the government decided to maintain the even tenor of society: to exact in a humane way a licence fee of 30s a month from the diggers to finance the administration of the fields, and generally assist rather than impede them in their search for gold. Prices of all commodities rose astronomically as diggers came in from the other colonies, labour in the towns and pastoral districts became scarce and the news of prodigious finds prompted the London *Times* to state, 'this is the Arabian nights over again'. In the main, the early days of gold in New South Wales, though marked with some unrest and resentment at the licence fee, saw all the romance and hardship which the lottery of gold digging entailed, together with stability and a quick return to normalcy when the early rushes were over.

Gold mining continued in New South Wales especially on the Turon River where the diggings were very rich. The golden period in the colony reached its symbolic apogee in 1871 when the world's largest reef-gold specimen was found in the Hill End area. It weighed 630 pounds and was brought up almost intact. One of the owners of the claim was Bernard

Holtermann, born in Hamburg in 1838, who later built himself a home in Sydney with a tower in which a stained-glass window depicted him standing beside the huge specimen. By his patronage and enthusiasm, Holtermann became the father of Australian photography, and the reconstruction of the historical period of gold about Hill End and Gulgong was possible from the photographs of those fields at their peak. The photographs which were used abroad to publicize the colonies of New South Wales and Victoria and encourage immigrants to come out to them were also made possible by his sponsorship.

While the first discoveries of gold were being made in New South Wales, Port Phillip was still reeling from the catastrophic bush fires of Thursday 6 February 1851, named Black Thursday because ashes fell in the Melbourne streets in 120°F heat. From Westernport in the east to across the border with South Australia in the west, in a vast swathe of country stretching beyond Mount Macedon, the awesome fire destroyed all in its path when, swept by high winds, it raced beyond control, but there was little loss of human life. Soon the rains fell and the earth became green with a refreshed and increased luxuriousness.

The news from New South Wales had drawn many workers from Victoria to the goldfields there, and Charles La Trobe waited anxiously for word of discoveries in his own domain. Wisdom should have indicated patience. New South Wales with its settled population, its established system of law and order, its seasoned administrators and its healthy treasury was able to handle a gold rush. Victoria was but an infant born on 1 July 1851. Nine days later, at Clunes, ninety miles north-west of Melbourne, gold in payable quantities was found. The rushes did not begin in earnest until late August when rich deposits were discovered at Ballarat. Within three months, the richest goldfields the world had ever seen were opened, especially at Mount Alexander where the diggings spread over an area of fifteen square miles and made Victoria the mecca for thousands from Europe.

The cold statistics tell little of what life was like in those golden days, but they reveal much of how gold affected Australia, and particularly Victoria. In the decade of the 1850s over 1000 tons of gold worth £110,000,000 came out of Victoria. New South Wales produced about 140 tons valued at £15,000,000 and Australian gold accounted for 40 percent of the world's total production in the 1850s. It remained a more valuable export than wool until the 1870s. But it was in the numbers of people that the big change took place, thereby laying to rest Governor George Gipps's fear that Australia would remain a vast sheep walk.

In the ten years of the golden decade, Victoria's population grew from

80,000 to half a million, while that of New South Wales rose from 190,000 to 350,000. Of the 600,000 who came to Victoria in this decade, over half stayed, but of those 86,000 who crossed from New South Wales almost all went home. This indicated where their long lasting emotional and economic roots were. Although the United Kingdom was the major source of the new population, the goldfields attracted 40,000 Chinese. Many of them were debtors who came to work, save their money and then return home. Their passing created a legacy of racism, which over a century later still showed its mark. As an indication of how money will be spent when available, the value of exports never exceeded imports into Victoria in the decade, and indeed in 1854 goods to the value of £18,000,000 came in while £12,000,000 worth went out. This caused a glut of unsaleable commodities, high rates of unemployment in Melbourne and the failure of many business houses.

Amongst the first on the goldfields were the ex-convicts and native-born, many of whom had been shepherds. Their presence initially alarmed the squatters, who foretold doom for themselves and anarchy for all, neither of which proved true. In fact, the squatters doubled their cattle numbers and did very well supplying mutton and beef to the fields and breeding horses for transport. In the wake of the early comers, bankers, tradesmen, parsons, lawyers, doctors, clerks, sailors, farmers, government employees, policemen and prostitutes followed. Alfred Tennyson would have come had his wife permitted him, and Henrik Ibsen wrote of 'Ballarat beyond the desert sands'. So many policemen left the ranks to become diggers that there were only two left out of a normal force of forty in Melbourne by the New Year of 1852. Their places were soon taken by ex-convicts and scoundrels.

The past life of the gold digger was of no consequence to anyone except himself. All that mattered was his ability to wield a shovel, to withstand heat and cold, water and mud, flies and fleas, dysentery and eye disease — meanwhile fortified by meat, damper and tea, with an odd glass of doctored grog because the government was too obstinate to permit licensed premises on the fields in the early years. The diggers were sustained by the search for gold, which rewarded a minority handsomely, kept others in moderate comfort and sent away about a third empty-handed. As a group, the diggers were young, unmarried, adventurous, of some slender means, better educated than the norm and Anglo-Saxon or Irish in origins. Equally, they were, in the main, law-abiding, God-fearing, hardworking and upright. Amongst them, however, there were some who possessed little of those qualities, and the goldfield population, which was never more than a third of the total

The diggers bitterly resented the methods of the Gold Commissioners who enforced the buying of licences. They rigorously policed the fields to ensure that everyone could produce a licence for inspection on demand.

Victorian population, was often judged harshly because of the behaviour of a rowdy or criminal minority.

In the beginning, the diggers merely scratched at the surface, taking what gold was readily available by panning in the creek beds and rivers. They then rushed to another place when word came of new finds. Millions of years earlier in the Tertiary period, volcanoes had erupted, twisting and turning the rivers and burying them, with their golden deposits, 60, 100 or more feet below the surface of the earth. By the end of 1852, at Ballarat, the diggers were going down and down through timber-lined holes searching for the deep leads. The holes quickly filled with water and the work was hard, unsafe and costly so they banded together in groups of eight to twelve, often of the same nationality, British, Irish or American, to work a common claim. Each claim was limited to 576 square feet. If they bottomed out on a lead they could win riches, even great riches, especially if they hit a spot where old river beds ran together. One such place was called the Jewellers Shops. It was on Canadian Gully at Ballarat where nuggets of 84, 93 and 136 pounds were found in January 1853. Alternatively the diggers could miss the lead or find it unproductive, so the heartbreaking work of shaft digging had to begin all over again.

With deep-lead mining a change came over the fields, for the diggers had to raise capital for equipment and daily necessities because they were forced to settle in the one place for months. As a consequence, the fields gradually took on the aspect of a stable community. Ballarat, by late 1854, was a thriving township with banks, shops, stores, hotels, theatres, libraries, churches, lawyers, doctors, a newspaper and a hospital under construction. More importantly, there were women and children, 15,000 of them in a total population of 50,000. Charles Hotham had recently replaced La Trobe as Governor of Victoria, and it was not a mob of uneducated vagabonds and assorted criminals that he had to deal with on the fields. On the contrary, they were mostly men who were literate, respectable and determined to be treated with dignity as upright citizens, and in many cases fathers of families.

The diggers had neither land nor votes, and they paid for their right to dig for gold by an extremely high tax of 30s per month. The tax was brutally enforced by a government bent on wresting every possible penny from them, while offering little in the form of services in return, especially in roads, bridges, transport and postal facilities or police protection from thieves. Increasingly the diggers began to agitate for their rights and at Ballarat, Castlemaine, in the Ovens River district and on the largest field, Bendigo, crowds of up to 12,000 met to protest and to refuse to pay for a licence to dig. The government compromised and reduced the fee in November 1853.

The event, called Eureka, of Sunday 3 December 1854 did not happen by accident. Goaded for three years by a repressive and corrupt administration at Ballarat, the diggers formed the Ballarat Reform League on 11 November. It demanded full civic rights together with abolition of the licence fee and proclaimed the doctrine that 'the people are the only legitimate source of all political power'. The editor of the local *Ballarat Times* called the League, 'the germ of Australian independence', while in London Karl Marx, when he heard of the goings on at Ballarat, prophesied that the movement there would be quickly suppressed. Marx was right.

On 1 December, a group of about 200 diggers gathered within a flimsy and hastily-erected stockade of logs near the Eureka lead. They were determined to resist, if necessary by arms, any further arrests for the non-possession of a licence, but they made no plans to launch an attack on anyone. Hotham and his Ballarat subordinates were equally determined to break the resistance of the diggers by the use of superior arms. They were convinced that the diggers' movement was organized by seditious foreigners. In fact the diggers were not in revolt and, apart from a few enthusiasts, they had no republican ideals. Essentially they demanded the fundamental right to be treated with respect, which time after time had been denied them when they were dragged from their damp holes and ordered to produce their licences. Failure to do so resulted in being forcibly carted off into custody where they were fined. Apart from the question of taxation without representation, which the licence fee virtually imposed, the diggers wanted a chance to settle on the land, most of which was still held by the squatters.

Over thirty of them died on that Sunday morning, when, outnumbered by more than two-to-one, they were attacked at dawn by police and troops, five of whom also lost their lives. It was later said that they died in vain because the freedoms and the rights for which they sacrificed their lives would have been eventually granted in any case. Reform did come about in 1855, when the licence fee was abolished to be replaced by an annual miner's right. This also gave an entitlement to stand for parliament and to vote in elections. The diggers' leader, Peter Lalor, bewailed the fact that the English so often found it necessary to baptize in blood the rights they granted. Public opinion in Victoria was clearly on the side of the diggers.

The men of Eureka left behind a legacy carried on in prose, poetry and painting and in the powerful symbol of their flag. H. R. Nicholls, who was a newspaper man, scorned the diggers as Irish drunkards, but Raffaello Carboni, the chronicler of those events of late 1854, saw it differently and he was able to plumb the symbolism of Eureka. To him, the flag, with its white cross and five stars on a blue background denoting the Southern Cross, was a thing of beauty under which free people could stand upright and proud. The Southern Cross flew briefly for those few days at Eureka but long and purposefully enough to win its place in the loyalty of many Australians. To them the stand taken by those who had fought beneath it was a promise of lasting democracy. With the passage of time, Eureka passed into mythology and its flag was seized by restless elements of the political and industrial left, which effectively put paid to its claim to be a universal symbol. But the legend remained to proclaim that, in the new land called Australia, the right to oppose tyranny and to be treated with respect, to have hope in and to work for a better future, was inalienable.

The already established society of the eastern colonies proved resilient to the coming of so many thousands in the 1850s because it was firmly shaped as white, male-dominated, hierarchical, dependent on Britain, closely governed and highly urbanized. The freedoms, inherited from

Britain, of religion, press and association were upheld and treasured by many. Law and order on the English model was accepted and, unlike California, the rule of the mob never took hold on the goldfields. The older popular movement which had helped stop transportation and was deeply involved in the demand for self-government was indigenous to Australia. The small elements of Chartism that came with the diggers refined it but did not change it. The diggers helped to strengthen the ethos that had become peculiarly Australian in a positive way. They had to support each other and find ways of confronting the problems thrown up on the goldfields. Their experience of the government officials on the fields, who so often acted without compassion or ordinary decency, caused many of them to become anti-authority. The repeated acts of brutality and corruption of the police enhanced a hatred that had its origins in chain gangs and convict hell holes.

The Australian characteristics of a fondness for strong drink, a readiness to take a risk and a general air of independence were reinforced on the goldfields as was racism, which, beginning with the blacks, now included the Chinese and had developed from contempt to loathing. The proportion of three males to one female had not changed much by the end of the 1850s but there were seven times as many females as before 1851. This made a difference to the whole fabric of society, as did the greatly increased attendance at schools and churches. Gold, with its ability to make the poor rich, to delude even the astute and to turn the sober into drunkards was a unique leveller. Servants left their masters; mistresses had to cook, clean and open doors. Men of no substance yesterday now rode in splendid carriages and drank fine wines. The hierarchical orders of old England, based on birth or distinction in the martial arts, found no role on the goldfields and little more in the society that grew around them.

Gold brought changes of enormous consequence to Victoria and New South Wales. With the threefold increase in population from 1851 to 1861, the rule of the squatters was threatened, though the squatters remained. The cry of the diggers to unlock the lands in Victoria was partially heard so that there were 13,000 farmers and market gardeners in 1861, mostly ex-diggers, compared to 3,000 a decade before. Gold built or made prosperous numerous country towns, which was more important than its contribution to the development of the cities. The towns brought to the bush those elements of civilization without which life can be brutish, and for which a week's holiday in the city for the races or an agricultural show never sufficed.

Some of the towns thrived to become cities like Bathurst, Ballarat,

Bendigo and Ararat, the only Australian city to owe its origins to the Chinese diggers who found gold there in 1857. Bendigo and Ballarat founded first-rate Schools of Mines and the technologies developed in them spread throughout Australia and into the Pacific. Everywhere settlements took root which were named by such simple expressions as the distance from the previous resting place — Five Mile, Ten Mile and Fifteen Mile and similar names were given to creeks and other watering places. Towns now forgotten sprang up overnight and had populations of 20,000 or more with numerous pubs and other amenities. They prospered while the gold lasted. In the end they became mere names — Hill End, Sofala, Mount Alexander, and others who had their fleeting moment in history. Out of them, and places like them, came the romance and hardship of gold. In and about them, and especially in Victoria's Golden Triangle, the great nuggets were found and often their names were enough to sum it all up — Welcome Stranger and Welcome Nugget of 2,284 and 2,217 ounces respectively — for there were many diggers who never saw a nugget.

The rise of new towns created a demand for new means of transport. The state of the roads was a guarantee of intense discomfort for travellers and heavy costs for goods. In 1853 a young American, Freeman Cobb, with his partners, founded a coaching firm in Melbourne called Cobb & Co., which provided speedy and reliable transport to the goldfields and eventually to towns right throughout Victoria, New South Wales and Queensland. The early drivers, called Yankee whips, were Americans, and the coaches were Concord Jacks of the thorough-brace type, imported initially from America. Only the best of horses were used, and the change stations were spaced about ten miles apart to provide fresh horses. Some of them, such as the bluestone stage at Buangor on the run west from Ballarat were imposing structures, while others left no trace. Cobb sold out at a large profit in 1856, but the name of his firm remained to be cheered by thousands, in the next eighty years, whose moderate comfort and speedy delivery at their destination was made possible by his enterprise.

Developments on land were paralleled at sea when steam was introduced onto the England to Australia route in 1852. The *Chusan* made the run to Sydney in eighty days carrying mails and passengers. The ship so delighted the citizens on her arrival that they created a new dance tune called the 'Chusan Waltz'. In 1854 the most important of all modern technical revolutions in communications arrived when the first electric telegraph line was installed between Melbourne and Williamstown. The telegraph quickly spread throughout the colonies. It annihilated distance,

The comparative luxury, the speed between towns and the general efficiency of their coaches with their skilful drivers, called 'Yankee whips', made the name Cobb & Co. famous. This form of popular transport survived in eastern Australia long after the gold rushes.

making joy and grief only moments away, but as the Melbourne *Argus* observed, its use was especially important to 'those engaged in commerce'.

Gold ended transportation to Van Diemen's Land and the possibility of it being resumed in any of the eastern colonies. In Van Diemen's Land opinion still had been divided between those who wanted the labour of convicts and those whose morals or pockets were threatened by their presence. Victoria had taken the drastic step of refusing entry to anyone from the island unless the newcomer could offer proof of his or her civil freedom. In England John Pakington, Secretary of State, decided it was time to act. On 14 December 1852 he wrote to William Denison,

Lieutenant-Governor of Van Diemen's Land, to tell him that no more British refuse would pollute Tasman's fair isle, partly because of the undesirable impression English criminals could gain by seeing their companions transported to 'an island in the immediate neighbourhood of the gold colonies of Australia'. On 26 May 1853 the last convicts to Van Diemen's Land landed from the *St Vincent* at Hobart to end that dark chapter in the history of the island. The last convicts to eastern Australia arrived at Norfolk Island in 1855. In the following year, 194 descendants of the mutineers against Bligh on the *Bounty* were taken from Pitcairn Island for resettlement on Norfolk Island where their own descendants flourish into the present.

Pakington was not one to deal in half measures. Gold freed Van Diemen's Land of convicts and so moved its citizens to reject the past that they changed its name to Tasmania in 1855. Gold also induced Pakington to take the other long awaited step and grant political freedom to the eastern colonies. He wrote to Charles Fitzroy, Gipps's successor in New South Wales, to tell him that the decision to grant self-government was prompted, not merely by listening to requests from the colonists but also, because of the 'extraordinary discoveries of gold'. The colonists could now go ahead and draw up constitutions for the approval of the Queen.

In his letter, Pakington said that there had to be provision for two houses of parliament written into the constitutions. The lower would be elected by the people and the upper one, preferably, nominated by the Crown. The colonists would be given control over land and finances. This was the crux of the matter as without such powers responsible government would be a sham. Pakington fondly hoped that such generosity would result in further cementing and perpetuating 'the ties of kindred affection and mutual confidence' between the colonists and the United Kingdom. It was a shrewd assessment for, although the colonists would bicker long and loud amongst themselves about the shape of their emerging freedom, they would never be permitted to forget its source. In vain did John Dunmore Lang, Daniel Deniehy, Charles Harpur and others cry for full independence from the Crown even if blood had to be shed to obtain it. The British statesmen had learnt how to give the needed inch. In any case, a golden age was not one in which to cry revolution. Most people had more pressing matters at hand and the pursuit of wealth had ever proved to be the handmaiden of conservatism.

Much argument followed in New South Wales about the exact shape of the new form of government, although little of it mattered. Wentworth generated a great deal of heat and comedy when he suggested that the members of the upper house, called the Legislative Council, should be given titles with hereditary rights to pass on to their successors. In itself the suggestion was a piece of nonsense, although it had been mooted earlier in Canada. It was quickly ridiculed by Deniehy, brilliant lawyer-son of convict parents, who burlesqued it in a speech of wit and invective and dismissed the idea of a 'bunyip aristocracy' with contempt. Wentworth, by now a proclaimed conservative, remained unperturbed. He failed to get his aristocrats, but few noticed that he got the nominated Legislative Council, which he, not wishing 'to sow the seeds of a future democracy', was determined to have as he hoped it would be a bulwark against the tide of radical change. Furthermore, the squatters, whose hold on rural electorates was secure, were ensured of retaining considerable weight in the new government. This was an assurance that change would never come about suddenly.

By the end of 1856, New South Wales, Victoria, Tasmania and South Australia all had self-government. The Victorians had decided to elect the members to their Legislative Council but, because its members and electors had to have wealth or education and preferably both, it remained particularly impervious to change and became a bastion of entrenched privilege. The secret or Australian ballot was used for the first time in the Victorian elections in March 1856 and progressively in the other colonies. Western Australia adopted the method in 1877. The South Australians also used the ballot box in their elections in April 1856. They also gave the vote to every adult male, which was an unprecedented stride to full democracy.

The ensuing elections in the four colonies went off with little fuss because the differences between the candidates generally amounted to little. There were no real leaders and policy formulation was unclear so that parties did not exist. When the new, nominated Legislative Council and elected Legislative Assembly met for the first time in Sydney on 22 May 1856, it was not remarked upon that a change had come about in the development of the colony of far greater significance than the much-vaunted existence of parliament and parliamentarians: there were now more females than males in Sydney's population of 53,118 persons for the first time in sixty-eight years.

John Dunmore Lang's political career was temporarily in abeyance as the Reverend Doctor had been lodged in Darlinghurst Gaol for six months convicted of libel, but there was one person of some stature elected to the Assembly. Henry Parkes was an English immigrant whose colonial career began in 1839 as a labourer in the employ of John Jamison. His talents soon stamped him as a man of the future, and his patriotism was shown when he supported England in the Crimean War against Russia. His enthusiasm for the war was shared generally, and a spate of place naming occurred, particularly around Ballarat, with battles such as those of Sebastopol, Inkerman, Balaclava and Redan being commemorated. Parkes had moved through various business and journalistic ventures, joined the radical elements of the reform movement striving for universal suffrage and land reform, flirted briefly with republicanism and finished as a liberal with his own paper, the *Empire*, founded in 1850 as the chief voice of the movement.

Vain, bigoted and blustering, there was also in Parkes a touch of greatness which made him stand above the crowd. His opposition to the old guard of colonial society, with its entrenched interests based on land, gave him entry onto the political stage. There he remained devoted to change, even when to conform may have served his own interests better because he was constantly in debt. Above all, Parkes was the embodiment of early Australian democracy, which grew from the middle classes, was stamped with their values and remained far removed from that supposed nightmare which Wentworth dreamt it could become. Colonial democracy posed no threat to Wentworth and his kind because the same, generally favourable, economic forces sustained them both.

In Britain, the Australian gold discoveries were a source of astonishment and, to some, profit. Fortunes were made in shipping and in supplying anything manufacturers deemed appropriate to fill the needs and fancies of the diggers. Overseas, Australia was on everyone's lips for a time and Ballarat and Bendigo became the chosen destination of thousands who wanted to go to the fields. Others came to the colonies because labour was short in the Australian cities and in the bush and the government was prepared to assist them to migrate by subsidising fares. The effects of the potato famine, which had reduced the Irish to 'a rag of a nation' were still being felt, and the large numbers coming from Ireland in the late 1840s kept up in the 1850s. Half of those who came in the 1850s were assisted and, in the main, they settled in the cities and towns, becoming labourers, craftsmen and servant maids, although the males perhaps spent an intervening stint on the goldfields.

In England, Caroline Chisholm had maintained her work of assisting migrants. She was not impressed by the news of the gold discoveries as she feared that they would cause instability in society. Her husband came to Australia in 1851 to work as her colonial agent, while Caroline kept sending families and girls from the British Isles, including a party of Jewish girls. Now famous and supported by such powerful figures as Charles Dickens, she decided to return to Australia in 1854. She was imbued with the optimistic but never proven idea that the health of a society lay in the settling of many, small farmers and she worked for the unlocking of the land. She died in poverty and obscurity in England in 1877. The inscription on her grave at Northampton reads 'The emigrant's friend' without recording the fact that her husband, whose bones rested with Caroline's, had shared in making her work possible by his faith, love and patience.

On another level, Caroline's work was aided by that of the Melbourne-born Mary McKillop. She was of Scots parentage and, with all the determination and grit of her forebears, she founded the Sisters of St Joseph in 1866, with the encouragement and guidance of a remarkable English priest-scientist, Father J.E. Tenison-Woods. After the Bishop of Adelaide lifted the excommunication he had put on her for alleged disobedience, she worked tirelessly for the education of the children of the poor, especially in the bush. She founded numerous schools and charitable institutions to that end up until her death in Sydney in 1908. In 1973, Mother Mary, as she became known, was the first Australian to be formally proposed in Rome as a candidate for canonization.

Some immigrants joined the native-born and old hands in concluding that both the system of land tenure and the policy of assisted immigration needed revision. There was unemployment in the mid-1850s in Sydney

The road from Adelaide to its port was opened in 1839 and McLaren Wharf was built in 1840. When steamers opened the Murray-Darling river system to transport in the 1860s the port flourished as a transit point for trade.

and Melbourne, which was caused by the arrival of diggers from the fields where a change to mining by companies was taking place. The constant influx of newcomers from the ships stirred up resentment against the government, employers, squatters, immigrants and Chinese. The *Operative*, a Sydney paper founded in 1854, struck a loud note calling for the cessation of any government assistance to immigration as well as the protection of the workers from the depreciation of the labour market by the 'introduction of inferior races', meaning the Chinese. On the goldfields the Chinese were often ill-treated, at times barbarously. In 1857 on the Buchland River in north-eastern Victoria, a mob of diggers drove the Chinese down the valley, destroying and burning their property and their joss-house. They were seen as economic competitors although opposition to them was often clothed in quasi-cultural terminology on the grounds that they threatened to dilute the British nature of society. By late 1861, Victoria, South Australia and New South Wales had passed laws restricting their entry.

The early years of the gold-rushes inspired ballads, poetry, art and some literature. Samuel Gill, an artist of great delicacy of line, left a lasting monument with his carefully drawn sketches, full of vitality, of life on the Victorian fields. Catherine Spence, preacher, reformer and feminist, published anonymously in 1854 her *Clara Morrison*, which dealt with South Australia in the days when gold lured many thousands away from the colony. A contemporary critic judged it the best work of literature yet written with Australia as its setting, and better than Alexander Harris's *The Emigrant Family* and the earlier *Tales of the Colonies* by Charles Rowcroft. The most important contribution to the gold period, however, was William Howitt's *Land, Labour and Gold* published in London in 1855. Howitt spent only two years in Australia but his gift for narrative and his incisive judgements on the bumbling ineptitude of Hotham's administration made his work a gold mine in itself for those who, later, wanted to know what life on the goldfields was like in the days of the great rushes.

The most formative element in the lives of literate Australians was the newspaper. Indeed, the editor of the newly-founded Melbourne *Age* said, with some truth on 17 October 1854, that 'The Newspaper has become the great teacher of the age' with more influence than either pulpit or school. It was opportune in the days of Eureka, and during the ordeal of the thirteen men put on trial for their lives after the event, that the *Age* held to a 'strong sense of popular rights' together with the conviction that, unless closely watched by the defenders of freedom, all governments would naturally tend 'to corruption and tyranny'. All the men of Eureka were acquitted. In Sydney, John West was appointed in 1854 as the first

4

~~Colony, who may be hereafter appointed a Judge *quamdiu se bene gesserit*,~~

~~shall be eligible to be summoned to the said Legislative Council; nor~~

~~shall any prelate, priest, deacon, or minister of any religious denomination,~~

~~whatever may be his title, rank, or designation, be so eligible.~~

*Hereditary title may
have a seat awarded
to them for life in the
Legislative Council.*

~~V. Whenever Her Majesty, Her Heirs, or Successors shall think~~ 5
proper to confer upon any Subject of the Crown of Great Britain, by
Letters Patent under the Great Seal of the said Colony, any hereditary
title of honor, rank, or dignity of such Colony, descendible according to any
course of descent limited in such Letters Patent, it shall be lawful for
Her Majesty, Her Heirs, or Successors to annex thereto, by the said Letters 10
Patent, if Her Majesty, Her Heirs, or Successors, shall so think fit, a
right to each original Patentee to be summoned to the Legislative Council
of the said Colony ; and every person on whom such right shall be so
conferred, shall thereupon be entitled to demand from the Governor
his writ of Summons to such Legislative Council, subject nevertheless to 15
the provisions hereinafter contained.

*When the holders of
such hereditary titles
amount in number to
fifty or upwards, the
present Legislative
Council to cease,
and a Council com-
posed of Patentees
for life, and of a
certain number of
elected persons hold-
ing such titles, to be
thenceforward the
Legislative Council.*

VI. Whenever the number of persons to whom such hereditary
titles shall have descended shall, together with the original Patentees then
under Summons to such Legislative Council, amount to fifty, or upwards,
the Legislative Council so nominated as aforesaid shall cease and deter- 20
mine ; and such original Patentees, together with all such persons to whom
such descendible titles shall have come, being of the full age of twenty-one
years, and not having taken any oath of allegiance or obedience to any foreign
prince or power, and being duly required by the Proclamation of the Governor
to be published in the *Government Gazette* at least one calendar month 25
previously to the day to be therein named for the election of Members to serve
in the said Legislative Council, shall assemble together at such place as shall
be directed in the said Proclamation, and the major part of the persons so
assembled, after appointing a Chairman for the occasion by a majority of
the votes of the persons present, shall proceed to elect twenty from the whole 30
~~number then existing of persons to whom such descendible titles belong,~~
and

Wentworth's proposal for hereditary titles in New South Wales was scorned by the
colonists and was withdrawn from the proposed New Constitution of 1856. However,
Wentworth gained his main objective in securing a nominated, rather than an elected,
Legislative Council.

117

official editor of the *Herald*. Since the publication of David Collins's *An Account of the English Colony in New South Wales* in 1798, little worthwhile Australian history was written until West's excellent *History of Tasmania* was published in two volumes in 1852. He was also the father of the anti-transportation movement as well as a firm believer that 'Australia was one', and thus an early federationist. West brought his strong convictions as a Congregational minister to the editor's desk together with a blend of liberal-conservative attitudes and moral stances and a rigid adhesion to principles.

In the early days of Sydney Cove, Phillip had noticed that there were numerous and admirable rock carvings about the harbour, some of which, he thought, were executed in a superior style. In white Australia, sculpture, before all other art forms, began badly. Lacking patronage, whether by state or church, sculptors could only deal in busts of the would-be famous, although Melbourne in the 1840s had two 'Madonna and Child' groups by Emil Todt. Todt, later, did a remarkable work depicting the gold diggers. In Tasmania, Benjamin Law sculptured two Aboriginal busts, one being of Truganini wearing the doomed look of a woman conscious that her people were dying. Teresa Snell Walker, Australia's first woman sculptor, also worked on the island. Thomas Woolner, an original of the Pre-Raphaelite brotherhood, sailed for Australia in 1852 and Ford Madox Brown painted the departing vessel in his *The Last of England*. Woolner remained only briefly, so the early palm goes to Charles Summers who first exhibited in Melbourne in 1854 though to show his true worth, Summers had to await a later tragedy when the story of Burke and Wills gripped the imagination of all Australians.

The most notable events of the period on an intellectual level were the founding of the University of Sydney in 1850 and that of Melbourne in 1853. Ironically, the very step of founding a university, and thereby proclaiming a commitment to liberal principles, almost caused Sydney's opening to be postponed. William Bland's was amongst the names put forward as original senators. He was a scholar, surgeon of high repute and a pioneer who had made a great contribution to the colony. He was also an emancipist, having been transported in 1814 for killing his opponent in a duel in Bombay. Robert Lowe publicly refused to sit on the Senate were Bland appointed, although Plunkett shared no such inhibition. It was a bitter affair with all the odour of the past about it. Bland's subsequent omission from the Senate indicated that old passions still ran deep.

Otherwise, Sydney's university, like some powerful elements in the society from which it sprang, was secular. Its teachers and governing body were all laymen. Its foundation indicated that the powerful and the wealthy would no longer tolerate the 'frightful dearth of Colonial education' that had persisted for over sixty years. Nor were they prepared to allow sectarian conflicts to mar the beginning of their University. Down in Melbourne, the already existing rivalry between it and Sydney would not permit any delay in founding a university, although some Victorians thought it an act of insane extravagance. Nonetheless, the price was not considered too high to give a colony not yet fifteen years of age an institution of prestige.

At a river crossing on the Murrumbidgee called Gundagai, the few hundred inhabitants were witnessing the growth of a flourishing community with moderate prosperity by 1852. Despite the warnings of local Aborigines, the township had been laid out on the river flats, which were clearly exposed to danger from flooding. On 25 June the river rose rapidly overnight, six families and a total of seventy-seven persons were drowned, homes and businesses were washed away and the community all but destroyed. It was noticed that very few turned to God to give gratitude for their survival. On the other hand, they were certainly mindful of the role played by an Aborigine who paddled out in a frail canoe on perilous trip after trip to rescue scores of them as they clung to roofs and trees. In a later time they erected a monument to commemorate Yarrie and his deeds of valour. On the plaque of honour they spoke of him as 'one of Australia's greatest heroes'. In one place at least, the black man, in the person of Yarrie, during the darkness of a night of swirling waters, became acceptable to the white community.

CHAPTER SEVEN

Change and Development

On 17 April 1861, at a desolate place in Central Australia, three men paused to bury the body of their dead companion, Charles Gray, in a shallow grave. It was an act of great courtesy because the survivors, Robert O'Hara Burke, William John Wills and John King, all stood unsteadily on their feet. Emaciated, bewildered and despondent, they now tasted bitterness after the jubilation of a few weeks previously when to them had fallen the honour of being the first white men to cross the continent — from Melbourne in the south to the Gulf of Carpentaria in the north. After the burial, they pressed on to their depot at Cooper Creek, but they found it deserted when they arrived on 21 April. The party which would have brought them safely back to Melbourne had left seven hours previously. Burke, the leader — brave, impetuous, unskilled and obstinate — and his loyal and honourable lieutenant, Wills, were dead from starvation by the end of June, while King, young and strong, lived on with the help of the Aborigines.

The remains of Burke and Wills were buried with great solemnity in Melbourne in 1863. In due course, a magnificent statue was sculptured in their honour by Charles Summers and the Royal Society of Victoria decided that an official title would be given to that successful but largely useless tragedy and it was called 'The Burke and Wills Expedition'. By them and many others the vast continent was walked upon — Sturt, Eyre, Oxley, Leichhardt, McDouall Stuart, Giles, the Forrests, Grey and the Gregorys — and their names were honoured by posterity. The sheep followed in their steps to the very fringes of the desert, and small towns and stopping places grew up in the outback. Yet the land remained largely unconquered and the names of Burke and Wills lived in legend as testimony to its supremacy.

With their much publicized and even flamboyant gesture in traversing the continent, Burke and Wills symbolized the passing of the early colonial period of which gold was the watershed. Those same days saw the departure of that period's pre-eminent representative in the person of William Charles Wentworth who finally retired to England in 1862 and died there ten years later. Brought back for burial his remains were interred near his home, and he was spoken of as Australia's 'greatest son'. Time had softened much, and even Parkes was contrite for his rejection of the eldest statesman, but Wentworth's legacy was permanent.

William Charles had fought for a whole range of causes: responsible government, freedom of the press, trial by jury and much else. Despite all his reforming work, the one thing that stood out was his struggle for the rights of the squatters which gave them a hold over their lands in effective perpetuity. As Wentworth himself changed to patriarch and consul from the days of his rebellious youth so too the squatters changed. Gone were the times of the rude dwellings, flimsy yards and make-shift shearing sheds. The squatters became graziers, and built fine houses with long drives of pines, elms, oaks and other exotic trees leading to well laid out gardens. Their shearing sheds became symbols of the squatters permanence for they signalled that on these vast acres the sheep would run in thousands and that each year the ritual of shearing the golden fleece would take place under the watchful eye of the master. But the squatters also had to struggle with the land for it could be full of caprice. Fine seasons were followed by others in which the clouds passed overhead to pour their abundance on distant mountains and seas, the earth cracked, the creeks dried up, the skeletons of stock whitened in the dust and crows cawed a requiem for hope.

The new forms of government in the east had helped to entrench the hold of the squatters, because it was clearly in the best interest of those with property to ensure the stability of the economy, and wool promised security while gold, to the astute, was a transient commodity. In vain conventions of delegates drawn from the landless met in Melbourne and Sydney in 1857, both to protest and to plan a suitable form of legislation for the future sale of land. One major obstacle to reform was that, although the best land had been taken up, there was still so much land to be occupied on the mainland. It was available to anyone with the will and means to push further out onto it.

Furthermore, it was apparent that with the entry of the colonies into a boom period in the aftermath of the gold rushes, most people were comfortably placed, although there were still pockets of unemployment in the cities. By the 1860s per-capita income and consumption was fifty percent higher than in America and 100 percent higher than in Britain while the external signs of prosperity were apparent with developments in business and the erection of imposing buildings. In short, it was not a favourable time for a reform movement. Yet, 'unlock the lands' became a catch cry upon which unity was achieved amongst the land hungry, or the merely discontented, and the politicians were quick to jump on the bandwagon.

It seemed, however, that little could be done about the squatters given their standing in a society which they had dominated for years. Their almost complete hold of grazing land on long leases, their political base in the parliaments, their favoured position in the eyes of British capitalists and their own industry, which allowed the most successful to double their capital every two to three years, made them the supposed enemy of the workers and excited jealousy in those city dwellers who were financially less well-endowed.

Much of the resentment against the squatters was wrongly based. Although their hold on land allegedly prevented the spread of agriculture, the nature of the pastoral industry was such that only the first comers who occupied the land without paying for it, or, later, the wealthy who could afford to pay, were successful. Economic viability required large holdings and the less fertile the land the larger they had to be. In western and northern New South Wales, in parts of Victoria and South Australia and even in eastern and central Tasmania, the pastoral runs resembled principalities.

To the extent that dreamers or malcontents envisaged the breaking up of the pastoral runs into farms for a yeomanry, they were deluded at best and unhinged at worst. A square mile, 640 acres, was a block scarcely sufficient under wheat or other cereals to provide even frugal comfort for a man and his family, while blocks of a lesser size invariably led to ruin and misery. In short, no one, except the squatters, knew what the land further out could support, while by the 1860s land closer in to the main centres was already taken up. Under such circumstances, the growth of the cities was inevitable because the gradual use of wire fencing, the provision of dams and the breeding of better sheep-dogs lessened still further the labour required to run the pastoral industry, while the running down of the goldfields added more to the number of those who saw no future outside an urban setting.

There were some powerful men prepared to attempt to break the monopoly of the squatters and the foremost was John Robertson. Since his arrival in 1822, as a child of six, Robertson had become as one with the native-born although London was his birthplace. As he grew to prosperity, he too became a squatter and defended his peers although he wanted to share the land with others. In 1861, he resigned as Premier of New South Wales to devote his energies to the cause. Dan Deniehy worked with him on drafting a suitable bill and in essence their proposal was simple but radical. Anyone with £80 could select a block of 320 acres in that half of the colony with a ten inch or better rainfall and get a title to it after three years provided he had his residence on it, improved it and paid the residue of £240 at the overall price of £1 per acre.

Two years previously, a Land Act had been passed in Victoria which proved a failure as land could not be selected until it was surveyed, and any form of effective survey would have taken several years to complete. The radical element in the New South Wales proposal was that the land could be selected before it had been surveyed, which meant that selectors could go practically anywhere and stake a claim to land. Robertson got the legislation through Parliament and on 1 January 1862 a period began in which unbridled rapacity was widespread. Selectors scrambled for land and squatters defended themselves by buying up the finest lots on their runs through dummies or by 'peacocking' the best land. The inmates of the old men's home at Parramatta were enlisted by squatters to act as dummies. By 'peacocking', many squatters got titles to river or creek fronts, thus effectively excluding others. To achieve all this, loans were sought by selectors and squatters alike and ruin was the outcome for many in both groups.

It seemed that the insatiable thirst to possess land — born out of ancient slaveries and feudal serfdoms, nurtured further by enclosure in England and dispossession of land in Scotland and Ireland — could not be curbed by an honest man's legislation. If anything it was sharpened — putting men at each others throats and defeating the admirable purpose the reformers, Robertson and Deniehy, had in mind, for in the end eight million acres were bought by less than 100 men and pastoralism remained triumphant.

Pressure for further reform in Victoria was strong as there was an increasing population and a temporary turn-down in the economy. In 1862, the Lands Minister, Charles Gavan Duffy agreed to reserve ten million acres for relocation as agricultural blocks of forty to 640 acres to be sold at £1 per acre. High-minded, like Robertson, Duffy had the additional encouragement of ensuring that Victorian diggers who were leaving the goldfields remained contented members of society. Later,

Duffy lamented the shameless manner in which the squatters had defeated the purposes of the law by perfecting the techniques their fellows had used in New South Wales. The upshot was that within two years about 100 individuals had bought two-thirds of all the land sold. Thus the original Selection Acts, to the extent that they were intended to release land for cultivation, were largely unsuccessful, although some settlement was achieved and some established small land holders were able to expand. With the introduction of the Grant Act in Victoria in 1869 matters improved. In the following decade about eleven million acres were selected, while in South Australia, by the 1880s, most of the agricultural land had been taken from the squatters.

The story of the selectors was generally one of constant hardship and frequent failure, and it could happen that even the most determined and experienced amongst them were unable to prosper. At the heart of their problem lay the inadequacy of the area of land they took up, but lack of finance or heavy borrowing, bad seasons, distant markets, ravages by pests and stock disease made the lot of even the most thrifty and industrious a burdensome one.

In the early 1880s some 200 Italians fled from the ill-fated venture of colonization initiated by the Marquis de Rays on New Ireland. Henry Parkes welcomed them to New South Wales, where they went onto small selections south of the Richmond River. The Italians, as a group, were capable, hard-working, thrifty and co-operative, and gradually they formed a happy community called New Italy. They grew most of their own necessities, built homes and a church, while the government provided a school, made their own wine and blended well with the local community to the extent that within a few years they were the backbone of the district cricket team. Nevertheless, they could not survive on the produce of their selections. The men had to go away for long periods to increase their income by cutting cane and felling timber. Gradually other selectors left and the Italians were able to enlarge their selections and turn to dairying. It was all to no avail as necessity required that the land holdings get bigger and bigger and within fifty years the community had dwindled to nothing. It was an experience repeated constantly throughout the colonies by other selectors.

All reforming land legislation was part and parcel of the fundamental flaw which caused men to regard land as a mere commodity to be exploited. In the beginning, this meant that the Aborigines were denied any right to that which they had been part of since their origin. The next step was to give the land away freely to a favoured minority or permit it to be occupied without asking by the squatters. Finally, the attempt was made to parcel it out to the needy in meagre lots, almost irrespective of climate and fertility. Through the whole process of its alienation the land remained, though ravaged by the ringbarking of trees which turned millions of acres into ghostly forests; the destruction of stands of timber around the headwaters of rivers and creeks; the consequent erosion which scarred and gullied countless acres and the exhaustion of soil through too frequent cropping. The land was ever eager to repair itself but in some measure it was changed beyond reclaim.

Arable and pastoral land in the south, and particularly in Tasmania, was becoming scarce, but in the north of New South Wales there was still a vast area of unoccupied territory. Starting 200 miles north of Brisbane and stretching for another 2,000 miles to the Cape York Peninsula, it comprised 670,000 square miles. Running inland from the coast there was a thousand miles of pastoral country, fit for sheep and cattle, which was finally swallowed in a forbidding desert, so that the area north and north-west of Rockhampton became known as 'The Never Never'. Nearly as large as France, Germany, Spain and Italy combined, the north was that part of the continent where contradictions abounded. Rainfall of stupendous proportions fell in tropical areas while in the interior there were years of drought. In the Channel Country the whole earth was laced with streams in wet seasons which were followed by periods when all things, even the air, remained dry. Lush vegetation with all manner of exotic flora gave way to great plains where the eucalyptus, emu and kangaroo flourished.

After the departure of the convicts, the settlement at Brisbane declined until John Dunmore Lang decided to send out 600 God-fearing and hard-working Scottish Presbyterians in 1849. They were intended to found the cotton industry, which Lang believed would help to absorb many immigrants. Although the government refused to give them land freely, as Lang had assured them would be done, their arrival did give an impetus to the district although the cotton industry still had a slow start. Brisbane depended in all official matters on Sydney, where Lang represented the territory in the Legislative Council, and from there he agitated for separation of the north from New South Wales.

Meanwhile, from the 1840s, the pastoral occupation of the Darling Downs pushed west and north. Leichhardt's journey in 1845 as far north as Port Essington on the Arafura Sea had opened up more country, and the squatting movement went on and on but not without resistance. In those parts, the blacks had decided to make a firm stand for what they held. Shepherds were killed, homesteads attacked, black and white alike died, and black, native police were used to hunt down and kill their own people. Despite the black resistance, nothing could stop the penetration of the country by the whites with their sheep and cattle. Ancient names with a pleasing lilt, Maranoa, Barcoo, Diamantina and Warrego were mixed with the absurd or merely pretentious, Comet, Charleville and Roma. The foundations of fine towns were laid because the distances were so great to Brisbane and Sydney that the scattered population had to rely on centres of commerce closer to their homes. Along the coast, Gladstone, Bundaberg, Mackay, Cairns and Townsville were amongst the places to which the people of the north eventually looked for the comforts of civilization. In 1858, 15,000 diggers rushed to the valley of the Fitzroy River near Gladstone, but the gold was worked out in a few weeks, and the men, mostly from Victoria, went away downhearted and impoverished for the golden days had not yet come to the north. Nevertheless, the abortive gold rush gave rise to the town of Rockhampton in 1859, which took its place with the other towns as urban centres in the north.

In Sydney, the Governor and his Council gave no serious consideration to separation, but, in response to petitions, London decided in 1855 to cut the north off and make it a colony. In December 1859, the colony was proclaimed and the sovereign, whose appetite had apparently been whetted rather than satisfied by the naming of Victoria, suggested Queensland as the name of the new territory. Parliament sat for the first time in May 1860, fittingly in the old convict barracks as unconscious recognition that this part of the continent was also opened by convict labour. The Governor, thirty-eight year old George Bowen, was advised by the London authorities never to permit his thoughts to stray from finance which was impressed upon him as the true basis of a prosperous state. With a mere seven-and-a-half pence in the treasury when Bowen arrived, it was good advice, and his twenty-eight-year-old Treasurer, Robert Herbert, needed a cool head to give the colony a good start. Implicit in that start was the power of the local squattocracy which, with its rough and ready style of conservative politics, indelibly etched the image and set, in part, the reality of public life in Queensland for the next century.

Right across the occupied areas of the continent a grid pattern was formed according to the size of the holdings and throughout the grids ran roads or tracks because the pastoral industry, and later the selectors, relied heavily on transport. The squatters needed efficient means to shift their wool from the sheds to the wharf from where it was shipped to England for auction. In the early days bullock teams were the main means, taking stores out to the stations and returning with a back-load of wool. Ex-convicts and the native-born proved the most reliable bullock-drivers as they knew the country and seemed to have the knack of controlling the large teams of sixteen or eighteen bullocks yoked in pairs.

Bullocks were essential to the transport industry until their replacement by horses and camels, and before the railways provided the outback with swift and cheap transport. The bullockies were colourful characters who made a significant contribution to the opening of the country.

After the explorers, squatters and drovers, the teamsters or bullockies helped to open up the continent. Their tracks became roads. Their stopping places, at about fifteen mile intervals were the beginnings of towns and hamlets, while many a landmark, creek or resting place was named where the teams halted, breakfasted, lost a bullock or merely recorded the distance from the previous settlement. Their colourful language, their clothing of red shirts with moleskin trousers and cabbage-tree hats, and their long-handled whips became the stuff of many a legend.

Gradually horses replaced bullocks on the long tracks in the outback, although the bullockies held their own for many years in the mountainous coastal regions. There were places where neither bullocks nor horses were useful and other means had to be sought for transportation. Thomas Elder and his brother-in-law, Robert Barr Smith, owned or leased more land in South Australia than the whole extent of their native Scotland, and Thomas concluded that the vast distances of the dry inland would be well served by camels. In the mid-1860s, he imported over a hundred of them and within a few years his original herd had grown to thousands. In the wake of the camels, Afghans came to manage and drive the camel trains which became a familiar sight in the outback with up to eighty camels per train. The camel was used successfully in exploration and in the building of the Overland Telegraph line from Port Augusta in the south to Port Darwin in the north which was completed in 1872. The first cablegram from Britain was transmitted on 22 October in that year. For eighty years, the camel and the Afghans were an essential segment of the transportation system in areas impassable to other means and the gentility and honesty of the Afghans remained in the memory of the outback long after the last of them had died or returned to their home-land. When it became possible to run a railway over the route the Afghans had pioneered through to Alice Springs, the train was named the Ghan in their honour.

The river boat trade on the Mississipi inspired the undertaking of a similar venture on the Murray and its connected river system. Melbourne in the 1840s had become the port to which wool was sent by wagon from the vast area around the Murray, Darling and Murrumbidgee Rivers. In South Australia the idea dawned slowly that if rivers could be served by steam boats, the natural overseas and intercolonial outlet for wool and for trade into the interior would be Adelaide. The opening of the Vic-torian goldfields made this even clearer as it was cheaper to transport goods by river to them than by other means over Victoria's atrocious roads.

Francis Cadell and William Randell were the first masters of steam-driven vessels to negotiate the snags, the sand bars and the long periods of low-water level of the rivers. From the 1850s the new form of transport burgeoned and ports sprang up from Wentworth to Albury on the Murray with Echuca and Wahgunyah as the main ones. On the Murrum-bidgee the major centres were Balranald and Gundagai and on the Darling they were Menindee, Wilcannia and Bourke. Pacific Island labour and the Chinese were often employed on the paddle steamers, which grew in length and often towed large barges.

The steamers carried all manner of supplies, including fruit, vege-tables, beer, lobsters, saddlery, doors, windows, equipment, clothing and books, for delivery to the stations and the gold-fields. After the intro-duction of fencing, some large stations shore half a million sheep by the late 1870s and produced 1,000 to 2,000 bales of wool, which were carted to the river ports by camel train or horse-drawn wagons. At its peak the Murray system had 300 steamers operating with the largest of them carrying 300 bales, and nearly 100,000 bales passed through Echuca in 1880 with the whole river trade worth over half a million pounds. In 1883 a severe drought combined with the expansion of the railways to affect river shipping adversely, and with their cargoes of iron rails and wooden sleepers, the river vessels carried the seeds of their own destruction. Gradually the steamers fell in numbers, the skippers retired and died, and the voice of the Darling was rarely broken by the splash of the paddles. The welcoming sound of a steamer's whistle was seldom heard again as only a handful of steamers survived into the twentieth century.

Until the gold-rushes and the consequent growth of inland centres, railway construction was negligible. A line from Sydney to Granville Junction, near Parramatta, was opened in 1855 and one to Newcastle in 1858 with all construction in the hands of the government. Victoria had put through a line from Melbourne to Port Melbourne in 1854 and then to Geelong in 1857. The development of the gold towns, Ballarat, Castlemaine and Bendigo, and the need to compete with the river trade, saw lines opened to those places, as well as to Echuca, by 1864. Lines from Sydney through to Wagga Wagga (1879), Albury (1881), and Bourke (1885) meant that New South Wales was linked in its main parts, and from that time progress was rapid.

The line from Sydney to Albury was opened in 1881. When the station was built, it had one of the longest platforms in the world. The link with Melbourne was made in 1883 and passengers could travel between the two capitals, changing trains at Albury because of the differing gauges.

Links were made between the New South Wales and the Victorian systems through Albury in 1883 and with Queensland at Wallangarra five years later, so that a traveller could go from Melbourne into Queensland on the railways but not without changing trains. The difficulty of having rival colonial administrations was apparent in the choice of railway gauges, although their reasons for selecting differing gauges, given the variation in terrain, the purpose for which the lines were built and the availability of finance bore some weight. The New South Wales government, after much dithering and obstruction, decided on a 4ft 8½in gauge, Victoria 5ft 3in and Queensland 3ft 6in, but South Australia showed its eclecticism by having all three major gauges with three others for small, private lines.

The development of the railways in all the colonies was closely bound up with politics and the exertions that vested interests could make to ensure that lines ran through places from which benefit for such interests could be reaped. Nevertheless, the opening of a line — with the attendant construction of stations, many of which were imposing edifices and some indeed works of true architecture — filled the locals with pride and gave employment to an ever-increasing workforce in which mere numbers were never an indication of efficiency. To those who saw romance and power in the trains with their mighty engines, who enjoyed the passing fragrance of coal smoke, who watched from afar the approaching light of a train at night and looked at passengers as they alighted at the end of journeys, the railways remained a source of pleasure. The railways never inspired a significant literature or art form, which was also true with the transition from sail to steam at sea. Nonetheless, the social transformation brought about by the railways was immense. People who had previously lacked the money to take private means of transport were now able to go from place to place for work, leisure or schooling. The 'Refreshment Rooms' at railway stations, where tea and other hot beverages, sandwiches and, eventually, hot pies could be consumed, became places familiar to generations of Australians as they awaited the signal to board the train again for destinations throughout the land.

Little progress was made with shipbuilding in Australia in the nineteenth century but, as a continent with a vast seaboard, transport across the oceans or on the coastal waters was always necessary. The Americans were the first to build the fast, softwood clippers, which were soon rivalled by British-made vessels. Some of the wool clippers and migrant ships on the England to Australia run became famous. In 1869 the *Thermopylae* left The Lizard in England, and arrived at Port Phillip sixty-two days later and the record under sail stood through the ensuing years.

Other famous sailing ships were the *Marco Polo* and the *Cutty Sark*. But the great days of sail gave way to steam which provided efficiency and safety but little romance.

Everything that the white settlers brought to Australia came across the oceans but not all of it was brought intentionally and some of it had undesirable effects that were long lasting or permanent. The sheep and cattle with their hard hooves tore at the frail surface of the ancient soil and unbalanced its vegetation. Birds, trees and flowers added beauty, but native grasses gave way to imported ones, while pests like the Capeweed, Bathurst burr and Scotch thistle proved impossible to eradicate. Fauna was also introduced — dogs, cats, foxes, ferrets, hares and buffalo — all of which competed with the native fauna, while camels, donkeys and horses often multiplied to pest proportions in inaccessible areas. Trout and redfin were let loose in rivers, lakes and streams and the blackfish, the Macquarie perch and the Murray cod declined in numbers as they tried to compete with the voracious or cannibalistic new varieties.

The worst of all pests, the rabbit, arrived with the First Fleet and then successively with other vessels. It prospered so abundantly in some places that by 1842 an island in Bass Strait was named after it. In 1859 the tide really turned for the rabbit with the importation of twenty-four wild ones for sporting purposes by Thomas Austin to his property at Barwon Park near Geelong. Within six years their numbers had reached such proportions that, having destroyed 20,000 rabbits, Austin calculated that he had 10,000 left. By 1880 the rabbits had crossed into New South Wales and South Australia, infesting agricultural and pastoral lands. In vain they were declared noxious and war was waged against them. They consumed the grasses, ringbarked young trees, ate seeds and left a desert in their wake throughout large areas. The females bred up to six litters annually in good seasons. The use of dogs, ferrets, fences, poisoning, trapping, fumigating and warren destruction saw the spread of devastated pastures as testimony to their ineffectiveness.

Before the 1880s the greatest threat to the pastoral industry was a disease caused by a parasite in sheep called scab. The very word was whispered for its presence in a flock could mean ruin. Annually, it killed hundreds of thousands of sheep. In Victoria alone, it caused millions of pounds in losses, despite the successful use of a dip with a tobacco and sulphur mix as its base. Scab, together with fluke and footrot, drought and fire, cold and wet, crows and dingoes combined to make the life of the pastoralist difficult. Nonetheless, the industry, still mainly based on the Spanish merino, continued to flourish so that from the stunted, hairy prototypes of fifty years previously over forty million fine-fleeced and well-bodied sheep walked the continent by 1870. It was amongst the most successful pastoral achievements of all ages which reached its annual climax when, across the sheds, vast and small, to the quiet click of the shears, the golden fleece fell from those millions. Out on the stations, women in increasing numbers accepted the land and its people while a minority rejected it bitterly. Sheep, wool prices, the seasons and shearing were always on the lips of the men. One English governess, employed on a station near Glenorchy in Victoria, found a great grossness of spirit and weakness of intellect amongst Australians, whom, together with the land, she professed to hate.

In the outback and in the cities, a generally dedicated band of pastors helped their flocks fill the void in the human spirit, caused both by the attainment as well as the lack of material success. They often did it discordantly, because between them lay vast valleys scooped out by the rivers of the Reformation. But the days had passed since religion was seen as little more than the handmaiden of a coercive state, although in some measure the same state was still clothed in Christian garments. Admittedly, state aid to religion was abandoned by the 1870s in the eastern colonies. But in matters of morality, such as divorce (which was avoided by having legal separation instead, until each colony passed its own divorce act, which they had all done by 1873) the state gave little offence to the churches. Queen, parliament, chapel and cathedral all seemed devoted to the one purpose of mankind's betterment.

Here and there an odd Irishman muttered unkindly about the Queen, but there were Irish Catholics such as Judge Roger Therry and Premier Gavan Duffy who were proud to be her knights. Equally, there were a few, even in high places, who professed themselves free from the chains of religion and proclaimed that, unaided, mankind could rise to unsurpassed heights of harmony, enlightenment and general well-being. Lacking cohesion or structure, the secular creed had little appeal and, for the thousands who invoked the name of Christ, only a handful knew of Voltaire or Rousseau.

Amongst the better-off there was a widespread conviction of the usefulness of something called 'a liberal education' which it seemed good to ensure for the male children if possible. Institutions of a superior type such as The King's School at Parramatta and Geelong Grammar on Corio Bay in Victoria were founded, as preparatory schools for higher education, social attainment and to avoid the need to send the boys to Eton and Harrow. Within their walls, it was reasonable to hope that students would at least be given a sound basis in loyalty and Anglicanism. At the other end of the scale stood the state and the denominational primary schools, which were still state-assisted throughout the 1860s. They all fought for funding and it was increasingly clear that even the strongest denominations could not meet the demand for places. Yet in the 1860s they educated twice as many children as the state system and they thought that their position was secure, despite the fact that, throughout the colonies, half the children under twelve could neither read nor write.

Whatever else Christianity and education managed to achieve, they failed to convince many of their beneficiaries that all human beings possessed equal rights. The Chinese, in particular, remained the butt of much odium, especially on the goldfields where their coming was likened to an influx of barbarians. Their habits were considered unmentionable by civilized people and their very presence feared, because they were regarded as alien, degraded and heathen. Paradoxically, the Chinese thought exactly the same of those who were not Chinese. The argument was put forward by some whites that, as they had discovered and settled Australia, no Chinese had any rights in it, and all manner of restrictive, fiscal legislation was passed to keep them out. This kind of thinking reached its climax at a locality called Lambing Flat in New South Wales in June 1861. The gold there had run thin and the European diggers resented the alleged success of the industrious Chinese. The diggers rioted and attacked them with great ferocity, cutting off pigtails, destroying property, beating them and terrifying them as they fled from the field. Troops were sent from Sydney to restore order and, later, a government commissioner, who said that he regarded the Chinese as deceivers. Nonetheless, he awarded claims to 706 individuals. But no pecuniary measure could heal the outrage done or received.

By 1858 there were one million white Australians. By 1863 some of them thought it proper to participate in the suppression of another people outside Australian territory. By the end of that year, 1,475 volunteers had sailed from Sydney, Melbourne and Hobart for New Zealand to participate in the Maori Wars that had been waged intermittently since 1845. In 1863 and 1864 the Waikato War, which threatened Auckland, saw almost 20,000 troops, including the Australians, engaged against a confederation of Waikato tribes numbering less than 3,000. As was the case in Australia with the Aborigines, the main cause of the conflict in New Zealand was justifiable Maori fear that their lands would be taken by the whites. In 1864 at least another 1,200 Australians, with their wives and children, sailed for New Zealand to act as military settlers on land taken from the Maoris. In due course the conflict was resolved in favour of the dominant power and the Maoris had no choice but to accept a settlement. Many of the Australian volunteers subsequently left the land to work in the towns or to go to the Thames gold-fields, which were opened in late 1866. The Maori Wars had indicated that colonial Australians would take up the call to arms willingly were Queen and Empire threatened and a volunteer from North Melbourne summed up the prevailing sentiment by signing himself, in a letter to the *Age*, as one, 'Who will shed his last drop of blood for his Queen'.

A more positive face of colonial Australia was shown by the gains made in social legislation. The right to strike, bitterly resented by employers, was recognized by law. Shop assistants, traditionally an exploited sector, benefited from early closing. By the mid-fifties, the creed 'eight hours labour, eight hours recreation, eight hours rest' had become widespread. Its partial achievement amongst stonemasons and others was acclaimed by annual festivities in Victoria after 1856. The workers were now heard through the use of the ballot box and the introduction of triennial parliaments. No government could now afford to ignore them. Some great institutions, such as the Melbourne Public Library, and lesser ones, such as the Mechanics Institutes, catered for the leisure of the workers, while a few informed voices spoke on their behalf. At the opening of the Melbourne Trades Hall in 1859, a speaker urged that, as well as reading and thinking, workers also needed to learn from and associate with each other and achieve their rightful place in society.

Unions, Guilds or Benefit Societies which had existed in most trades before the gold-rushes had been broken up by the consequent dislocation but they soon began to regroup and the gains they won, especially in reducing working hours, convinced them that they led Britain and Europe in achieving satisfying living standards. They probably did not realize that the wealth of the country and the need for labour had rendered the employers powerless, temporarily at least. In Victoria their efforts were symbolically crowned in 1859 when Charles Jardine Don was elected to the Legislative Assembly for the seat of Collingwood as the representative of the Political and Social Labour League. He claimed, probably correctly, that he was the first worker to represent his class in any legislature in the British Empire.

Don was a stonemason, who worked at his trade on Parliament House by day and sat in it as a member at night. The city in which he worked embodied in stone the motif of the age of progress. Buildings of the most pretentious and ornate design were rising, climaxed by the magnificent Treasury Building with its Italian Renaissance style. Nevertheless, Parliament House was not far from 'radical and riotous' Collingwood with its terraces, which dwindled away into blocks of decrepit weatherboard cottages and smelly tenements. Already the fierce civic pride of the residents and their rivalry with neighbouring Fitzroy was evident. On one important level it expressed itself with the founding of the Britannia Football Club in the late 1870s, which became the famous Collingwood Football Club in 1889.

The houses of the upper-class spread south of the Yarra to St Kilda, which, by the end of the 1860s, had become the most attractive place to live where the wealthy, the merchants and the professional men built their imposing homes. The dwellings of the workers in the Melbourne suburbs were much more humble, but the land still had to be bought, the houses constructed and services provided, all of which required massive capital. Manufacturing industry provided little investment capital as its exports were minimal, so the whole financial edifice rested on gold, wool and British loans.

The times of 'jam and honey' for the workers had commenced and no one could foresee their ending. Colonial beer was threepence a glass and the workers drank it in great quantity. There was a gay and independent spirit everywhere and, even in Melbourne, the streets were thronged at night in summer with men dressed in shirt sleeves and women in light dresses. Singing and music until midnight was not unusual. An English visitor in 1869 thought that he was in another world where each man considered himself as good as any other. He had no difficulty in believing that once Australians 'become acclimatized, they scarcely ever leave the country, and, if they do, they often return'.

In both Melbourne and Sydney, there was another face to progress. A report on the condition of Sydney's working class in 1860 was damning in its condemnation of the conditions under which the urban workers lived. The older tenements were 'unfit for the occupation of human beings', and high rents caused over-crowding: seventy people were found in one lodging-house of six rooms while 315 Chinese were found in another. Neglected and vagrant children roamed the streets. For some of them, their condition was another legacy of the dislocation to family life caused by the gold-rushes. Some parts of the city saw the erection of a better class of house for the worker with 'indoor sinks, fitted pantries, suitable stoves and clothes' closets', but the slums in Woolloomooloo, for example, showed all the worst aspects of the older cities of Europe. The report concluded that, despite their living conditions, the generality of Sydney's workers, for their 'honesty, intelligence and sobriety', were 'a credit to the country'.

Colonial governments were loath to involve themselves in relief measures for the poor, believing that social provisions by the state undermined self-reliance and fostered pauperism. Governments, instead, encouraged charitable organisations to assist the hungry, the homeless and the sick aged. The Melbourne Ladies Benevolent Society virtually controlled all non-denominational outdoor relief in the greater Melbourne Area. The Benevolent Society of New South Wales, founded in 1813, cared for the chronically ill, the blind, the paralytic and the mentally-ill. By 1862 the New South Wales government took full responsibility for the aged and destitute who required residential facilities, but the Benevolent Society continued to function with government subsidies. The mentally-ill were a group which suffered from neglect until the arrival of F. N. Manning, an English medical practitioner, who initiated reforms that were finally reflected in the New South Wales Lunacy Act of 1878. Manning encouraged visitors to the Tarban Creek hospital for the mentally-ill and ignorance and prejudice were slowly broken down.

Henry Parkes was especially concerned about the state of the Sydney Infirmary and Dispensary. He appealed for help to Florence Nightingale for trained nurses, and in 1868, a remarkable woman, Lucy Osburn, arrived as superintendent of the Infirmary accompanied by five other nurses. Pretty, slim and with a 'bright ingenuous manner', Lucy won Parkes's complete trust and she threw herself into the almost impossible task of cleaning up the crumbling, foul-smelling, vermin-infested buildings. She met opposition from the doctors and the Board, and she was lonely and often dispirited. But she stuck to her task and by 1874 she had partially succeeded. By the time the institution's name was changed to the Sydney Hospital in 1880, Lucy had achieved her objectives and she returned to England, where she died in 1891.

The 1860s were a period of consolidation and progress brought about by the increase in population due to the gold-rushes. The Scottish-born William Arnott found he made more money selling his own pies and bread on the Turon than by panning for gold. He and his brother David later opened a factory in Newcastle, and soon they were shipping tons of biscuits weekly to Sydney. Arnott had his own dairy farm where 200 cows produced the milk for his popular milk arrowroot biscuits, but he died before his most famous biscuit, the Sao, was put on the market in 1906 by his sons. Maria Ann Smith grew apples from Tasmanian seeds in Sydney in 1868 to produce a new strain called the 'Granny Smith' which was eventually exported, as was canned meat, to England. On 23 December 1861 two horse-drawn tramcars started to carry passengers along Pitt Street in Sydney. They excited much attention from the passers-by, not surprisingly, as they were painted bright yellow and named 'Old England' and 'Young Australia' respectively.

Before the paddle steamers, all transport was slow and costly over wretched roads. The steamers opened trade to the Victorian goldfields and to the pastoral runs west of the Darling and through to Bourke. The railways finally replaced the steamers as the normal means of transport for goods and passengers.

Sport and communications were other aspects of progress. Regular cricket matches between New South Wales and Victoria began in 1856 and attracted much interest and mild inter-colonial rivalry. Horse racing had fast become a favourite pastime of both the high and the lowly and most towns had their own racecourse. In November 1861 the Melbourne Cup was run for the first time. It was won by a horse called Archer which had been walked down from near Nowra in New South Wales for the event. In the same week Brisbane was linked by telegraph to the other eastern capitals. Hobart could be included in the link as there was a submarine cable running from Melbourne. Amongst the items carried by the telegraph to Brisbane was news of the largely victorious visit of an All-English cricket team which had given much pleasure to the sport-minded citizens of Sydney and Melbourne. Of these and other matters the inhabitants of Western Australia, cut off by a distance of more than 1,500 miles by land or by the waters of the Australian Bight from the nearest colonial capital, remained largely oblivious, but they too were making progress.

The last of the convict colonies had benefited by transportation to a marked degree. The convicts blended well with the assisted free migrants who came with them. Convict labour on public works, roads, bridges and other public amenities was so valuable that many citizens preferred to see hardened criminals brought in, who would be forced to spend long periods constructing public utilities, rather than lesser criminals, who would quickly be released on tickets of leave to work for themselves. The British government maintained the large convict establishment and as a consequence paid for public buildings such as the large Fremantle Jail. The town prospered to such an extent that its free citizens were encouraged in 1854 to request, unsuccessfully, that the seat of government be transferred there from Perth. The convicts remained at Fremantle where the old, barbarous discipline of floggings and solitary confinement on bread and water in dark cells for periods up to fifty days still persisted into the 1860s.

While the convicts in the West toiled on the public works, the free grew wool, bred horses for the Indian army, cut timber, went whaling, explored the inland, and found lead and copper deposits. It was increasingly clear in Britain that free immigration and transportation could not together continue for long. The colony would soon want some form of responsible government and in 1865 the decision to stop transportation was made. Amongst the last transportees was a group of sixty Fenians of the Irish Republican Brotherhood, who arrived in 1868 and, as political prisoners, faced long terms in maximum security doing hard labour. By 1876 only a handful of them remained in custody at Fremantle and on Perth Regatta Day, 17 April, six of them made a daring bid to join an American whaler, the *Catalpa*, which had been purchased in the United States in order to aid their escape. After a skirmish with the government vessel *Georgette*, sent to intercept her, the *Catalpa* sailed for home and the Irish to freedom in New York where they were given a heroes' welcome.

About 10,000 convicts had come to Western Australia and in 1867 just over a half of the 20,000 inhabitants had been or were still in bondage. One English visitor in that year described Western Australia as a vast English prison rather than a colony. He berated the whole system of transportation as vile and corrupting, a judgement in which he was partially right. Yet his view was that of a passer-by who had no concept of the contribution of convict labour to the settlement and development of Australia. If transportation brought a stain, it was not one of moral infamy in the societies that grew from it for, in general, the emancipists were indistinguishable from those who arrived free. The stain was red in blood from the floggings, dark-hued from the misery, despair and shame meted out to those 160,000 who from 1788 to 1868 were sent to Australia. Those stained were the people responsible for the whole bloody system.

CHAPTER EIGHT

The Making of Australians

Australians made the journey 'home' to the British Isles by the Great Circle route before the opening of the Suez canal in 1869. Even with the advent of steam, they still had had to face much tedium and some danger as they crossed the oceans. The sea provided a sense of security by throwing a barrier around the continent. It cut off Tasmania though, which felt isolated and neglected by the other eastern colonies. In contrast to the sea, the bush remained changeless, solid and full of mystery. From the earliest days, the bush became part of legend and literature. Stories with titles like Henry Kingsley's 'The Lost Child', Marcus Clarke's 'Pretty Dick' (who was found after six days dead in the bush 'lying on his face, with his head on his arm') and Barcroft Boake's 'Where the Dead Men Lie' all spoke of the relentless harshness of the bush and of 'the wastes of the Never-Never'. Nonetheless, there were some few who sang of its peace and beauty.

The bush was simply that part of the country where settlement was sparse or non-existent. It ranged from thick forest to eucalyptus scrub and then on to almost treeless plains, from the Barrington Tops and the Atherton Tableland to the Pilliga scrub and the Gibson Desert. But it was always called the bush. Out there, free of parson, priest or police, and, in large measure, of women, the old hands, who had come as convicts, did odd jobs about the stations — shearing, fencing, clearing scrub and, with horses and scoops, making dams and tanks. They stuck close to their mates because they had no one else. As they passed, their places were taken by new chums who, filled with hope, had come to the land of opportunity and ended up in the bush. Unwilling, or unable, to settle on the gold-fields working for wages as miners, they had drifted further out, where they became indistinguishable from the old hands. Then there were the native-born, mostly of convict stock, who were more adept than all in the ways of the land and especially those of the pastoral industry. They shared with the others a rejection of authority, an inability to settle long in the one place and a tendency to earn just enough money with the least trouble. This, in a practice known as 'knocking down the cheque', they spent in a bush shanty on a drunken carouse.

White civilization crept tentatively into the bush with the development, in the 1870s, of better means of communication. It brought with it elements of commerce and culture associated with the settled life of the inner districts and the cities. Religion and education, bankers and doctors, streets and stores, the post office and the telegraph, newspapers and books — all these, together with women and children, became part of life in the bush. Before this wave the old hands disappeared into obscurity. Some of the brave, when word came of new gold-fields in Queensland and Western Australia, joined the rush. Others went on the tramp carrying their few belongings: a pair of blankets rolled in a swag, a billy to make tea, a few ounces of flour for a damper, perhaps a trap to catch rabbits and little else. From station to station, the 'swaggies' went; avoiding the towns and the law when possible; begging a meal, often fruitlessly, from a station owner or manager; doing a little work here and there; but never settling until, in some lonely place, they finally met with destiny. They were the last of their tribe, and in them the legend of the bush was born and metamorphosed. It was a legend that rarely spoke of endless scrub; chains of dry waterholes called rivers; stunted mountains; desolate and derelict station buildings; the harshness, frequent brutality and servility of life in the shearing sheds; the ignorance and prejudice of the bush workers and the hopelessness of the life of the swaggies.

The white, restless tribe was moulded by the inhospitable land and, with the years, they became part of it. With their lack of concern for tomorrow, their inability to hoard, their constant movement over the land, partly living from it while refusing to possess it, and their intimate knowledge of it, they became as much Australians as the Aborigines had always been. The tragedy for both races was that, in the early days, no creole race was born, which, elsewhere, was the source of a new and vital people. In the end, the white nomads became the basis of a legend woven from a longing for what might have been, a lost sense of identity with the land, a guilt for its raping and a passionate urge to be different from the old European societies. The legend was a tribute to the land and those born from it.

The rising waters of a distant past had cut off Tasmania and its people

Truganini died at Hobart on 8 May 1876. Fearful lest her body be mutilated by surgeons she said before death, 'Don't let them cut me but bury me behind the mountains'. In 1976 her bones were cremated and the ashes scattered on the D'Entre-casteaux Channel, near her birth place.

from contact with the mainland. When the whites arrived in the early part of the century, the Tasmanian Aborigines were isolated on their island and there could be no escape. On the islands of Bass Strait a new race was born from the union of sealers, whalers and Aboriginal women. Also out there, onto Flinders Island, a remnant of the mainland blacks were taken, where they survived briefly. Originally 300 in number, they dwindled to a handful as, ravaged by pulmonary disease and demoralized by the loss of their past, they eked out a miserable existence at a place called Wyballena. In 1842 a fruitless attempt was made to save the race by transferring a handful to Port Phillip. In that same year their leader in the person of proud Woorraddy was lost. He had remained Aboriginal in all things. In him thousands of years of tradition perished.

The government chose Oyster Cove, on the mainland south of Hobart, in 1847 as the last resting place of the forty-seven individuals who had survived the years of exile at Wyballena. They came back home to die out slowly, painfully and shamefully of disease and drink. Of that forty-seven, by July 1871, only Truganini remained, sole survivor of a people who had numbered perhaps 5,000 less than seventy years previously. Surviving her husband, Woorraddy, by thirty-four years, she died in 1876. With her passing, it was thought that the problem of the Aborigines of Tasmania was solved, although the last 'full blood' died later, on Kangaroo Island, in 1888. The whites had not deliberately engaged in genocide, but they achieved it nonetheless. European diseases and cruel, wanton slaughter coalesced with the inability of most whites to understand that the Aborigines possessed their own culture and had a sense of fierce independence and a determination to live according to their own traditions. The Aborigines were deprived of a purpose for existence once their land was lost. For a time, few cared to remember that there were still those on the islands of the Strait in whom the blood of their ancestors flowed.

As its old inhabitants passed, the white man consolidated his hold on Tasmania. In a manner comprehensible to those who had shared the nostalgia of the exile or the shame of the felon, Tasmanian society took on, where possible, the shape of its parent societies. Place names, the architecture of the homes, the hedgerows, the gorse bush (which itself became an ineradicable pest) and the forms of government, all combined to give the outward appearance of another England, with some Scottish and Irish tones. Yet with the beauty of its coastal regions, the untamed wilderness of its south-west, the islands of its bays and the huge timbers of its bush, Tasmania was a unique jewel and its inhabitants, jealous in their own internal rivalries, were as one in their attachment to the island. In homes such as 'Panshanger' and 'Entally', the gentry entertained graciously, while at 'Gala' on the east coast, where hospitality was warm and generous, the hardy Scots survived with dignity on country which made the narrow strip of fertile land of the north-west appear a paradise. At Ross and throughout the midlands, the squatters lived on big estates of 10,000 or more acres, refining their wool and stud flocks year by year. 'Tasmanian blood' was highly prized on the mainland. The great squatters became haughty, entertaining one another in their gracious homes and turning their backs on the local towns. In the north the *Examiner* was their favoured newspaper while in the south they read the *Mercury*.

Tasmanians argued about their first railways, but the discovery of mineral deposits settled the question as to their need. After 1871, when the richest tin mine in the world was discovered at Mt Bischoff on the north-west, and gold, coal and silver deposits were found at Waterhouse and Fingal, the railways were rapidly developed. The economy, fallen into disarray when Tasmania did not share the gold boom of the mainland, recovered as people realized the extent of the mineral wealth of the island. New arrivals, no longer in convict garb, began to exceed departures and females rose to equal proportions with males, which changed entirely the composition of the old society of the 1840s. Nevertheless, the past was not forgotten and literature helped to keep it vivid. Marcus Clarke, a young English writer living in Melbourne, spent a month's research in Tasmania in 1870. The result, initially published in serial form, became the classic of the convict era with its story of pain, degradation, inhumanity and sorrow intertwined with love and hope. Clarke's monumental *For the Term of his Natural Life* opened for thousands a mental gateway to the grim past of Van Diemen's Land, although it passed unnoticed that Clarke's convict hero, Rufus Dawes, was innocent of any crime. In those days, it was not possible to make a hero of a true criminal.

Marcus Clarke, who wrote about the event with wit and impertinence, was not amongst the thousands of Victorians who went wild with delirium when Prince Alfred, Duke of Edinburgh, visited Melbourne in November 1867. The occasion was such that electric light lit up the outside of Parliament House, apologies were made that the Australian accent may seem offensive to the royal ears, and throats were drowned in loyal toasts to the young gentleman and his mother, Victoria. In the following March, Alfred attended a public picnic at Clontarf, Sydney, which gave a mentally deranged Irishman, Henry O'Farrell, the opportunity to shoot and wound him. Despite the Duke's efforts to have his life spared, O'Farrell was hanged and Henry Parkes used the affair to raise a groundless and absurd scare of revolution by Irish republicans and Catholic Fenians. Hysteria reached such proportions that the New South Wales legislature, known locally as the 'Bear Garden' given its notoriety for dirty play, passed an Act which made it a crime to refuse to drink a loyal toast or to use insulting language of Her Majesty, while other zealots wanted to change the name of New South Wales to Alfredland.

Parkes's Fenian scare, deliberately engineered and falsely concocted, was all part and parcel of a wider conflict in society about the role of religion in education. In 1866 Parkes had managed to have his Public School Act passed, which set up a Council of Education to control both the state and denominational systems and stopped funding denominational schools. The Act heightened tensions and pushed many Catholics, hitherto practising their religion as a private affair, to take their convictions into the public arena and to accept the idea, proposed by Marsden in the early 1800s, that Catholics were different from the rest of the community — a concept that the members of Orange Lodges and other anti-Catholics had never found any difficulty in both believing and propagating. In the long run, a colonial community divided on a central issue was the fruit.

By the 1870s, it had become clear to all the colonial governments that their purses could no longer afford to support two systems of education. Parallel with and justifying such a conviction was the development of the notion that religion was divisive and obscurantist in the face of modern thought. The argument was put forward that a solid education needed to be based on a liberal and scientific foundation which had to be available to all children who, for their own and for society's good, ought to be submitted to it. Such ideas were easily put into a slogan and 'secular, compulsory and free education' at the primary level became the catchcry of the reformers.

The embodiment of the slogan in a system meant that the state entirely stopped funding denominational schools, which happened in Victoria in 1872 and in all the colonies by 1895. Catholics were prepared to follow the lead of their pastors in this matter at least, although very considerable personal sacrifice was entailed. They supported a separate system staffed by the free labour of men and women of religious congregations. In New South Wales the debate was heightened by the response of the Catholic bishops, led by the English Benedictine monk, Roger Vaughan, Archbishop of Sydney, who prophesied that the new secular schools would breed future immorality, infidelity and lawlessness. To the extent that truth lay in such an assertion, Catholics, but more especially the bishops, carried some share of responsibility, because their absence from the public system helped push it down the long road to indifference and then to aggressive secularism.

Most of the Irish were at the bottom of the social scale except in

Queensland, where, first in the cotton and then in the sugar industry, it had been found necessary to acquire a source of coloured labour suited to climatic conditions which were alleged to be too trying for the white worker. Sugar was first grown, for a brief period only, at Port Macquarie in the 1820s, but the industry did not develop until the late 1860s, by which time there were eight mills near Brisbane. Later, cane was grown extensively in the north of the colony. As early as 1847, Benjamin Boyd, who controlled 2,500,000 acres of land on the Monaro and in the Riverina imported 200 Pacific Islanders to work his properties, but most of them were sent back before the year was out as humanitarians and workers combined to reject their presence. Ironically, on a visit to the Solomons in 1851, Boyd himself was very probably eaten by the inhabitants of those islands he had intended to exploit for his own use, but his early example in the employment of islanders was not forgotten.

By the 1860s the labour shortage was acute, and the owners of cotton and sugar plantations imported natives from Java, Ceylon and the Pacific Islands. The unmarried, well-behaved, hard-working islanders, known as Kanakas, were mostly induced or duped into leaving their home islands, to work in Queensland for ten shillings per month, plus keep, although some left willingly and did not want to return. Some high-minded individuals judged their use as slave labour and there was certain proof of 'blackbirding', as the kidnapping of islanders was called. Amongst the blackbirders was the former medical practioner James Murray, who had searched for Burke and Wills and spent time with the Leichhardt Ladies Expedition in search of the explorer before turning to blackbirding. As a blackbirder he was involved in the massacre of a group of Polynesians in the late 1870s.

The use of the Kanakas was seen by many as an underhand measure designed to bring in coloured labour to the detriment of the European workers at a time when assisted immigration had, between 1875 and 1890, reached 213,000. The numbers of Kanakas were initially small, with fewer than 2,000 arriving over five years, but the opposition, especially from missionaries, was intense. The numbers grew rapidly, however, and 50,000 had come in by 1895 and had died at a rate three times faster than other Queenslanders. The whole episode of Kanaka labour was sordid and it fostered a racism in the workers' movement, which was based on fear of cheap competition. It also strengthened the determination of the southern colonies to keep Australia free from all Asiatic or coloured races.

Racist sentiment was one aspect of a new but rapidly developing nationalism that had its visible expression in bodies such as the Australian

Natives Association, which restricted its membership to the Australian-born. It was founded in 1871 as a mutual-aid body to promote the welfare of Australia and to oppose non-white immigration. Nationalism also developed on the gold-fields, which knew no colonial boundaries. The gold-fields extended from western New South Wales to Queensland, where Charters Towers and the Palmer River flourished in the 1870s and Mt Morgan became the country's richest goldmine. In northern Australia workers on the Overland Telegraph found gold; in the Kimberley region in the north of Western Australia, gold was mined in the mid-eighties, and at Kalgoorlie in the nineties. In Victoria, at Bendigo and Ballarat, Walhalla and other places, the great quartz crushers pounded on and on throughout the whole period.

All the fields attracted an itinerant workforce, largely made up of men who considered themselves neither Tasmanians, Queenslanders nor anything else but Australians. The same happened with the development of other mineral deposits. In South Australia the copper mines gave work to 20,000 people. Sapphires and diamonds were dug for in many places. Tin was mined at Inverell, Glen Innes and Tenterfield in New South Wales and Stanthorpe and Herberton in Queensland and Mt Bischoff in Tasmania, making Australia the world's largest producer of tin from 1873 to 1882. In 1883 a German-born boundary rider with an interest in minerals, Charles Rasp, stumbled across an immense outcrop of iron-stone on a broken hill in desolate, arid country 800 miles from Sydney. The Broken Hill Proprietary Company was founded and in a century the 'Hill' produced 120 million tons of silver, lead and zinc ore. Meanwhile the Tasmanian silver and gold, copper and tin fields continued in production.

The men who worked the mines increasingly brought their wives and children with them and they settled where prosperity, old age or mere contentment beckoned. What mattered to them was not the divisions of the past but the land that gave them an opportunity. Transformed rapidly from Cornishmen, Irishmen, Scots or Cockneys, they wanted to know no other land and they joined those others — urban dwellers, squatters, land selectors, farm workers and nomads — to whom Australia was already home. The miners carried with them traditions of unionism, mateship and a fair-go for the underdog and a sense of the family as the heart of society, and so, with time, they became similar to the other colonials in accent, vocabulary, and likes and dislikes in food, drink and dress.

In the cities an increasingly industrialized workforce settled to urban life. They made goods ranging from clothing, textiles, machinery,

Bad lighting, unhygienic conditions, long hours and low wages often made women's work onerous, until the introduction of effective Factory Acts. In many cases, women worked at home for even lower payment and this practice, called 'sweating', was not easily eliminated.

furniture, building supplies and saddlery to food and drink, and used products marked 'Australian made'. Amongst them many rejoiced in a standard of living which they ranked as the best in the world while others, especially in the factories, were exploited and made to endure physical hardship, much in the manner of their counterparts in Britain. Nevertheless, out of all this amalgam of miners, bushmen and city dwellers a form of nationalism grew which expressed itself by calls for the building of a defence force, especially after the withdrawal of the British regiments in the 1870s, the proliferation of scares of a Russian threat and demands by the Australian Natives Association that New Guinea and the New Hebrides be annexed to Australia. Indeed, some New South Welsh politicians were so taken with the idea that a new nation was in process of formation that they wanted to assert their rights over it by calling their colony 'Australia.'

The Industrial Revolution, although it caused widespread and complex changes in societies, tended also to produce uniformity of thought. This meant that little room was left for people to choose consciously a way of life that was distinctive. Developments in technology caused the same phenomena to be repeated across societies. Steam brought powered ships and railways, electricity produced the telegraph and street lighting spread rapidly after the Edison method of incandescent lighting was first used to illuminate the Sydney General Post Office and Circular Quay in 1880. That same year the Melbourne telephone exchange was opened connecting forty-four subscribers and the new method of communication was soon widely accepted. Refrigerated meat was first shipped to London in 1879, causing the *Times* to hope that a normal meal for an English family would soon be Australian fresh meat. Education and the press, with newspapers now readily available to those even of slender means, produced common ways of thinking.

Partly as a consequence of its formation as a society in the nineteenth century, Australia was unlike others in which millenia had permitted and geographic and climactic conditions encouraged regional developments in language, with varying dialects and accents, variations in clothing and food dependent upon locally available commodities, and a growth of high and popular cultures with regionally distinct forms of song, literature, art and social relations. Furthermore, Australians came for the large part from the one British society with variations for the Scottish and Irish. The Chinese and Kanakas were regarded as complete outsiders from whom nothing could be gained and with whom little could be shared, while the Aborigines were deemed by many as scarcely belonging to the human race. Inevitably the society that developed in the nineteenth century had an element, perhaps a grey element, of sameness about it.

By 1880 the United Kingdom was the birthplace of less than one in three Australians so that the population was markedly and increasingly indigenous. In general, they spoke the same language with the same accent, ate essentially the same food and drank similar beverages — tea and beer. Their clothes only differed in minor ways with the changes in climate. It was noticed in Brisbane that the men discarded their coats and displayed their shirts to the world. While some visitors to Australia were struck by the differences between the old societies and the new one, especially in the alleged lessening of tensions between the social classes, they rarely remarked on differences within Australian society itself. Indeed to Australians themselves, differences that did exist scarcely mattered. It was possible to travel within the country and not be affected by them. Rivalry between Sydney and Melbourne and between Hobart and Launceston, varying railway widths, border posts between the colonies and other minor variations did exist but they were either curiosities or irritants and not significant in themselves.

If anything it was the land itself that was capable of shaping a new society because it was so old, brooding, mysterious, threatening and embracing. Interminable in its distances, washed with the same blueness of sea and sky, covered with the strength of its flora, the puzzling quaintness of its fauna, passing from the richness of its coastal regions with their wild and beautiful coasts and their mountain chain called the Great Divide, to the seemingly limitless deserts; the land gave at once a sense of sameness and wonderment. The land had to be won by the white settlers, who used it, abused it, and made it productive in the things that were precious to them but only scarred rather than changed it. In its use they came to know it and gradually an interaction between settlers and the land took place so that those who had been newcomers in 1788 had become part of the land a century later.

In 1877 a poet, James Brunton Stephens, wrote, 'She is not yet' when expressing a yearning for a form of national unity that would result in the 'girdling seas alone' becoming the boundaries of all Australia. With this expression of hope no element of jingoism was mixed, but Stephens did not realize that, by the time he wrote, Australians had already forged a unity amongst themselves which later political measures would merely sanction but not strengthen. A year later, Peter Dodds McCormick wrote 'Advance, Australia Fair' thereby accepting the unity between the people themselves and with the land they inhabited.

The attempt by some urban Australians to define their distinct identity revealed itself clearly in sport, art and literature. Australian cricket had its origins and most of its later development in Sydney, where it was played from the earliest days and where the long summer made it a particularly acceptable game. In 1868 it became an international phenonemon with the despatch of an Aboriginal team to England from the Western District of Victoria. The team went through a strenuous tour winning and losing fourteen matches alike, and its champion Mullagh was proclaimed by English critics as a batsman of high merit.

Two England elevens came to Australia in the 1860s, including a tour in 1873–74 captained by W.G. Grace who combined the trip with his honeymoon. The Australians had developed their skills considerably in the previous decade and Grace's team was beaten three times. At Melbourne in March 1877, a combined Australian team from New South Wales and Victoria played England in the first ever Test Match. The locals won by forty-five runs. In the following year, a win at the Oval in London caused the team to receive a national welcome on its return home, while the names of Spofforth, Bannerman, Blackham and Gregory became immediately famous. In 1882 the 'Ashes' of English cricket were symbolically created when Australia won a Test at the Oval by seven runs and the 'Ashes' became thenceforward the coveted prize between the two cricketing nations.

The Victorian gold-fields in the 1850s gave rise to a unique code of football based on the Irish game, which was codified in Melbourne in 1858 in a primitive form. Thomas Wills was one of those who drew up the rules. He was a son of Horatio Wills who had named Mount Ararat.

Thomas survived the massacre of his family by Aborigines in Queensland in 1861. Called 'Australian Football', the game made use of open space and freedom of movement and developed its own terminology drawn from the gold-fields, with expressions such as 'lead', 'shepherding' and 'pockets'. Carried by the diggers and miners to South Australia, Tasmania and Western Australia, the game never became international although played in New Zealand. Identification with it was purely local, but the first intercolonial game was played between Victoria and South Australia in 1879. Neverthless, its popularity, the fierce suburban and country-town loyalties engendered, the increasingly large crowds in attendance and its rapid spread through the southern colonies gave the Australian game a form of national prominence. Despite the native origins of 'Australian Rules', it has never displaced Rugby Union or, since 1907, Rugby League in New South Wales and Queensland. In those parts of Australia, both games retained their dominance and their proud following with overseas touring teams called the Wallabies for Rugby Union and the Kangaroos for Rugby League.

Rowing, sailing, sculling and swimming rapidly became favourite sports of a maritime people. When Edward Trickett returned to Sydney from England in 1876 as the world champion sculler and Australia's first world champion in any sport, there were scenes of unbounded enthusiasm. After Trickett came such sporting heroes as William Beach and Henry Searle so that, gradually, Australians began to realize that on the field and in the water they could match the best, and a particular pride in beating the English at their own games was widespread throughout the colonies.

Apart from the episode of the Maori wars, none of this sporting expertise was translated onto the field of the martial arts until a contingent of 552 New South Welsh infantry and 212 mounted men sailed from Sydney in March 1885 to take part in the Sudan Campaign in North Africa. By the time of their arrival, the conflict was almost over and they saw little action although three were wounded and six died of other causes. The experiment proved, ominously, that, when the glory of England and the defence of the Empire was invoked, Australians would be amongst the first to exchange their bats and oars for guns and bayonets.

In a society struggling for permanence, and where the wealthy were mainly concerned with the pursuit of more wealth, the fine arts were paid little attention before mid-century. There were no great personages, no ancient buildings, no scenes or battlefields pregnant with history to commemorate and the landscape was so unfamiliar initially as to defeat those who wanted to draw or paint it. Conrad Martens arrived in Sydney in

The Association Ground Lawn Tennis Club, now the Sydney Lawn Tennis Club, was formed in 1878 and is the oldest in Australia. Service was always underhand and women wore a long pinafore, with a pocket for holding balls, and a white underskirt. Miss Mayne was the New South Wales women's champion in the late 1880s.

1835 and for the following thirty years his constant theme was the Harbour and its surroundings. His water-colours were of a high order, but he saw the landscape in unreal colours and shapes which resembled those of Europe.

A change took place with the arrival of Abram Louis Buvelot in 1865, because the Swiss-born painter had an instinctive sense of light and tone that allowed him to touch the reality he saw and, in particular, the plains of Victoria's Western District. He was recognized as the father of Australian landscape painters by those who followed him in the 1880s. Buvelot left an unchallenged legacy, which flowered after his death in 1888. Eugene von Guerard was given the honour of becoming the first instructor at Victoria's National Gallery instead of Buvelot, but the latter's *Waterpool at Coleraine* remains, with other paintings, as testimony to his artistry and vision.

Thomas Henry Kendall, whaler, clerk, horseman, swimmer, derelict, bankrupt, dypsomaniac and poet was the sweetest voice of colonial Australia. He was born at Ulladulla on the beautiful south coast of New South

Wales in 1839 and lived his entire life in Australia until his death at the age of forty-three. He loved the bush, sang a delicate song and possessed deep emotional forces, which were never more evident than in the lament for his dead infant daughter entitled 'Araluen'. As a lyricist, whose poems rang gently with the sounds of the bush, Kendall is a unique witness that in less than eighty years the land had produced a testimony to itself. With the balladist Adam Lindsay Gordon, whose span was even briefer (1833–70), Kendall needs no comparison as a poet. Gordon, supreme horseman, temporary politician and one hurt in his being by injury and despair, always remained an Englishman and an alien who loved Australia without helping to mould her. 'The Sick Stockrider', 'How We Beat the Favourite' and other ballads, the flamboyancy and physical courage of his life and its tragic end at his own hand won the hearts of many Australians, but his bust is in Westminster Abbey where it is at home.

Marcus Clarke thought that Henry Kingsley's novel, *The Recollections of Geoffry Hamlyn* (1859), was the best Australian novel ever written. It dealt with squatting in the pre-gold period and its assumption was that the true leaders of colonial society were the pretentious English gentry, which was the precise element in it that caused Joseph Furphy to dismiss the novel as trash. Thomas Browne also thought that Kingsley's work was 'immortal' but Browne, Kingsley and Clarke were all English-born. Browne himself, under the pseudonym Rolf Boldrewood, wrote a work of far greater merit, *Robbery Under Arms*. Browne was only five when he arrived in Australia. He eventually took up a run in Victoria until drought forced him to become a police magistrate at various places in the bush in New South Wales. He drew on his experiences to write a masterpiece of superb story-telling with characters that are Australian and with the use of a bush vernacular. Serialized weekly in the *Sydney Mail* newspaper in 1882 and 1883, *Robbery Under Arms* was eagerly read by Australians, in both the bush and the city.

There were developments of importance in the study of the various branches of science. Government astronomers — H.C. Russell in New South Wales, R.L. Ellery in Victoria and Charles Todd in South Australia — continued the systematic study of the southern skies which Governor Brisbane had begun in Sydney. They provided the colonial time services, assisted the land surveyors and made important contributions to the study of meteorology. In 1877, using information provided by the telegraph, and after consulting with Ellery and Todd, Russell began issuing daily weather charts to the press, which later served as a rudimentary guide both to city and bush dwellers. Throughout the nineteenth century

Before Federation, border posts were set up to collect customs on goods passing between the colonies. They were an irritant to travellers and their existence helped the move towards Federation.

until 1896 time was all local, taken from the overhead position of the sun at noon. In 1896 three Standard Time Zones were introduced for legal, social and railway timetable purposes. In the eastern colonies, which based their time on the 150th meridian east of Greenwich, there was uniformity and South Australia and Western Australia were respectively one and two hours behind Eastern Standard Time. In 1899 South Australia and the Northern Territory changed to being only half an hour behind Eastern Standard Time.

The botanical work begun by Joseph Banks and Daniel Solander and continued by Robert Brown, Allan Cunningham and other explorer-scientists was systematized by George Bentham who, assisted by Ferdinand von Mueller, published the monumental *Flora Australiensis* between 1863 and 1878. Von Mueller's work in botany greatly helped Australian science gain international recognition, but he is locally more often remembered as the foundation planner of Melbourne's botanical gardens. The geologist, Rev. W.B. Clarke, and zoologist Gerard Krefft of the Australian Museum both corresponded with Charles Darwin and supplied him with evidence to support his theory of evolution, but in Australia Darwin's theory was either fiercely opposed or regarded at best with great suspicion. Clarke's great pioneering geological work was continued by many distinguished scientists including Father J. E. Tenison-Woods, A.R.C. Selwyn, Robert Etheridge Jnr, and T.W. Edgeworth David who in 1886 discovered the important Greta (New South Wales) coal measures. When a visiting Cambridge zoologist cabled a terse message in 1884 to the delegates at a meeting in Canada of the British Association of Science that the platypus and the echidna were egg-laying mammals, he caused a mild sensation and an eighty-year-old mystery was solved.

Scientific effort was strengthened by the foundation of societies which had their model in the Royal Society of London (founded 1662). By the 1860s Royal Societies had been formed in New South Wales, Tasmania, Victoria and South Australia; 1874 saw the Linnean Society of New South Wales established for 'the cultivation and study of the science of natural history in all its branches'; the Royal Geographical Society of Australasia was founded in 1883; and the peak of nineteenth century scientific organization was reached in 1888 with the holding of the inaugural conference of the Australasian Association for the Advancement of Science (now ANZAAS) in Sydney.

In the earliest days of settlement convicts frequently absconded into the bush, where, unable to live off the land, they turned to robbery to support themselves. By 1805 they were called bushrangers, while in Van

Diemen's Land, where their violence and daring were unsurpassed, they became known as bolters. The most famous bolters on the island were Michael Howe, Matthew Brady and Martin Cash. Cash was one of the very few who managed to cross the neck of land at Port Arthur, with its ferocious guard dogs, and escape. He went bushranging later but died a respectable man in 1877. On the mainland the early bushrangers were also runaway convicts. Bold Jack Donohoe was made famous in the ballad named after him, and Governor George Gipps forbad it being sung in taverns lest others be led to emulate his deeds. Jackey Jackey Westwood, Davis the Jewboy and Yankee Jack Ellis were others long remembered in New South Wales. They all lived in the pre-gold period when bush-ranging had become almost a profession amongst those who put little store on their own or others' lives.

In the gold-rush period, the native-born began to turn to bushranging. Apart from the excitement and the bravado, it was a handy trade for young men who found living off the produce of the gold-fields without actually doing the labour an attractive way of life. There was always a stagecoach or defenceless travellers on the roads who were easy prey, and, at anytime, a foray could be made into the towns or to homesteads. At the latter, good and fast horses, and sometimes racehorses, were often taken because the bushrangers relied heavily on the reliability and speed of their transport to evade the law. In general they were ensured pro-tection, shelter and food amongst their own families and friends. The 'bush telegraph' or quickly relayed word of mouth brought notice of police movements, while their daring won admiration from those who stood to loose nothing by their depredations.

In central-western New South Wales, the Weddin mountains were a favourite refuge for small gangs of bushrangers who raided the towns, roads and homesteads and then were able to retreat into the mountains with impunity. A particularly audacious act was the holding up of the township of Canowindra for three days by a gang led by Ben Hall in 1863. Little was taken, but they entertained the locals to free food and drink and left without hindrance. Two years later, Hall, then aged twenty-eight, was betrayed, ambushed and shot down by the police. For the main part, an early death by shooting or hanging was the lot of the bushrangers.

One notable exception was Frank Gardiner who, after a series of hold-ups and robberies not involving the loss of anyone's life, was sentenced to thirty-two years' hard labour in 1864. Released in 1874 on the condition that he go into exile, Gardiner lived until 1903, having run the Twilight Saloon in San Francisco for some years. His release, however, had caused the downfall of a government in Sydney for the Parkes ministry had to resign over the handling of the affair. The general behaviour of the bushrangers did not entirely alienate the people of the bush, although amongst them there were a few murderous madmen. By the late 1860s bushranging was largely over, and the killing of Frederick Ward, known as Captain Thunderbolt, on 25 May 1870, closed a chapter of colonial history apart from a few isolated phenomena of the seventies.

Australia's most famous rebel was Ned Kelly, son of an Irish, emancipist father. After his father's death in 1866, the family moved to a small selection at Greta in the north-east of Victoria, where young Kelly soon fell foul of the law. By 1873 he was on a hulk at Williamstown serving three years. He emerged to find the old bush days gone, with the electric telegraph and the railway linking the north-east to Melbourne. The home selection was too small to support the family. Ned found work for a time locally but then turned to horse and cattle stealing. Such activity was not simple criminality but also a protest by the landless and the unsuccessful against the large squatters, who had increased their land holdings, despite the Land Acts of the previous decades.

Kelly may have faded into obscurity had the police not shown their determination to bring him and his companions to heel. High ranking police officers had become alarmed when the Premier, Graham Berry, sacked some 300 judges, police magistrates, coroners and other public servants on Black Wednesday, 9 January 1878. The sackings had been brought on by the refusal of the Legislative Council, bastion of landed and merchant power, to grant supply, as they wanted to stop the payment of members of Parliament which had recently been introduced as a reform measure. Captain Standish, who incompetently ran the police force from the comfort of the Melbourne Club, decided it was time to prove his own value to society and what better way than by picking off the Kellys.

A false accusation of the attempted murder by Ned of a constable led to the arrest of Ned's mother, her son-in-law and another innocent man, and rewards were put out for Ned and his younger brother, Dan. In an ambush, three police refused to surrender and were killed by Ned. Outlawed, the brothers with two mates Joe Byrne and Steve Hart, took to the bush for twenty months emerging on two occasions to hold up banks at Euroa in Victoria and Jerilderie in New South Wales. In June 1880 they made a stand at Glenrowan near the old Greta homestead, where, in the ensuing battle with the police, all but Ned were killed. Sentenced to death, Ned was hanged in Melbourne on 11 November 1880.

Kelly, clad in the iron armour he wore at Glenrowan, became in time the archetypal legend of Australia's folklore with the expression 'as game as Ned Kelly' the byword of indomitable courage. The legend was rejected by those whose values sanctified property, authority and the law and who accepted the police version of Ned as a terrorist and cold-blooded murderer. Others saluted Ned's identification with the land of his birth, his rejection of despotism clothed in law and his thirst for freedom from tyranny, because they saw that he was the first of a new Australian breed. Ned's monument was his legend, kept alive in ballads, prose, poetry, films and paintings.

CHAPTER NINE
Prosperity and Depression

One hundred years of settlement had bred a basic conviction in the minds of the white inhabitants which marked them off from their forebears and many of their contemporaries in other lands. They grew up with the expectation that, with moderate effort, life could be sustained, families raised, fed and clothed in some degree of ease, and the cycle repeated. The subjection experienced by a European workforce and peasantry to factory owners and landlords, who could make or break individuals and families, was simply unacceptable to most Australians. In the natural course of events some Australians were not survivors, whether as small selectors or factory hands, but it was not the norm to go under because work of some kind was available to the willing. In particular the workers' movement was convinced that, with proper organization and unity, a balance could be achieved between capital and labour to the benefit of all concerned.

A labour movement embracing both bush and urban workers was already a necessity, because the rural dream, in which a high percentage of the population would live comfortably on small holdings, had turned sour. The squatters maintained their dominance and, although there was an itinerant workforce especially of shearers, large properties employed permanent and settled workers, almost all of whom were males. On very large stations it was not unusual to find eighty or more employees. Over seventy percent of the population were on wages or salaries while more than a third of the people of New South Wales lived in Sydney and approaching half Victorians were Melburnians. These were the Australians whom the trade union movement had to represent.

If worker representation was necessary for the males, it was imperative for the females and children. By the mid-eighties, twenty percent of the workforce was female. In shops or factories they worked in industries many of which previously had their base in the home — food, drink, textiles and clothing. The first Act regulating hours of work and conditions for females was passed in Victoria on 11 November 1873. Despite that Act female workers in Victoria and elsewhere often worked for sixty to seventy hours a week, and in factories their wages were normally less than half the male rate. Sanitation and ventilation were ignored as were health and safety issues. In the clothing industry they often took work home at night which meant that, after nine hours in the factory, they did three more at home. Women who were unable to leave the home because of commitments to the children took work in, and, under the process known as 'sweating', they worked as long for less pay making it difficult for the factory women to claim higher rates.

Children were similarly exploited with cases of youngsters aged ten and eleven working sixty hours for 6s per week — about one-sixth of the adult male rate. Often children fainted from exhaustion and the apprentice system was little relief being no more than exploitation as apprentices in many trades were not paid at all in their first four years. With compulsory education far from realizable, many youngsters became 'street Arabs' begging, selling matches and trinkets, wandering the streets or gathered as 'larrikins' in 'pushes', which were mostly a nuisance but sometimes a terror as they marauded through the city and suburbs.

No clearly structured political parties had emerged, partly because the concept was strong that a member of parliament was responsible primarily to his electors rather than to a party. The main, divisive, issue in politics was whether free trade or protection of local products was preferable as a policy. Victoria became the stronghold of protection because the decline in revenue from taxes on gold inclined the government to listen to the voices of the farmers, who wanted to protect their wheat from imports, and, the founders of new industries who had to compete with products made elsewhere. By the late 1870s, a twenty to twenty-five percent duty had been placed on imports into Victoria.

Protection caused no marked growth in industry, but a large domestic market was created on account of the population rise and in the thirty years from 1861 to 1891, the number of factories in Victoria grew from 400 to 3,300, and the growth rate of the urban sector was higher than that of the rural. In New South Wales, three times the size of Victoria, the continued revenue from the sale of Crown Lands meant that protection was not as badly needed, so free trade was espoused. Nonetheless, protection appealed not merely to pockets but also to emotions as it gave a

The tradition of carrying banners in processions was brought to Australia by British craftsmen. The first Eight Hour working day procession took place in Melbourne on 12 May 1856.

sense of security from competition, initially economic and eventually racial, and it was adopted in the other colonies. The fact that free trade took hold and survived in New South Wales was a tribute to its exponents because it was based on belief rather than practicality, and Australians had never shown much faith in political dogmas.

With politics largely confined to the intricacies of the free trade versus protection debate, the workforce, whether rural or urban, could not look to party representation for help as no distinct groups existed with a defined policy on industrial or rural sector matters. Furthermore the old form of the state, with its origins in the penal period, still prevailed, making it the key factor in all enterprises wherever large capital was required, such as railway construction, education and immigration. State policy, especially in regard to assisted immigration, necessarily had an effect on the workforce and there was a hardening of attitudes against immigrants amongst the leaders of the workers.

Although there were pockets of unemployment, especially in the mid-eighties the seventies and eighties were periods of general prosperity and there seemed no need for a theoretical blueprint upon which to construct social policies for the future. Trade union activity was based on crafts and directed at wages and factory conditions. In 1882 a strike on wages and piece-work occurred amongst the 4,000 women employed as tailoresses in Victoria and received widespread union and community support. The tailoresses formed their own union, the first union amongst females in Australia, and the employers capitulated. The voices of the unionists were joined by those of reformers (a few of whom were manufacturers although the majority were opposed to reform) and by the Melbourne *Age*, so that Factory Acts regulating conditions were passed in Victora in 1885 and 1896 with the other colonies following suit in the 1890s. The struggle for reform was long and slow however. Inadequacies were everywhere apparent because, without factory inspectors, only the good will, often markedly lacking, of owners could be relied upon to ensure reform took place.

In the same period the formation of trade unions went ahead, and, more importantly, central bodies were formed to assist in the coordination of their activities. By 1885 there were Trades and Labour Councils in Victoria, New South Wales and Queensland and intercolonial congresses had been held since the first in Sydney in 1879. At Coolgardie, Western Australia, a congress was held in 1889 at which compulsory arbitration was put on the agenda and thought was given to a political programme. Finally, when the Australian Labour Federation was formed in Queensland in 1889, it clearly indicated that organised labour realized the need for unity to perfect its development.

The most significant step towards one strong union covering a whole industry was the formation of the Amalgamated Shearers' Union of Australasia (A.S.U.) at Ballarat in 1886 under the presidency of the indefatigable organiser and populist, William Spence. He had previously formed the Amalgamated Miners' Association of Australasia and, turning his attention to the pastoral industry, Spence managed to unionize shearers in the eastern colonies. By 1894 the A.S.U. had combined with the Amalgamated Workers' Union of Queensland and a shed hands' union to form the Australian Workers' Union (A.W.U.), which eventually became the most powerful workers' organization in the whole of the continent.

While the workers sought to organize, a symbol of those years of prosperity was rising with the building of 'Marvellous Melbourne', where the population increased, in the decade before 1891, from 268,000 to 473,000. Tramways, railways, bridges, schools, hospitals, offices, factories and homes, all rose as the suburbs spread out from the centre. The people went to the races, cricket and football, gambled and drank and, on Sundays, they worshipped God in the churches they so proudly built. Great edifices based on administration and commerce — Parliament House, the General Post Office, and the Rialto — all added to the lustre of the Exhibition Building which was opened in 1880. Called by a visitor 'The Metropolis of Australia' the city abounded with libraries, parks, galleries, theatres and bookshops, including the famous Coles Book Arcade. In 1888 two million people visited the Centennial Exhibition. The city also abounded with slums, which were evil-smelling and ill-lit with unpaved streets and makeshift dwellings.

As it grew Melbourne also became an octopus. Ballarat's and Bendigo's mining exchanges, manufacturing concerns from foundries to breweries in the country towns, bush people with ambition — all were affected by the growth of Melbourne, which became the centre of economic and commercial activity and the place to seek work or skills. Above all, the city became the heart of the financial activity of the whole continent, and indeed beyond into the Pacific, so that a network of bankers, managers, clerks and civil servants grew apace.

The peopling of the city meant land development with housing and shops, gas and water, and the linking of the suburban centres by railway. The inner city was served by a cable tram system after 1885. By May 1888 there were 112 new land and investment companies registered in Victoria, and one of them declared a dividend of 66.6 percent before selling any land. Within eight months land sales totalled more than £13,000,000 and the building industry had begun to use seven-tenths of business profit, which resulted in a boom. Millions of pounds were lent, thousands of acres developed, prices rocketed and capital in seemingly limitless amounts flowed in, especially from Britain, as if it were another gold-rush. Greed had overcome sense, speculation replaced wisdom and unbridled optimism dimmed well-founded hope. The land boom burst in a few short months, and by the early 1890s thousands were left with valueless allotments and shares worth less than the carefully enscrolled paper upon which they were recorded. Just as Melbourne's growth was a symbol of prosperity based on the catch-cry of progress and on imported capital, its collapse and stagnation served as the yardstick for the widespread economic downturn of the 1890s which had an effect on all Australians.

In the twenty years from 1871 to 1891, Australian governments had borrowed £126,000,000, but by the end of 1891 British capital was almost unprocurable because of a series of events which originated in Argentina and caused the leading financial institution in London, Barings, to fail. Colonial governments could no longer borrow and it became the case of the country riding out the storm alone as the eastern colonies witnessed failure after failure of respectable financial concerns. Corruption on a large scale was revealed, even amongst leading politicians in Victoria, and the confidence of the public was shattered. Next hit was the pastoral industry, which by 1890 had doubled all other exports in value. Over-production brought on a partial slump in wool prices, and the desire of the squatters to turn their runs into freehold properties entailed fencing and other improvements which combined with high labour costs to cause many squatters to mortgage their properties. Furthermore large sums of capital had been outlaid on marginal lands, especially in western

The wheat fields of South Australia were the granary of the colonies until towards the end of the century when agriculture developed in New South Wales and Victoria. South Australia also saw the development of the Ridley stripper, based on John Wrathall Bull's experiments in the 1840s.

New South Wales, which proved expensive in artesian water schemes and unprofitable as fleece quality fell. Droughts, rabbits and new land legislation all helped to increase costs and speculation in pastoral properties had meant greatly inflated values. After 1891 a continuing fall in wool prices worsened an already critical situation.

The long-established backbone of the economy, pastoralism, went into decline and sheep numbers dropped by a half from the late 1890s due mainly to the onset of a great drought which began in 1895 and lasted for seven years. Agriculture, principally wheat production, was based chiefly in Victoria and South Australia, which supplied most of the needs of the whole country. In the 1870s farmers in South Australia had moved out beyond the line set down by the Surveyor-General George Goyder, which approximately marked the twelve inch rainfall boundary. Goyder was proved right in his estimate that productivity could not be sustained beyond his line and with falling wheat prices many farmers went broke. Too often they had overworked the land in vain, on country with insufficient rain to grow regular crops. They left shifting sand and arid, wind-swept clay pans as evidence that nature's limits could not be pushed with impunity.

The economy could probably have survived had the financial institutions, with government backing, remained firm. But the long period of prosperity had led Australian banks and other lending institutions to over-lend. This contributed to the slump as business could borrow too freely but then could not repay the loans. The business would then fail, productivity would be lost and people put out of work. The diverse and uncontrolled practices of the banks meant that they could not save themselves, nor could government intervention once the productive basis of the economy was shaken. Panic set in after the Commercial Bank of Australia suspended operations in April 1893 and a run on the banks commenced. By May only three large banks, the Union, the Australasia and the Bank of New South Wales, and six lesser ones, were able to operate.

Commercial life and the community itself were in chaos as the distressed banks converted savings into shares, accounts were frozen, wages and bills were not paid, and many of the retired or unemployed lost overnight any savings they had accumulated. Sensible government intervention with co-operation from the banks could have reduced the effects of the collapse but, although the banks passed into a period of so-called reconstruction, the damage was done and the country was gripped by depression. Workmen's wages fell by over a quarter, some of the unemployed roamed the country looking for work, evictions became common and people slept in the streets or in public gardens such as Sydney's Domain.

Australia's period of prosperity in the aftermath of the gold-rushes was over. The economic structures were in tatters, capital had ceased to flow in, labour relations were strained or non-existent and the claim that here was 'a good place for a steady man' had become hollow. In three years, 50,000 people left Melbourne and in some suburbs the streets were deserted. Some of those who had previously been wealthy and many more poor starved. Thirty percent of the workforce was unemployed. As no direct government assistance of any kind was available, the spectre of misery and hunger overshadowed thousands of homes, although some charitable organizations struggled to help ward off starvation. A few schemes of piecemeal work were initiated and co-operative settlements were founded in Victoria and New South Wales. Victoria lost 100,000 citizens in the decade, mostly to the West Australian gold-fields to which they took their spirit of independence and their love of Australian Rules Football. Finally, nature added its own measure of flagellation to a society already on its knees as the great drought showed no sign of lifting.

Western Australia in the 1860s had seen the development of the vast areas of pastoral country in the north-west beyond Geraldton with about six million acres running 40,000 sheep while the east and south-east were further opened and about nine million acres were under lease by 1870. Concurrently the end of the convict period in 1868 saw in office a governor of some foresight, Frederick Weld. He directed the development of the telegraph and the construction of roads, and in 1874 the first public railway was commenced, although it was not until 1879 that the railways began to expand in a measure commensurate with the needs of the colony. Pearling, timber, especially the splendid jarrah and karri woods, sandalwood and wool were the basis of the economy and the pastoral industry was given further impetus with the leasing, by 1883, of about forty-eight million acres of country in the Kimberley region. The colony was enormous in extent, one-third the area of continental Australia and larger by far than Western Europe, but the centres of long established political, social and economic power were still in the east. The opening of the Golden West was another element in the swing away from the coastal emphasis of the cities towards the inland and its gold-fields and bush.

Consequent upon these developments, it was finally decided to give responsible government to Western Australia and on 30 December 1890 the first Parliament was sworn in, with an upper and a lower house as the colonists had resisted a single chamber parliament which the Colonial

Private charity was the principal form of relief for the needy poor in the nineteenth century. The absence from this illustration of able-bodied men perhaps indicates that they were ashamed to proclaim their poverty openly.

Office had wanted to give to them. The discovery of immense deposits of gold at Coolgardie and then by Paddy Hannan at Kalgoorlie in June 1892 was followed by the opening of the 'Golden Mile' at nearby Boulder. Gold transformed the colony economically and socially. Thousands flocked to Western Australia thereby quadrupling its population in a few years, otherwise the mass of unemployed could have caused chaos in the eastern cities. Lured by profits British capital was abundantly available for

Western Australia and some of it was transferred to the east. The net result of the gold discoveries was that the eastern colonies were helped to get through the depression, while Western Australia itself went through a period of catching up and then mild transformation.

During the depression labour and capital in the eastern colonies engaged in a protracted and hard-fought struggle. The labour movement emerged chastened and defeated, but with the need for unity and political representation more clearly established. In August 1890 a maritime strike took out 50,000 workers in transport and mining, for a period of two months, while the shearers in New South Wales went out for a week as a defensive measure. The strike began over claims by marine officers for better accommodation and increased pay, which the shipowners refused to discuss until the officers were prepared to disband their own union. Meanwhile wool shorn by non-union labour was arriving at the wharves, and in a matter of days, marine officers, seamen, wharf labourers and coal lumpers all had gone on strike both to support the marine officers and to prevent the loading of 'black' wool. The Pastoralists' Federal Council and the Steamship Owners' Association fought on the right of capital to organize a workforce as it saw fit and, in the case of the former, to break Spence's already loosening hold on an industry in which they regarded the 'closed shop' principle as an affront.

The unions quickly ran out of funds, men saw their jobs taken by non-union labour and it appeared as if the employers, with strong support from government and the law, had won. In fact the workers' movement had been pushed so far that no alternative remained but to organize direct political action. In May 1891 three labour candidates won seats in the South Australian Parliament and in the June elections of 1891 thirty-five nominees of the New South Wales Labour Electoral Leagues, which were the true founders of the Labor Party, were returned to Parliament and a party was formed in New South Wales. The Party differed in New South Wales from that in Victoria where liberals could be relied upon to pass reforming measures; it suffered internal discord, and only very gradually formulated clear policies except on the exclusion of coloured labour. In 1890 Henry George, American writer, lecturer and visionary economist, whose book *Progress and Poverty* (1879) had been read by many thousands in the colonies, visited Australia and seeded some of his ideas on a tax on land into the movement. Old Chartist ideals and the concept of mateship had survived the golden days and they blended with faint traces of socialism popularised in the newly founded papers of the labour movement, the *Radical* (1887), the *Worker* (1890) and the *Hummer* (1891).

The 'Great Strikes' of 1890 affected the transport and shipment of wool and were decisive in the formation of the Labor Party. Horse wagons were used to bring wool from the Sydney railway station to Circular Quay. This illustration shows a wool wagon in Pitt Street, Sydney during the strikes.

Nonetheless, the Labor Party lacked any blueprint for society, and therefore relied upon practical achievements to win and hold support. Its pragmatism made it a suitable vehicle to represent the society which gave it birth and the workers and small farmers rapidly looked to it as their party. Catholics, most of whom were working class, became the party's backbone, because they saw its concern for the poor and oppressed as an indicator of hope in their own depressed economic and social conditions.

Most Australians shared the conviction that conditions for all could become increasingly better provided the state settled for the correct legislative measures. It was an innocent conviction resting upon a belief in progress and perfectibility. Men of principle from the workers' movement combined with liberal progressives to achieve a three year duration for parliaments and the abolition both of plural voting, by which property owners could vote in more than one electorate, and property qualifications for either candidates or voters. Payment of members of parliament was also introduced, and women were given the vote in South Australia in 1894 and Western Australia in 1899, followed later by the other colonies.

Some of the old guard politicians passed from the scene unable or unwilling to work with powerful Labor minorities. George Reid in New South Wales found no such difficulty and he was able to pass social reforms, aided by the Labor leaders Watson and Hughes, whose careers were shaped in the hardy days when Labor was forced to compromise in order to exist. In Victoria the liberals were so powerful, held views so close to those of the Laborites and contained such talent as Alfred Deakin and Isaac Isaacs that the fledgling Party could only give them quiet and effective support.

On 1 December 1899 the Labor Party in Queensland formed the famous 'first Labor government in the world' under the leadership of Andrew Dawson. His minority ministry did not receive the support it expected from the liberals, and the government lasted less than a week. Tasmania, lacking trade unions of any consequence, left the field to the liberals and conservatives and no Labor Party existed there until 1903 nor was there one in Western Australia until 1900. In South Australia a group of business and pastoral interests forced genuine liberals to coalesce under the leadership of John Downes, who worked with the Labor members to legislate in a markedly radical way. Independents were practically gone from the political arenas and factions no longer existed anywhere except under the label of parties. With the advent of the Labor Party, politics had taken on aspects of organization and discipline unrecognizable to the more relaxed but nonetheless devoted figures of the 1850s who had laid the foundations of Australian democracy.

In this atmosphere, Factory Acts became widespread, sweating of labour done in private premises was attacked but not stopped, and the first steps were taken towards compulsory arbitration, although the depressed economy put the owners in a strong position. Taxes on land and incomes, and the introduction of non-contributory old-age pensions in Victoria and New South Wales seemed to give the Australian colonies the right to be called a 'social laboratory' where progressive ideals were translated into legislation for the good of the poor and the powerless. In reality, the truth lay in a widespread recognition that all sections of society, including the owners of capital, benefited when the sources of discontent were alleviated.

There were some idealists who proclaimed in mildly socialist publications that socialism would make all men 'mates', which, for most of their readers, was only a pious hope. In 1890 William Lane stated his faith in a youthful Australia which was also wise with the wisdom of the generations and therefore had a right to be foremost amongst the nations. He soon became convinced that he would never see his utopia in Australia, and in 1893 he led a party of followers to the wilds of Paraguay to found the perfect settlement. Instead he discovered that greed and envy held sway also in the jungle. His community broke up in discord and Lane left it in 1899 for New Zealand where he became a conservative imperialist.

While there was abundant proof that Australians were prepared to experiment with the shape of their society, there was little proof that they wanted to tamper with its loyalties and allegiances. Despite some public unease at royal appointments, titles and courtesy titles such as 'Sir' and 'Lady' and the other assorted regalia of Empire, republicanism was always a fragile if not exotic plant in Australia. The distant but overwhelming presence of majesty in England's Queen, whose life had been dignified and imperial and to whom numerous statues were erected in 1887 and 1897 to mark her anniversaries, made loyalty a prerequisite of public sanity amongst colonial Australians. Little proof was needed that all were loyal children of the British mother, but when loyalty was called for with the outbreak of the Boer War in 1899, it was forthcoming with spontaneity and pride. The response puzzled only that vocal minority who, knowing the Empire was in no danger and suspecting that the retention of British mining interests was relevant, condemned the way in which 16,000 young Australians departed to fight for England under banners such as 'For Queen and Country' and 'The Empire Right or Wrong'.

Henry Lawson, already widely accepted as a writer of stature, proclaimed himself ashamed of his fellow Australians, and William Morris Hughes and others in the Labor Party called the war immoral, needless and unjust. Their voices were scarcely heeded. It seemed that the chance had come to prove that male Australians were really men and that the country had come of age. Up to the peace treaty of 31 May 1902, the Australian volunteers numbered 16,175 men, the dead, 518, the wounded, 882 and six Victoria Crosses had been won for valour. The other face to valour was seen in the concentration camps where Boer families were held while the British forces burnt their homes and farm buildings. Harry 'Breaker' Morant, who had been a bushman and horse-breaker in Queensland and had later tried his hand at poetry, found peace for his 'soul world-weary' when he and his friend Peter Handcock were court-martialled and executed for shooting Boer prisoners. Their deaths helped to soothe the conscience of the British high command, which had begun to agonize over the whole dirty business it was involved in.

Meanwhile the opening of the land in Australia had gone ahead despite the depression and drought. Wool and gold had tended to obscure the contribution of agriculture to the economy as well as to the development of the country itself. Wheat was the principal grain both for home consumption and export especially when, with the repeal of the Corn Laws in Britain in 1846 which lifted tariffs on imported grain, Britain became the largest importer of wheat in the world. In South Australia; the Riverina; on the Darling Downs; south of Perth; in a vast area of South Australia and Victoria called the Mallee; and south of it again on rich soils called the Wimmera; wheat cultivation became intense from the 1890s.

Technological progress in the wheat industry was impressive. Farmers cleared the land with the Mullenizer, which pushed over the scrub with a roller; prepared the soil with the stump-jump plough; and the better-off harvested with the newly released McKay 'Sunshine' harvester. Most farmers began to understand the soils better, they improved fallowing, controlled weeds, varied their wheat strains, began to use super-phosphates and worked hard. New South Wales farmers laughed at Victoria as a cabbage garden where small farmers called 'cockies' ate treacle on their bread and grew wheat on miniscule plots, but in the 1890s New South Wales began to feed itself for the first time and trebled its acreage under wheat. The very size of the contribution of the golden grain to the economy made farming respectable and the land selectors who went into the Wimmera and Mallee, including Germans from South Australia who settled around Horsham, gave solidity and permanence to townships which helped Victoria survive the depression of the nineties.

The grape, with so much else, had come with the First Fleet, but despite the pioneering work of the Macarthur family, it was not until James

The vast spaces of Australia encouraged an early interest in flight. Lawrence Hargrave's experiment with box kites lifted him fifteen feet above the ground at Stanwell Park, NSW in 1894. His work was an historic step in the development of flight.

Busby imported many varieties from Spain and France in 1831–32 that an industry was firmly established at Kirkton near Singleton and Dalwood near Maitland. Hunter River wines quickly began to gain a reputation for their lightness, fragrance and taste. By 1895 over 7,000 acres were under cultivation in New South Wales, but in South Australia the area was almost double that and its wines were praised at the Paris Exhibition as early as 1854. Victoria had rapidly become the leading wine colony after William Ryrie began a commercial establishment at Yering, near Geelong, in 1840. Development continued even after the appearance of the dreaded vine disease phylloxera in Victoria in 1877, brought in on a vessel to the port of Geelong. In South Australia the industry began to flourish under the direction of families like the Lindemans, Penfolds and Seppelts in the Barossa and Clare valleys, near Adelaide, and the future greatness of the South Australian industry was thereby laid.

Over 30,000 acres were under vines by 1895 in Victoria. Further out-breaks of phylloxera caused a gradual decrease in production, although the colony still led the industry at the end of the nineteenth century and names like St Hubert became famous. At Mildura and Renmark on the Murray the beginnings of viticulture were connected with two Canadians of Californian experience , George and William Chaffey, who pioneered irrigation in the area and made vine and fruit-tree growing possible. Their contribution, together with the discovery from 1879 onwards of vast artesian deposits covering over a third of the continent, made agri-culture and pastoralism possible in places where the lack of water resulted in 'hissing deserts' and uninhabited wastes.

Despite an outbreak of foot and mouth disease as early as 1804 and later ravaging by pleuro-pneumonia in the 1860s, cattle herds for meat and milk grew immensely. By the 1890s there were about four million head in New South Wales and Victoria; most were derived from the English Hereford shorthorn and polled Angus breeds. In Gippsland and the Western District of Victoria, dairy herds rapidly became common. Although in Gippsland, where huge forests had to be cleared and few good roads or other forms of communication existed, derelict farms tes-tified to the general hardship experienced by selectors.

Queensland, after the opening of the Condamine and McIntyre river districts, became the home of the cattle industry. The industry spread to the Northern Territory in the 1870s, giving life again to its small settle-ments and opening up a short-lived trade with East Asia between 1892 and 1897. The Durack family overlanded cattle from Queensland to the Kimberleys in Western Australia in 1883–85, settled Argyle Downs and eventually controlled 6,000 square miles of property. They helped pion-eer an industry and establish a legend of endurance and of urbanity as well as of civilized relations with the Aborigines who, as a versatile and dedicated workforce, there and throughout northern Australia generally became central to the cattle industry. The cattle tick was an added hazard to the industry after its introduction, probably with Brahman cattle in the 1870s, and it killed up to ninety percent of some herds and helped to reduce stock numbers in Queensland from seven million to four million in the decade after 1890.

The long boom of the 1860–90 period and the subsequent depression had contributed to the birth of the Labor Party as a distinctive political expression of the Australian experience. In literature and the arts there was a similar attempt to create a spirit, centred both upon the land and its people, which would be equally distinctive. In literature this spirit fos-tered elements of insecurity and arrogance that helped breed a sentiment of intolerance, which was particularly ardent in the Labor Party. This intolerance was not merely towards the 'coloured' races, the Chinese and the Japanese but also towards European, and more particularly, English immigration. In the 1890s, given Australian economic circumstances, immigration had dropped to a mere trickle.

The Sydney-based *Bulletin* was founded in 1880 by John Haynes and Jules François Archibald who were shortly afterwards joined by William Traill. It rapidly became the literary embodiment of Australian jingoism and chauvinism, expressed by 'Australia for the Australians' and, from 1908 to 1960, by its banner 'Australia for the White Man'. Its forays into racism, radicalism, anti-imperialism, republicanism and thinly-disguised larrikinism served to delight many, confuse others and enrage some. Archibald was a rare soul who, as well as being an insufferable autocrat, had the great gift of fostering the talents of others. As a consequence under his direction and then that of Alfred Stephens and, later, James Edmond, the *Bulletin* became 'The Bushman's Bible' read by people in the outback all over the continent, although the *Sydney Mail*, the *Australasian* and the *Worker*, together with the *Town and Country Journal* were more widely read by the workers in New South Wales, while the sporting novels of Nat Gould were read throughout the colonies.

The *Bulletin* was also appreciated by thousands in the cities to whom the bush had already become the symbol of a nostalgic yearning for a pioneering past. The black-and-white artists, Hopkins, May, Norman Lindsay and Souter, enlivened its pages with graphic wit and invective, while verse and prose offerings from readers, many of which were printed on the famous Red Page, poured in. Their reflections on their experience of life in Australia literally kept the *Bulletin* going as most of the contributors were never paid. However, there was enough revenue in 1892 for Archibald to send Henry Lawson to the bush with £5 in his pocket. It was the best used 'fiver' in Australia's literary history, for the Joe Wilson stories, 'The Union Buries its Dead' and other enduring masterpieces of Lawson's genius as a story teller came from those few months in the bush, when the drought which was gripping the country heightened Lawson's own tendency to gloom.

Other writers made their contribution, both in the *Bulletin* and elsewhere, notably the master balladist and poet of the horse, 'Banjo' Paterson. His *The Man from Snowy River and Other Verses* (1895) became an instant best seller and gave Paterson the right to be regarded as the composer of the national song 'Waltzing Matilda', which was first sung publicly in an hotel in Winton, Queensland, in that same year. Ethel Turner published her *Seven Little Australians* in 1894 and Joseph Furphy

Separated from his wife, driven to attempt suicide, in and out of gaol for failure to pay maintenance and several times in a mental hospital, Henry Lawson was already a wreck by 1910. He died of alcoholism in 1922, aged 54, but his stories and ballads and his legend endure.

wrote his novel *Such is Life* (1903), which was set in the Riverina and northern Victoria. In Furphy's words, the novel had a 'democratic' temper and an 'offensively Australian' bias. Steele Rudd (Arthur Hoey Davis) began his *On Our Selection* in the *Bulletin* in 1895. His figures of Dad, Dave, Joe, Mother and Kate became immortals of Australian literature and made the struggles of the poor selectors part of the national heritage.

In those same years, several artists began to assert their understanding of the native land when they attempted to paint Australian scenes. One of them, Arthur Streeton, said that an enduring theme was to be 'the quiet, beautiful wealth of the "Bush" that we must still endeavour to work'. On 17 August 1889, Streeton, Charles Conder, Tom Roberts and Frederick McCubbin held an 'Exhibition of Impressions' in Melbourne at which they showed their paintings mostly done on the lids of cigar boxes. Their work was roundly condemned by leading critics. The painters were a neglected little band whose work sold for a pittance with the Sydney Gallery buying George Lambert's 'Across the Blacksoil Plains' for £105 and Streetons's 'Still Glides the Stream' for £70. On his return from Europe in 1885, Tom Roberts had formed a group around him named after the outer Melbourne suburb of Heidelberg. With McCubbin, Streeton and Conder, the 'Heidelberg School' began to acquire cohesion, vision and increasing fame. Pioneering life, the pastoral industry and the bush were their particular subjects and their intuitive grasp, bred in them from infancy, of Australian light, colour and form gave their work a quality which has rarely been equalled. Their paintings also helped to reinforce the legend of an innocent past which the people of the cities could look back to and treasure. They avoided the turmoil of the cities, they were scarcely aware of any social conflict and neither the Aborigines nor the convicts had any role in their vision of the past.

Prior to the 1850s Australian music was practically non-existent, but the gold discoveries provided a market for the theatrical impresario, the piano importer and a flourishing sheet-music industry. Music of local or topical interest was often produced like Charles E. Horsley's setting to music of a Henry Kendall poem in 1870. The European musical tradition in Australia was pioneered by various regimental bandmasters and composers, among them Vincent Wallace, John Phillip Deane and Isaac Nathan. Their work was enhanced by the development of philarmonic societies and the Liedertafel movement. In the 1860s and 1870s choral music was very popular. George S. Coppin remained a major figure of the Australian stage, bringing many performers to the country and there was widespread support for W.S. Lyster's opera seasons in the eastern colonies. After Lyster's death, J.C. Williamson became the stage and musical entrepreneur and his 'Firm' dominated the Australian stage for several decades. In 1888 two works were commissioned for the Melbourne Centennial Exhibition, Leon Caron's *Australian National Cantata* and John A. Delaney's *Captain Cook*. This latent musical nationalism was vigorously championed by Henry Tate, Percy Grainger and Alfred Hill. Hill's music was influenced by Maori and Australian Aboriginal musical folklore.

The writers and painters of the nineties sought a distinctively Australian ethos in things which they thought would endure and for them the bush stood for virtue, mateship, hardship and spirit of place. But the nineties marked the end of old, white Australia. Her poets, story-tellers and artists cried out to her to become again an Australia which neither then nor later could ever be recreated. In 1896 Joseph Furphy admitted the hopelessness of the task when he wrote 'there is no Up the Country for us now'. The *Bulletin* was itself an ending rather than a beginning because the economic forces evident during the 1890s were already effectively changing the isolated continent and her people. Those forces were making Australians part of a wider world but it was a world that remained within the spiritual, social and economic ambit of Victorian England.

To some extent that wider world was also aware of Australia because from the 1830s visitors had been attracted from overseas. They departed with their varied impressions and, at times, left something behind of value. In an age when the spoken word was still the principal means of communication, the lecture was much in vogue both as entertainment and education. Visitors of note went on widely attended lecture tours throughout the colonies and were given good press coverage. Annie Besant (theosophist), George Augustus Sala (war correspondent), H.M. Stanley (African explorer), Sidney and Beatrice Webb (Fabians), 'Arthur Sketchley' and 'Max O'Rell' (lecturers), Ben Tillett (labour leader), General William Booth, and the novelists and poets Anthony Trollope, David Murray, Gerald Massey and Mark Twain — all passed through the colonies. Robert William Dale, the Congregational theologian, was joined by the musicians Frederick Cowen and Charles Halle; actresses Mrs Scott Siddons and Sarah Bernhardt; and entertainers, Lola Montez and J.G.F. Blondin. Joseph Conrad, R.L. Stevenson and Rudyard Kipling made brief visits as did Samuel Plimsoll, 'the sailors' friend', and Captain Joshua Slocum (in 1896 on his way to becoming the first solo yachtsman to circumnavigate the globe). The world had begun to embrace the ancient continent.

CHAPTER TEN

White Australia

By the end of the nineteenth century, the signs of white occupation of the Australian continent were everywhere apparent, except for that third of it where the deserts made settlement unprofitable. In the coastal regions there were cities and large towns, green pastures, gardens and other signs of a civilization brought from afar. Roads and tracks criss-crossed the countryside, although their condition was deplorable and became even worse with the coming of the railway. Fences now separated properties, trees had been ring-barked in millions and stood like grey ghosts of the past, gullies were eroded, the red cedar forests remained mainly in furniture and dust blew on pastures which overstocking and rabbits had thinned back to the clay. With imported trees, shrubs, flowers, weeds, animals and birds, with sign posts, railway stations, bush schools, churches and post offices, the evidence of white settlement was clear. In the cities some people lived and died without ever having seen a kangaroo, wallaby, koala or Aborigine.

Most changes were not for the worse. Sheep and cattle roamed in millions, thousands of square miles were under cultivation, the coasts were opened to shipping and there was regular contact with Europe. Colonial governments functioned smoothly, public services operated to the benefit of many, some form of education, although often rudimentary, was available to most whites and the civilizing effects of Christianity restrained many of the greedy and wilful. Social life had been transformed by the telegraph and railway, and the imprint of the latter was enormous. Journeys which had taken days and even weeks were reduced in time and immeasurably increased in comfort. People could move from one colony to the other, as well as within a colony, for business, pleasure or family reunions. City newspapers arrived in country districts on the day of printing, luxuries like ice as well as necessities were delivered to remote railway sidings and the days of bush lawlessness were over.

In much that the white people established, whether of the mind or in material things, there was little attempt to innovate on the ideas and forms that they brought with them. This was especially evident in the buildings, public and private, although the homes of the workers and the poor showed some distinctive variations from those of the past in the old countries. In the first decades of settlement necessity had also forced some variation from preconceived forms. Trees were plentiful so homes were built with timber footings and exteriors, bark roofs and earthen floors; the slab hut became the first symbol of the penetration of the continent. A roofed verandah was introduced, which proved effective in combating the heat of summer, provided a place of respite and enter-tainment in the evenings and a ready-made beginning to additions when another room or sleep-out was needed.

Bark for roofs, being porous, was unsatisfactory, so it was replaced by wooden shingles and they, in turn, by galvanized iron which, by the end of the nineteenth century, was giving way, in part, to terracotta tiles. The roof proved a useful catchment area for water, which was collected in tanks, both above and underground, and, given the low rainfalls and meagre creeks so prevalent in many inland areas, such a method proved vital to even reasonable domestic comfort. By mid-century weather-boards had replaced slabs for walls and clay had given way to floorboards so that the construction of the Australian home was settled. It varied from its English counterpart in the materials used and the addition of the ver-andah, while the widespread use of galvanized iron, even for walls, introduced an element of ugliness that only time and rust could soften.

The interior of most homes was simplicity itself with a centrally placed passageway from which, normally, four rooms ran off although two were often as many as the poor could manage. The kitchen had become part of the house by the 1890s and, in the sewered areas of the cities, the lavatory had moved into or adjacent to the bathroom. In the suburbs each house had a backyard with a clothes-line held up by a clothes-prop, a few fruit-trees and a patch for vegetables. Out the front of the house, if space permitted, exotic flowers, shrubs, trees and perhaps a lawn were estab-lished.

The older, inner suburbs had their rows of terraces, where life was enhanced due to proximity to markets and places of entertainment. The rough but efficient furniture of earlier times was being replaced with imitations of English styles, while prints of scenes familiar only to those

A REAR VIEW OF GLOUCESTER ST SHOWING CONSTRUCTION OF HOUSES
THE JOISTS ARE LET INTO THE ROCK ON ONE SIDE & ON THE OTHER ARE RESTING ON SIDE WALL OF HOUSES IN STREET BELOW
THE ROOFS ARE USED AS BACK YARDS FOR THE HOUSES ABOVE

All the cities had slum areas and this one in Sydney indicates that, despite the availability of space in Australia, economic conditions and habit resulted in close living in physically degrading circumstances.

born in, or who had visited, England and Europe adorned walls. In the homes of the more affluent there was a piano around which entertainment of a genteel kind prevailed while in others they made do with a fiddle. At Christmas, families groaned and sweated before turkey, roast chicken and plum puddings, and the heat was mocked by holly, strewn on a tree branch in the corner.

The main variation from the houses of the British Isles was in the tendency to build lightly-framed, semi-permanent structures in wood although the first brick veneer structure in the world was built at Swan Hill, Victoria, in 1850. The inner walls of houses were often made by covering the studs with hessian and then pasting paper over the hessian to keep out the wind and give some semblance of comfort. Such houses were built as cheaply as possible and they could be abandoned if unsaleable. It was not uncommon to move them from one place to another, as happened when gold-fields ran down. The vastness of the country, combined with the readiness of its inhabitants to pack up and move on, contributed a sense of impermanence to dwelling places and to aspects of life itself. Immigrants from countries where there was a solidity of houses, even if they were little more than slums, often found the Australian experience both different and daunting.

In some instances homes and public buildings of genuine beauty were constructed in sandstone, bluestone and other materials of a lasting nature that were locally available. The earliest building of merit, Old Government House at Parramatta, was begun under Hunter in 1799 and completed by Macquarie in 1816. It was a colonial replica of the country mansions of eighteenth century England, and, with chaste lines, classic portico and standing on a magnificent domain, it was a reminder of imperial authority in the days of penal servitude. Later governors in the other colonies built stately mansions none of which surpassed that at Parramatta for its quiet dignity.

The wealthy, who had become so from commerce or squatting, built imposing residences in town or country — Como in Melbourne, Carthona in Sydney, Ralahyne in Brisbane, and perhaps the finest of all, Booloominbah at Armidale in New South Wales. They all could have stood their own with the homes of the lesser gentry in England. In the cities, along Macquarie Street in Sydney, North Terrace in Adelaide and Collins Street in Melbourne, commerce and government constructed buildings of impressive grandeur, while the buildings of provincial towns, especially Bendigo and Ballarat, rivalled and in some measure surpassed those of the capitals. In Tasmania the simple Georgian houses of St John Street, Launceston, were a tribute to the restrained dignity of their owners. Nevertheless, nothing of all this said as much about the Australian experience as did the humble, flimsy bush home.

Church architecture soon developed into rudimentary Gothic as can still be seen from the ruins of the Anglican church at Port Arthur. St John's Catholic church at Richmond, Tasmania, began as a gem of colonial simplicity but was Gothicised in the late 1850s by alterations and a tower was added. Gradually the Gothic revival spread and some fine cathedrals were built in the capital cities, while the country towns rivalled each other with their smaller versions of the same. In Bendigo, the Catholics were able to draw on the financial legacy of a remarkable Prussian-born priest, George Backhaus, to construct a cathedral which is the finest ecclesiastical building in the land and only needs a genius working in paint or mosiacs to make it stand with some of the glories of Europe.

The familiar, the venerable and the proven had won in architecture. In only one type of building, the hotel, did the purely functional achieve a distinctive form before the end of the century. It was immediately recognizable to whoever was seeking refreshment, a meal or a bed or all three, as was often the case in a land where distances counted little and so many were on the move. The larger hotels were generally of two stories with the upper having a balcony, often encased in the ubiquitous cast-iron lace painted black or white. On the ground floor there were one or more bars, a private parlour for guests, a ladies lounge, billiard room, dining room and kitchen with the pervasively sweet odour of drink greeting the thirsty everywhere. Out the back stood the stables and perhaps a row of rooms for lodgers and the display of wares by commercial travellers. Upstairs the rooms were let, with shared bathrooms and lavatories in the middle of the corridor.

Some hotels were monuments to the affluence of a period, like Craigs in Ballarat and the Shamrock at Bendigo, which were built in the great days of gold. They were fit to lodge royalty or Australia's great singer Nellie Melba herself. In the smaller towns, the pubs, like the School of Arts Hotel, at Roma in Queensland, were the mecca for farmers and their wives on a Friday after shopping; to Catholics after Sunday Mass; to all for wedding receptions, club activities, electioneering and the exchange of news on the weather, wheat and wool prices, and the general woes and joys of life.

The Australian pub also enshrined the ethos of a society that, outside the home, revolved around the male and his need for companionship with his own kind, which had had its origins in the early pastoral period. Shouting by buying rounds of drinks in turn was everywhere prevalent and was regarded by some as the foundation stone of drunkenness and alcoholism. Marcus Clarke called Australia 'a nation of drunkards' and became one himself, while a steady stream of overseas visitors, so many of whom put their repetitious reminiscences in print, went out of their way to deplore the demon drink. Priests prayed, parsons railed and ladies ran temperance tea-and-cake parties to wean their men onto less potent

Hotels such as this one at Toronto, New South Wales, were a principal feature of all country towns. They served as centres of hospitality and community life, as well as resting places for travellers.

beverages. Meanwhile cordial factories and breweries abounded with every town of any consequence boasting one at least. Refinements in the brewing process and the use of refrigeration, which began in Victoria, gradually spread and beer replaced spirits as the staple drink, causing less harmful effects to the health and sanity of its devotees.

Three-quarters of the total population of 3,750,000 at the turn of the century were Australian-born. With two-thirds of that total being resident in New South Wales or Victoria, only one in three of its inhabitants living outside a city or town, Australians, in the main, were urbanites and easterners. Whatever minor differences arose amongst them, they generally shared a dual allegiance to Australia and Britain. Australia, to most, was the land of their birth but Britain was still called 'Home', even by many who had never visited there. Statues of Queen Victoria were common especially after her death in 1901. Little local tradition had been created so in the schools the teaching was necessarily British in content. The

Union Jack was run up on flagpoles outside schools on Monday mornings. Maps of the world, at school or in the homes, were splashed with a vast swathe of red to denote an Empire encircling the globe, with the high seas controlled by a 'Glorious Navy'. British symbols from bulldogs to Kipling, from Shakespeare to Dickens, war heroes from Drake to Wellington and the great universities of Oxford and Cambridge were treasured as part of the Australian heritage. The Irish did not stand aloof from all of this, especially in country areas where they normally attended government-run schools and, although they still heard stories of Ireland's woes, such things counted for little in a society where time, distance and some affluence had blurred memory, love and hatred.

The one thing that seemed to be lacking as Australia moved towards the new century was the administrative and political unity it had enjoyed in the days when the Governor of New South Wales was also governor of the whole. An attempt to revive this unity was made in 1851 when Charles Fitzroy was appointed Governor-General of all Queen Victoria's Australian possessions. The position had lapsed by 1856, but the idea of unity was taken up subsequently by some to whom colonies were unwholesome divisions. The differing fiscal policies created friction, especially between New South Wales, South Australia and Victoria, and local jealousies based on political factors negated any steps towards bringing the colonies under one government.

Interest in union was revived in the early 1880s, because external pressures engendered the fear that Germany had designs on New Guinea and that France had designs on the New Hebrides while her intention to make New Caledonia a convict base was regarded with suspicion. Internal developments also helped — the railways linked the eastern, mainland colonies, manufacturing ventures embraced an intercolonial market, and some newspapers and journals had a continental reading public. The trade unions were no longer local institutions but had become powerful inter-colonial bodies which saw themselves as representing workers throughout Australia. The lesson of the depression had pushed the middle classes into a realization that economic management needed inter-colonial co-operation rather than the rivalry which had been increasingly evident in tariff barriers and sterile competition.

The first step towards federation was taken with the formation of a Federal Council in 1883 with legislative powers over Australian relations with the Pacific and over the influx of criminals from New Caledonia. New South Wales, suspicious of the other colonies, stood aloof so that the existence of the Council was inconsequential and it last met in Melbourne in 1889. In that year the need for adequate defences was pressed home

The presence of many of the 'Founding Fathers' at this Federal Conference in Melbourne 1890 made it an important step towards federation. The participants were (l. to r.) *front row*: W. McMillan (NSW); J. Hall (NZ); J. Macrossan (Qld); D. Gillies (Vic); J. A. Cockburn (SA); J. G. Lee Steere; *back row*: A. J. Clark; Cap. Russell (NZ); S. Griffith (Qld); H. Parkes (NSW); T. Playford (SA); A. Deakin (Vic); B. S. Bird (Tas); G. S. Jenkins (Sec.).

by a British military advisor who feared that the continent would be vulnerable were it attacked, although he left it unclear by what power. On 24 October 1889 Henry Parkes seized the opportune moment to propose a conference to discuss a federation although neither he, nor anyone else, including the vast majority of the inhabitants who already thought of themselves as Australians, had any firm ideas on what it all meant.

Nevertheless, the Australian Natives Association in Victoria, some recently formed bodies in New South Wales called Federal Leagues and organizations with commercial interests gave the movement impetus. Over all the deliberations which ensued hung the shadow of depression, bank crashes and drought which made the economic motive of making Australia a safe place for investment strong. Nationalism, which already implied unity, had little to do with the whole development.

A conference was held in Melbourne in February 1890 attended by political leaders from all the colonies, including New Zealand, and it was agreed that tariffs were the main obstacle to federation. Parkes, with a fine turn of phrase about 'a crimson thread of kinship' running through them all, boosted hopes and it was decided to hold a convention to work out the exact nature of the proposed federal body. In March 1891 the convention met in Sydney, with Parkes in the chair, and a draft constitution, largely the work of Samuel Griffith, Premier of Queensland, was accepted. Griffith's draft was substantially adhered to throughout all the debates of the ensuing decade.

The central concept which governed all the deliberations was the need to retain autonomy for the colonies once they became states. The federal body was required to co-ordinate such vital matters as customs and defence, postal and telegraph services, currency, immigration and foreign affairs. Lawyer-politicians dominated the proceedings. In 1897–8 a bill, based on Griffith's original of 1891, was drafted to constitute the Commonwealth of Australia. Parkes, who died in 1896, never saw his work come to fruition, but he had firmly held that 'Australia ought to be Mistress of the Southern Seas'. With personal wealth per head considerably higher than in America it was safe to assume that his hope was well founded, temporarily at least.

The workers were not so sure of the future and spokesmen of their movement warned that federation would cause the Labor Party to be overwhelmed unless the proposed constitution was thoroughly democratic in electoral divisions. Unsurprisingly business interests saw much benefit from federation with one of their number saying it would provide them with 'a market as large as the whole of Australia', while imperial statesmen in Britain, realizing that there was no hope of bringing the whole Empire into an imperial federation, gave cautious assent to Australian federation.

After two referenda, five colonies voted in favour of the Constitution Bill with Western Australia waiting to see the outcome of the vote in the east. The Bill then passed through both Houses at Westminster between May and July 1900. Western Australia, led by its cautious Premier John Forrest, who had been one of the country's greatest explorers, joined at a referendum on 31 July. There was an overwhelming 'Yes' vote from the gold-fields, where a petition had been got up for separation if the Western Australians did not vote for federation and where most of the diggers were unaware that hitherto they had been anything but Australians. Although the Queen had some misgivings about the use of the word 'Commonwealth', preferring 'Dominion' instead, she consented to an entity called the Commonwealth of Australia coming into being on 1 January 1901.

Andrew Dawson was Queensland born and became a miner, editor and politician. As Premier of Queensland for a week in December 1899 he led the 'first Labor government in the world'. He became Minister for Defence in Watson's federal cabinet in 1904 but died estranged from the Party to which he had made a significant contribution.

The Constitution, on one level, was a triumph for common sense and it was partially modelled on the Canadian and United States experiments. On the other hand, recognition that Commonwealth meant a unity of separate bodies with their own sovereignity in internal matters was crucial to acceptance of the new federation. The number of members in the House of Representatives from each state was to be proportional to population, but the Senate was to have equal representation from each state in the hope that senators would serve the interests of their states rather than those of a party. It was an ideal to which the reality of political life soon put paid.

Federation did not come about quickly or easily, especially in New South Wales where a combination of uncertainty on the part of politicians, unease within the Labor Party and a reluctance to abandon free trade helped to confuse the electorate. In South Australia some manufacturers were unhappy about unrestrained competition from Victoria and their employees shared their fears. The negative vote in Queensland, where over forty percent of the voters who participated in the referendum were against federation, remained inexplicable except on the canefields where many workers did not feel themselves to be a part of Australia at all.

The majority of Australians were federationists although few got emotional or excited about the whole affair. The creation of the Commonwealth was a simple, public act ratifying what they internally accepted, the reality of white Australia. They had always been able to move from one part of it to the other, where they met the same kind of people, speaking the same way and eating, drinking and dressing with only minor variations. They were all proud of Melba as she won acclaim in the opera houses of Europe, of their cricketers as they beat the England team and of their soldiers who, like lion cubs, had 'rallied to the dam' in South Africa. In vain the *Bulletin* called the new flag of Union Jack and Southern Cross a bastard symbol of Australia. To most Australians the symbol was insignificant and nothing was made of the fact that federation, the most significant long ranging step in Australia's white history, had been achieved without any civil discord of an extreme kind. Only thirty years before a much smaller country, Italy, had won its unity after centuries of struggle and bloodshed.

There were three main groupings in the first Parliament. Edmund Barton, an urbane Sydney lawyer, was Prime Minister and leader of the Liberal Protectionists, who were convinced that progressive but judicious reform was the right path to progress. The Labor Party held the balance of power in both Houses. Led by John Watson, it differed from the

Liberals in that it wanted more radical and rapid reform, but Barton could rely on its support to govern. George Reid led the third group made up of Conservative Free-Traders. In effect they became the opposition and had little to say except that they were against protective tariffs, which meant that they were opposed to the Liberals, and that they would have no truck with socialism, by which they meant the Labor Party. There were some very able men in the first Cabinet — Deakin, Lyne, Turner, Kingston and Forrest — who added considerably to the prestige of the new Federal Parliament.

The days of early, penal Australia were also represented in the person of William Groom, member for the Darling Downs. Groom had come to Australia, aged sixteen, as a convict on the *Hashemy* in 1849. Six years later he was sentenced again on a charge of stealing gold and served time on the roads. Notwithstanding his past, he was six times mayor of Toowoomba and sat for over thirty years in the Queensland Parliament. His time was short in the Federal sphere as he died on 8 August 1901. His passing symbolized the end of an era — convict Australia was dead and buried and most Australians preferred to forget that it had ever been. William Groom, member of the House of Representatives, had reminded them briefly of its importance, although the last imperial convict, an original Fenian from the days of the *Catalpa* incident in Western Australia, was not pardoned until 1906.

Lacking its own place to sit, the Federal Parliament met in Melbourne although the Constitution had decreed that its eventual site was to be in New South Wales but at least 100 miles from Sydney. All those elected to Parliament showed a determination to keep Australia British, and all but two were bent on maintaining it as the possession of an exclusively white population. Barton knew that if they could run financial matters smoothly, deal firmly with the question of non-white immigration and leave the old colonies, now called states, to run their own affairs all would be well. In his resolve to keep the country white, Barton was ably assisted by his Collingwood-born Attorney-General, Alfred Deakin, who was member for Ballarat.

Deakin's temperate racism was oddly quirked as he wanted to deny entry to the Japanese because of their good qualities, which he feared would result in their outstripping the more leisurely Australians in endeavour. Labor, backing Barton to the hilt, had members who talked about the danger of making 'a mongrel nation' if 'the coloured sheep' were not culled to preserve its 'racial purity', and there was general agreement in the Parliament on these propositions. The decision to introduce a White Australia policy was a conscious one with which the vast majority of Australians agreed. It had its economic overtones, but no one reading or hearing the debates in the Commonwealth Parliament could have mistaken the general thrust of the arguments for the exclusion of non-whites — they were essentially racist.

Asiatics and the hapless Kanakas, who it was decided would be refused entry after 1904 and who were to be returned to their home islands by 1906, were the main butt of the exclusionist argument but colour itself was proposed as the forbidden factor by the Labor members. Those Kanakas who were born in Australia or who had been residents since 1879 could remain. Some of the rest had come voluntarily, a few happily, and there were those who feared to go back to the islands, but the law took its course. They were black and hence unwanted, and in the end 4,269 were returned 'home' while 1,654 were permitted to stay. For other coloured races the Parliament devised a dictation test of fifty words in a European language which could be given to unwanted immigrants. To appease the Japanese, European was later changed to any prescribed language, but the effect, in its power to exclude non-white or other undesirable entrants, was the same. In this way the Commonwealth, now ruling over a continent which 113 years previously had been the exclusive domain of a black race, ensured that, temporarily, its citizens would only be whites.

The Aborigines, depleted by disease and murder and disheartened at the loss of practically everything that had made them a people, had all but vanished from large parts of the continent. The remainder, nevertheless, continued to resist being submerged in the culture and social structures of the whites. The pernicious idea of the Great Chain of Being which placed the blacks one degree above brutes, the pseudo-scientific pronouncements of phrenologists who measured skulls and attempted to prove that the intellect of the black was inferior, and Darwin's survival-of-the-fittest theory combined to soothe the conscience of those who, for their own material gain, had contributed to the decline of a whole race. The tragedy of the part-Aborigines who could not merge into either society was apparent in the history of the Breelong blacks with the violent outbreak led by Jimmy Governor in north-central New South Wales in 1900. In 1972 Thomas Keneally's novel, *The Chant of Jimmy Blacksmith*, told the Governor story powerfully and brutally, and in 1978 it was made into a film.

In places where they still lived on in significant numbers, it was decided that protection was the best means of allowing the Aborigines to die out in peace and with some dignity. Reserves were set up in which they had to live unless they were permitted to take approved employment else-

An undated photograph of Aborigines in Perth Gaol. The custom of chaining blacks around the neck was common although this was not done to the convicts. Federation brought no change to the status of the Aborigines. They remained non-citizens of the new Commonwealth.

where. They were legally in the charge of their protectors, they could not receive old-age pensions and they had no status as citizens, which meant that they could not be counted in a census. Above all they were subject to the constraints of institutionalism and were often under the control of inept and unsympathetic bureaucrats. It was almost as if, now that the whites had taken all from them, the Aborigines were judged to be unable to cope for themselves in a land whose fullness they had once possessed.

The Aborigines were granted a form of equality in one area of importance to the whites. When their skills could be used cheaply, they were welcome in the workforce and the reserves became nurseries providing a cheap source of labour, for the pastoral industry in particular. The union movement, so resolutely opposed to coloured labour, encouraged them to join its ranks and, because of their particular aptitude, they were welcome as shearers and some participated in the shearers' strikes of the early 1890s.

At Broome, Beagle Bay and La Grange in the Kimberley, Christian missionaries had worked amongst the Aborigines since the 1880s. They had been treated badly as stockmen in the outback and even worse as pearl divers in the polyglot community which grew up around Broome. The efforts of the missionaries, whether Protestant or Catholic, were often without apparent success. Bishop Gibney of Perth thought the Aborigines were a 'splendid race' and another missionary said they were industrious, co-operative and friendly. Daisy Bates, her first marriage to 'Breaker' Morant now long in the past, worked with Gibney for the betterment of the Aborigines and lived herself amongst the Kimberley blacks for some months. Her vast, personal knowledge of Aboriginal languages, customs and beliefs, and her dignity as a white woman who went to live amongst them caused the blacks to name her Kabbarli or grandmother.

Many later critics took pains to decry the work of the Christian missionaries, condemning it as harmful and destructive at the worst and mere paternalism at the best. The missionaries did, however, perform one priceless task in that they awakened some form of conscientious response to the Aborigines amongst the whites. Without their civilizing influence there would scarcely be any full-blood Aborigines left as the missionaries worked at a time of unenlightened governments and a white community imbued with barbaric ideas which could have, as in Tasmania, resulted in the virtual extermination of the blacks.

In the same way as the population retained the major aspects of the parent societies in the British Isles, so also the religious denominations repeated in Australia the composition and flavour of their origins, and their beliefs were preached with the same emphasis and accents of their homelands. Religion was observed in a quiet and orderly manner without outbursts of fervent enthusiasm because the ostentatious, the unusual or the foolish was not the way of Australians. Methodism went through periods of restrained revivalism in New South Wales and South Australia, and its daughter the Salvation Army, first established in South Australia in 1881, grew rapidly and had representatives in all the colonies by 1891, when its founder, General William Booth, visited Australia to see for himself the progress it had made. No sects were born of any consequence, no martyrs made, and no saints proclaimed but every so often a bigot declaimed against the Catholic Church and its largely Irish adherents. Yet when the Archbishop of Sydney, Cardinal Moran, stood, unsuccessfully as it happened, as a candidate to represent New South Wales at the Constitution Convention in 1897 he was supported by many Protestants.

The secularization of education and of the state was carried out by men of principle who remained firmly committed to the Judaeo-Christian

tradition with its accompanying moral standards. They were also committed to the idea that church and state needed to be separate, although
they did not recognize that the virtual elimination of the Bible from the
schools would result in future generations losing one of the most precious
well-springs of their culture. In this society there was a determination to
bury forever the patronage, power, hatreds and divisions that had so
marked the history of the old world, but the spirit of Christianity
remained alive and only one person in 500 stated that he or she had no
religion. Nonetheless, the diverse denominations claiming to be Christian
resembled a spiritual Tower of Babel as they ranged from Bush Baptists
to Calathumpians with every other shade in between.

Hospitals, for which the governments met the capital costs, were
mainly run by charitable organizations and staffed by women — lay and
religious — and countless acts of unsung private charity sustained the
needy, especially in times of hardship like the 1890s. The positive change
in religious attitudes and the adherence to Christian values in England
after the middle of the nineteenth century had an effect on social legislation as many convinced Christians immigrated to the colonies. Votes
for women, factory acts, pensions and other similar enactments, often
hailed as indicative of a new spirit at work, had their basis in Christian
morality. Amongst those who thought, worked and made sacrifices of
time and money for the 'good' society, there were many who found
inspiration in Christian socialism. Edward Bellamy, whose influence on
the early Australian workers' movement through his novel *Looking
Backward* was greater than that of Karl Marx, taught that Christian socialism was the fulfilment of Christ's teaching on love for thy neighbour, and
many Australians worked with that as their ideal.

As a result, in the trade unions, throughout the Labor Party and
amongst the Liberals, there were many men and women prepared to
stand up not only for the poor and disadvantaged but also for the right of
the ordinary citizen, by virtue of work and frugality, to enjoy an ensured
and decent standard of living. The voices of Marx and other justifiable
exponents of international solidarity amongst workers were heard, and
in their wake followed claims to universal economic equality. Such claims
aroused unfilled hopes amongst some and moved others, who saw their
own wealth threatened, to attempt to negate the gains made by the
workers and their representatives.

By beating up the hare of international socialism, conservatives were
able to create unity amongst themselves and arouse groundless fears
amongst timid Australians. The Labor Party, while embracing wide
divergences of opinion within its ranks, settled down as a valid represen-

The undergraduate procession in 1903 was a joyous and colourful event for the students at Sydney University. By that year, there were four universities: Sydney (1850); Melbourne (1853); Adelaide (1874) and Tasmania (1890). Queensland (1909) and Western Australia (1911) soon followed. The early establishments were influenced by the Scottish universities and Trinity College, Dublin, and had a strong tradition of high-level pass degrees.

tative body of the generality of Australians and its, not infrequent, flirtings with doctrinaire creeds were always of short duration. Those ardent spirits whose purpose was the destruction rather than the containment of capitalism found the Labor Party a weak vessel and deserted it while others, no less ardent, remained in the Party to defend the defenceless and help to bring some measure of relief to the weak.

The signs of a new age were everywhere apparent: in the extension of street lighting to the large country towns, together with water, street curbing and guttering, although drainage and sewerage, even in the cities, were often lacking. The cinema and the motor car, X-rays, fast dances and fancy drinks all vied with the horse and buggy, the theatre, the quack, stately waltzes and rum. With the introduction of the hydraulic lift, higher buildings became feasible and in 1889 the construction of the twelve-storey Australian Provincial Life Assurance Building on the corner of Elizabeth Street and Flinders Lane gave Melbourne one of the tallest buildings in the world. The bicycle had become the most popular means of transport with the introduction of low wheels and pneumatic tyres, and by 1900 there were two cycle paths in Sydney. In the bush the bicycle meant that workers no longer had to walk from place to place in search of a job. Progress, sacred to some and acceptable almost to all, was ascendant and to stand against it was useless.

On 9 May 1901 Melbourne staged the opening of the first Federal Parliament in its Exhibition Building. The honours were done by the Duke of York, 'Australia' was sung and Tom Roberts painted the scene. In the House of Representatives a formidable group of members took responsibility for the new Commonwealth. Very few of them were new to politics, because ten had been premiers of their colonies, twenty-two had been ministers and fifty-eight were experienced as former members of colonial parliaments. Proud that they were the foundation members of the new democracy, they undertook their task with much seriousness and, because Christianity was still the firmly accepted religion of the majority of the people, they began their deliberations with a plea for God's help and the recitation of the Lord's Prayer.

Despite the pageantry and the optimism, all was not well in the Commonwealth for the longest of all droughts had not broken and sheep numbers had dropped by half, but gold, sugar and wheat helped hold up the economy. Nevertheless, there was much optimism, for unity had been achieved without much rancour or division and the social cohesion that existed was the product of material success. Spiritually, the new Australia was an infant because no great cause, no overwhelming catastrophe, no response to a sign transcending the mundane had contributed to its birth. Australia had been federated because a few men of commonsense, motivated by high motives of patriotism and lesser ones of profit, had said, 'Let there be an Australia'. It was left to others to consummate the vision.

CHAPTER ELEVEN

The Fledgling Commonwealth

The first, and for a short time only, Commonwealth public servant was Robert Garran, who was appointed on 1 January 1901 as secretary to the Attorney-General's Department and parliamentary draftsman. He acted as his own clerk and messenger, wrote the first *Government Gazette*, personally delivered it to the printer and then, almost single-handed, organized the first federal elections without the benefit of an electoral law to guide him. He said that he felt reasonably sure that justice had been done to the contending parties. As seven out of nine of the first Cabinet were lawyers, he probably felt that he was being closely scrutinized. In his spare time, Garran saw to the setting up of the first Commonwealth departments.

A totally new structure had to be developed at the federal level. It could draw upon the previously existing colonial departments in the case of the new Commonwealth Departments of Customs, Defence and Postmaster General's. The others — Prime Minister's, Home Affairs, Treasury, and Attorney-General's itself — were entirely new. Garran worked indefatigably, and he was chiefly responsible for the smooth beginning of the Commonwealth structure, while his insistence on 'clear, straightforward language, free from technical jargon' became for a time a model which others imitated. In collaboration with John Quick, Garran wrote the classic *An Annotated Constitution of the Australian Commonwealth* (1901) and by his retirement in 1932 he had served as permanent head of a Commonwealth Department for thirty-two years and had been the trusted counsellor of sixteen governments.

A Public Service Commissioner was appointed to ensure that entry into the service was competitive and that promotion was based on merit

rather than patronage. It was readily accepted that, if the federal structure was to work effectively, judges had to be appointed to the new High
Court with the skills necessary to determine the meaning of the Constitution. The matter was particularly important in the sphere of state rights

When Nellie Melba came home to Australia in 1902 she received a tumultuous
welcome and the takings at one concert in Sydney reached a world record figure. John
Norton's accusations that she was a drunkard, publicised in the Sydney *Truth*, caused
outrage. Melba ignored him.

given that each state was to retain a large measure of self-government. By 1903 the High Court was set up. Its prestige was enhanced by the fact that Barton resigned as Prime Minister to sit on it as Senior Judge, Samuel Griffith, who was the principal framer of the Constitution, was Chief Justice and the third member was Richard O'Connor, who had also worked on the Constitution. Therefore the first High Court was in a position to interpret a document which its members had helped formulate.

Meanwhile, the fledgling Commonwealth was watched closely by the custodians of the parent society in Britain. Some saw evidence of 'racial decline' proved, in their eyes, by the relentless pursuit of wealth, a mania for sport, lack of an intellectual life and an appalling pronunciation. In their judgement the eight-hour day and trade union activity had led to laziness, which, incredibly, bore as its fruits the depression of the 1890s. Despite their acquisition of voting rights in the federal sphere, Australian women in general were accused by some observers of lacking education and refined manners. Since her debut at Brussels in 1897, Nellie Melba had been successful on the continent and at Covent Garden. She came home to a tumultuous welcome in 1902 and made £21,000 from concerts in Sydney and Melbourne alone. She noted that the country was still gripped by drought and that much in it was crude and antiquated. She was pained to find that people everywhere had little appreciation of their proper role in society; this was particularly true of female servants, which her cook proved by refusing to work on a Sunday. Nellie failed to observe that most female domestics still worked in harsh conditions with keep and wages as low as 10s per week for up to a hundred hours work. In her turn the English writer and commentator on social conditions, Beatrice Webb, said that bad manners, pretentious dress and a marked lack of refined taste were predominant amongst women everywhere she deigned to go.

Amidst the rhetoric there were serious voices, including that of the former Victorian Minister for Education, Charles Pearson, who said that Australia, with its reliance on state interference in the economy and social life, the increasing public debt and the swollen growth of the cities was a deplorable example for other white peoples. In general the common denominator of English opinion was that somehow Australia had been wayward. It had not become another England, it showed every sign of being turbulent and, above all, it had mismanaged British capital. John Fortescue, previously noted as a military historian, summed it up by saying that worshipping state socialism was an inevitable road to disaster, although the effective survival of Australia through the depression silenced him.

Despite these criticisms, it was clear that there would be no social revolution in an Australia where the reformers were apace with, if not ahead of, organized unrest. After all the talk of a social laboratory, it was ironical that when Tom Mann, the British trade union leader, was in Australia he was disappointed in 1904 at the way in which the leaders of the Australian workers, whether trade unionists or in the Labor Party, seemed bent on 'civilizing' rather than destroying capitalism. Those leaders were conscious that their strength lay in votes and persuasion. They were prepared to use power sensibly when given the chance, but as yet the Labor Party could not govern alone. John Watson's first Labor government in 1904 lasted four months, which proved that without a majority in Parliament power was so transient as to be futile. Clearly the road to a majority was to persuade enough voters that Labor would govern in the best interests of all. As the Brisbane *Worker* said, it was possible to do greater harm to capitalism with a vote than with a strike.

One remarkable feature of the early years of the Commonwealth was the resilience of rural Australia during the long drought. Nothing had prepared squatters and farmers for such a catastrophe. With sheep numbers fallen so dramatically, the wheat crop yielding less than a tenth of the pre-drought harvest, rabbits eating what feed remained, and dust clouding the skies, many small settlers left their few acres with all hope lost. Their wives battled the hardships alongside their menfolk, working long hours inside and outside the homestead and trying to make ends meet when there was a shortage of food or clothing. Often the survivors on large properties were unable to tap a source of capital to tide them over. As a consequence, they were forced to run up debts with local stores and mortgage their land to stock and station companies. The drought was generally eased by 1904 and good times came again, but its effects were not forgotten, especially in the inland parts of New South Wales and in Queensland although in coastal areas the effects were not as bad.

Amidst such matters as drought and depression and the return of the troops from the Boer War, only a few of the more serious-minded noticed the warning of the eminent statistician Timothy Coghlan that the birth rate had been in decline since 1870 when it was thirty-eight per 1000 to twenty-seven in 1900. A Royal Commission into the matter blamed the decline in births on selfishness and stated that white Australia could not be maintained unless the rate of national procreation went up. The depression and unemployment, the previously unrestrained development of grim suburbs and the increasing cost of maintaining a family under a policy of compulsory education were not seen as other factors contributing to the decline. Nevertheless, with its own statistical analysis, the Commission was not wide of the mark in predicting that, with such a trend, there would only be seven million Australians in 1948 and twenty million would not be achieved until the year 2017. The economic climate persuaded trade unionists to oppose any widespread immigration, including that from Britain, in the first five years of the Commonwealth, so no one hoped for relief from that quarter.

The young Commonwealth attempted to continue the work on social legislation begun earlier in the colonies, particularly in the field of disputes between employers and employees. Labor politicians saw indus-

Australians were to be united in a Federal Commonwealth on and after the first day of January 1901. The *Australia Act*, 1986 removed the last constitutional links between Australia and Britain although the position of the Queen as Queen of Australia remained unaltered.

trial legislation as the means to ensure good conditions and adequate wages, while the more conservative view was that such legislation served only to restrain employers or employees from harming the community by lock-outs or strikes. The problem for the Commonwealth was whether it possessed powers in a dispute which was restricted to one state. In 1903 a strike amongst railway workers brought the role of the Commonwealth to the fore.

Labor, holding that the states were powerless in disputes affecting industries with an inter-state element such as the seamen and the railway workers, wanted an arbitration system which would apply to the whole continent. Deakin held out for state rights, but when George Reid became Prime Minister in 1904 he managed to establish a Federal Court of Conciliation and Arbitration, which, as required by the Constitution, only had power over interstate disputes. The very creation of the Federal Court helped to clarify the relationship of the Commonwealth to the states. It also gave the trade unions a more public and responsible role and brought out the great talents of Henry Bournes Higgins, who became the second President of the Arbitration Court.

Higgins brought down the most far-reaching decision in Australia's industrial history on 8 November 1907. The facts in the case were simple but the social ramifications immense. For each harvester made by H.V. McKay at Sunshine in Victoria, McKay had to pay the Commonwealth £6 in excise duty, unless he could prove that his workers received 'fair and reasonable' wages. This requirement was part of Deakin's 'New Protection' which had been introduced to ensure that manufacturers who benefited from tariffs on competing imports should charge reasonable prices and pay reasonable wages, as well as ensure decent conditions for their workers.

In Higgins's view to tell a Court to interpret 'fair and reasonable' was an act lacking both qualities, but he brought in his judgement nonetheless and ruled against McKay. He decided that profits did not enter into the matter, likening the hiring of labour to buying raw materials. Taking as his norm the requirements of an unskilled labourer with four dependents who needed to live in 'frugal comfort' in a civilized community, he ruled that such a man ought to be paid £2 2s for a six-day working week. Higgins ignored the fact that many men had no dependents, or more or less than four. Equally he ignored women with dependents, many of whom worked in factories for less than £1 per week. In effect, his judgment enshrined the principle of a male minimum wage based on the need of the worker to receive rather than on the ability of industry to pay. It also established the family as the central unit of the industrial workforce and, as a corollary, the dependence of women on men. The history of wage fixing in Australia for nearly seventy years always looked back to the Harvester judgment. Over the years, it assumed legendary status, almost in the way Magna Carta had done in the disputes between the king and the barons.

The second Prime Minister, Alfred Deakin, was first and foremost a philosopher but he threw himself wholeheartedly into politics. He never reaped the rewards that sometimes befall those whose gifts are unsurpassed by their peers. Needing the support of Labor to govern, he found that he could only apply his principles provided Labor concurred. In some ways he led, in others he was pushed, but in the end, dispirited and broken in health, he had nowhere to turn for constant support except to that group of so-called liberals, protectionists and conservatives which he assuredly despised. They had already discovered that by making noises against the 'socialist tiger', which, in the words of Reid, would turn 'the free citizens of the Commonwealth into members of one great Government gang', they could awaken a response in those who feared socialism. Deakin was sensible and just and he realized that Labor's posturings about collective ownership of the means of production were unrealistic and, to the extent that they were not, would be rejected by a staunchly conservative electorate, which applauded moderate change when it served its own interests.

Labor itself was beginning to sense that the time to govern in its own right was coming as its vote kept increasing at succeeding elections, the trade union movement was growing and the Catholic vote was solidly behind it. In 1908 the Party withdrew its support from Deakin and Andrew Fisher formed the second Labor government. Under this pressure, Deakin fused his liberal followers with those who had previously espoused Free Trade and a new Liberal Party was born. The result was that Labor could not maintain its majority, and after only six months in office, Fisher, bemused at the turn of events, was out of office. Deakin's act inaugurated the beginning of two party politics and thereby gave the electors some chance of knowing where candidates stood on policy issues. Furthermore, the 'Fusion' clearly identified the Labor Party, for the first time, as a distinctive force in its ownright. Under these circumstances the Labor Party had no choice but to try to win sufficient support from the electorate to govern securely without support from other parties. To embark on such a course was to ensure that the voices of the socialists who still remained within the Party would henceforth cry in the wilderness of pragmatism.

For the third and last time, Alfred Deakin was sworn in as Prime

Minister on 2 June 1909, and he continued to foster and implement moderate and progressive policies. By his life's work, he deserves to be remembered as the part creator and foremost defender of federation. In his resistance to state aggression, his bridling of centralist tendencies and his promotion of harmonious relations between the Commonwealth and the states, he remained firm to those qualities of the Constitution which were lasting in value. Charming, brilliant and totally committed to the welfare of his country, Deakin was also, according to Garran, utterly sincere and straight-forward and he hated 'political tricks, manoeuvres and opportunism'. In Deakin, genuine liberalism had meaning because he believed in destroying class privilege and in abolishing laws against trade unionism. His ideal was a just and progressive Australia in which the poor, the sick and the old would all be protected, and policies implemented to give equal political rights to all citizens without regard to wealth or standing. With his passing as Prime Minister in April 1910 and his retirement in 1913, Australia lost the services of one of her greatest sons.

During the first decade of the Commonwealth, Australians began to perceive that their future was bound up, not merely with the mother country but also with other countries in the region. It was being realized that Australia was a large island continent with a small, white population situated in the south of the vast Pacific and Indian Oceans. In any case, Britain had its own worries with the emergence of a powerful Germany, which was increasing its presence in the North Sea. The Boxer Rebellion had broken out in China in 1900 and 451 volunteers from New South Wales and Victoria left to help put it down but, surprisingly, no fears were raised of a Chinese invasion of Australia. Closer to home, there was, however, concern about the responsible administration of Papua. As early as 1883, Queensland had 'annexed' the south-eastern portion of New Guinea but Britain refused to ratify the act, and in 1884 it set up a British protectorate there based on Port Moresby. Four years later Britain formally annexed the territory itself and, under the moderately enlightened rule of William MacGregor as administrator, the urge of the settlers and traders to exploit the natives was at least curbed.

The Commonwealth reluctantly undertook responsibility for British New Guinea in 1902 and in 1906 it became the Australian Territory of Papua. However, effective Commonwealth control was spasmodic and chaotic until the appointment of John Hubert Plunkett Murray as Lieutenant-Governor in 1908. Murray was a generally benevolent ruler who supported the settlers while remaining friendly with the natives, whom he defended and encouraged. Australian involvement in Papua, how-

John Hubert Plunkett Murray (third left) succeeded F.R. Barton (head of table) as administrator in Papua in 1908. He was liberal and humane, and at his death in 1940 the Papuan people mourned him.

ever, could not disguise the fact that other nations had firmly entrenched interests in the Pacific. The Germans were in charge of north-eastern New Guinea, New Britian and New Ireland, the Dutch had held the western half of New Guinea since 1828 and France's involvement in New Caledonia and its interest in the New Hebrides were well known. All of these were distant, European powers but Japan was geographically located in the Pacific and it was undergoing change.

Britain had signed a treaty with Japan in 1902 which, ironically, made Japan Australia's ally in the Pacific. In 1904 the Japanese inflicted ignominious defeats on the Russians, which aroused fears that Japan was no longer a slumbering volcano but one awakening and likely to erupt the 'Yellow Peril' down upon Australia and endanger its white people and its peaceful prosperity. Henry Lawson begged in vain 'Hold them, Ivan', for it was already clear that Russia, a major European power, was no match for the Japanese. With no foreign policy of its own, no defence forces of significance and no diplomatic representatives overseas, Australia left concern for its security to Britain. Nevertheless, a first, scarcely noticeable, crack in the bond of imperial relations took place in 1905 when

Deakin said that 'next to our own nation we place our kindred in America' and tentatively looked to the Americans as possible defenders in the Pacific. This role was refused but the visit of the sixteen ships of the 'Great White Fleet' from the United States in 1908 reassured all Australians that American dominance in the Pacific was sufficient to dispel any fears from Japan.

Despite the cries of nationalists at the time of federation, it was decided to continue hiring an Australian squadron from the British Navy, thereby avoiding the huge cost involved in having one built. Likewise, it was agreed that a small standing army would be sufficient for defence, although it had to be commanded by an Englishman, Major-General Edward Hutton, as the Defence Minister thought it proper to get 'one of the best men in the Empire to start this machine'. The title 'Royal Australian Navy' was made official in 1911, and in 1913 an Australian Navy of seven vessels sailed into Sydney Harbour, led by the battle-cruiser HMAS *Australia*. Under Vice-Admiral Creswell, who rightly became known as the 'Father of the Royal Australian Navy', it was no longer under British command. The event was one of much national pride, of avowals of loyalty to England and of the determination to maintain responsibility for Australia and thereby contribute to the 'fabric of Empire', which was held to be the guarantor of peace in the world.

If there was minimal strategic significance in such a minuscule navy, it was clearly possible to build a citizens' militia, as distinct from a standing army. The Labor Party, with William Morris Hughes beating the drum of national defence, had included compulsory military training in its platform, despite opposition from members of the trade union movement, who asked what it was that the working class found worthy of defence. They were threatened with prosecution and reminded that sufficient individuals, invariably sanctified with the title 'the people' on such occasions, were in favour of compulsory military training, which made all opposition absurd. No one needed reminding that a policy as odious to other races as the White Australia policy may eventually require to be defended in ways that were not merely verbal.

The British Field-Marshal, Kitchener, arrived by invitation in 1909 and visited the military installations in each state. He set the seal of authority on the planned militia, and 1911 saw military training made compulsory for all males aged twelve to twenty-five. Isolation from any form of organized and militant solidarity amongst workers, the prevailing ethos of pragmatism and loyalty to Empire, and the already formulated plans of German mobilization in Europe had turned the ears of the Labor leaders away from those voices proclaiming the insanity of war. Temporarily, opposition to compulsory military training on the part of a minority was silenced by grossly unjust and repressive measures, which resulted in nearly 28,000 prosecutions and 5,732 citizens being imprisoned in military gaols in the following three years.

Rumours of war did not prevent the government proceeding with other developments in the new Commonwealth. In early 1913 the valley of the Molonglo River, nestling amongst gentle hills on the southern tableland of New South Wales, was still a place of much solitude, as well as being in a drought. By Wednesday 12 March, all had changed. The river was swollen and the land green and lush from rain. More significantly, the tranquillity had gone forever because on that day the new capital of Australia was launched and christened with its ancient Aboriginal name of Canberra. The choice of the site had taken until 1908 with much travel, restless nights, banter and bandwaggoning amongst federal politicians and their staffs. Dalgety, Tumut and the Yass–Canberra area were the final contenders and the latter won by six votes over Dalgety in the House of Representatives and by two over Tumut in the Senate.

The Minister for Home Affairs was King O'Malley. Of uncertain origins, possibly Canadian or American, he fluctuated from the sane and wise to the flamboyant and unbalanced. Two of his ideas for the new Capital Territory were of the latter variety, for he wanted to call it 'Shakespeare' and keep it dry of all alcoholic beverages. He succeeded with his wowserism — to the intense discomfort of a generation of residents of the capital who had to travel to nearby Queanbeyan to quench their thirst. The proceedings by the Molonglo on 12 March failed to impress many Australians, who thought that the whole undertaking of building a capital city was insane, extravagant and pointless. The die was cast, however, and the bush capital was started in a place of such natural beauty that others eventually concluded that only Providence could have guided politicians to choose it. As a symbol the capital was already one of white supremacy, for the old Aboriginal people of that region had long since departed, leaving their traces only in the lilting softness of its place names and in some of their mixed-blood descendants.

The generality of Australian citizens went about their business paying little heed to the doings of their politicians except at election time. After the introduction of compulsory voting in Queensland in 1914, the practice spread to the Commonwealth in 1924, and then to the other states, although South Australia resisted the move until 1942. Such a procedure caused the citizens at least to go through the formality of casting a vote.

Sometimes voices were raised about the expense of maintaining seven separate Parliaments, six Governors and the Governor-General, all of whom were imported from Britain to keep up the vaunted ties of Empire. The voices went unheeded. The growth in rulers, both elected and nominated, was matched and outstripped by a greater one in public servants very few of whom, on the federal level, were located in Canberra for many years to come.

The growth in the public sector was partly due to the determination to maintain the full apparatus of government in the colonies until 1900 and, latterly, in the states. It also came about because of the successive waves of new people who had come to Australia since the 1830s. In the ten years 1904–14, the reawakened desire to populate the continent saw another wave of 400,000 immigrants from Britain. Their reliance on government assistance, in most cases both for their passage and settling, helped the growth of the public sector as had been the case in previous generations of immigration.

This influx of immigrants, of whom half were assisted by state governments, depended upon the boisterous economy. This was the result of a remarkable regrowth of flocks after the drought, which yielded a record clip of 1,400,000 bales of wool in 1906 that was mostly sold to Britain. The management of flocks on such a scale would have necessitated a much increased workforce had it not been for the remarkable development in the breeding of border collie and kelpie sheep dogs in the 1870s and 1880s. Notable among the developers of the kelpie was John Quinn of Cootamundra who won a sheep-dog trial at Temora, New South Wales, with a black-and-tan kelpie, Clyde. This dog sired the legendary blue kelpie, Coil, which won trial after trial and became the progenitor of a noted strain of prize-winning working dogs.

In time it became possible for comparatively large flocks to be managed by one man, mounted on a horse and accompanied by one or two dogs. The unity and understanding of man and dog in the control of sheep became a fundamental feature of the whole pastoral industry. It soon became a pastoral axiom that a good sheep-dog was worth two men and the skill and faithfulness of the drover's dog was commemorated in verse:

> And whether its Toby, or Toss or Nell,
>   And whether its wool or meat,
> He will work all day, and at night as well,
>   Till the pads wear off his feet.

There were similar and equally valuable developments in the breeding of dogs for the cattle industry. The Australian blue-heeler cattle dog, the only pure-bred cattle dog in the world, evolved in the 1890s from crossing the smooth-haired Scotch collie with the dingo, dalmatian and kelpie. The blue heeler fulfilled all the requirements of a cattle dog. It proved capable of working with horses and bullock teams, as well as looking after stock in the wild bush, and guarding the owner's property, in days when stealing horses, saddles and bridles was a lucrative profession. As with the flock owners, cattlemen said 'a good cattle dog is a man's living.' The cattle dogs proved especially valuable with the opening of the Canning Stock-Route in Western Australia in 1906. It was the longest stock-route in the world stretching for more than 900 miles and on it cattle could be overlanded from Halls Creek in the Kimberleys to the railhead at Wiluna by passing through some of the most arid regions of the continent.

The increase in the production of wheat was due in no small measure to the work of one man, William Farrer. He arrived in Australia in 1870 and worked as a tutor at Campbell's property, Duntroon, at Canberra, which in 1911 became the site of the Royal Military College. Farrer settled near Queanbeyan in 1886 to devote his life to improving wheat strains, as he was convinced that many of the types then in use were not suited to Australian conditions. Without any specialist knowledge of genetics, he cross-bred Indian, Canadian and older, established Australian strains to produce one he called 'Federation' in 1901. It became the basis of wheat growing for many years across the continent. Farrer was never entirely successful in developing a fully rust-resistant strain, but his devotion and skill put wheat growing in a position from which it never looked back for eighty years, especially when it was combined with the introduction and then the widespread use of superphosphates and chemical fertilizers.

Despite the introduction of migrant workers, the demand for labour remained high, especially in places, like Western Australia, where railway construction was still going ahead. Nonetheless, unemployment still failed to fall below a six percent national average, as much labour was seasonal and many young people were still drifting to the cities, causing industrial unemployment despite the rapid development in the manufacturing and building industries. Unemployment caused resentment amongst a workforce which thought that state expenditure on immigration was foolish and strikes took place at Broken Hill and on the coalfields in New South Wales. The Labor Party expressed concern at these trends and seemed to sound the right note with the electorate, because it was the first party to achieve a majority in both Houses when in the elections of 1910, with 49.97 percent of the votes, it won over half the seats.

Andrew Fisher, as Prime Minister, implemented the decision taken at

Racial prejudice, especially against the Chinese, was deeply ingrained into the ethos of White Australia. The prejudice was revealed sometimes in accusations that non-whites were carriers of such lethal diseases as leprosy.

the 1905 Labor Conference which decreed that Cabinet be elected by all the Labor members in Parliament — the caucus. It was a procedure which became a source of irritation and frustration to successive Labor Prime Ministers. Faced with an array of ministers chosen on factional, state or mateship lines the Prime Minister could do no more than designate their portfolios and hope that time and luck would prove him right. Fisher retained the Treasury for himself and made Billy Hughes his Attorney-General. Although Scottish in origin and formerly a coalminer by trade, Fisher decided to order a motor car for his use, unlike Alfred Deakin who either rode a bicycle or took the tram to Parliament daily. Fisher was a man of wide, sound and moderate views, and he fondly hoped to see women representatives in the Federal Parliament, a hope which was not realized in his lifetime.

The Labor government lasted until 1913 and oversaw a period of hitherto unmatched reform. In the minds of many of its members, there were memories of the bank crashes of the 1890s and they were determined to avoid any repetition of a catastrophe which had brought much suffering to the poorer classes. As a result, they were committed to the foundation of a Commonwealth Bank, which King O'Malley in particular had spoken of for years, and legislation for its foundation was passed in 1911. The new, government-guaranteed, savings bank was a competitor with the private banks for deposits. It introduced a national currency and thereby displaced the notes put in circulation by private banks. With the addition in 1913 of the role of a trading bank, it was financially profitable and it was directed by a governor appointed by the Parliament, to which he was responsible. For a time, its very existence, like that of the Labor Party, helped to restrain capitalism in some of its excesses.

As the first Labor government of any consequence, Fisher's had a chance to implement in its own right a series of policies, some of which derived from the Deakin era while others were distinctively its own. Old-age pensions were extended, those for invalids started and a maternity allowance of a £5 'baby bonus' was granted in 1912, though Aboriginal, Asian and Pacific Islander mothers were excluded from receiving it. Piecemeal arrangements were made to solve federal and state financial relations, with the states being compensated £1. 5s per capita of population for their loss of revenue from customs and excise. Railway construction was undertaken to the extent that Australia ranked first in the world on miles per head of population and in 1912 construction began on the line from Port Augusta in South Australia to Kalgoorlie in Western Australia so as to link east and west.

In 1910 the first Australian coins were minted to replace English coins, and in 1913 the first Australian postage stamps were introduced when the Commonwealth took over from the states the whole of the postal services. The government courageously implemented a land tax on un-improved properties worth more than £5,000 in order to break up the large holdings into small farms. Much resentment was aroused at this measure despite the fact that it achieved little in land reform, but some urban holdings were affected and the revenue raised was considerable. Fisher was irritated that the Constitution restricted the powers of the Commonwealth in industrial disputes and, wanting to extend its control over trade and nationalize monopolies, he tried twice, unsuccessfully, to have it changed by referendum.

The members of the Constitution had ensured that no one could idly tamper with their legacy to the nation. To this end they had written clauses into it which safeguarded its text and meaning by requiring that it could only be changed when a majority of the electors in a majority of states voted in favour of a change. In these instances, on trade and on monopolies, as in so many subsequent ones, the electorate voted against change, although narrowly in the second instance. No one had ever asserted that the Constitution was engraven on stone; equally no one henceforth imagined that it could be toyed with at will, or even that it could be changed at the wish of a majority of Australians, which even-tually resulted in many of its clauses being anachronisims.

The early years of the Commonwealth widened the horizons of poli-ticians and public servants, who hitherto had seen themselves as respon-sible for one or other colony only and their new concerns were partic-ularly evident in regard to the Northern Territory and the Antarctic. The settlement of the Northern Territory, an area of half a million square miles, had been one of fits and starts since 1849, when Port Essington was abandoned for the second time. In 1863 it was annexed to South Aus-tralia although it retained its name of Northern Territory. The govern-ment in Adelaide, with that zeal for good order and land development so evident in the previous thirty years, proceeded, unsuccessfully, to intro-duce Wakefieldian theories into settling the sub-tropics. The town of Palmerston was renamed Darwin and became the main centre, but all interest in the north was lost after the gold discoveries at Pine Creek and other places in the 1870s. In the appalling conditions of heat, distance, lack of water and general amenities on the fields, only some Chinese survived to help found the cosmopolitan population of Darwin. Meanwhile, the north remained unattractive to white settlers.

It was agreed that without a railway linking north and south no pro-gress in developing the north would be made so, gradually, a line crept from Darwin to Pine Creek and from Adelaide to Oodnadatta leaving a not inconsiderable gap of 1,800 kilometres. In 1907 South Australia gave up the burden of trying to administer the north and passed the whole Territory to the Commonwealth. This step finally took effect on 1 January 1911. The Australian taxpayer thereby incurred a public debt of over £10,000,000 while the total annual revenue from the lease of 150,000 square miles of the Territory was a meagre £9,000. It was not an auspicious beginning to Commonwealth control although great pastoral properties running cattle herds had flourished, especially on the Barkly Tableland, since the 1880s. An administrator with a staff of nine was appointed to run the Territory, but further development of any consequence had to await the beginning of World War II.

For well over a century, there had been interest in the vast land mass to the south of the Australian continent but it was spasmodic and ineffective. Few even knew anything practical about Antarctica, although its connection with the origins of white Australia was close. On his second voyage of discovery, Cook had left Cape Town on 23 November 1772 and struck south. A few weeks later his small vessels were surrounded by

The Expedition to the Antarctic led by Douglas Mawson 1911–13 was regarded as the greatest and best executed of all and marked him as one of the most prominent explorers of modern times. This lantern slide of the *Aurora* was taken by John Hunter, biologist of the expedition.

islands of ice and, penetrating these, they crossed the Antarctic Circle on 17 January 1773. Twelve months later Cook ventured even further, where he rightly claimed that no man before him had gone further south. His Antarctic voyages sealed his reputation as one of the greatest navigators of all the ages.

After Cook, intermittent voyages were made in the nineteenth century but it was not until 1895 that a party of Norwegians landed at Cape Adare and Carsten Egeberg Borchgrevink was the first man to set foot on the Antarctic continent, an area twenty percent larger than Australia and the coldest, highest and windiest of the continents. Among those that followed were Amundsen, Scott, Shackleton, Edgeworth David and Mawson. Professor Edgeworth David claimed the whole area for the British Empire when he and Mawson reached the south magnetic pole on 16 January 1908. By 1911 the Antarctic was the object of attention by parties from Britain, Japan, Germany and Norway, so Mawson was commissioned to sail south and hoist the flag on land deemed to be geographically Australia's own province. Mawson was Professor of Geology at Adelaide University but his interest in the Antarctic was such as to link his name with it for all time. He set up headquarters at Commonwealth Bay and his party suffered great hardship but much useful exploratory work was done in the next two years, including a survey of a thousand miles of the continent's coastline. As a result, the Australian public, already aware of the Antarctic through the tragic loss of Scott, began to think of it as closely connected to their own continent, although what use it would ever serve was not readily discernible. In 1936 an area comprising forty-two percent of the continent was declared as the Australian Antarctic Territory, and eventually three permanent bases were established there for scientific purposes. In 1991 the Antarctic Treaty, signed by some thirty nations, will come up for review, when Australia's future in the Antarctic will be decided.

Throughout the Australian continent, the motor car was already the chosen means of transport for the people of more ample means, while those with less often used a motor cycle. Cars had rapidly captured the general interest and their use resulted in changes in women's clothing, as bustles and trains were uncomfortable on the seats of T-model Fords. Furthermore cars so disturbed pedestrians and horses as to warrant them and their drivers being required to have licences and the Automobile Club of Australia was founded to protect motorists' interests. Melbourne's Harley Tarrant managed to start a local car industry, but competition from overseas importers, especially Ford, restricted his market so that he only built sixteen cars. His Tarrant was clearly suited

The Dunlop Trial from Adelaide to Melbourne in 1905 had only one woman entry, Mrs Thomson of Adelaide. She drove a Wolseley two cylinder and arrived sedately, to a gracious welcome.

to Australian conditions, and its prototype came equal with imported cars in the 1905 Melbourne to Sydney reliability trial over roads that were still so primitive as to be little improved on the bullock tracks of half a century before.

Amongst the most creative of all Australian inventors was Henry Sutton, born in Ballarat in 1856. Although without formal scientific education, Sutton proved to be a prodigy in the scientific and technical field. He was the first Australian to experiment with heavier than air materials for flight, his electric motor contributed substantially to the growth of the electrical industry and his work on the electric storage battery was widely acclaimed. He improved on Bell's telephone so much that the inventor visited him in Ballarat to see the complete system Sutton had installed in his own home. Independently from Thomas Edison, Sutton had successfully experimented with a carbon lamp. He invented a mercury air pump and a vacuum pump, and, by the late 1880s, claimed to have designed an instrument which would televise the Melbourne Cup and show it in Ballarat, but he did not construct it. Engraving, colour photography and car carburettors were other interests and he built a portable radio set with a range of a little under 500 yards. In the midst of all this work he engaged in the family musical instrument business, Suttons Pty Ltd, to die in 1912 with no one sure of his greatness because he had taken out very few patents as he wanted 'to benefit fellow workers in science'.

By 1914 Australians could take a ticket by post in Tattersall's lottery based in Hobart, go to a night out at a rudimentary moving picture show or perhaps listen to the gramophone at home. They avidly read the adventures of the Linton family in Mary Grant Bruce's 'Billabong' series of stories although the author had decided that there should be no love interest in them. They could read, in any of the more than 1,000 newspapers, that Norman Brookes had helped beat the Americans four times in the Davis Cup and that an Australian had no opposition when winning the first air race from Botany to Sydney in 1912 as his American opponent had refused to trust the weather. The telephone linked Sydney and Melbourne, mail was flown between the two capitals in July 1914, electric power was spreading from lights to trams and the first official wireless station was opened in Melbourne in 1912. Speed — in measures hitherto unsuspected and applied to communications and transport — became a reality accepted, if scarcely understood, by all.

Increased prosperity made leisure the prerogative of all except the very poor. Such festivals as the Melbourne Cup and the Royal Shows attracted huge crowds and an international exhibition of women's work was held in Melbourne in 1907. The weekend had started to emerge in 1909, when workplaces began to close on Saturday afternoons and suburbanites in thousands went to see their teams play Australian Rules in the southern states. In New South Wales, Queensland and Western Australia glorious beaches and fine weather attracted people, surfing became popular, the 'Australian crawl' (used for centuries in the Pacific Islands) was learnt and voluntary lifesaving clubs were spreading from Sydney where they started at Bondi in 1906. In January 1907 the future airman Charles Kingsford Smith was the first rescue with a primitive reel and line.

Some clerics warned of hedonism and were especially alarmed at mixed bathing but there was much seriousness in life also. Education was extending very slowly to the secondary and technical levels. Only one student in twenty went on to secondary schooling while a mere handful graduated at a university. The first woman doctor had been registered in 1890 and the first woman lawyer graduated from Sydney University in 1902. She was excluded from practising until 1921 after the passing of the Women's Legal Status Act. A universally free, secular or even fully compulsory education system was still a sought after ideal. Teacher training was inadequate and of the 867 teachers registered in the secondary system in Victoria only nine were properly trained. The beginning of the Commonwealth Literary Fund, the opening of the Mitchell Library in Sydney and the offering of tutorials by the Workers' Educational Association, which stood for an alliance between 'Labor and Learning', all helped to contribute in the field of adult education.

Despite apparent prosperity, the poor still went hungry, wages were often insufficient and home ownership was, for most, only a dream. In many factories, conditions remained primitive and exploitation of women by sweated labour continued despite the legislative acts to prohibit it. An outbreak of bubonic plague had caused great consternation in Sydney in 1900, which had led to measures being taken to clear up slums, although the work went ahead slowly. Pure Food Acts did not operate with much effect until 1912, pneumonia killed the young and the strong, as well as the old, and diphtheria ravaged the lives of many children. Blood poisoning after operations, especially for appendicitis, was a common occurrence, and it was vividly illustrated when the nineteen-year-old Barney Kieran, who held practically every world swimming record, died in Brisbane during the Australian swimming championships in 1905. Life for many was still brutal and short but throughout the continent the ideal of Australia as a paradise for the workers was maintained, especially by those with something to gain from its acceptance.

Very few were alarmed at an apparent constitutional crisis in 1914. By now political choice was clearly narrowed to the two parties — Labor and the conservatives, who were often known as Liberals. Joseph Cook led the latter. He too was a former coal miner and had alternated between Labor, Free Trade and Protection to settle down as a conservative Prime Minister when, in the federal elections of May 1913, Labor lost its majority in the House of Representatives. Cook had a majority of one in the House of Representatives which he used to over turn Labor legislation giving preference to unionists in Commonwealth employment. The Senate, with a strong Labor majority, rejected Cook's bill twice and the Governor-General, faced with a lack of precedent, decided that Parliament could not function and dissolved both Houses. After an election in September 1914, the Labor Party, under Fisher, returned to govern with thirty-one of the thirty-six Senate seats and forty-two out of seventy-five in the House of Representatives. In the meantime, events had taken place in Europe which were to test the proclamation of the Australian Natives Association of 13 December 1913 that 'Our home is Australia'.

CHAPTER TWELVE

The Loss of Innocence

Compulsory military training, the acquisition of a navy, and the setting up of a college to train army officers at Duntroon in 1911 and an aviation school at Point Cook in Victoria had all helped to prepare Australia for participation in a war. Involvement in the Sudan and Boer conflicts combined with an increasing interest in European and Pacific affairs to develop public opinion on Australia's readiness for war. The psychology of a pioneering society had also done its part. Australians, it seemed to many, had faced hardship and sacrifice with manifest endurance and won some control over a new land. Pride in manhood, the ability to struggle and improvise against the odds, widespread use of the horse, rifles and shotguns, and the emphasis placed on sticking to one's mates were other factors shaping a mentality that was not adverse to war.

In literature and legend, the 'glories of war' had been held up as an ideal to young Australians and many took it for granted that the true worth of a people was tested in battle. Over-riding all other considerations was the bond of Empire forged in blood, sentiment and commerce. Since 1905 Australians had solemnly celebrated Empire Day on 24 May and pledged themselves to stay loyal to their British origins. In 1910 the Catholics in Sydney claimed that 'Australia, not England, is our motherland' and they decided they would call 24 May, Australia Day. Despite some minor differences, the vast majority of Australians were bound in some way to Britain. That bond was the decisive factor that determined Australia's participation in the First World War. There was unbounded enthusiasm for, and apparent unanimity in, the cause of the 'Mother Country', England. A nation that had begun its origins tainted by convictism could perhaps prove that the stain was finally eradicable in blood.

Joseph Cook was still Prime Minister on 5 August 1914 and it fell to him to announce that war with Germany was now a reality because 'when the Empire is at war so is Australia at war'. The wider implications of that reality, and Australian involvement in it, seemed apparent to none at the time. A few days earlier, when Labor leader Fisher had promised to come to the defence of Britain with 'our last man and our last shilling', no one remarked that such a wildly profligate offering of blood and resources may not have lain in Fisher's, or anyone else's, keeping. The thing that seemed to cloud rationality, inflame passions and stir anger, even in the breasts of the peaceful, was the allegedly barbaric behaviour of the Germans as they 'raped' Belgium.

Other causes of war, ranging from unbridled nationalism to the desire for territorial conquest and more trade outlets, were scarcely considered. Britain was at war with a nation of so-called primitive 'Huns'; Australia would come to her aid with her little navy and, as an initial token of support, 20,000 men. Few voices questioned the wisdom or justice of it all except those on the far left like the Industrial Workers of the World (to whom war was the bloody exploitation of the workers by the capitalists), a few feminists and other 'small voices' such as the Quakers, who regarded war as the antithesis of Christ's teachings. When the Labor government came into power in September and showed every sign of wanting to prosecute the war with enthusiasm, the consciences of most dissidents were eased and, temporarily, there was unity.

Australia threw herself into the conflict with such a will that it was claimed the very first shot of the war was fired to stop the German steamer, *Pfalz* as she was about to pass through Port Phillip Heads. This occurred at about noon on 5 August and it was the only act of belligerence on Australian territory during the war if one excepts the episode in which two Turks died after attacking a train at Broken Hill. Germany did, however, have naval forces in the Pacific of two large cruisers and a strong squadron, and garrisons in New Guinea, while there were potential spies in Australia itself. The capture of Rabaul was the first significant act by Australian soldiers. The fleet put to sea to hunt the German warships and those Germans of military age in Australia were interned. Amongst the later internees was the Sydney brewer Edmund Resch, who had neglected to take out Australian naturalization, unlike his brother Emil, the first managing director of Carlton and United Breweries, who remained free.

No pleas needed to be made for volunteers, with over 50,000 men enlisting as rapidly as they could be processed. By 1 November thirty-eight transports, with 20,000 Australians and New Zealanders aboard, were ready and sailed from Albany in Western Australia. The fears of Asiatic hordes were set aside as Japan, Australia's ally, provided a powerful escort cruiser, the *Ibuki*. A few days later, a naval engagement took place near the Cocos Islands where the Australian cruiser, *Sydney*, destroyed the German raider, *Emden*. The news of the successful episode caused great rejoicing and pride throughout Australia.

Turkey's entry into the war in October had caused concern for the safety of the Suez and the Anzacs (Australia New Zealand Army Corps) were diverted to Egypt rather than go on to England, where they were to be trained on Salisbury Plain. There, about the Pyramids, they trained and in Cairo gambled, drank and whored on 6s a day to the consternation of the British command and of some of the locals. With their loosely fitting khaki uniforms, hats swept up on the left and the badge of the 'Rising Sun' worn proudly, they were a formidable group of men eagerly awaiting action. They had little time to wait, because Winston Churchill and others in England had decided to conquer the Turks on Gallipoli Peninsula and thereby free the Dardanelles to the Allies and relieve pressure on the Russians. On 25 April 1915, at a place they called Anzac Cove, the 3rd Australian Infantry Brigade of the Australian Imperial Forces (AIF) came ashore at dawn.

The Australians scrambled up the slope from the beach under the ceaseless fire of the Turks positioned on the heights. Cries from the dying and wounded, anguished appeals to mates for help and the incessant whirring, shrieking and thudding of bullets and shells filled the air with ear-shattering noise. The ancient ritual of blood was enacted on the young Australians, far from the peace of the old continent of their origins. They were in a place which had seen all this through the ages as men had killed men for land, money, religion or other causes. The Australians were at Gallipoli, they had been told, to defend an Empire. By nightfall their steps were irretraceable, for 16,000 had been landed with over 2,000 casualties and they had nowhere to go except into the earth. Many of their forefathers had been diggers and now the sons dug in to hold an alien soil. At home, ministers of religion visited houses to tell of the dead and wounded, while the names went up outside newspaper offices, where wives, mothers, parents and friends stood to grieve and only partly understand. At last, it seemed, white Australia had a history.

By early 1915 all Australians had learnt a good deal about involvement in a war. Prices had risen considerably and a marked decrease in shipping and overseas trade combined with uncertainty in the manufacturing sector to cause unemployment. Imports, especially from Britain, were scarce and wages were frozen, which caused many workers to become resentful as it was clear that some people were making huge profits. Meanwhile, there was another of those perennial hardships to be faced, drought, which began in 1911 and lasted until 1915. Patriotism in many guises gripped scoundrels and the decent alike. Anyone or anything to do with Germany, whether person, place or product suffered discrimination or internment, name change or rejection. In South Australia forty towns or districts with names of German origin were changed and Germanton in New South Wales became Holbrook in 1915.

Another face of patriotism was shown in the extraordinary level of recruitment, partly engendered by the news from Gallipoli. June (12,500), July (36,000) and August (25,700) were its peak months with the British calling for more and more troops and the Australian authorities drumming them up with recruiting campaigns. The numbers, however, began to drop away and a group of men who were determined to see the war prosecuted to a successful conclusion formed the Universal Service League. The principal creed to which it subscribed was that only con-scription for military service would fill the ranks of the dead and wounded and thereby win the war against the 'Hun'.

The landing at Anzac Cove in April 1915 and the subsequent bloody and unsuccessful campaign on Gallipoli gave Australia its most enduring legend.

August 1915 saw the Australians assault and take Lone Pine on the south of Gallipoli Peninsula, but fresh British toops had failed tragically at nearby Suvla Bay because of indecisive command, and the whole bloody campaign, in which both sides engaged in brutalities, was in jeopardy. Hamilton, the British commander was replaced, and, in London, the War Office was at last ready to cry 'enough'. In a manoeuvre remarkable for ingenuity, 20,000 Australians were withdrawn from the Peninsula under cover of darkness on 18 and 19 December 1915 with the loss of only two lives. They left behind 8,708 Australian dead near Anzac Cove while nearly 20,000 had been wounded. Major-General Bridges, commander of the AIF, died as a result of wounds he received on Gallipoli and his body was brought home to rest at the Royal Military College, Duntroon, of which he had been the first commandant. The British and Indians lost 27,000 men, the New Zealanders 2,701, the French almost as many as the Australians. The Turks, who defended their land with great courage under a valiant commander, Mustafa Kemal Ataturk, counted 86,000 dead, but to them, presumably, the whole campaign had not been a waste as they had successfully defended their homeland. Seventy years later the Turks named the place Anzac Cove and they erected a plaque there with the words of Ataturk inscribed upon it: the Anzacs were called heroes who now lie 'in the soil of a friendly country' and their mothers were reminded that their sons, who 'have become our sons as well, now rest in peace'.

The courage and endurance of the Anzacs had been staggering as, shrouded in sardonic good humour, they endured the impossible. The New Zealanders had fought alongside the Australians and suffered their own awesome meed of sorrow which formed a bond of lasting trust across the Tasman. The words 'Anzac' and 'Gallipoli' were etched in the memory of the nation while the dead of the Peninsula became, in time, the symbol and measure to test its quality. From the agony of those months, no nation was born or forged, because such a thing happens only through the unity of a people with its land. Yet of the Anzacs the legend speaks truly for they walked upright, fine and noble of bearing as they went to death, to maiming and defeat. They carried in their persons the legend of the bush and they lived by its values. No people could have asked more, permitted more or expected more of their sons and received such a response. It was fitting that a non-combatant, John Simpson Kirkpatrick, 'the man with the donkey', who brought in the wounded day after day amid fierce shrapnel fire, became the enduring legend and symbol of the pure, selfless and heroic at Gallipoli.

The debacle of Gallipoli was of minor consequence in London, where victory on the Western Front was seen as the key to a final triumph. By

English-born, John Simpson Kirkpatrick became a swaggie, cane cutter, miner and sailor in Australia. He landed at Anzac Cove on 25 April 1915 and was shot dead on 19 May of that year. With his donkey, 'Duffy', he became the best-loved figure on Gallipoli as he carried the wounded to the dressing station.

1916 the opposing armies had dug in along long lines of trenches and the war had become one of attrition of human life. Territorial gains were minimal, but both sides hoped that the death toll and the bleeding of their respective economies would cause the other to capitulate. The summer of 1916 was seen as the time for a decisive strike by the Allies and more men were needed. In Australia a census showed that there were still 600,000 able men available, so Hughes, who became Prime Minister in October when a dispirited Fisher resigned to go to London as High Commissioner, called upon them to help crush 'Prussian military despotism' for all time.

Hughes was a complex character, who was born in London in 1862 although he always claimed to be of Welsh origins. After a sound secondary education, he taught in England for a while and arrived in Australia in 1884 to become in turn a fettler, seaman, shearer, and actor. Later he studied law, owned a book shop, organized strikes as a union leader in the 1890s, helped found the New South Wales Labor Party, entered Parliament, became a federal member in 1901 and later a King's Counsel. He managed to contain in his own diminutive person a spirit whose elements were explosive in passion and enthusiasm, including a love for Empire, a fierce loyalty to Australia and a penchant for militarism.

To Billy, as he was known by thousands, there were plenty of men to draw on in Australia and he wanted 50,000 without delay and a further 16,000 each month. He claimed that those who opposed recruitment were 'foul parasites' on the body of the Labor movement, knowing 'no nationality, religion or principle'. It was an unwise way to confront a movement in which many were already suspicious of his refusal to hold a referendum for price control by the Federal Parliament. They saw this as craven capitulation to the forces of capitalism which were growing fat on war while the workers were called upon to fight it. By 1916 prices had risen by twenty percent, real wages had dropped by ten percent and unemployment, despite the number of males who had enlisted, stood at six percent.

Many were largely unaffected by the war preferring football matches, horse racing and sundry other diversions, although inflation was constantly rising, war loans were being called for, and, adding to other increased taxes, the first federal income tax was introduced. Manufacturing grew due to the opening of munitions factories and the need to make other necessities no longer available by import. Broken Hill Proprietary Limited opened a steelworks at Newcastle and the production of pig-iron rose from about 130,000 tons to over a million during the war years. The drought was over by 1916 and farmers and wool growers were benefiting by British demand for their products.

Hughes had failed to find any remedy to rising prices but wages did not go up commensurably which caused the workers to think that they were being asked to bear the burden of the war, both at home and at the front. Trade union leaders, despite being reviled as disruptionists of the war effort, called for strikes on the water front, and amongst metal workers, coal miners and shearers in 1916, resulting in 1.7 million working days lost. By then the war appeared to be dragging on interminably and the workers were less and less inclined to be swayed by the heady rhetoric of Hughes, who called for greater and greater sacrifice. Easter 1916 saw a rising of insurgents in Ireland which was followed by the execution of James Connolly and other Irish leaders by the British. It was not a happy event for the Irish in Australia to ponder on while their sons were being called to put their own lives at stake for the Empire.

Early in 1916, Hughes visited England, where he arranged for the purchase of fifteen ships by the Commonwealth to carry freight to and from England, helped formulate a tough line on how the Allies should deal with Germany once victory was secured, stomped the country preaching total war, and was feted and applauded by royalty, politicians, the wealthy and the powerful. He also met the Australian troops in France where, affectionately, they called him the 'Little Digger'. He had left the Western Front before their first disaster at Fromelles on 19 July, and was on his way home to receive a hero's welcome. The British commander, General Haig, had persisted in trying to breach the German lines on the Somme. In and about Pozières, two months of late summer and early autumn saw 23,000 Australian casualties with the gain of about one mile in territory.

Gallipoli was another world away compared to the ferocity and horror of the Somme. The sheer enormity of the slaughter, the dreadful noise of the shells, the stench, poison gas, mud, filth and finally the uselessness of it all drove the men into shock and depression from which some never recovered. In its own way, the Australian army was never the same again. Distrust in the British High Command, almost contempt for the British troops, bitterness at the loss of so many lives, hopelessness as no avenue of escape was possible from further horrors; all overwhelmed the men. So many of the finest of the nation soaked their blood into the fields of France that Australia, in that generation at least, suffered a grievous blow.

Despite some heartening news from Egypt that Henry Chauvel's Light

Horse had forced the Turks back into Palestine, all was not well at home. Women sent white feathers to men who had not enlisted and the recruiting officers did their best, but the number of volunteers fell from 22,000 in January 1916 to 6,000 in July, which was said to be far short of the numbers demanded. On his return Hughes said that 32,500 volunteers were required immediately and 16,500 a month thereafter which was unrealistic and provocative. If realized, it would have caused industrial and agricultural chaos with the loss of a third of the able-bodied male workforce in a year.

Undaunted Hughes pressed ahead with a proposal to hold a plebiscite on conscription for overseas military service. He did not have the numbers in Parliament to enforce conscription by legislation, and he paid no heed to the clear signs of resentment in large segments of the Labor Party, both federal and state. As a result of his determination to pursue conscription, he found himself, together with his fellow Labor conscriptionist, William Holman, Premier of New South Wales, expelled from the New South Wales state branch of the Party in September, and the same happened in other states as well. With a further rash act of provocation, he called up young men for home service and announced a plebiscite for October. It was a step which dramatically divided the people — after all the claims that involvement in war had united them.

The basic reason for the division stemmed from two broadly divergent concepts of Australia. One held that Australia was white, civilized, British, mostly Protestant and part of a great Empire which itself was God's gift to mankind. To people who held this concept, the Germans threatened the very bastion of civilization — the Empire — and it was difficult, if not impossible, for them to comprehend how anyone but a traitor could disagree with conscription, the logical extension of their belief, given the military situation. Practically every public figure in Australia, the press, except for publications of the broad Labor movement, the judiciary, all but a handful of the Protestant clergy, and the wealthy held this view, often fiercely. They were joined by many thousands whose sense of patriotism and loyalty to Empire inclined them to vote for conscription. The press inflamed passions with the *Age* castigating those who failed to enlist as 'muddy-mettled wastrels', while David Low and Norman Lindsay used their brilliance in the *Bulletin* to draw cartoons showing the miserableness of the anti-conscriptionists and the glory of the soldiers fighting to defend civilization from the 'Hun'.

The other concept of the nation was held by a numerically significant sector, represented particularly in the Labor movement and the Catholic Church. Australia to them, while part of the Empire, was also an entity in

David Low used his genius as a cartoonist to foster the Yes vote in the Conscription plebiscites during World War 1. Much of the propaganda against the Germans was directed at women.

itself. Their emotional ties with Britain were weaker than those of the conscriptionists. Indeed, for many Catholics, led by Archbishop Daniel Mannix of Melbourne, the bloody reprisals taken by the British in Ireland after the Easter Rising had effectively severed the ties. To such people, whether of the Labor movement or not, it was not as easy to represent the Germans as the embodiment of all evil, nor the war as a holy crusade to preserve civilization. Furthermore, with the losses in casualties since April 1915 and the daily news of increasing slaughter in France, the idea was increasingly held that Australia was doing enough in manpower and resources.

In the main the anti-conscriptionists were not against involvement in the war, although many held deep-seated convictions on the evils of militarism, which they saw embodied in conscription and some, such as the resolute and courageous Quakers, were implacably opposed. Amongst the workers, there was also the fear that military conscription would be followed by industrial conscription, the importation of coloured labour and perhaps the repression of the trade union movement. Many women, stiffened in their resolve to resist the blandishments of those who exhorted them to make further sacrifices of their husbands and sons, were determined to vote 'No'. To these groups was added the voting strength of some farmers whose concern was with their harvests and the manpower needed to reap them, while small businessmen and factory owners feared that a further depleted workforce would endanger their economic interests. Such people, having voted against conscription, could return to their traditional conservative political allegiance.

Much passion, ranting and pathos confused the issues in the two conscription campaigns of October 1916 and December 1917. Alfred Deakin was so ill he could not speak publicly, but the old patriot wrote the sorriest document of the whole affair. He begged Australians to vote 'Yes' to keep Australia 'white and free for ever' — to vote to save civilization. He concluded with a plea and a promise, (both of which remained sterile): 'Let our voices thunder "Yes", and future generations shall arise and call us blessed'. A very narrow majority of 72,476 out of nearly two and a quarter million voted against conscription in 1916, but the majority increased in 1917 and Victoria joined New South Wales, Queensland and South Australia in opposition. At the Front the soldiers on active service were almost evenly divided, as if to say that it was bad enough in France for those who went there willingly.

The first important consequence of the conscription era was a deep and lasting split in the Labor Party, having its origins in past differences which were heightened by the war. In the labour movement there were some who saw the Labor Party as a vehicle of social change, but whose commitment to the cause of the working masses was either emotional or merely one of convenience in that it gave them a stage to work on. Conscription forced them to evaluate their position and act on it. After the first plebiscite, Hughes replied to a caucus motion of no confidence by saying, 'Let all who support me, follow me'. He walked from the party room with twenty-four followers out of the sixty-five present. By January 1917 he had formed the Nationalist Party with the support of his former Labor colleagues and the parliamentary opposition. Holman did the same in New South Wales and the Labor Party was divided in all states except in Queensland. Frank Tudor was elected federal Labor leader and went onto the opposition benches with forty followers. Labor was changed in that it now relied almost completely on trade union and worker support.

Daniel Mannix, Catholic Archbishop of Melbourne from 1917 to 1963, was a fearless opponent of conscription in World War 1. Few figures in Australian public life have earned as great opprobrium from some and admiration from others.

Another consequence was that many who stayed with Labor, whether as parliamentarians or voters, were Catholics. The Party was seen for many years afterwards as Irish and Catholic, which was sufficiently true as to arouse sectarian fears that were given added strength because, after 1916, some Australians regarded Catholics as traitors. Finally, radical elements of the workers' movement — inspired by the Russian Revolution and convinced that the solution to the ills of society lay in the overthrow of its dominant capitalistic structure, which they judged the Labor Party incapable of achieving — went off to form the Communist Party of Australia in 1920. Reduced in numbers and with the press against it the Labor Party, with an untried leader and much of its base eroded by jingoism, lost the federal election called by Hughes in May 1917. The Nationalists, who campaigned effectively under the banner 'Win the War', dominated the seventh Parliament having more than twice Labor's numbers, and patriotism seemed the preserve of those who were anti-Labor.

Meanwhile the war went on relentlessly with little yielding of ground, although the Australian Flying Corps joined with other Allied airforces to bomb German positions effectively. Haig, who never seemed to weary of the butchery, had a victory when five miles were gained in October 1917 near Ypres. Both sides lost half a million men — the Australians, 38,000 in four months. The Australian soldiers now called each other 'diggers', and the survivors became more embittered as they watched their comrades being maimed or killed. The only note of optimism was the entry of America on the Allied side. At Villers Bretonneux five divisions went over the trench tops on 8 August 1918 assisted by two Australian squadrons in the air and 450 British tanks. French, Canadian and British troops fought along a thirty-two kilometre front and it was Germany's blackest hour. The Australians took thousands of prisoners and saw their final engagement in France on 29 September, as the war drew to a close.

In France, the Australians won the respect of their allies and their enemies as they had on Gallipoli and in Palestine, where their mounted troops had helped to gain victory and took Damascus on the morning of 1 October 1918. On leave in Egypt, France and England, the troops had enjoyed themselves, to the not infrequent discomfort of their hosts. Amongst them there were some mutineers, deserters and malcontents, but the majority were the pride of their officers and a source of confusion to the British commanders, who often found them discourteous, insolent and undisciplined. The Australian dead numbered 60,000 out of the 330,000 who had served in theatre-of-war zones and their overall casualty rate at 68.5 percent was the highest of the Allied forces. The news of the

Armistice of 11 November was heard with happiness and relief throughout Australia, but in many homes hearts were broken. Mute, material relics of Australia's passing on Gallipoli remained for generations, as its memory did in the homeland itself. Time perhaps healed much sorrow as it did the broken earth of Flanders' fields where poppies grew on graves. In the words of Australia's official historian of the Great War, C.E.W. Bean:

> What these men did nothing can alter now. The good and the bad, the greatness and smallness of their story will stand. Whatever of glory it contains nothing now can lessen. It rises as it will always rise, above the mists of ages, a monument to great-hearted men; and for their nation, a possession for ever.

Tarnished permanently in the minds of some by his conscription stand and by his destruction of a Labor government, Hughes, nonetheless, revealed himself as the incomparable exponent of Australia's traditional foreign policy. As the nation was determined to remain white, coloured races had to be excluded and, as an island far removed from its cultural roots, Australia had to be defended. The former was to be achieved by ensuring that no exceptions were made to the policy on colour, and the latter by preventing any hostile, or potentially hostile, power from getting a foothold close to Australia. Despite the fact that it had been an ally, Hughes remained uneasy about Japan as a Pacific power, and he was determined to keep Japan at bay.

At the Paris Peace Conference in 1919, Hughes firstly established Australia's right to speak as an independent signatory in the name of 60,000 dead. When the Japanese tried to have a racial equality declaration proclaimed, Hughes saw it as a threat to the White Australia policy and would have none of it, so Wilson, President of the United States, refused to accept the Japanese proposal. The Japanese claimed, and were granted, a mandate to control the north Pacific islands formerly held by Germany. Hughes objected unsuccessfully, but he did, however, succeed in his main objective of obtaining a mandate for Australia to control the former German colonies in the south-west Pacific and especially in New Guinea. He thereby ensured that there was a barrier between Japan in the north and Australia in the south. Hughes was satisfied and came away from Versailles feeling victorious, to be acclaimed by large crowds at home, who wildly cheered him on arrival.

To a small nation of five million people, a war debt of £350,000,000 was huge. Admittedly, most of this money had been spent in Australia to

the benefit of the public utilities in every state. The opening of the trans-
continental railway through to Perth in 1917 was an example. Furthermore, the economy had prospered with assured markets for wool,
metals, wheat, butter and other primary products, sold mostly to Britain.
The inability to import many items resulted in a wide variety of articles
being manufactured locally, ranging from ships to Aspro tablets. There
were other effects of the war which, though not as tangible, left a lasting
legacy and served to put the negative aspects of Hughes's prime-ministership in perspective.

At the very start of the war, Hughes introduced a War Precautions Act
that gave the Commonwealth wide powers which he played down at the
time, but eventually the implications of the Act became clear. The Act
covered aliens and, although they were rarely treated with the harshness
shown on Torrens Island in South Australia where 300 harmless Australian-born Germans were flogged and in other ways treated in-
humanely, the paranoia caused by the war ensured that to be an alien of
any kind was to suffer a sorry lot. By 1917, an incident occurred in
Queensland which showed how Hughes's enthusiasm for the war had so
unbalanced the Prime Minister as to cause him to behave like a despot by
misuse of the Act.

Thomas Ryan was an extremely able politician and Premier of
Queensland, which was the last state to retain Labor in power in wartime.
Ryan's government brought in a range of reform measures of lasting
benefit such as a mandatory eight-hour day and state controlled enterprises which competed with privately owned concerns. Moreover, Ryan
was a forthright opponent of conscription, and he spoke strongly against
it in the Queensland Parliament. Hughes decreed that the *Hansard* containing Ryan's remarks could not be processed by the Post Office. Ryan
repeated his statement outside the Parliament and was charged under
the Act with making statements prejudicial to the war effort, for which he
was tried and acquitted with costs against the Commonwealth. At the
time Hughes was in Queensland and, when making a speech at Warwick,
he was hit by an egg. A sergeant of police refused to arrest the egg-
thrower, Patrick Brosnan, which so enraged Hughes that he returned to
Melbourne and set up the Commonwealth Police Force. That body
proved to be the forerunner of future organizations, which operated in
secret, culminating in 1949 with the establishment of the Australian
Security Intelligence Organization (ASIO). The purpose of such bodies
was always the security of the country, but they often proved to be a
source of concern to some Australians who were innocent of any subversive acts.

By the end of the war, Hughes's War Precautions Act had been invoked to launch a wide variety of successful prosecutions. They included exhibiting the red flag, showing disloyalty or hostility to the Empire, disturbing loyalist meetings, giving shelter to unnaturalized Germans and dyeing military overcoats. Such prosecutions by the Commonwealth were scarcely a good precedent for its behaviour in peace time. Governments, once having secured wider powers in the name of an emergency, invariably show a remarkable reluctance to relinquish them once the crisis has passed, and the Australian government was no exception.

The nation at war was subject to much industrial disharmony despite the prevailing attitude that all strike action was disloyal. On the extreme left, the Industrial Workers of the World preached a highly idealistic doctrine with violent undertones, which had the destruction of capitalism as its purpose. They kept hysteria high by allegedly plotting to burn Sydney down, helping Tom Barker, editor of their paper, to escape from prison and generally conspiring to incite sedition. Twelve of them were arrested and were sent to prison for long terms. A judge enquired into the

Sixty-eight percent of Australian troops who engaged in combat were killed or wounded — a greater proportion than that in any other part of the Empire. Those wounded in the Battle of the Menin Road in France on 20 September 1917 were among them.

matter in 1920 and found that their convictions rested on Crown wit-
nesses who were 'liars and perjurers', which resulted in ten of them being
released.

In 1917 Hughes blamed the Industrial Workers of the World, Sinn Fein
and other allegedly disloyal elements for inciting a general strike in New
South Wales. It began amongst railway and tramway employees who
refused to accept a new system of recording work done. A total of 70,000
men were on strike by the time it was halted when volunteers and other
assorted 'loyalists' helped to fill the vacant jobs. The Premier, Holman,
enunciated the uneasy principle that there were times in which the state
was supreme over the individual, without delineating the exact terms in
which that principle operated. His statement indicated that the war had
so increased the power of government that in some minds it bordered on
the absolute. The general strike itself was a psychological response to the
bitterness caused by war with its losses and deprivations, to the conscription plebiscites and to the way in which Hughes had partially destroyed the Labor Party.

After the war, there were so many strikes that it seemed as if the battles
of the Western Front were being fought again in the factories and on the
wharves. Members of trade unions and returned soldiers rioted over their
respective loyalties to Russia or to the British Empire, to capitalism or
socialism. In Brisbane nineteen people were wounded when returned
men attacked the office of the Russia Association, while the Returned
Soldiers League, founded in 1916, played its part in ensuring that nothing
which resembled a Bolshevik Revolution would take place in Australia.
Despite these upheavals, Lieutenant-General John Monash, the most outstanding Australian military commander of the war, directed a remarkably smooth operation by which some 160,000 servicemen
returned home in eight months. By November 1919 all except 14,000
were in employment while another 20,000 were receiving technical training.

To the returned men, much had changed in Australia since they left.
Some had gone to war in hope and determination. Many were swayed by
a spirit of adventure because — to lads who had perhaps never been
beyond Tasmania's north-west coast, the northern rivers area of New
South Wales, Victoria's Wimmera, the wine-growing valleys of South
Australia, the Darling Downs or the wheatbelt towns of Western Australia — it was a chance to see the world. They came home with a new
way of looking at things, for they had seen their friends killed and many
had themselves taken human life; they had been close to a world old and
wearied in its ways with little hope of renewal. As many of them saw it,

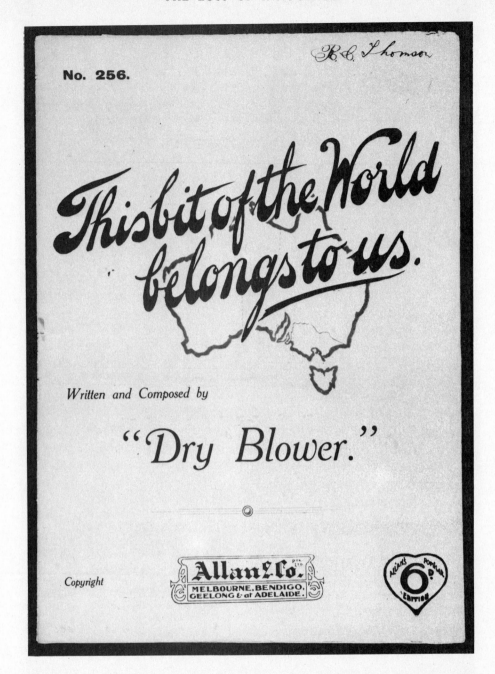

Patriotism in song, verse, cartoon and theatre was fundamental to the lives of most Australians in World War 1. The mounting casualty lists, bitterness over conscription and sheer war weariness dulled the edge of patriotism as the war dragged on until late 1918.

they had fought for the integrity of Australia and the Empire, but on return they discerned, here and there, the signs of an Australia that had lost its conscience and direction with everyone seeking the best for themselves irrespective of others.

Australia was no longer an isolated island, even to disease. The diggers brought the Spanish influenza with them which forced the wearing of masks, closed public buildings and killed 12,000 people in 1919. In politics, there was a new creation called the Country Party, which began informally when it won its first seat at the Corangamite by-election in the Western District of Victoria in 1918. The Party relied on the simple slogan of 'Production first' and the vote of those farmers who believed that the city and all those who represented it were against them.

Initially the closing at six p.m. of hotels in several states may have seemed trivial to the returned men but it was a symbol of the passing of the old ways. Since the 1830s the temperance movement had never lost its drive, but even its most ardent supporters could not have dreamt what a golden chance the war would give to their cause. In early 1916, at Liverpool near Sydney, 15,000 troops mutineed in protest at their prolonged training hours. They rioted, consumed vast quantities of liquor, fought amongst themselves and against civilians, one soldier was shot dead and there was general disorder in Sydney's streets. In June the people voted to close the hotels at six o'clock, so New South Wales joined Victoria, Tasmania and South Australia in the practice.

In this way the degradation called 'the six o'clock swill' began. It saw men line up in hotel bars after leaving work to get down as much beer as possible before 'Time, gentlemen please' signalled the closure. Ninety percent of beer consumption took place in the one hour between five and six and bottled beer, previously ill-favoured as a beverage, became universally acceptable. Six o'clock closure was an undignified, narrow and fruitless response on the part of wowserism to what certainly had long been a social problem in Australia — the over-consumption of alcohol. The swill produced more drunkards in the ensuing generation than any other single factor and was not got rid of in Victoria, heartland of wowserism, until the 1960s.

Australia welcomed the returned men with fervour and genuine gratitude. In every city and right through the land, even in the small country towns, stone monuments to the memory of the fallen were quickly erected, or were being built, for it was agreed upon everywhere that permanent recognition had to be made of the sacrifice of the diggers. Often the monument was a single figure, upright, rifle and bayonet in hand, slouch hat shading fixed eyes. There was little attempt at religious symbolism, with classical models chosen by preference to avoid sectarian differences although Moruya on the south coast of New South Wales failed to erect a monument because of religious tensions. On the plinth a roll call proudly listed the names of those who had served and every list had its dead. Sometimes there were brothers and cousins, for many families were doubly stricken. Around the monument the townspeople and the returned men gathered on 11 November, 1919 to observe two minutes silence for all the dead.

It was Anzac Day, 25 April, the day of the landing at Gallipoli, that overshadowed memory and made all new and vital in significance for it was seen as the day on which the nation had shaken off the bonds of subservience and Australians had come to know themselves. Billy Hughes saw it a little differently. To him victory in the war meant national safety, liberty and the safeguarding of the White Australia policy. Despite some signs to the contrary, Hughes was still convinced that Australians were 'more British than the people of Great Britain'. The two views of the nation revealed so clearly on the conscription issue had survived the war. Time would reveal their respective validity.

CHAPTER THIRTEEN
The Mirage of Progress

Australia came out of the war with a new sense of its identity and its people were aware that the ways of the past were changed irrevocably. The application of technology to the purposes of war, on land, at sea, in the air and in the factories at home, meant that a large proportion of the population had grown accustomed to developments in science, communications, medicine, engineering and transport. The involvement of the nation in war had radicalized those who rejected violent conflict as a means of solving international problems, while many, who previously had seen Australia with the eyes of patriots, now looked upon her as more firmly embedded than ever in the web of Empire. That development was notable in the *Bulletin*, which joined the newly-founded *Smith's Weekly* as a voice of conservatism and firm devotion to the British and their Empire. In the case of the *Bulletin*, this development had been foreshadowed by its founder, Archibald, who said in 1894 that it had started as a 'clever youth' but that it would become 'a dull old man.' Conservatism was notable too in the new legend of the digger as the bearer of the national legend. The digger showed the old virtues of his forerunners in the bush and on the gold-fields, but he added conformity and imperialism to them, which blunted the creative urge and made the 1920s for many a period of material but not spiritual development.

The role of women underwent some changes during the war and with differing roles came developing attitudes. Some served as nurses in the Armed Services, but at home they were employed in greater numbers in shops, banks, and light industry. They worked as typists and telegraphists and generally where the lack of manpower or, given the differential wage structure, the avarice of employers made their employment convenient.

Nevertheless, two women became police officers in Sydney in 1915 and five female doctors worked for the Victorian Education Department. Participation in the workforce gave many women a personal understanding of how society operated outside the home, but their overall position remained one of subservience to males. For the minority who were married, the need to organize a timetable to fit in a day's work with child-minding, leaving the home environment and dressing up to do so, the contact with others, and finally the acquisition of a wage helped towards a greater understanding of their own value. The conscription struggle had radicalized a few women who began to take more interest in union activity and to work for women's rights.

Nevertheless, the role of wife and mother still dominated and marriage was seen as the acceptable norm to which young women were educated, but there were some changes. Domestic service was no longer where most of the female workforce was employed, because industrialization continued after the war and by 1925 females made up half the workforce in light industry. A typical woman worker was young, unmarried and received half the male wage. If widowed with children, her burden was severe because there were no child-minding facilities, no national health scheme, and no child endowment until 1927, and then only in New South Wales.

For the young and independent woman, life offered avenues of fulfilment and enjoyment not open to her elder sisters of the pre-war period and still not available to most women in rural areas, where distance, the lack of amenities, the need to work on farms and the absence of female companionship made life hard. The divorce rate doubled in the decade from 1911. The imbalance in the sex ratios, plus the hospitalization of so many returned men — 23,000 in 1926 — combined with wider knowledge of birth control techniques to reduce the birth rate. In 1931 there were over a third less births by percentage of population than in 1921.

Reaction to the war years, with their deprivations and sorrows, took place in many material ways. Dress styles changed with the introduction of short skirts, silk stockings and lower bodices. Mixed bathing in increasingly revealing costumes became popular, while dancing the foxtrot, Charleston and waltz was a favoured pastime in public halls and cabarets. Women smoked, often using long cigarette holders, rode pillion on motor bikes, a few learnt to drive cars and all went to the pictures where romance dominated as the theme, culminating with the excitement of the 'talkies' in 1929, when enthralled thousands listened to and watched Al Jolson in *The Jazz Singer*. Picture palaces of vast and often sumptuous proportions and style were built and Australians became the world's

During World War I, many women were employed in offices as clerks and typists. The war helped the transition of women into the workplace and, on their return home, some men found employment difficult to obtain. The scene is Myer, Melbourne.

most regular patrons of the film with attendances reaching 126 million in 1929. The popularity of the cinema helped to develop a local industry, although it began to wane in the late 1920s due to competition from imported American films.

Middle class and some conservative women joined organizations such as the Country Women's Association, the Australian Women's National League and a host of others which had their counterpart in the religious world, where the evergreen Temperance bodies still survived. In 1921 Edith Cowan became the first woman elected to an Australian parliament when she won the seat of West Perth for the Nationalist party. She uttered the sentiments appropriate to its ideology of conservatism and nationalism, but she also proclaimed that she would stand by women and demanded their right to vote in union ballots to prevent strikes; she worried about class consciousness and wanted the shilling impost on prams carried on public transport to be removed. The minister promised to comply immediately with her last request. In 1922 a deputation of women from several organizations complained to the New South Wales Premier that single men were receiving a basic wage based on a family component. They claimed that such a wage was absurd in that it ignored the needs of large families and harmful because it encouraged birth control and sapped the health of the community. The Premier promised to deal with the matter 'later on'.

The middle class, urban dwelling woman of the 1920s was, in general, as distant in the fruits of progress from her mother of thirty years before as she in her turn was from the woman of the seventeenth century. Technology and work had wrought the change for both, and the war was a turning-point for modern women, while steam power and industrialization had been responsible for the earlier changes. Time payment meant that a range of appliances including washing machines, electric irons, stoves and kettles, hot water services and radiators were procurable while gramophones and radio sets, of which over 300,000 were licensed by 1929, provided music in the home. The poor enjoyed few if any of these amenities, but the gradual spread of electricity, even into the bush, helped to bring about change.

For children, life was an orderly process governed by parents who insisted on set patterns of behaviour in the home as much as teachers did in the schools. A church service was followed by the Sunday roast and then an 'outing', possibly to visit relatives when children were often called upon to recite or sing. Clothes were handed down and fruit eaten sparingly. After school, jam was spread on bread sometimes with cream to top it off, but at the main meal there was usually a pudding of some kind, even if only of rice or sago. American contributions in the form of sundaes, Life Savers and Kellogg's Cornflakes came on the market and were occasional treats by the early twenties. 'The health food of a nation', Peters ice cream, appeared in 1929.

In many schools, the children still used slates, the readers contained the long-after remembered stories of awakening consciousness, while sums, parsing, spelling and tables were everyday fare for home work, which, depending on economic circumstances, was done in exercise books or on brown paper. Boys grouped in 'gangs' in which the shanghai, a Y-shaped, hand-held catapult, was a favourite weapon, while, after school or on Saturdays, to go rabbiting or yabbying (called lobbying in Queensland) for small, freshwater crays was always a source of excitement for both boys and girls. In the bush, children rode horses to school, often two or more to the one horse. On cold mornings, a warm, bare back was preferable to a cold, stiff saddle.

Inevitably, elders asked children the question, 'What are you going to do when you grow up?' which implied that the precious days of childhood were only preparatory to the real stuff of life. The answers from the boys were mostly fanciful — fireman, policeman, sailor, farmer, or whatever happened to be in vogue such as aviator. The girls had only one choice — marriage — perhaps preceded by a career as a nurse, shop assistant, school teacher, office worker or whatever was deemed a genteel task. Yet for children to grow up in the twenties was to sense security. War was over and had not yet come again, the economy seemed to work moderately well and the phenomenon of the broken home was rare. At the end of the year came seemingly endless summer holidays when it was always hot and Santa Claus was looked forward to eagerly, although in every school room, there was the child sceptic who declared Santa to be a fraud. Above all childhood was a time in which to go to bed dog-tired and wake up looking forward to another day, when 'to go out to play' at some time, was a normal expectation.

The predominant factor which affected the lives of the thousands of young men who came home from the war was the need to settle back into society and find a role in its economy. Preference for jobs for returned men was accepted federally and in all the states except Queensland where trade unionists always came first, but unemployment rose to twelve percent in 1921 and varied from five percent to eleven percent during the decade. The unmarried men rapidly spent their deferred pay and gratuities but behind all the returned diggers stood the Returned Soldiers League which had 30,000 members by 1925 and eventually built clubs in the suburbs and country towns, especially in New South Wales.

The League rapidly became a powerful body with access to government, and it ensured that the provisions of the Repatriation Act of 1917, designed to help the returned men, were followed. The League fiercely propagated the legend of the Anzacs, held to a hard line on White Australia and generally took an anti-radical stance on matters it failed to understand or accept, such as Bolshevism. Its contribution, and that of the non-political Legacy movement founded in 1923, to the welfare of the returned men and to the widows and children of the dead, was immense.

The old myth of an empty land, with vast numbers of nameless Asians poised with grasping hands to people it, still held strong amongst the people and the planners in Australia. The land, it was thought, could produce abundantly, which would help people Australia and keep out any would-be invaders. By exporting the produce of the land the economy would thrive. To get all this going a few things were needed — suitable land, people, credit, roads, water, railways, determination and hard work — the rest would follow. It was a neat and circular argument given shape in the phrase 'Men, Money and Markets' and had its remote origins with Hughes who had postponed the dream of Australia as a social laboratory in order to get on with the war. Pragmatism had replaced ideals, and, by the time Billy had come back to his senses, there were other men with different ideas, based essentially on the market-place, ready to take over affairs.

Amongst the new men was Earle Page, a medical practitioner from Grafton, New South Wales. He was elected to the Federal Parliament in 1919, where he joined and led ten others who represented the Country Party. The Country Party was essentially conservative and had its origins in the conviction that city-based politicians would invariably neglect the needs of 'the man on the land', but the Party managed for a while to work in moderate harmony with Hughes. Under Hughes, Parliament stumbled along, with its most useful acts being the acquisition of control of the Commonwealth Oil Refineries and Amalgamated Wireless. The Prime Minister irritated the Melbourne and Sydney financial establishments by his attacks on their power; but he placated all conservative elements in society in late 1919 by forcing the expulsion from Parliament of Hugh Mahon, Irish-born Labor member for Kalgoorlie, on the grounds that Mahon had uttered seditious and disloyal sentiments in referring to 'this bloody and accursed Empire'.

Hughes could only maintain the uneasy alliance between Nationalist and Country Party members by offering sops to both rural and industrial interests. He introduced a tariff bill which effectively wanted to make protection the basis of domestic policy. Few seemed aware that such a step was also a fundamental act of foreign policy for to protect one's own industries was to disadvantage others. Fearing protection because farmers wanted to buy agricultural machinery and items such as fencing wire at the lowest price, irrespective of their origin, Page and his members were pacified by subsidies to local production which was another form of protection. As a result, Australian citizens paid to keep both primary and secondary industry economically viable and to retain the levels of employment in both. Another consequence was that secondary industry had little incentive to improve its efficiency or to compete for sales on overseas markets.

Given the fickle support of the Country Party, Hughes decided to bolster his position in late 1921 by appointing the National Party member, Stanley Bruce, as his Treasurer. Bruce, though born in Australia, was in all respects English. Melbourne Grammar, Cambridge and the British Army, in which he fought at Gallipoli with distinction, formed his spirit; an Oxford accent and the best of English fashions cloaked his exterior. His inscrutable calm and air of detachment hid a mental agility of which Hughes seemed unaware. Bruce and Page combined to forge Billy's downfall and the former Laborite was forced to step down from being Prime Minister by the quintessence of Australian conservatism.

To the Country Party Hughes had become too radical for comfort so they refused to maintain the coalition, which left him without the numbers to govern. Although Bruce had openly pledged his support to Billy as his leader, he accepted the post of Prime Minister, made Page his deputy, and five of the eleven cabinet posts went to the Country Party. Billy neither forgot nor forgave, and he went to the back bench probably uncomforted by the thought that his undoing had been his inability to rid himself of some of his Labor principles. Reviled and called a 'rat' by many in the Labor movement, Billy's tragedy was his exaggerated patriotism which had led him into conflict with those to whom, at heart, he always belonged.

The new government, formed in February 1923, set about implementing Bruce's policy of 'Men, Money and Markets'. In essence, it meant populating the rural areas with settlers, whether native-born or immigrants, providing the money for settlement, and finding the markets for the wool, wheat, dried fruits and other produce. The states, again all under Labor governments except Victoria (where the Country Party held too great an electoral advantage), were wary of immigration given the unacceptable levels of unemployment. Nevertheless, Bruce went to London and negotiated an agreement whereby £34,000,000 was made available to assist British migration. In the following decade 261,000 Britons arrived of whom eighty percent were given assistance and a quota system saw a few thousand Italians arrive, many of whom went to sugar cane farms in Queensland.

The greater part of the British immigrants remained in the cities and towns helping to produce and, in large measure, consume the increase in manufactured goods, which rose by one third in value from 1919 to 1929. Light industry, chemical, metal, engineering and electrical firms, all prospered, helped by cheap coal and steel, high tariffs and electrification of the suburban railways. Tariff-protected secondary industries made goods for the Australian market, thereby swelling profits for some and raising living standards for many, but the increasing trend to place almost total reliance on primary exports to service national accounts was apparent. Any marked fall in overseas demand and prices for primary exports could spell ruin. In the decade before 1930, borrowing, mostly from Britain, amounted to £250,000,000, and after 1925 no year had a favourable balance of trade. Very few saw this imbalance as an ominous sign for the future.

If the new immigrants, like their predecessors in the nineteenth century, were unwilling to risk life on the land, the returned soldiers showed no such reluctance, and 37,000 of them, with their wives and families, decided to give it a go. A market seemed assured in Britain for tinned and dried fruit, wheat, wool and hides, and the fatal myth was peddled that the land could be worked cheaply. A former politician stomped about

Broken Hill Proprietary Limited began steel making at Newcastle in 1915; by 1925 production had risen to over 300,000 tons annually. BHP also acquired collieries around Newcastle and bought its own shipping fleet.

proclaiming 'A million farmers on a million acres'. The Commonwealth was prepared to put up £1000 per settler but the actual settlement process was left to the states, which also incurred huge costs thereby. Often the selected land was infertile, acreage too small, improvements too costly, labour too expensive and livestock, or trees for fruitgrowers, unsuitable. Nevertheless, the settlement scheme went forward with reckless disregard for either planning or consequences.

In the Mallee, in Gippsland, in the Western District and in the Goulburn Valley in Victoria, on Queensland's Darling Downs, in the west and around Griffith in New South Wales, in the north-west and in the Tamar Valley of Tasmania, new settlers tried to wrest a living from the land. The experiment proved a costly failure in public and private money, in torn emotions and misery, with appalling conditions in which families frequently lived on rabbits and parrot stew. In Western Australia, the group settlements for British immigrants equally turned out to be a failure, although a dairy industry was established. The whole episode of post-war rural settlement should have learnt from the experiences of small selectors in the 1870s and 1880s. The miracle was that about half the settlers somehow survived, although for many it was a short-lived

The 'No. 1 Rabbit Proof Fence' in Western Australia ran for 1,176 miles from near Esperance to east of Port Hedland. Other states also built fences but these proved useless in stemming the tide of the rabbit. On the Western Australian fence, a worker and his camels are pictured heading south for Christmas, 1926.

reprieve because the Depression of the following decade saw many more leave their blocks.

A judge was asked to examine the settlement scheme and explain why it failed, especially as the states lost well over £200,000,000 as a result and rural debt was high. He saw some evidence that hard work and persistence had been rewarded and cited the Murrumbidgee irrigation areas and parts of the Victorian Mallee country as instances. Without malice, he stated bluntly that many of the men were unsuited to farming, but suited or not, they could never have succeeded on inadequate land, little or no capital, mortgages and falling prices for their produce. Notwithstanding this, the rural myth persisted with its unshakeable promise to keep out the 'hordes' and bring home the bacon. To balance the ledger somewhat, more land had been opened to the plough and for the fruit tree. More importantly for the future, some insight had been gained into how rural settlement could be successfully undertaken.

Bruce, impeccable in word and manner, was essentially a prudent man, whose concern was to make the federal system work. He was especially troubled in the area of industrial relations, with the workers wanting higher wages as prices rose and the employers intent on increasing profits. Arbitration, intended to temper both drives, could work effectively only while a careful equilibrium was maintained. When employers or trade union leaders pushed the scales too far in one direction, lock-outs or strikes followed. If industry couldn't expand because wages were too high, the economy suffered, while workers in a period of rising prices were always disadvantaged. It was an intricate maze to Bruce, especially at a time when Labor premiers appeared to favour the workers.

In Queensland, where Labor was in power from 1915 to 1929, Premier E.G. Theodore brought in a living wage, unemployment insurance and abolished the Legislative Council. His plan to expand the economy with state steel works and coal mines was defeated when London bankers refused him £9,000,000 in loan money because he proposed to increase rents on pastoral properties. As a result, unemployment rose in the state to nearly twenty-two percent and there was a recession until Theodore capitulated on pastoral rents. Jack Lang became Premier of New South Wales in 1925 and was accused, wrongly, of flirting with socialists and 'Reds'. In fact he abhorred both. His government introduced widows pensions, compulsory insurance paid by employers, child endowment, abolition of fees in secondary schools, a Government Insurance Office and better conditions for rural workers. All of this seemed to threaten social equilibrium when viewed from the conservative standpoint.

Another source of concern to conservatives was that the Labor Party itself appeared to be tainted by socialism given that its 1921 Federal Conference had set as an objective 'the socialisation of industry, production, distribution and exchange', although the Conference carefully refrained from stating in which millenium it was to be achieved. Conservative anxiety was heightened when a series of strikes occurred, including some by public servants and school teachers in Western Australia in 1920 and by Melbourne policemen in 1923. Rioting and looting took place during the police strike, and a right-wing group of militants, called the White Guard, was formed under the direction of Sir Brudenell White, retired chief of the general staff of the A.I.F., to resist the advances of Bolshevism, which he considered a threat to Australian society. Under these circumstances, Bruce was assured of widespread support. The fact that future economic stability was jeopardized by continued and large overseas borrowing in London and New York was not yet apparent. Nonetheless, Bruce formed a Loan Council to control public borrowing and the electorate showed good sense by agreeing at a referendum in

1928 to give centralized powers to the Federal Government which made the Premiers accept a curb on their spending.

In 1926 Bruce had decided to tackle the arbitration question head on by increasing Commonwealth powers, but he lost a referendum on the matter, basically because the electorate was unsure of what was proposed. Undaunted, he went ahead with legislation designed to curb union power and sharpen the teeth of the Commonwealth Arbitration Court. By this time union strength had risen to sixty percent of eligible workers and the Australian Council of Trade Unions had been formed to present a united front to employers and the government itself. Union reaction was predictable and a worker's life was lost during riots on the Melbourne waterfront in 1928. It was a period of direct conflict between capital and labour with a mounting number of days lost in strikes everywhere. In the upshot, Bruce decided on a remarkable turn about. He would pass all power in industrial matters to the states, retaining for the Commonwealth, control over its own territory, its own employees and those engaged in overseas and interstate shipping.

Hughes seized his chance and moved to amend Bruce's bill, winning by a single vote. This led to an election being called for October 1929. The electorate had not understood either Bruce or his motives but had trusted him when the feeling was widespread that he knew what he was doing. He lost the election, miserably, with Labor winning forty-six of the seventy-five seats including the Prime Minister's own blue ribbon seat of Flinders. It was good for Bruce and his country that he lost because he had become a centre of extreme discord. Bruce, despite the spats and the voice, was a patriot and a man before his time with an urge towards moderate interventionism, a feeling for technocracy and a realization that governments had to be structured on an objective rather than emotional basis. He served Australia well as High Commissioner in London, where he spoke the language of power to perfection, and elsewhere as a roving diplomat. In his latter years, Bruce accepted the first Chancellorship of the Australian National University, and, when he died in London in 1967, he asked that his ashes be scattered over the bush capital, Canberra, which he had helped found.

In May 1927 the Federal Capital moved to Canberra, the city which was the dream child of an architect of rare genius, Walter Burley Griffin. From America, Burley Griffin had admired the radical developments in politics and social legislation of the young Australian democracy, and, in response to an international competition, he planned a capital to express those ideals. He came to Australia to oversee construction of the city but by 1920 Griffin, himself a difficult and unyielding character, had become disillusioned at bureaucratic interference and he departed to leave others to fulfil his plan. He was absent when the Duke of York opened the new Parliament in a temporary but pleasing structure amongst the gum trees. Nellie Melba led the singing of the national anthem by 9,000 whites and the whole proceedings were watched by a solitary Aborigine, who left no record of his reaction to the ritual.

Bruce took seriously the need for research into problems besetting the rural sector, and in 1926 the Council for Scientific and Industrial Research was firmly set up and properly funded. It helped in the elimination of the prickly pear, a pest which had ravaged millions of acres of good land, especially in Queensland. To eradicate it, the cactoblastis insect was brought from South America and did its work of destruction so efficiently that grateful farmers at Dalby in Queensland, which had been particularly affected, erected a monument to the insect. Despite the high sounding name of the research body, the rural myth was strong in its ranks also and very little attention was paid to the needs of research for secondary industry. Manufacturing lagged behind developments elsewhere, which affected profitability, made export difficult and shored up the accepted tenet that the country rode on the back of the sheep.

As early as 1894 Lawrence Hargrave had become airborne with the help of four box kites at Stanwell Park, New South Wales, although he was never able to adapt his great invention of a compressed-air engine, powered by three rotating cylinders, for use in flight. Australians remained fascinated by the progress made in aviation and by the 1920s it was an area of great technological advancement. Again the rural sector benefited greatly with its need for fast, safe transport and reliable communications. In 1928 John Flynn, a pastor of the Presbyterian Church, established an aerial medical service in the north-west of Queensland with headquarters at Cloncurry. Communication with outback stations was possible by means of a pedal wireless, and the Flying Doctor Service treated patients on the spot or flew them to the closest hospital. It was a service unique in the world and its contribution to the people of the outback was immense in the social, medical and educational spheres.

In 1928 Bert Hinkler flew the longest solo flight in the short history of aviation. In a small, single-engine plane, he flew from London to Darwin, and his epic and courageous journey earnt him £10,000 as well as a dahlia and a soup named in his honour. Shortly afterwards, Kingsford Smith, Charles Ulm and two Americans flew from San Francisco to Brisbane and then across the Tasman. By the time of Hinkler's great feat, the

John Flynn, 'Flynn of the Inland', was a Presbyterian minister who gave his whole life
to the people of the outback and founded the Flying Doctor Service. He took radio to
the inland in 1925 and is here pictured in that year, bogged near Alice Springs.

Australian continent was already criss-crossed with airmail services,
Qantas had linked the outback towns of Queensland since 1922 and the
conquest of the air was a reality.

Holden's Motor Body Works at Woodville, South Australia, was producing over 20,000 car bodies by 1924 to fit an American chassis, while at
Geelong, Victoria, Ford, in conjunction with General Motors, began
assembling and was soon producing 36,000 bodies annually. The T-
model Ford had come into widespread use. By the end of the twenties,
half a million cars carried six million passengers to work, leisure and
romance, whether in the Ford or in a more stylish model — Renault,
Essex, Chandler or Chrysler. The horse still held its own in country areas,
although tractors in small numbers had begun to shatter the silence of the
bush. Car transport meant that roads had to be upgraded, but sealing
them was costly, accounting for a quarter of public expenditure by the
end of the decade, which added to overseas debt.

Henry Lawson died on 2 September 1922. Lost for years in the mists of
alcohol and eking out a miserable existence on charity, his literary talents
were spent. For countless Australians, his passion for hopelessness
entwined with endurance was epitomized in the dying words of his
famous character, the woman of the bush, Mrs Wilson, who told her

children to feed the pigs and calves and 'to be sure and water them geraniums'. Lawson became the symbol of the embattled visionary whose sad but all-embracing eyes had looked on a world in which the sounds were gradually muted by increasing deafness and in which, to him, neither the flora nor fauna had mattered. Lawson had seen through to the land and its people both in city and bush and there was a frailty in all he wrote which resembled the land he loved. Like it he left a gentle but indelible mark on those who peopled it.

Gladys Moncrieff became known affectionately as 'Our Glad' to all Australians after she sang the lead role in *Maid of the Mountains* at the Theatre Royal in Melbourne in 1921, for the first of her 3,000 appear-ances. In the following year Jack O'Hagan's song 'The road to Gundagai' became popular after it was published in sheet music by Allen and Com-pany. Arthur Hoey Davis, creator of *On Our Selection* lived on but wrote little as his Dad and Dave became celebrities of stage and screen, while 'Banjo' Paterson passed from memory for a time. Only Christopher Brennan — his head filled with languages, literature, scholarship, laughter and love — strode on, for he was a poet who belonged neither to time nor place. In the end he was struck down in the place of his birth, Sydney, to which he had given all his great qualities of mind and heart. In 1925 Sydney University dismissed him as associate professor and head of the Department of German and Comparative Literature for adultery and drunkenness. Its gesture was symbolic of an age in which many of those who loved life seemed to be outsiders threatening the stability of entrenched morality and order.

The great literary work of the period was the trilogy, *The Fortunes of Richard Mahony*. It was written by Ethel Robertson who called herself Henry Handel Richardson, and it had the golden days of the 1850s as its setting. The main character, based on her father, struggled between an old world and a new one and found rest in neither, much as W.C. Wentworth had done. The book remains a poignant testimony to those whose lives were broken because Australia to them never became home, whether in heart or in mind. Because he was wholly Australian, John Shaw Neilson achieved what eluded Robertson and he wrote of the mystery and lure of his native land with mastery. Half-blind, often appearing to be stupid, Neilson grew up at Minimay in the Victorian Wimmera and worked around Sea Lake in the Mallee until the late 1920s. Unmarried and lonely, his verse was tender and delicate and 'in that poor country' he was no stranger, for he neither knew nor longed for another. Neilson's pen was matched by Elioth Gruner's brush for Gruner painted the landscape with the same delicacy. Margaret Preston was the Brennan of the brush, turning into still life the eternal truths the poet had put into verse.

Millions of Australians had never heard of Neilson or Gruner, but they all knew something about Ginger Meggs, of Ginger's girl friend Minnie, his enemy, Tiger Kelly, his rival for Minnie's affection, Eddie, his mates, Benny and Ocker, and Mrs Meggs, the archetypal mother of strength and stability. James Bancks was the Sydney-born cartoonist and creator, in 1922, of the lovable figure of Ginger with his mop of red hair and his black waistcoat, who at one moment was wheedling ice-cream from an Italian vendor and the next was softening-up two 'sooks' named Cuthbert and Wentworth. Through thousands of escapades in the Sydney *Sunday*

Raymond Longford directed *The Dinkum Bloke* starring Lottie Lyell (1923). Longford was the greatest of the early Australian film directors but when the local industry declined he became unemployed and worked as a watchman on the Sydney wharves. He died in 1959 and was buried at the Northern Suburbs Cemetery, Sydney, in the same grave as Lottie Lyell who had been his mistress.

Sun and other papers, Ginger was an essentially urban larrikin, philosopher, battler and humorist. Children and adults laughed with him, worried about him, hoped and dreamt with him. On the twenty-fifth birthday of his appearance, the occasion was celebrated in children's wards of state hospitals. Ginger bore the stamp of his creator Bancks, who was generous and warm, and Ginger carried also the old legend of the bush in his reactions to figures of authority — parents, policemen and schoolteachers. At his death in 1952, Bancks left Ginger as a legacy to a generation of battling Australians who had gone through war and depression with him and came through in the end to the good times.

To an increasing proportion of Australians, especially adherents of the Reformed Churches, religion was steadily more closely identified with such matters as opposition to drinking, gambling, and Sunday violation, and the rejection of anything that threatened stability in the social order. Publications such as John and Ezra Norton's weekly *Truth*, with its emphasis on sexual, domestic and political scandals, alarmed them, but it was widely read nonetheless. Sectarianism had been given a new dimension through the involvement of Catholics with the Labor movement. In New South Wales the unhappy story of the flight of a young, deranged nun from a Wagga convent in 1921 caused waves of resentment and thinly-veiled hate to flow over the embarrassed Catholic community. Catholics seemed a race apart with their preoccupation about birth control, divorce and feminine immodesty. They were protected in their own schools and adult organizations such as the Holy Name and Vincent de Paul Societies, while Freemasons often denied in covert ways their entry into business institutions. The teaching orders directed them into professions and the public service, but in the main they lived alongside Protestants in peace, played the same sports, suffered the same anxieties and worshipped the same God for the Australian Commonwealth was still, professedly, in large measure, Christian.

Probably less than one in ten white Australians had seen an Aborigine, and perhaps one in ten thousand knew anything about them that was not derisory. An academic Association for the Preservation of the Native Races was founded, and Professors Baldwin Spencer and A.P. Elkin had become useful advisors to state and federal governments. In 1927 an Australian Aboriginal Protection Society secured the abolition of Aboriginal child labour, but the Aboriginal population throughout the continent had shrunk to about 60,000 full bloods. Around the towns the blacks were an irritant to the righteous, but on some government reserves and mission stations there was a measure of good will, if at times ill-directed, and they could live there peacefully, unmolested by those who now inhabited their land. In the north the cattle industry relied heavily on their labour, and in the south many part bloods were itinerant workers. Many children grew up without parents or race for the government decided to separate part-Aboriginal children from their Aboriginal mothers in an attempt to integrate them into white society. It was an exercise in inhumanity that bore its fruits in sorrow for decades.

In some places in the desert, in the Kimberley, at Cape York and on Arnhem Land the Aborigines still lived in the ways of their ancestors, and like them they were subject to the same barbarisms from the whites, although now only spasmodically. In 1926 a police party killed eleven Aborigines and burned their bodies in the Kimberley and probably killed another thirty in the same year. Another atrocity, again implicating the police, took place in the Northern Territory in 1928 involving the killing of thirty-one Aborigines. The day had passed when such behaviour was

From 1901 to 1927, when Parliament House in Canberra was opened, the Commonwealth Parliament sat in Melbourne and the federal public service was centred there. The charabanc belonged to Pioneer Tourist Coaches which later sold out to Ansett.

acceptable and there was a sense of outrage amongst whites in southern and eastern Australia, but no white man was brought to trial for the murders. Nevertheless, after 139 years of intermittent slaughter, the last atrocities of that nature closed a chapter in the history of the Aboriginal race.

Until the late twenties, it was possible to look back on the decade as one of development after the years of the Great War. The value of production rose, the work force grew, home ownership was slowly becoming a reality and 260,000 immigrants had arrived from Britain of whom eighty percent were assisted. The population, over six million by 1928, saw signs of progress everywhere. The Melbourne tramway system was under electrification, as was the railway line from Sydney Central to Oatley, and the first traffic lights were installed in Melbourne. Vegemite was produced and gradually accepted, Anna Pavlova came on a ballet tour, Melbourne University Press was founded and the gangster 'Squizzy' Taylor was gunned down in Carlton, Victoria.

Other signs were not so promising. The birth rate fell, prices rose, unemployment hovered from six to eleven percent, the cities grew but the rural population fell, while a submerged urban poor suffered without much comment. Over two million koala skins were exported from the eastern states, resulting in the virtual extinction of the animal in Victoria and New South Wales. There had been unprecedented conflict in industry, militancy grew, right-wing elements took shape and there was much bitterness between capital and labour. Despite the efforts of the Loan Council, the states had continued to over-borrow, and, generally, Australians over-spent as if there would be no day of reckoning. The twenties, outwardly so full of gaiety and promise and underneath marked by harshness, tinsel and a lack of seriousness, had brought progress but they also gave a hostage to fortune which the next decade would be asked to redeem.

CHAPTER FOURTEEN
The Unforgotten Thirties

T he whole thrust of Australian nationalism had been realized in the person of James Henry Scullin. Son of a railway worker, Scullin was born in 1876 at Trawalla, near Beaufort in Victoria, and educated to primary level. He was the product of the Western District of Victoria and of Ballarat, where he won prizes as a public speaker. His ideals were shaped by the bush, trade unionism, the Labor Party, the conscription conflict and the Catholic Church. The influence of the latter was never obtrusive nor in his whole political career did he ever work directly in favour of that Church. The essential platforms of the Labor movement — humanity and justice — were the forces that motivated him but they were frail weapons in the battle for survival Australia was about to enter.

Elected federal leader of the Labor Party in April 1928, Scullin made many speeches in Parliament warning of impending economic disaster as shown by rising unemployment, unfavourable trade figures, a large national deficit, mostly owed on loans raised in London, and the parallels with the economic downturn that led to the depression of the 1890s. Just as his cry of doom seemed vindicated, he succeeded Bruce as Prime Minister. Stock prices were falling and London investors were becoming shy of lending; wheat and wool prices fell by a half and a quarter respectively; industrial conflict on the coalfields and waterfront abounded; a drought had begun; and no solutions seemed in sight. Scullin's government took office in late October 1929 during the very week which saw the collapse of Wall Street in New York with a catastrophic drop in share prices and a loss of confidence amongst investors causing a spate of suicides. The same happened on the London Stock Exchange and the

Great Depression had begun. Its paralysing impact on the economy and workforce was readily apparent, but few understood its causes and fewer still had any clear idea as to how it could be combated.

In Australia the effects of the Depression were clearly discernible in both the private and public sectors. The Federal Labor government was reduced to a shambles of conflicting factional interests with those on the right and left having diametrically opposed solutions, roughly summed up as spend less or spend more. In the centre of the Party stood Scullin and his Treasurer, Ted Theodore, who opted for a little of both. Meanwhile, the conservatives sat back, effectively opposed any legislation they deemed unsatisfactory by using their huge Senate majority to block bills, nibbled away at the waverers in the government, and waited for the whole sorry edifice to collapse.

The private sector, like its public counterpart, was divided. The poor, the unemployed, the small businessman whose economic base was shattered, the shopkeeper who no longer had customers or who had to extend credit beyond his resources, the professional whose services could not be afforded, the entrepreneur who had gambled and faced unpayable debts, the farmer who had overcapitalized in hope and had walked off his property in despair; all these suffered deprivation to a greater or lesser degree. On the other hand, the rich whose capital was safe, the employed whose jobs were not at risk and especially those in government services, the clever who had enough capital to take advantage of those who were forced to sell a home or a business; all of these survived and some prospered. Those on salaries could absorb cuts because the drop in commodity prices compensated. To such people, the Depression was a stage on which they played a part, but as mere observers, although some were not even that as they remained sheltered in their affluent suburbs, with their rounds of social events, where misery did not penetrate. The rich, the employed and the secure did not join the ranks of those who bore the marks of the Great Depression for a generation, and passed its memory on as a caution to their children.

In the pyschology of the nation, the gap that opened between promise and reality was the deepest source of concern. Since the days of the goldrushes, with the one exception of the 1890s, there had always been the assurance of steady progress. Only the heartless or the obtuse ever denied the existence of both rural and urban poverty in that triumphal march towards the workers' paradise. Yet the unemployed had never previously averaged at least twenty-four percent of the workforce, which it did for five long, hard years from 1930 to 1934, with over twenty-eight percent out of work in 1932. Only Germany topped that figure, and it says much for Australian resilience and common sense that there was no shift to the totalitarianism which took place in Germany with the rise of Hitler.

Nevertheless, unrest caused some to turn to utopian solutions. The Communist Party increased in numbers rapidly and fought valiantly for people evicted from their homes because they could not keep up rental or mortgage payments. As a result of their manifest concern, Communists were elected to key positions in several important trade unions. Meanwhile, the followers of Social Credit propounded a doctrine of supply and demand probably only understood by its originator, Major Douglas, and his devotees. Some Sydney Rotarians formed the 'All for Australia League' with business and professional men at its core and a rapidly growing membership in New South Wales, Victoria and South Australia. The League was especially concerned at the ineptitude of politicians, and it determined to rid the political arena of those elements it disliked, which, after the League's merger with the opposition parties, were seen to be chiefly in the Labor Party.

Another sign of unrest was apparent in rural areas where the Country Party was dominant. In Western Australia the Wheatgrowers Union adopted some of the organization and tactics of industrial unionism to fight foreclosures for debt. In New South Wales, both in the the Riverina and in New England, movements aiming at the setting up of new states flourished, because Sydney was seen as the source of mismanagement and neglectful of people's interests, especially those of country dwellers. In time such moves for separation came to nothing. The White Army continued in Victoria. In New South Wales some returned soldiers, alarmed at what they saw as a thrust to demoralize the institutions of democracy, associated themselves and others in a body called the New Guard. Armed, enthusiastic and secretive, they were a pale imitation of Mussolini's Blackshirts and their numbers grew to about 60,000 in Sydney. The Guard busied itself mainly in the violent disruption of meetings it suspected to be communist inspired. Its one original act took place on 19 March 1932. The newly-constructed Sydney Harbour Bridge was the pride of the city and its future symbol. Premier Jack Lang had decided that he was the most worthy person to cut the ribbon at its opening. The New Guard leadership had decided equally as determinedly that neither Lang nor his followers were the appropriate representatives of the law-abiding, Empire-loving citizens they claimed to defend. As Lang was about to cut the ribbon, a Guard member rode forward on horseback and slashed it with his sword. He was promptly removed to a centre for the mentally deranged. The ordinary citizenry of New South Wales and

The Great Depression of the early 1930s affected the lives of millions. Many of the homeless slept in places like the Sydney Domain.

throughout Australia stood bemused at this event which implied that the state itself was unable to preserve its own integrity.

During the Depression, there were bankruptcies and suicides, heart-breaks and anxieties, which bit deep into psyches, especially when the loss of work meant the loss of a home. Men, married and single, tramped the roads, rode the rattler between the towns, begged and hawked trinkets, while cynics suggested that the depressed times gave some men an opportunity to flee their marital and paternal responsibilities. Dole queues of men lined up for 7s per week if single, 14s if married and an additional 7s for each child. It was no longer a crime to dye an army overcoat and the government itself issued thousands of surplus coats left over from the war but now dyed black. Wearing one became an outward sign of misery and defeat. In the ranks of those who wore the old army cast-offs was John Ryan, who had marched with the 'Kangaroos' from Wagga to Sydney in 1915 to enlist and won the Victoria Cross during the attack on the Hindenburg defences in the last weeks of the war. After his return home, he had adjusted badly to civilian life, and by 1935 he was destitute and on the road again seeking work. At his death in 1941, John Ryan, VC was a victim of both war and Depression.

State governments financed the dole and some public works, in part, by a wages tax, but their support for the unemployed was inadequate and partly grudging. In Victoria the Shrine of Remembrance, the Yarra River Boulevard and the Great Ocean Road are monuments to the Depression because men working on sustenance, called 'susso', built them. Some of those who lost their homes often went with their families to shanty towns, like 'Happy Valley' in the sand hills near Sydney's La Perouse, where they erected ramshackle dwellings from bags and beaten-out kerosene tins and where they at least enjoyed fresh air and were given unsaleable produce by the local fishermen and the Chinese market gardeners. There were such places in the other big cities and none worse than Jolimont at Melbourne, where homeless men lived in conditions that many of them had seen paralleled on the Western Front fifteen years previously.

In country areas, gold prospecting became much more than a pastime, while the rabbit filled many a pot and empty stomach. A sustenance worker, Jim Larcombe, found the last of the big nuggets, the Golden Eagle weighing 78 pounds, in Western Australia at Coolgardie. At times there was violence when the unemployed marched in protest in the cities, but mostly acceptance of their lot was the norm. For those who could get government assistance, survival was reduced to the purchase of basic necessities. Bread was spread with dripping in many a home, onions became a staple, hotels induced drinkers with a free sandwich, blankets were replaced with wheat bags in the bush, and in the cities cardboard covered holes in footwear. The horse came back into its own as a means of transport and traction, replacing cars and tractors.

Many children born in the twenties grew to the age of reason and then lived as teenagers in the thirties without knowing either affluence or much comfort for there was still ten percent unemployment in 1939. In the cities their parents moved from one boarding house to another, while the father tried to earn a quid by selling something, possibly one of the new gadgets such as a sewing machine or a vacuum cleaner — mostly bought on hire purchase. Moving from school to school, the children picked up the rudiments of an education, but above all they learnt to survive without revealing their poverty to their better-off school mates. In the bush some children grew up rarely wearing shoes, eating the plainest of food and working on the family farm for hours before and after school. The children of the Great Depression were a generation that endured to go into another war, only to see the semblance of good times come with the 1950s. For many it was too late for enjoyment.

One prominent Melbourne citizen was amongst those who did their utmost to combat the Depression. Sidney Myer was born Simcha Baevski of Jewish parents in Russia in 1878. He joined his brother Elcon in Victoria in 1894 and prospered as a merchant, initially at Bendigo, and then in Melbourne. By 1930 the Myer store in Bourke Street was renowned throughout the state with its only rival in Australia being Hordern's vast Italianate emporium on Brickfield Hill, Sydney. Myer issued shares to his staff, but cut their and his own wages in 1931 so that no staff need suffer retrenchment. He gave an example to other capitalists of how to stimulate the economy by selling Australian made goods, enlarging his own premises, donating over £20,000 to the Yarra Boulevard scheme and holding a vast Christmas dinner for the unemployed on Christmas Day 1930. Myer's life was one marked by philanthropy, love for and encouragement of the arts and education. His quiet revolution in the retail

The Christmas shopping at Myer's Melbourne. Sidney Myer was born of Jewish parents in Russia in 1878. He was a philanthropist and patron of the arts as well as a leading retail trader.

trade changed Melbourne in a way that made him one of the outstanding figures of his period.

Labor's short period of office, 1929–31, was eventful. Scullin's overwhelming numbers in the House of Representatives, forty-six to twenty-four, ought to have ensured a moral ascendancy despite his lack of a majority in the Senate. The capabilities of Theodore, Brennan, Lyons, Fenton and Anstey in his Cabinet ought again to have given him the human agents through which to govern well. A few steps were taken to relieve the general economic situation — personal income tax on the better-off was raised in order to boost government finances, defence expenditure cut, tariffs raised and the gold market controlled. Scullin was faced with a hostile Senate and an unco-operative chairman of the Commonwealth Bank in the person of Robert Gibson, who was determined to make goverments balance their budgets. More importantly, he and his Cabinet, lacked clarity as to what course to follow. The Prime Minister turned firstly to the farmers whom he exhorted to grow more wheat in the hope that increased production would compensate for falling prices. Wheat in abundance was grown, but prices remained low and it proved impossible to ensure the promised 4s per bushel of wheat, which consequently alienated a whole generation of farmers from the Labor Party. Despite the huge wheat crop, export income in 1930 was half the 1928 level. The basic wage had to be dropped by ten percent.

Scullin's other course of action was to invite, reluctantly, an expert from the Bank of England to advise on the Australian economic situation. The expert, Otto Niemeyer, duly arrived in the winter of 1930 and, after investigation, advised the government, with some degree of ingenuity, that Australians had been living beyond their means, that they now had to cut back in public and private spending, that governments had to run their affairs without borrowing and that wages had to be reduced. Federal and state governments made vague promises about balancing their budgets, which they, and Niemeyer, knew was unrealistic because to do so at the time would have resulted in even greater social disorder. Niemeyer's financial advice was simple but his political impact was considerable, because he personified the very thing that many Australians abhorred — subjection to England and her bankers. On the other hand, to many wealthy and comfortable Australians, Niemeyer was the embodiment of respectability, decency and financial integrity.

Ted Theodore was Scullin's Treasurer and many contemporaries considered him highly competent and capable of creative innovation in financial matters, but he was lost to Scullin when charges of fraud allegedly committed while Premier of Queensland forced his resignation from the Cabinet in 1930. In any case, the climate was such that Theodore could not have survived as he favoured an inflationist approach to the economy by stimulating it through bank credit, public works, a reduction in incomes and a devaluation of the currency. Lyons replaced him as Treasurer and Scullin made the grave mistake of leaving the country to its own destiny between August and January 1930–31.

Scullin attended an Imperial Conference which helped define the status of the dominions, travelled around Britain and Europe, and persuaded an unenthusiastic monarch that it was appropriate to have an Australian-born Governor-General represent him in the person of Isaac Isaacs. The Prime Minister arrived home in mid-January 1931 to find his government and Cabinet in such disorder that recovery seemed impossible, although further useful steps were taken by increasing tariffs and devaluing the Australian pound by almost a third against sterling. These measures rapidly helped to reduce imports by two-thirds. Within weeks the two men who had run the country during his absence, Fenton as acting Prime Minister and Joe Lyons as Treasurer, resigned from the Cabinet when Scullin reinstated Theodore who had been exonerated over the fraud charges.

Economic policies were the principal cause of the divisions within the Labor Party and the labour movement generally. The more cautious elements were determined to cut spending and acknowledge the financial obligations to overseas creditors, especially Britain. Responsible members of the government agreed with such measures but saw the need for some inflation and extension of credit while the left had a range of solutions from socialization to the repudiation of debts. In New South Wales matters were further complicated because Jack Lang had led Labor back to power in the state elections of October 1930 and by March 1931 he was trumpeting debt repudiation to London on the grounds that the Depression was a gigantic swindle by capital to force the workers to their knees. Lang's rhetoric was mostly heady nonsense, but it met a positive response amongst the left elements of the labour movement. Scullin found himself isolated from both left and right when he met the interest payments owed by New South Wales in London.

Gibson, still reigning supreme as director of the Commonwealth Bank, had threatened to cut off loans to the governments completely unless they reduced spending. A meeting was held in Melbourne in June at which the federal and state governments agreed to reduce pensions and cut public service salaries by twenty percent — a lead readily followed by private enterprise. In the meantime, business interests centered on Melbourne had decided to form a new party under the leadership of Lyons called the United Australia Party. When Scullin lost a confidence motion in the House in November and went to the polls, the result was a foregone conclusion. Lyons, less than a year before Labor Treasurer, now became a conservative Prime Minister. Nonetheless, the Depression continued and by the middle of 1932 unemployment was close to thirty percent.

Scullin had tried to grapple with the financial and social problems thrown up by the Depression but he failed. The Australian electorate was unable to associate Labor with financial expertise — a quality more readily seen in their opponents. Furthermore, the Labor Party had not been in power since 1917, and it came to the Treasury benches precisely when the profligate spending in the 1920s had begun to reap its fruits to the extent, as Niemeyer pointed out, that Australia's credit rating was lower than India's. Nonetheless, the inability of the Federal Government under Scullin to present to the electorate a carefully thought-out plan for economic recovery, even were it defective, was a major cause of its downfall. In New South Wales two parties calling themselves Labor were in existence by the time of the federal elections, and the official federal party won only three seats in that state. Scullin's government was destroyed not merely by a coalition between conservatives but one which, for the temporary purpose of destruction, included those segments of the Labor movement who saw Jack Lang as the saviour.

In New South Wales, Lang commanded a huge and enthusiastic following which failed to recognize that his determination to default on interest owed to Britain on loans, while fine and flamboyant rhetoric, was an untenable position to take in the circumstances. Australia was so closely tied to British finance that to default would have brought worse and more long-lasting economic ruin. In 1932 Lang's followers remained convinced of his courage and wisdom in sufficient numbers as to persuade him to repeat his act of repudiation of interest due on loans in London. The Commonwealth again picked up the bill, but this time it decided to recover its money by a new Financial Agreements Enforcement Act, and, in April 1932, it used those powers to take over the revenues of New South Wales despite Lang's having the state Treasury barricaded.

When Lang instructed public servants not to pay money into the federal Treasury, as the law required, the state Governor, Sir Philip Game, sacked him as Premier on 13 May 1932. In June the electorate returned a United Australia and Country Party coalition to power with a resounding victory and the reign of Lang, the 'Big Fella', was over. He went from office convinced he was right, and placards all over the country and the largest crowd in Australia's history of 300,000 people in the Sydney

Domain testified to his alleged rectitude. Right he may have been in that his action of repudiating debts, if followed at the federal level, would have so alienated Britain and Australia from each other that some form of an Australian Republic could have eventuated. Despite his record of legis-lation in social matters, he was justifiably remembered by many Labor supporters as a decisive element in the destruction of the Scullin gov-ernment. He lived on until 1975 after his re-admission to the Labor Party in 1971.

Despite the rigours of the Depression, there were still ways in which the generality of the people could find some outlet and enjoyment. The picture theatres never failed to attract crowds to films which allowed those present to escape into the unreality of Hollywoodian opulence, while on the stage the inimitable Roy Rene, known simply as 'Mo', with his earthy humour, brilliance and humanity, gave a universal touch to an essentially Australian performance and delighted audiences in Sydney and Melbourne. Outdoor recreation, especially on the beaches, was in-expensive, although seven fatal shark attacks in 1934 made many bathers unenthusiastic. Attendance at football and cricket and listening to them on the wireless continued, while perhaps having an illegal bet on the races, with the local starting-price bookmakers. The automatic totalizator (tote) had also come into widespread use since its introduction at Clon-curry Park racecourse in Perth in 1916.

To go to the races was an event in itself, and it was a rare pleasure to watch the skill and knowledge with which the course bookmakers set a field. Racing's event of the year was the Melbourne Cup, held annually on the first Tuesday in November. Declared a public holiday in Mel-bourne, the Cup attracted huge crowds, and, by the mid-thirties, a few minutes silence descended on Australia as people everywhere listened to it on the wireless. The Cup always attracted the best trainers, jockeys and horses in Australia and New Zealand, including Carbine — who carried ten stone five pounds to victory in 1890, beating the largest ever field of thirty-nine horses — and Peter Pan who won in 1932 and 1934.

In 1929 a New Zealand bred horse, Phar Lap, ran third in the Mel-bourne Cup, won it in 1930 with Jim Pike as jockey, but was weighted out of a chance with ten stone ten pounds in 1931. The horse won thirty-five times in thirty-nine starts in two years and died suddenly in California in 1932, where he was taken to prove he was the best. His death, possibly by poisoning, reminded Australians of the death of the young boxing cham-pion Les Darcy by blood poisoning in the United States in 1917. During Phar Lap's short career, he had given a little hope and pride to countless Australians in those depressed times, when a small wager on him could

During the Depression, the New Zealand bred horse Phar Lap gave heart to millions of small punters with a remarkable streak of wins, including the 1930 Melbourne Cup. He died in America and some Australians were convinced he was poisoned.

return the price of a Sunday roast and his name became a lasting legend.

During the same period, a human wizard was carving his own legend. Many old-timers still spoke in awe of the 'immortal' Victor Trumper, whose artistry with a cricket bat had held crowds spellbound both in England and Australia in the early years of the century. In 1930 Don Bradman, aged twenty-one, returned to a hero's welcome after an outstanding season in England. Unlike Trumper, to whom every stroke was a creative act, Bradman had one single purpose — to score runs. He had done this so effectively on the tour of England in 1930 that he had

Donald Bradman was the greatest run scorer of all time, establishing batting averages that are unlikely ever to be surpassed. He has become part of Australia's cricketing legend.

scored 974 runs, including four centuries, in seven Test innings with an average of 139, and a highest score of 334.

Bradman's equal had never been seen, and the English cricketing hierarchy knew that he had to be tamed were England to win the test series in Australia in the summer of 1932–33. The method used, bodyline bowling, was against the spirit of the game, but it proved effective. It consisted in fast bowlers concentrating their deliveries on the body of the batsman who had to choose between ducking under the ball, weaving away from it, being injured or being caught out to a packed leg field. England won the series amidst widespread recrimination, but Australians were diverted from their own worries while the bodyline series was played. Bradman was temporarily subdued, averaging fifty-six runs per innings, but he went on to become the greatest batsman of all time scoring 6,996 runs in fifty-two test innings at an average of 99.94.

Other heroes helped to lighten the gloom of the Depression. Walter Lindrum, whose skill at billiards was never equalled and for whom the rule book was constantly rewritten, held fifty-seven world records when he died in 1960, but his greatest feats with the cue took place during the early thirties, including a world record break of 4,137 in 1932. Jack Crawford won both Wimbledon and the French tennis singles in 1933. 'Bobby' Pearce won the Diamond Sculls at Henley in 1930, a gold medal at the Commonwealth Games in Canada in the same year and Olympic gold medals in 1928 and 1932. Every Saturday saw thousands go to football grounds to watch Rugby League, Rugby Union and Australian Rules.

In the very height of the Depression, 6 June 1932, a record crowd of over 70,000 watched Australia lose a Rugby League test to Great Britain at the Sydney Cricket Ground. South Melbourne won the Victorian Football League's premiership in 1933 despite the absence in America of their champion forward flanker, Austin Robertson, who was also world professional sprint champion. The players were happy to receive an average of £3 per match throughout the season, and total payments weekly to the team and coach rarely exceeded £75. South Melbourne's win was an historic event in itself for during the following fifty years it failed to win another premiership. In 1982, forced by economic pressures, it went to Sydney to become the Sydney Swans. In the 1930s club and suburban loyalties shared by players, officials and spectators were the basis of all football codes, adding cohesion both to sport and society itself.

No great literature was published during the Depression, although a few writers later drew inspiration from their experiences during it. Kylie Tennant and Christina Stead tried to give literary expression to poverty and the slum dwellers. Xavier Herbert began to grapple with the plight of the Aborigines in his great work *Capricornia*, but few Australians at the time were able to share either his love for the land or his respect for her original people. It was not until 1964 that one of the finest novels of the Depression came out with George Johnston's *My Brother Jack*. Unlike the novelists, who needed time to distil their experiences, the artists could express the reality and their sense of it directly, but they had nothing to say in the face of a society in trauma and they produced little of value, except for Noel Counihan's work in a later period with his harsh but truthful rendering of the despair of the helpless.

In 1925 an American visitor informed his Department of State that Australians, lacking any significant historical event, had no soul. He thought that an attempt by any of the states to secede from the Commonwealth might sharpen perspectives and enliven the general scene of acceptance of the status quo. Since 1906 the 'yell of the secessionist' was loud in Western Australia, and in 1933 the farmers in the West outvoted the gold fields two to one in a referendum to secede and become an independent part of the British Empire. The farmers' vote was based on the fact that they had to sell their wool and wheat on a competitive international market and buy Australian secondary products which were protected by high tariffs. The Premier, James Mitchell, said that the West was the victim of 'Protection that does not protect and Free Trade that is neither free nor fair'. A visit to the West by Lyons and Hughes had done nothing to pacify feelings, and a plan to throw Hughes into the Swan River misfired.

In the election held at the same time as the referendum, the same people who voted to secede also voted out of office the conservative government that had put the referendum to them. Mitchell and his Attorney-General both lost their seats and the Labor Party came back into office. In this way the majority of electors in the West protested against the neglect of Canberra by voting for secession and against their own government for its failure to take decisive action to lessen the effects of the Depression. There was little interest or concern in the affair, whether in Canberra or at Westminster. A Committee set up by the British government decided that it was not proper to receive the petition to secede, which proved that once a colony had become part of the Commonwealth there was no escape from it by constitutional means. Although there was a Fremantle Sugar Party which planned to throw sugar into the harbour in the manner of the Boston colonists at their Tea Party, unlike the Americans, no one in the West was prepared to take up arms to make secession a reality.

A similarly apathetic attitude was taken to the Statute of Westminster, which was formulated in 1926 and gave independence in domestic affairs to the dominions while at the same time requiring common allegiance to the Crown. It was ratified at the Imperial Conference in 1930, passed by the Imperial Parliament in 1931, and rapidly put into legislation in the other dominions, but remained a dead letter in Australia until 1942. Some Australians thought that implementation of the Statute would weaken the ties with the Mother Country, but, in the main, most Australians saw no need to assert their national independence in the face of a Crown which for 150 years had been looked to as the cornerstone of unity and the guarantor of safety.

There were occasions when the Australian government was prepared to question British foreign policy in the Pacific. The appointment of R.G. Casey to the new post of Australian Liaison Officer in London in 1924 and an improvement in the status of the External Affairs Department in the early thirties helped to make information available to the government. The awareness of Australia's lack of defences and the possibility of an eventual war involving the Pacific region led to a slight reassessment of the traditional relationship with Britain and a realization of the need to speak up, even if in hesitant and respectful tones, on Australia's behalf. In 1933 a complaint was lodged with the British Foreign Secretary when Britain unilaterally embargoed the sale of arms and munitions to China and Japan. In 1934 John Latham, Minister for External Affairs, told his Japanese counterpart that any attempt to land an army on Australian soil would result in Japan finding that she had 'a very lively nest of hornets' on her hands. The argument was clearly put to Britain that unless the Japanese were allowed to expand in their own region, specifically in Manchuria, they would probably soon turn their attention to the South Pacific, and the Americans were told that, if they continued to neglect Australia's interests, its government would have no alternative but to continue to appease the Japanese.

Latham was, furthermore, aware of the need to develop good relations with Australia's near neighbours. The lack of diplomatic links and the existence of only minor trade relations made close contact difficult, except with New Zealand, although an attempt was made to keep contact with the Dutch government in the East Indies. Despite the broadening of Australian attitudes, no realistic assessment was made of the preferential treatment given to Britain in trade, which was further extended reciprocally in 1932. This completely ignored the growth of Japan as an industrialized nation and Australia's favourable balance of trade with Japan in primary products.

Lyons had come to office determined to balance the federal budget and thereby give a lead to the states. He embarked on a rigorous programme of salary cuts including, creditably, those of politicians; he reduced the number of persons entitled to allowances and pensions; and, in an almost revolutionary move, he slashed tariffs. By mid-1932 the figures revealed that the objective of a balanced budget had made considerable headway, both federally and in the states except New South Wales, and that the trade balance had begun to register a surplus. Such developments did little to relieve the misery of the unemployed, and the 1933 budget was noteworthy for the way it favoured the affluent and the rural community. Census figures showed that one in four of the nation's breadwinners were unemployed or on a pension. More starkly still, two-thirds of the male bread-winners had no income or received less than £3 per week, while three-fourths of the female breadwinners received nothing or less than £2 per week.

Nearly thirty years previously Henry Bournes Higgins had set the basic wage at £2 2s per week, which proved possible in a time when the economy was booming and there was almost full employment. The Depression revealed the frailty of the Australian social laboratory and its inability to withstand a world-wide recession. Yet even during it, there were those who denounced 'subsidized idleness' and predicted that, come prosperity, the evil would continue because there would be a generation reared on doing nothing which would want to remain in that state of alleged bliss. To the Melbourne *Argus* the hope of the unemployed was in the restoration of 'profitable private enterprise', which was partially true but did not recognize the fact that the principal enterprise which helped people survive the Depression was the government and the public service, funded certainly by taxes, but staffed by citizens of the Commonwealth who for the larger part remained in work.

One lusty child of the Depression which endured was the Australian Broadcasting Commission (A.B.C.). From the beginning, radio stations had been supported financially by listeners' licence fees or by advertising. The government decided to take over those stations financed by fees, and, in 1932, the A.B.C., modelled on the British system, was set up with eight metropolitan and four regional stations. By the end of 1932, there were fifty-five stations and 370,000 radios, and Australians had become avid listeners to soap operas, plays, sport and classical music. The establishment of studio orchestras in all states in 1936 opened the way for the development of symphony orchestras in the following decades. The people in far-flung or inaccessible rural areas were thus given the benefit of entertainment and of the informative and educational aspects of radio.

An elderly lady in Western Australia, who had come to Australia on a sailing vessel in 1857, listened in awe to the coronation of King George VI in London in 1937. The goverment permitted those stations funded by advertisements to enjoy wide autonomy, but, whether through an act of providential genius or merely to protect private interests, the A.B.C. was debarred from advertising or sponsorship. Generations of Australians looked back on that decision with relief.

The Depression did not prevent Reginald Ansett from founding an empire in the field of transport. He was born in Victoria in 1909 and, using a second-hand Studebaker car, started his own business, Ansett Roadways, running a passenger service between Maryborough and Ballarat in 1931. He had obtained a pilot's licence in 1929, and, when legislation restricted road services, he turned to the air by opening a line between Hamilton and Melbourne in 1936, which became Ansett Airways Ltd. Despite the unfavourable economic climate, his enterprise flourished and developed further into Ansett Transport Industries. It later became Ansett Airlines of Australia and the private sector of the government's two airline policies. In private enterprise, the other Australian who made a very considerable contribution was Edward Hallstrom with his Silent Knight kerosene-powered refrigerator. Even during the Depression, it sold in thousands, bringing comfort to homes in the city and rural areas, although most people still used ice chests and some the primitive but effective Coolgardie safe, which cooled the contents of the chest by water evaporation.

Another, more fanciful child of the Depression was Lasseter's Lost Reef. Lewis Hubert Lasseter was an Australian-born dreamer who claimed to have located 'a vast, gold-bearing reef', 14 miles long, in Central Australia at some indeterminate date between 1897 and 1911. Gold had the added attraction of being a quick means of achieving wealth in bad times, so an expedition was formed, which set out in July 1930 to find the reef. After a three months unsuccessful search, the party returned, but Lasseter remained behind and died in the Centre a few months later. He was clearly unbalanced, and it is extremely doubtful whether he had ever been in that part of Central Australia previously, but he had probably read some of the earlier novels based on gold finds in the central desert. In September 1931 Ion Idriess published his *Lasseter's Last Ride* which stirred the popular imagination, and it went through seventeen editions by 1935. It turned Lasseter into a myth, perpetuated by the name of the Lasseter Highway between Alice Springs and Ayers Rock.

The signs that the Depression was lifting because of economic restraint showed faintly in 1933, and the following years saw a gradual but dis-

When Jack Lang, Premier of New South Wales, was about to cut the ribbon at the opening of the Sydney Harbour Bridge, 19 March 1932, a member of the fanatical New Guard anticipated the act. Lang is pictured here, with Lady Game (left), Mrs Lang, and Sir Philip Game, the Governor who would later remove him from office.

cernible improvement. Five years of economic recovery followed with revenue exceeding expenditure, balanced budgets on both federal and state levels, tariffs slightly reduced, and credit restored in London, where Bruce had been able to persuade British bond holders to accept a cut of twenty-five percent in interest. The mining industry, especially gold, but not including coal, prospered and the upturn in manufacturing after 1934 was remarkable, resulting in a slow increase in industry's share of national productivity, the creation of an industrial base for later years and the reduction of unemployment to eight percent by 1938. After the Depression, the overall standard of living rose. The old virtues of thrift, hard work and prudence had been learnt by many Australians at the price of much suffering.

Many other Australians, however, never recovered financially and wheat farmers, struck by lower crop prices and accumulated debt, were the worst hit of primary producers. Later debt-adjustment schemes were able to help only a few, although most farmers managed to hang on through a long period of deprivation. Wool growers fared better with firmer prices and greater demand, but dairy-farmers, with an increasingly restricted British market, suffered badly. By the mid-thirties jobs, especially in the manufacturing industries, became more readily available, and some children in the cities who had known only bleakness began to find that life could hold the promise of better times.

Through all the days of Australia's misfortunes, little Billy Hughes had battled on with an ever-alert eye cast on the world outside her shores. Reinstated as a member of Joe Lyons's Cabinet as Minister for Health and Repatriation, he published a book in 1935 entitled *Australia and War Today: the Price of Peace*. Billy looked out from Canberra and saw that 'The East, roused from its age-long slumbers, has awakened'. For years he had been crusading for the need to prepare for war, and he saw Australia endangered by Japan with its uncontrollable military and naval oligarchy. Lyons was embarrassed and sacked him, but Billy had the better insight, because he realized that Australia's long dependence on the British Navy, as an assurance against aggression, was drawing to a close.

CHAPTER FIFTEEN

War and
Changing Alignments

In 1938 an attempt was made to celebrate the 150th anniversary of white settlement in Australia, but no one showed much interest in the proceedings except in New South Wales where the anniversary had some meaning. A re-enactment of the landing of the First Fleet took place, accompanied by a protest by a group of Aborigines who refused to rejoice in the '150 years of misery and degradation imposed by the white invaders'. Despite these differing views of the meaning of the festivities for whites and for blacks, one thing was certain — Australians of whatever origin were irrevocably bound to live together and to find a common destiny. As always that destiny was inseparable from the decisions made by more powerful nations, and the 1930s had made Australia's dependence even plainer than in previous generations. Dependence heightened insecurity and combined with the aftermath of the Depression to make Australians feel insecure about their role in the world.

It was increasingly clear that little had been learnt from the experience of the Great War and some nations, notably Germany and Japan, were gearing up their military machines with aggression in mind. In those countries the same kind of reaction that had led to Australian conservatism after the Depression was in the process of consolidating regimes which developed such a reaction to fatal extremes. The fascist movements of Mussolini and Hitler were born of the wrecked hopes of millions, to whom the suffering and humiliation of their countries after the Great War was intolerable, and they looked to their dictators to restore their national and personal dignity.

Inevitably, Australians began to take an interest in the development of the fascist regimes and, equally inevitably, differing views were held on them. Generally those whose view of the world revolved around the desirability of moderate, structured progress governed by law and order looked upon them benignly and some people commented on them favourably, especially on Mussolini and fascist Italy. On the other hand, those who regarded social change as demanding the recognition of human rights and the involvement of all sections of the community in the democratic process were cautious and critical. That small minority who looked to Soviet Russia as the model for all countries to follow rejected fascism outright.

Despite these differing attitudes, there had been widespread displeasure in Australia when Italy used its vastly superior military power to invade Abyssinia in 1935. The government followed Britain's lead in the largely useless step of applying sanctions on Italian trade, which, nevertheless, met general approval in the electorate. Lyons, a man to whom peace was paramount, held strong pacifist and anti-conscription convictions which he managed to enforce on his Cabinet. Perhaps his pacifism led him to trust Mussolini, and, at the Imperial Conference in London in 1937, he said that Mussolini had expressly requested him to say that Italy wanted peace and most especially friendly relations with her old ally, Britain. Although Mussolini had already proposed an alliance between Italy and Germany in 1936 and signed the Anti-Comintern Pact, together with Japan and Germany, in 1937, it was still possible that the Italians would have chosen to remain an ally of England but little was done to ensure it.

Germany was proving much more aggressive and recalcitrant than Italy, and Lyons was determined to add his government's voice to those who wanted to appease Hitler. Although he was horrified in 1938 at the barbarities perpetrated on the German Jews, Lyons was as anxious to deter Britain from entering into a war against Germany on behalf of Czechoslovakia as he had been in 1936 when Germany asserted its sovereignty over the Rhineland. Australia retained the long-held belief of its foreign policy — any threat to Britain was a threat to Australia, whose involvement in the defence of the 'Mother Country' would be automatic. Nonetheless, it was recognized that if Britain found herself at war in the European theatre at the same time as Australia was involved in the Pacific it would prove difficult for either country to help the other. The steady deterioration of Australia's relations with Japan, Japan's military and naval build up, together with its alliance with Germany and Italy; all gave point to Australian concern about the future.

In Canberra it was felt that a Pact of Non-Aggression signed initially by Japan, the United States, Canada and Australia would ensure peace in the

Pacific. President Roosevelt readily gave warm support to the idea of a Pact in 1937, but Japan was lukewarm, especially so its naval warlords, who regarded the navy as the spearhead of any future thrust into the South Pacific. Furthermore, Japan had withdrawn from the League of Nations, consolidated itself on the Chinese mainland with the seizure of Peking and Tientsin, and showed signs of moving into the same fascist ideological orbit as Germany and Italy. Unsurprisingly, the Pact of Non-Aggression came to nothing, and the British government made it plain that in the event of a war with Germany, accompanied by Japanese involvement in the Pacific, priority would have to be given to the European zone and the war won there first. An assurance was, however, given of maintaining a 'defensive policy in the Far East' of which the essential feature would be 'economic pressure'.

No one was clear what this 'defensive policy' meant, although there was general agreement amongst British and Australian military authorities that Australia would be incapable of repelling a full-scale Japanese invasion, unless the British fleet based on Singapore were to intervene. John Curtin, Labor leader since Scullin resigned because of ill-health in 1935, thought that the sensible course to follow was to engage in an immediate build up of the Australian Air Force, which he considered the only effective form of defence for Australia. Curtin was doubtful whether Britain's naval base at Singapore would prove to be invulnerable, and he saw air power as a partial answer to Australian exposure to occupation. On one issue the Labor Party remained unmoved — it rejected all forms of conscription, while maintaining its determination to defend Australia against aggression from any source.

Curtin was a quiet, determined leader who was bent on healing the divisions in his Party caused by Lang and his followers and maintaining its unity despite the widespread diversity of opinion within it. The first inklings of a repercussion within Australian society to international events had taken place in 1937, when there was conflict between Catholics in the Labor Party who regarded Franco as the saviour of Spain, and those on the left of the Party who judged him to be a mere tool of 'the military captains of capitalism' that were bent on destroying a genuine workers' republic. There were very few Australians actually committed enough to Franco or the Republic to volunteer to go to Spain and fight in the civil war there, but the division within the Australian labour movement was sufficiently deep to indicate that, were a choice to arise involving conflicting ideologies, the democratic process upon which the Party was based would be in jeopardy. Curtin was fully aware of the danger of a split in the Party were the Spanish issue pressed too far, so he carefully avoided permitting it to come to prominence.

Australia's wartime Prime Minister John Curtin formed a strong partnership with the American General Douglas MacArthur to defend Australia from the Japanese. Curtin died before victory in the Pacific was won.

A negative reaction to Communism had been building up for some years, bolstered by the conservatism of a society bent upon economic recovery. There was a zeal to exclude Communists altogether, which led to a ludicrous situation in 1934. Egon Kisch, a Czechoslovakian agent of the Comintern, arrived to attend a Congress against War and Fascism. Kisch was refused entry, but he leapt from his ship onto the Melbourne wharf, broke his leg and was later subjected to a test in Scottish Gaelic as a condition of obtaining entry. Unsurprisingly, he failed the test, but when taken to the High Court his case was upheld on the grounds that Scottish Gaelic was not a European language. Kisch was given another test and failed. He was deported after attempting to convert others to his view of the world, but the case illustrated to some the ineffectiveness of the democratic process in attempting to curb those bent on its subversion.

At the same time, the censorship of books, conducted by clerks in the Customs department, resulted in 5,000 titles being banned on the grounds that they would tend to offend morality or good order. Their authors ranged from Defoe to Hemingway, and it was axiomatic that works by Marxist theorists were regarded as unfit for public consumption. This repressive atmosphere resulted in a reaction amongst intellectuals, some of whom started to move to the left. Another variation of the old 1890s nationalism was revived. P.R. ('Inky') Stephensen, a controversial writer and publicist, appealed to other Australian writers to turn from Britain to their own country as the true source of their creative spirit, while his follower Rex Ingamells founded the Jindyworobak movement to foster the same aim, as well as to encourage Australians to draw inspiration from the culture of the Aborigines. Stephensen himself went on to found the extreme nationalist movement, 'Australia First', which, through its journal the *Publicist*, expressed pro-German and pro-Japanese sympathies in 1942. This resulted in the suppression of the movement and Stephensen's internment for the duration of the war.

Living a simple life with his wife and large family at the Lodge in Canberra, Lyons was perhaps faintly aware that one of his colleagues sensed his frailty and was determined to succeed him as Prime Minister. Robert Gordon Menzies was his Attorney-General and they appeared to get along well but events in Europe were gradually convincing Menzies that strong leadership was needed in Australia. He took it upon himself to mention his conviction publicly in a climate fraught with rumours of war. The news of settlement of the Czechoslovakian crisis reached at Munich in September 1938 between Hitler, Chamberlain, Daladier and Mussolini seemed to promise 'peace in our time'. The passengers on the Sydney–Melbourne express, forced to change trains at Albury because of the differing rail gauges, congratulated each other when they heard the news.

Other news from Germany caused alarm because the pogrom against the Jews, involving confiscation of property, deportation and death was now widely known about. It was called by Melbourne news commentator, Denys Jackson, 'a new form of barbarous fetishism'. Its human evidence was soon apparent in the Jewish refugees who arrived in Australia on the *Dunera* in 1939. Australian concern had been shown when attempts were made to found a Jewish homeland in the Kimberley, but they proved abortive, although 7,500 of the 15,000 Jews Australia had promised to receive arrived before the outbreak of war. Despite their exposure to overseas events, there was general ignorance amongst Australians on foreign affairs with few commentators of any quality able to

The Advisory War Council, headed by Menzies, was formed on 28 October 1940. The Council brought together a group of men, six of whom, at one time or another, served as prime minister of Australia.

proffer informed opinions. The country was isolationist and overseas news was filtered through Britain. The government timidly followed British policies closely and any suggested departure from them was quickly dubbed as disloyal.

Lyons died of a heart attack on Good Friday, 7 April 1939. His life as Prime Minister had been full of distress and he wrote to his wife some time before, 'I wish they would defeat us and we'd be out of our misery and get a little happiness.' Except by those zealots in the labour movement to whom he would always be a 'rat' because he left the Party, Lyons was a widely-loved figure. There was some slight truth in his words to his wife, Enid: 'Neither you nor I can put everything right and we saved Australia from ruin. Think of the homes that are happy because of what we did and realise that no-one is unhappy because of what we did'. He was buried in his native Tasmania and three weeks later Menzies became Prime Minister.

Clearly Europe was moving towards war and, were Australia to be involved, the support of the workers would be needed. Menzies's position was not helped by the opposition to him taken by a now revitalized trade union movement. To them he was known as 'Pig-Iron Bob', because, when Attorney-General, he had tried to use the law to force striking wharf workers at Port Kembla on the New South Wales coast to load pig-iron for Japan. The government's position was strengthened, however, when it became known that Germany and the Soviet Union had signed a Non-Aggression Pact in August 1939. Many conservatives were delighted at the news of the Pact as it seemed that both the Nazis and the Communists were now in the one camp, thereby simplifying matters, although Australian communists were confused and not much enlightened when one of their leaders tried to explain that the main concern of workers everywhere was to preserve the Soviet Union.

The Depression and the consequent downturn in imports had sown another seed which bore fruit in preparing for war, because Australian industry had expanded very considerably. Under the direction of Essington Lewis, Broken Hill Proprietary Limited had been modernized and diversified, and its steelworks were developed so as to rival its European counterparts. General Motors and Ford had expanded to the degree that by 1939 most cars bought in Australia were made there, although the engines were still imported. A mill at Burnie was turning out excellent paper entirely made of Tasmanian hardwood, while the first Australian war plane, the Wirraway, was built by the Commonwealth Aircraft Corporation set up by Lewis. Munitions were in production at several government-owned factories. There had been an increase in skilled factory workers who now worked a forty-four hour week, although the unions had already tentatively begun to agitate for a reduction to forty hours. Finally a national register of all males aged eighteen to sixty-four had been introduced, which the Labor Party opposed because it seemed a first step towards industrial and military conscription.

Britain and France declared war on Germany on 3 September 1939 after her invasion of Poland, and no one was surprised when Prime Minister Menzies went on radio that same Sunday to inform Australians of the melancholy fact that their country was also at war. He elaborated this position with the words, 'where Great Britain stands, there stands the people of the entire British world'. There was no jubilation, because, after the Great War, most Australians knew what was entailed in a bloody international conflict. Most calmly accepted the fact, although it was realized that, unlike 1914, the question of national security was involved. Tears were again shed in some homes where the sorrows of Gallipoli and Flanders were remembered, but, generally, people accepted Menzies's advice of 'business as usual' and life went on.

Recruitment of a Second Australian Imperial Force began quickly, but the main problem was where to deploy the available troops. Initially the war was fought only at sea with no British troops committed to the European theatre. The conflict was quickly dubbed a 'phoney war', especially by segments of the trade union movement and communists who wondered whether the Allies were serious in their fight against fascism. Behind the problem of whether to send the troops overseas lay the preoccupation about Japan's intentions. The British Secretary of State, Anthony Eden, assured the Australian government that Japan would remain neutral 'for a time', and the British government promised to defend Singapore and Australia from any attack by Japan, although an invasion of Australia was regarded as unlikely given the lengthy supply lines which would be involved. With these comforting assurances, two Australian divisions left for Palestine in early 1940. Meanwhile, an Empire Air Training Scheme got underway in Australia, England and principally Canada which prepared Australians to fight as air crews in the European zone.

By the end of June 1940, all talk of a 'phoney war' was over. Northern Europe was in German hands, Paris had fallen, Mussolini had entered the war as Hitler's partner and the British Expeditionary Force was withdrawn from Dunkirk. These developments heightened Australian fears, because, with her ideological allies winning in Europe, it could only be a matter of time before Japan struck in the Pacific. R. G. Casey, recently appointed as the Australian representative in Washington and thereby Australia's first accredited diplomat to a foreign power, strongly advised that the Japanese had to be appeased in regard to their claims to Chinese territory because 'beggars cannot be choosers'. Concern was further strengthened by a message from London stating that no additions could be made to the fleet based on Singapore, because all available British naval strength was needed in the Mediterranean as well as on the home seas.

Australia, it seemed, had herself become a 'beggar' with no one to defend her. The navy was committed in the Mediterranean where the sinking of the Italian cruiser, *Bartolomeo Colleoni*, by HMAS *Sydney* made Australians cheer. The successes of the Australian army in Egypt against the Italians, of whom 40,000 were captured, added further to local pride, and the troops were convinced that their cause and their qualities were as good as those of their fathers. A sense of reality was brought home when 6,000 Australians of the Sixth Division were killed, wounded or captured in Greece and on Crete in April and May 1941; but the defence of Tobruk through 194 long days by the 2/13th Battalion of the Ninth Division, in unison with British and Polish units, added another legend to that of Anzac. The port's defenders became known affectionately as 'the rats of Tobruk' and took their place with the heroes of 1915.

When Germany invaded Russia in June 1941, the still illegal Communist Party decided that the war effort, in which it could now join, was in the best interests of the Soviet Union. With a new and different attitude taken by the previously condemnatory press to the Communist Party, it grew in numbers to reach a peak of 23,000 in 1944, when the only self-declared Communist ever elected to an Australian parliament won a state seat in Queensland. Throughout Australia there was much enthusiasm for the Russians, and a campaign to procure 'Sheepskins for Russia' was launched. As time passed, the Soviet Union and its courageous people, shunned both physically and mentally since 1917, were regarded as valuable allies.

The great majority of Australians were now united in the war effort. It was easy for the government to introduce press and radio censorship and price control over consumer goods, and to extend the National Security Act's already wide powers so that individuals could be directed to contribute their services and property to advance the war effort. Essington Lewis was appointed Director-General of Munitions Supply, and Keith Murdoch was given a similar role in directing war-time propaganda and information. For their part, the farmers were urged to grow more wheat and wool. Daylight saving started, petrol rationing was introduced and the A.B.C. employed its first female announcer in order to free male announcers for active service.

As wartime leader, Menzies did not enjoy the confidence of the electorate, given his previous ambivalence to the Fascist regimes. His own party was divided, the coalition shaken and, when he appealed for a National Government in mid-1941 as the Japanese moved into Indo-China, Curtin's refusal on behalf of the Labor Party brought the Prime Minister's resignation. Fadden, leader of the Country Party, became Prime Minister for six weeks but resigned in October so that, after ten years in opposition, the Labor Party was back with John Curtin as Prime Minister. The brilliant, impetuous, but erratic H.V. Evatt, having resigned from the High Court to enter Parliament, was made Attorney-General.

It was Curtin's burden to become leader at a time without precedent in Australia's short history. The Japanese were moving quickly, without a declaration of war, and their successful attack on the main American naval base at Pearl Harbor in Hawaii on 7 December 1941 brought the immediate entry of the United States into the war. Within days, Thailand, Malaya and the Philippines were invaded, Hong Kong bombed and the pride of the British Navy, the battleship *Prince of Wales* and the battle cruiser *Repulse* sunk, thereby opening Singapore and, consequently, the Australian north to invasion.

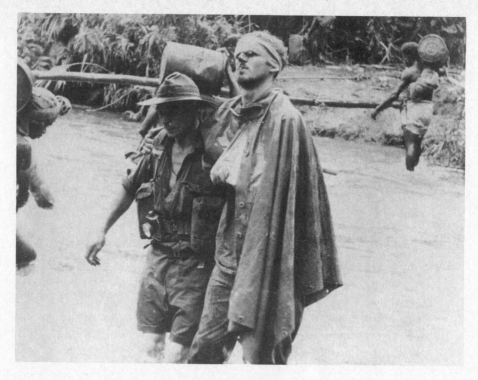

The campaign against the Japanese in New Guinea in World War II caused many Australian casualties and the battle for the Kokoda Trail became famous.

Australians heard of all this with foreboding. The government, not waiting for British approval, declared war on Japan on 9 December. Japanese forces took only weeks to occupy most of South-East Asia, driving the Australian, British and Indian troops back into Singapore. By mid-February, the so-called impregnable fortress of Singapore was in Japanese hands, together with 15,384 members of Australia's Eighth Division. Subsequently, a third of them died on the Burma Railway and in Changi Prison Camp, thereby earning for the Japanese a reputation for cruelty that would take decades to erase and which was exacerbated during the early part of the war by the hate campaign conducted by propagandists in Australia itself. More than 2,700 Australian troops were captured in Java by March, when the Allies surrendered there, and by April the Philippines and the Dutch East Indies had fallen. Rabaul was captured in the same month. The ancient cry of the enemy at the gates had become real for Australia.

Even before Singapore fell, the Japanese advance meant that, unchecked, it would lead to Australia at a time when three of her trained divisions were in the Middle East. As early as 1936, Curtin had said, 'The dependence of Australia on the competence, let alone the readiness, of British statesmen to send forces to our aid is too dangerous a hazard on which to found Australia's defence policy'. On 27 December 1941, Curtin made it plain that necessity had irrevocably shifted the balance of Australian dependence from Britain to America. His end-of-year message, published in the Melbourne *Herald*, bluntly stated, 'Australia looks to America, free of any pangs as to our traditional links or kinship with the United Kingdom'. British reaction was not recorded, but President Roosevelt was ill-pleased to find his country so unequivocally adopted as Australia's sheet anchor.

The Japanese stepped deftly and quickly from island to island and they were soon in a position to threaten the Australian mainland. The first of sixty-four bombing raids on Darwin took place on 19 February 1942 with the loss of 243 lives, eight vessels sunk in the harbour, and the town, airport and port damaged extensively, but the severity of the first raid was concealed from the general public. This decisive event convinced Curtin that his prime responsibility was the defence of the nation, and he refused Churchill's request that the Australian Seventh Division, which was on its way home, go to Rangoon and help prevent the Japanese take Burma. Churchill's opinion that Australia was temporarily expendable was not shared by the Australian government nor would it have been by the people had they been aware of it.

The bombing raids on Darwin, Broome, Wyndham and Townsville early in 1942, the laying of mines by submarines and raiders off the coast, the sinking of seventeen vessels on the east coast with the loss of 80,874 tons of shipping and 503 lives between 1942–43, the attack by three midget submarines against shipping in Sydney Harbour, and the shelling by submarines of Sydney and Newcastle in May and June, although played down by the government, had nonetheless an enormous impact. Even before these events, at schools and in many backyards trenches were dug. Public air raid shelters were built, black-outs enforced, beaches and headlands fortified and anti-aircraft guns and searchlights erected in the cities. In Queensland there was a virtual state of panic and in some northern towns, such as Ingham, many homes were deserted as people fled to the south. Plans were made for an evacuation were the Japanese to invade. Other plans were made to resist, and the Japanese would have met a type of guerilla warfare in Queensland before which, even with their superior forces, success would have been dearly bought. Rupert Lockwood published *Guerrilla Paths To Freedom* in 1942 and used

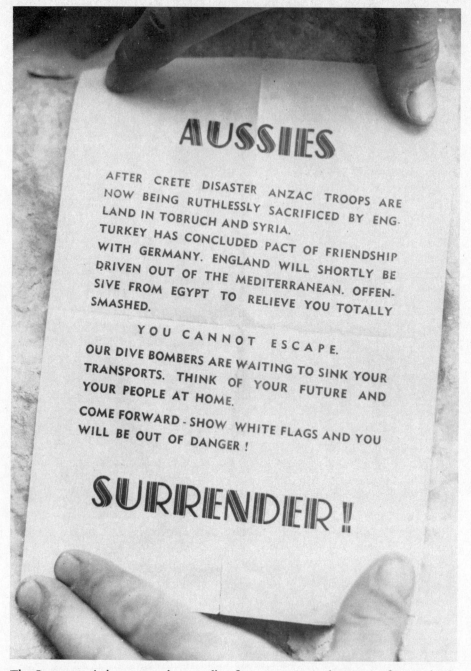

The Germans tried propaganda, as well as force, to remove the Aussies from Tobruk.
None of them showed 'White Flags' and the Rats of Tobruk, as they became known,
joined the Anzacs as bearers of the legend.

Mao Tse-tung, Garibaldi, Ned Kelly, the Soviet Army and others as models for Australians to 'terrorize and demoralize' the Japanese invader.

In the event, there was no invasion, and the arrival of American forces commanded by General Douglas MacArthur, who had made good his escape from the Philippines, was partly the reason. As he travelled from Alice Springs to Melbourne by train on 20 March 1942, MacArthur was shocked to learn of the small numbers of American troops, in all only 30,000, and the general weakness of the Australian forces. He said, 'God have mercy on us', when he was given an outline of the situation but his tumultuous welcome in Melbourne cheered him and he spoke at Spencer Street Station of his great admiration for the Australian soldier and promised to 'keep the soldier faith'. Many Australians said, 'Thank God for Mac'. MacArthur, despite his long-held conservatism, formed close ties with Curtin, who had been imprisoned for his opposition to conscription in the Great War. To MacArthur, Curtin was 'the heart and soul of Australia'.

The first units of the Australian divisions arrived home in March, and, when added to the number of enlisted men who had not gone overseas, there were over 100,000 fully-trained Australian soldiers available to MacArthur by the middle of the year, half of whom had seen action in the Middle East. To these were added the Americans, who now numbered 120,000. The Americans represented a great military power and their affluence as well as their access to luxuries — cigarettes, liquor, silk stockings and chocolates — made them welcome in homes, and, to the chagrin of some Australian men, also in the hearts of many local girls. One wit lamented that the Americans were 'overpaid, oversexed and overhere'. Riots and brawls erupted at times between Australian and American servicemen, especially in Brisbane where MacArthur's headquarters as Commander-in-Chief in the Pacific were located. Generally, however, the presence of the Yanks, as they were known, did much to create a relationship of understanding on both sides and particularly in America, where previously Australia had been practically unknown.

The general population suffered severe restrictions which, beginning in 1942, lasted until after the war. Identity cards were introduced and food, including meat, clothes, tobacco, liquor, but most severely petrol, were all rationed. Few grumbled seriously except at the black marketeers, who seemed to be able to provide anything at a price from Scotch whisky to silk stockings and, with the coming of the Yanks, nylon stockings. Many motorists compensated for the lack of petrol by attaching huge and awkward charcoal burners, called gas producers, to their cars.

With the Director-General of Manpower in control, the Australian Women's Land Army was formed in July 1942. Its 2,500 permanent and 630 auxiliary members worked principally in fruit, vegetable and cotton growing, dairying and poultry farming and made an important contribution to the war effort.

Even in cooking, the ability of Australians to make do with basic ingredients became apparent when women concocted dishes such as the Austerity Loaf and Austerity Beef. Morale, nonetheless, remained high, bolstered by such things as community singing in halls, theatres and on the radio, by newsreel segments in picture theatres, which gave war news with much emphasis to victories, and the gradual realization that the danger of invasion had receded.

In the Pacific, the war turned against the Japanese when they were contained in the Coral Sea and Midway Island naval battles in May and June 1942, although they remained on the offensive in 1943. In May 1943, they sank the hospital ship *Centaur* off the Queensland coast with the loss of 268 lives and bombed installations at Exmouth Gulf, Western Australia, which was their most southerly attack on the Australian mainland. On land, the struggle was long drawn-out and costly in men and 'material' on both sides. A key event had occurred on 2 November 1942 when, after grim fighting, the Japanese were driven back from near Port Moresby along the Kokoda trail, which added its name to Tobruk in the recent history of Australian war legends. With some opposition in the labour movement — notably from Arthur Calwell, Minister for Information, who, like Curtin, had memories of the anti-conscription campaigns of the Great War — the Labor government introduced conscription for the South-Western Pacific zone in early 1943 and the now respectable Communist Party supported the measure.

Although the Australian commander, General Thomas Blamey, found it an irksome experience to serve under MacArthur, the two armies fought together amicably enough, especially in Papua and New Guinea, which MacArthur regarded as the true battleground for the safety of Australia. To back up the campaign in the islands, the Americans engaged in huge construction works in Australia in roads, bridges, air fields and buildings, and Australians saw bulldozers, brought by the Yanks, for the first time. With this kind of support, the armies in the islands gradually gained the upperhand, although the Japanese fought grimly, gave no quarter and knew nothing of surrender. Their desperation was apparent on 5 August 1944, when, in the largest outbreak in the course of the war, 234 prisoners and three Australian guards died in a mass, suicidal attempt at escape from the prisoner-of-war camp at Cowra in New South Wales.

In the islands, Australians servicemen came into contact with peoples whom they had not encountered before. Many remembered with gratitude the assistance given in New Guinea by some courageous and generous sections of the local population who became known as 'fuzzy-wuzzy angels', although others collaborated with the Japanese. In Timor many locals made great sacrifices to help the Australians which was not forgotten in the 1970s when East Timor was again in trouble. Generally the Pacific War was marred by the continuation of 'mopping up' operations throughout the islands long after there was any need for them. They caused unnecessary deaths and injuries to both combatants and non-combatants and served only to glorify the commanders in charge of them.

In early 1943 the Germans were defeated in Africa in battles such as that of El Alamein, where the Australian Ninth Division helped conquer Rommel's Afrika Korps. In Europe the war slowly turned in favour of the Allies in the west and of the Russians in the east. By May 1945 Berlin had fallen and Hitler's Third Reich had collapsed in ruins with death and destruction as its legacy. The Japanese continued to fight on in the Pacific until the destruction of Hiroshima and Nagasaki, by atomic bombing in August 1945, brought about their formal surrender. Into the future there were arguments as to whether the act of annihilation of civil populations by such total means was ever justifiable.

The RAAF had contributed gallantly to the defence of Britain, with many Australians fighting with the RAF and several squadrons operating from Britain, the Middle East, North Africa, Italy and Corsica under Australian command. As the war developed in the Pacific zone, the RAAF was called upon to contribute in the air, which it did with great effect until the very end. A total of 190,000 men and 27,000 women enlisted in the Air Force and there were nearly 14,000 casualties of whom over 10,000 died.

In all the zones in which it operated, but notably in the Pacific, the small Australian Navy of nearly 40,000 men and women made a great contribution, but suffered a major disaster when HMAS *Sydney* was sunk, with the loss of all hands, by a German raider off Western Australia in November 1941. The Australian army suffered the loss of over 20,000 dead. The total of 33,826 dead of the armed forces was about half the dead of 1914–18, although this did nothing to appease the grief of those who lost their loved ones. The wounded and injured came to 180,864, and 23,059 had been prisoners of war while the monetary cost of the war was over £200,000,000. Six years of sacrifice, austerity, determination and grim resolution had seen the Australian people united as never before.

The social and economic effects within Australia of the war were far reaching. The demands of a wartime economy, at its peak in 1942–43, meant that forty percent of the national income was spent on the war

Women entered the workforce in large numbers during the war and took their place in skilled and light industry, contributing immeasurably to the war effort.

effort, and the federal government took over all personal income tax collecting using the pay-as-you-earn (P.A.Y.E.) method after 1943. As a result, there were no longer anomalous discrepancies in tax ratios between the states as had previously been the case with Queensland having a maximum level of 15s in the pound and Victoria only half that amount. Another important consequence was that henceforth the states had to look to Canberra for their main source of revenue. This step gave the federal government centralized control over state development.

To help further in raising revenue, a tax on company profits, a pay-roll tax and an entertainment tax were imposed but, with the cessation of hostilities and the removal of the need for their imposition, they remained in place. A National Welfare Fund was established to provide a pool from which social security benefits would be funded and a child endowment payment for families with more than one child under 16 and a widow's pension introduced. Finally Aborigines were given social service payments and many worked on construction projects in Northern Australia at award wages while others joined the Army and one became an officer. As a consequence a few Aborigines began to enjoy, very slightly, some form of equality with white Australians.

The demands on manufacturing industry during the war were such that a genuine quantum leap was taken, especially in the making of all kinds of arms and munitions, vehicle and aircraft engines, as well as optical glass, without which many weapons would have been useless. Under the direction of Essington Lewis, to whom both Menzies and Curtin gave enormous power, industry contributed to the war effort in a way that helped make Australia an effective partner with America in the Pacific. The chemical industry advanced rapidly in petro-chemicals and synthetic rubber, and also in drugs, vitamins and other products, often produced from native shrubs. In steel making, power production, in heavy and light engineering and in electrical goods there were also advances. To assist in all of this development and to maintain productivity, especially in the rural sector, over 200,000 women entered the workforce. Together with the 52,000 women who joined the services and the other half a million already in the workforce they were able, at least for the duration of the war, to feel that their contribution was necessary and valuable, and all Australians recognized it as a highly significant social development.

Despite the acquiescence of most people in the imposition of wartime restrictions, they were prepared to tolerate curtailment of their freedom for the period of the war only. Although Curtin won a resounding victory in the 1943 general elections, including a win in the Senate, a referendum held in 1944 to continue Commonwealth government control over the labour force and the economy was lost. Undaunted, Curtin worked on and, looking to the future, he set up a Ministry of Post-War Reconstruction under John Dedman in 1945. Unnoticed except by those who were closest to him, his health was breaking under the strain, but his whole-hearted leadership of Australia had won the respect of all, including that of Churchill with whom he had so strongly differed. John Curtin died in Canberra on 5 July 1945 without experiencing the joy of seeing the end of the war in the Pacific.

CHAPTER SIXTEEN

A New Wave

A few days before the end of the Pacific War, Arthur Calwell, with the new title of Minister for Immigration, spoke in the House of Representatives. He was the embodiment of the now venerable traditions of the Labor Party in that place, where it alone had been represented continuously since federation. Nevertheless, he had a policy to propose that ran contrary to the firmly-held traditions of his Party. Long before the days of the organized labour movement, the workers had always been uneasy about governments assisting migrants to come to the Australian colonies. It seemed too easy for employers to use such people as a weapon to break down working conditions and to lower wages. Such, in fact, had never happened, but the mythology was strong, and the trade unions and, later, the Labor Party itself had generally opposed assisted migration.

Despite the past, Calwell, with the full approval of the Party and the acquiescence of the unions, proposed a scheme of assisted migration on a large scale. Calwell's scheme was introduced in 1946 with the aim of achieving 70,000 immigrants annually by 1948. Those from the United Kingdom were expected to pay £10, with the British and Australian governments making up the rest of the passage. The whole scheme was so successful that the government was forced to cut back the intake from 170,000 in 1952 to less than 80,000 in 1953. In 160 years the population of Australia had grown to less than eight million. As a result of the realization of the vulnerability of the country with its small population, the most remarkable and far-reaching effect of the Second World War was to increase that number as quickly, efficiently and smoothly as possible.

Calwell was as committed to the White Australia policy as any purist of the past had been, and it was initially intended that only immigrants of European extraction would be welcome. Few Australians had any real objection to the British or, as they were called, Poms, but many took a different attitude to southern Europeans. A survey, conducted in 1948, indicated, with signs of deeply ingrained ethnic bigotry, that Germans were more acceptable than either Italians or Jews. When it became clear that not enough migrants were available from northern Europe, especially the British Isles, Calwell turned to the south for more. Moreover, the European war had cast up vast numbers of displaced persons who were not Anglo-Saxon in origin but who possessed the qualities to settle in new lands and over a million of them were prepared to do so. The Australian government was willing to take some of them despite a degree of local disapproval. Calwell went to work — obtaining the shipping necessary for transport; touring the camps of displaced persons; setting up offices in European capitals to facilitate the selection process and preparing the climate amongst Australians to receive the new settlers.

The success of the scheme was astonishing. With their skills and determination to make good in Australia, the immigrants helped lay the foundations of a labour force with which to build manufacturing and construction industries and to secure economic prosperity for the next twenty years. By 1949, when the Labor Party lost office, 500,000 immigrants had been welcomed. Only a third were from the British Isles, and many of the rest were 'Balts', 'Dagoes' or 'Reffos' — nicknames which did not necessarily imply either suspicion or rejection but merely an acceptance that the 'new Australians' were different to those of the old variety. Many of them had to go into camps, where they often experienced hardship, and most were obliged to work in specified jobs for two years, frequently in work unsuited to their qualifications so that doctors became ward attendants and scientists were put to work as laboratory cleaners. Indeed, the medical profession proved to be a 'closed shop' for the great majority of medically-qualified immigrants who found that their only pathway into the profession was by repeating their training at an Australian university. One profession which proved to be open handed and just in its dealings was engineering. Careful scrutiny was made of qualifications, and those who satisfied the criteria were accepted as engineers. In the main, the immigrants eventually settled in the new society, with varying degrees of acceptance on their own part and that of the 'old' Australians.

As with other waves of immigrants in previous decades, the great majority began in a lowly way, living in the less desirable suburbs, taking the jobs least sought for by others and enduring the hardship of rele-

Arthur Calwell is remembered by many as Minister for Immigration in the immediate post-war period. Other Australians better remember his anti-Vietnam war stance, taken as leader of the Labor Party. He is pictured (centre) at a reunion of Jewish immigrants.

gation to second-rate and third-rate citizenship. European women in particular found the new society strange and integration, especially for those who remained at home, was slow and, at times, heartbreaking if indeed it ever occurred at all. With time, the rest settled even if painfully, and their differences, whether of language and accent, food, drink, outlook or cultural attainment, blended with and gradually transformed the society they entered. The great majority learnt to speak English, perhaps in a broken way, with the accent forged since the first settlement at Sydney Cove.

The experiment in nation building in the post-war period had no parallel in Australian history. The gold-rushes saw more people, as a proportion of the population, arrive in Australia, but that wave was unplanned and mainly Anglo-Saxon in origin. This time the initiative rested with the government, and non-Anglo-Saxons were in sufficient numbers to make them noticeable. The fact that the Labor Party, which had pledged itself to full employment, accepted the risk that a vastly increased workforce posed to its policy, made the whole scheme more significant. With this development, Australia entered the third phase of its history. Up to 1850, the theme had been one of survival and settlement. After 1850, consolidation of the Anglo-Saxon dominance was the aim. From the mid-1940s, perhaps unwittingly, diversification in the origins of the immigrants became the keynote. Arthur Calwell little knew that the policy of 'populate or perish' he so passionately and effectively made work, would lead inexorably to the eventual dismantling of the White Australia policy, which had been fundamental to the idea of federation.

In 1946 Ernest Burgmann, Anglican Bishop of Goulburn, (later Canberra and Goulburn), asked in prophetic tones whether the time had come for Australians to be more concerned, in planning their future, with culture rather than colour. He courageously suggested that a finer race would emerge if, overcoming prejudice, there was 'a gradual infiltration of other colours into the blood stream'. In this, as in so many of the social policies he supported, Burgmann was ahead of his time, but when he died in Canberra in 1967 his dream of 'infiltration' was about to take place.

At the same time as the new immigrants were arriving, the 700,000 Australians who had served in the war had to settle themselves into a way of life vastly different to the one they had grown accustomed to in the services. Their experience of travel inside and outside of Australia, the exposure of many to learning and culture, the work of the Army Education Service, the rank they had held and the authority they wielded had opened up expectations that made them a new generation. When they entered civilian life some were dependent for the first time upon their own ability to earn a living in a workforce. Many had to readjust to the demands, as well as to the warmth and comfort, of family life. Little things such as the six o'clock closing of hotels, which remained the law in New South Wales until 1955 and Victoria until 1966, proved irksome to men and women who considered that they had made enough sacrifices.

Cigarettes, clothes and luxury items were scarce and rationing of clothes and meat continued until 1948. Housing was very difficult to obtain and some of the new homes were built of fibro sheeting for the exterior walls, which made them hot in summer and cold in winter. The deference shown to the uniform disappeared and few people outside immediate family circles wanted to hear tales of the exploits, the heroism, the horror, or the mere monotony of life in action. Fortunately, the prediction made by some economists that the post-war period would see up to eight percent unemployment did not materialize, and grants given to returned men to further their education at any level, including university, were readily available and eagerly accepted. With the influx of returned servicemen into the universities, especially Sydney and Melbourne, an intellectual and political ferment began to emerge which in retrospect seemed a golden age to many later students.

While the rural economy had suffered from a severe drought in 1944 and 1945, the demand for wool and wheat in countries ravaged by the war brought a speedy recovery, and the outbreak of the Korean war in 1950 increased the demand for primary products. The price of wool increased from 2s per pound in 1947 to 12s in 1950, and graziers running superfine merinos sometimes got the hitherto unheard of price of 20s per pound. The acreage under wheat increased, as did the price of wheat, and 20,000 tractors were bought by farmers in 1952. Under the direction of a newly-established Wheat Board, which guaranteed a minimum purchase price, farmers who had been through hardship and drought began to prosper so that they were enabled to replace run-down equipment and engage in improvements to their properties. The scientific use of superphosphates and trace elements in deficient soils also helped to boost productivity.

The main factor creating employment and boosting the economy was demand for goods produced by industry. During the war, Australian industry had of necessity rapidly developed skills and efficiency and proved that it could produce quality goods. After the war, industry responded to demand, most markedly in the automobile sector. Inspired by the drive and foresight of Lawrence Hartnett and with the full backing of Prime Minister Chifley, the Holden car, to the accompaniment of a ten-piece orchestra, was launched at Fisherman's Bend, Victoria in November 1948. It was a sign of Australian progress and independence, because no American money was used to finance the venture. The on-the-road cost of the six-passenger vehicle was £760, it did thirty miles to the gallon (that is, 10.6 kilometres to the litre) and had a maximum speed of eighty miles (129 kilometres) per hour. Long waiting-lists quickly exhausted the flow of 20,000 units a year and to own a Holden became a badge of prosperity and nationalism. By 1962, when Australians had become the fourth largest car-owning people in the world, a million Holdens had been manufactured but in the first years of production its cost was prohibitive to most Australians as it was double the annual average wage.

The initial period of recovery was under the Labor government led by Ben Chifley, who was determined not to allow the economy to run on unbridled. Personal income taxes rose with the need to pay for social services but, because the medical profession still blocked a national health scheme, the poor, who could not contribute to private health funds, continued to suffer. The use of X-rays to make an early diagnosis

combined with a government campaign brought about the virtual elimination of tuberculosis, which had been the greatest cause of death for the
twenty to forty year olds. Poliomyelitis continued to ravage the young
until the Salk vaccine effectively wiped it out after the mid-1950s.

The Labor government also initiated the most comprehensive construction scheme in Australia's history, which began in 1949 under the
direction of the Snowy Mountains Hydro-Electric Authority. By a system
of tunnels and dams, the scheme was designed to generate electricity and
irrigate dry land for food production at half the cost of power stations
burning coal or oil. The Authority attracted 5,000 to its workforce, most
of whom were immigrants, and its low record of labour unrest was probably due to high wages and the community spirit engendered by the
almost pioneering conditions under which the men worked. When the
scheme was completed twenty-three years later, its objectives had been
completely achieved.

Part of the Labor government's commitment to an overall objective of
post-war reconstruction was expansion of the tertiary sector in education.
In 1946 the first significant step was taken with the founding of the Australian National University to which a group of eminent, expatriate
scholars was attracted to found its research schools. In the following
years, the older universities were transformed by an injection of funds,
thereby augmenting staff numbers as well as teaching and research facilities. Trans-Australia Airlines was set up under government ownership to
compete against private carriers on internal routes, and, in 1947, the
government bought Qantas from Qantas Empire Airways as the national
carrier on international routes. The necessity to buy vessels to transport
migrants after the war led to the establishment of a national shipping line,
which helped to maintain a ship-building industry and provided a mer-
cantile marine service.

These steps were acceptable even to those who regarded every move
into the private sector as another expression of Labor's design to socialize
the economy. As the people at large were enjoying a new prosperity, it
was, however, difficult for Labor's opponents to make much headway by
cries of socialization. With the general introduction of the forty-hour week
by 1948, there was time for a variety of pursuits and the money to enjoy
them — to go regularly to the pictures on a Saturday evening while the
kids had been to the matinee shows in the afternoon, to take the family to
the beach or to the mountains, to have a picnic on a Sunday, to visit
relatives and generally resume the activities that war had interrupted.
Even so, there was still the reminder of the austerity of war because petrol
rationing was retained until 1950. More children stayed on at school, and

the universities began to see entrants who were neither wealthy nor on scholarships. Furthermore, there was the chance to take some pride in Australia as a minor power in peacetime, rather than to look back at war as the testing ground of the nation.

With Evatt as Foreign Minister, a policy emerged which was not solely connected with Australia's defence. New Zealand had always been regarded as part of the family as well as a friendly neighbour so it was logical to cement the bonds in 1944 with an Anzac Agreement designed to ensure the two nations co-operated in furthering their common interests. Having helped in the creation of Israel, Evatt was elected President of the United Nations in 1948; he surprised those Australians who thought that he was under communist influence, and earnt the displeasure of the Russians, by his protests against the treatment of Cardinal Mindszenty in Hungary. He fully supported the independence of India and his initially reluctant but finally firm stand for Indonesia in its bid for freedom from Dutch rule, enthusiastically backed by the Waterside Workers Union which banned Dutch supplies, gained him and his country the warm gratitude of the Indonesians, which long afterwards, in less amicable situations, was not forgotten.

When China became communist controlled in 1949, Evatt insisted that such a situation should not preclude commercial and eventual diplomatic relations with her, although his own government did not recognize the new Chinese one. Nonetheless, he was genuinely concerned at the development of the communist movement in Asia and also in Europe where Russia had begun to extend its control over most of the Eastern states. Evatt was probably swayed by these considerations when he agreed to the formation of a secret body, later called the Australian Security Intelligence Organization, which eventually and ironically helped cause his own downfall.

Australians did not want any form of national independence for themselves and in 1947 a Gallup poll indicated that sixty-five percent, as against twenty-eight percent, preferred having British nationality to a separate Australian one. Eighteen months later, another poll showed that Australians ranked first of six nations (the British ran third and the French last), in response to a question as to whether they were happy which possibly meant that happiness accompanied a lack of concern about larger questions than personal fulfillment. In any case, the fact that the retention of British nationality, and consequently British passports, was increasingly meaningless was not as important to Australians as the symbolic tie with Britain, but in 1949 the Nationality and Citizenship Act became law and Australians ceased to be British subjects.

H. V. (Doc) Evatt (right) succeeded Joseph (Ben) Chifley (left) as leader of the Labor Party although, unlike Chifley, Evatt never became prime minister. Evatt's best work was done as a jurist, statesman and historian.

The Labor government attempted to retain its sense of responsibility for the direction of the economy despite the good times, and amongst Labor members there was a determination to control the banking system. Some of them had youthful memories of the bank crashes during the depression of the 1890s, and all retained a taste of bitterness from the days of Niemeyer and Gibson in the 1930s with their reminder that the Australian government was helpless in the face of the banks. Chifley tried to reform the system in 1945 by abolishing the Commonwealth Bank Board and making the Bank responsible, through a governor, to the Federal Treasurer. All banks were required to deposit a proportion of their reserves with the Commonwealth Bank which set interest rates. Finally, only those banks controlled by government could be repositories for the accounts of all Commonwealth, state and local goverments and their instrumentalities. There was a degree of outrage at this measure, which the Melbourne City Council challenged in the High Court in August 1947 and it was found to be invalid as contrary to the Constitution.

Chifley's reaction was impetuous and rash given that the electorate was still prepared to trust Labor provided it restricted its control to areas not generally accepted as fundamental to private enterprise. He persuaded his colleagues that the only course of action was to bring the whole banking system within the ambit of the Commonwealth Bank, in effect to nationalize the banks. The outcry was immense despite the fact there was no evidence that public or private money was in danger. An avalanche of propaganda, orchestrated by the press, fell on the government, which was portrayed as only one step removed from ushering in a socialist state. A year later the High Court again found against the government, and the decision was upheld by the Privy Council in England. This meant that the Commonwealth Bank, while retaining its centralized powers, was no more than one other competing agency in the banking market place.

The domestic argument about the banking system highlighted the concern about socialism which the tensions of the Cold War made evident on the international scene. The success of several leading communists in winning important trade union elections had fostered a considerable attitude of reserve in the Australian electorate towards any organization showing left-wing tendencies. This was heightened in June 1949, when the communist-controlled Miners' Federation called a strike in New South Wales. They wanted a 30s weekly rise in wages plus three months paid leave every seven years and they claimed that their request for a thirty-five hour working week was not being processed rapidly enough. As the strike spread to other states and stocks of coal ran low, electricity usage was rationed, firms laid off their workforce for weeks, and the country was thrown into industrial and domestic chaos.

The government froze the union's funds, some communist leaders were imprisoned and troops were sent to work open-cut mines. To the left wing of the labour movement this proved that their leaders were mere tools of capitalism. To many other Australians, the attempt to nationalize the banks and the strikes seemed to show how unsafe the country was under Labor. The anti-communists exploited this feeling and sought to alarm voters. It was also unfortunate that, at a time when many voters were enjoying their new Holdens or imported cars, Chifley insisted that petrol rationing was still needed to maintain the exchange rate and help Britain with her trade balance. The electorate was fed up with wartime controls after a decade of restrictions and welcomed promises by Labor's opponents to remove them. For all these reasons, the end of 1949 was not a good time for Labor to go into an election.

Menzies went to the polls proclaiming that to vote for Labor was to bow under the yoke of socialism, an 'alien and deadly growth'. He had a basket of choice offerings for the electorate labelled 'putting back value into the pound' which ranged from the abolition of petrol rationing to the banning of the Communist Party. The results of the elections were a handsome reward for the coalition parties, who were able to take office knowing that they were governing in a period of prosperity not enjoyed since the 1880s. The fact that Australian troops, a mere five years after the end of World War II, began to arrive in South Korea in September 1950 and went into action almost immediately did nothing to dispel the air of contentment. When the war began to take its human toll, it went almost unnoticed except in the families of the 1,396 casualties and 277 dead before the armistice in 1953.

There were some promises that Menzies stuck by, although he was only able to deliver less than half of his electioneering basket. Child endowment was extended to the previously excluded first child in a family, milk distributed to school children, and medical care given freely to pensioners. In 1953 Earle Page was able to introduce a modified version of Labor's envisaged Medical Benefits Scheme, when he persuaded the medical profession that neither their wealth nor their social position would thereby be endangered. Compulsory national service training for selected eighteen-year-old males was introduced as there was concern that the Cold War in Europe would lead inexorably to real war. Harold Holt, a young protégé of Menzies, who had become Minister for Labour and National Service, explained that the six months' period of training would improve the physical fitness of the trainees, and many of the youths in question subsequently agreed.

To his and the coalition's credit, Menzies continued the Labor government's immigration programme, and he warmly praised Calwell for his initiative in setting it up. Holt was also Minister for Immigration and, in January 1951, he enthused publicly about the benefits of taking in close to 100,000 immigrants annually. Holt thanked the trade unions for their co-operation and noted that even militant unions had accepted immigrants with ten percent of the workers at the Newcastle and Port Kembla steelworks being displaced persons. The remarkable thing about the whole programme, however, was the way in which the Australian people, led by government, churches and neighbourhood groups had accepted, or at least tolerated, the new wave of immigration. For Labor the irony was that many of the displaced persons had fled from Europe with a horror of communism, which made them disinclined to vote for a party that cynics and opportunists, and some honest persons, labelled as procommunist.

In April 1950 Menzies brought in a bill to ban the Communist Party, seize its assets and declare persons who belonged to it 'unlawful'. At the time there were about 10,000 communists in the country and only a small fraction of the electorate ever voted for communist candidates, but it was unquestionably true that communist strength in key trade unions was marked. It was also true that most communist trade union leaders had a deep sense of responsibility to their fellow workers, which was the main reason for their election to such positions. As a secular creed, communism or Marxist-Leninism had begun to fill a void in the minds of many intellectuals to whom Christianity, often untried but found wanting, was pernicious or merely irrelevant. Within the Labor movement, there were some who, impatient with mere reformism and the long struggle to tame rather than overthrow capitalism, looked to the kind of more decisive action which they saw exemplified in the Soviet world. Yet neither they nor the communists, who, for the larger part, were loyal Australians, wanted to destroy the existing structures of government and society by force, although the chairman of the Communist Party, Lawrence Louis Sharkey, was sentenced to three years' imprisonment in 1949 for having stated that Australian troops would welcome Soviet forces were they to enter Australia 'in pursuit of aggressors'. Probably a majority of Australians genuinely thought that the Communist Party should be banned nonetheless, although it never became clear why, except to a group of militant Catholics who had been tireless in denouncing communism as far back as the days of the Spanish Civil War.

In 1931 Archbishop Mannix encouraged a group of Victorian Catholics to form a society which they named after an English Jesuit martyr, Edmund Campion. By examining the history and intellectual heritage of their faith, they realized its universality, which over-rode its Irish-Australian content. To them it seemed clear that the main, contemporary threat to the Church was international communism. They published a vigorous weekly, the *Catholic Worker* and eventually Industrial Groups were formed to contest for union leadership against communists which, with Labor Party blessing or mere tolerance, were often, and increasingly, successful. The Labor Party had a long history of opposition to communists involving themselves in union affairs — based as much on political expediency as on the desire for ideological purity — and the Industrial Groups thereby fitted into a well-known category to be tolerated as long as they proved convenient.

Understandably the success of the Industrial Groups bred opposition to them by some powerful members of the Labor movement. Seeing their base in the industrial sector eroded, they were quick to deny to Catholics who opposed them in the Labor Party the right to political activity they had temporarily granted to communists. B.A. (Bob) Santa-maria, a young Catholic lawyer, led a secretly organized Movement which stood behind the Industrial Groups. To the extent that it was an official body of the Church, criticism of it and the Church itself was valid. Otherwise criticism of Santamaria's Movement was an expression of bigotry, or was based on the desire to retain factional and personal power within political Labor and the union movement.

Within the Labor caucus, there was a solid Catholic minority which shared Santamaria's attitude to communism. Chifley as leader and Evatt as deputy realized that the unity of the Party was threatened and decided to compromise on Menzies's Communist Party Dissolution Bill which the Senate eventually passed. Evatt appeared for the Waterside Workers before the High Court in a case against the Act which caused accusations that he was soft on communism. The Court ruled that the Act was unconstitutional and the upshot was a double dissolution, with Menzies promising a referendum which, if successful, would give Parliament power to ban the Communist Party and all its followers.

In April 1951 the Liberal-Country Party coalition won the election and took control of the Senate. A state ball was held in June to celebrate the Golden Jubilee of the Commonwealth Parliament, but Chifley, re-elected leader of the Party, remained in his Canberra hotel to work. Weakened by strain, worry and work he died that night leaving behind a legend as the Labor leader par excellence — loyal, intelligent, determined and always a worker. But above all he was an Australian who, in his own words, had seen 'the light on the hill' and struggled towards it. His other legacy was H.V. Evatt whom caucus elected as leader. With Menzies's referendum set for September, the caucus choice was one which, in the long run, would admirably suit Menzies.

Those who remembered 1917 saw in essence a re-run of how a com-munity can be divided on a moral issue. Again the powerful organs of the media were lined up to persuade people to vote 'Yes' and thus ban the Communist Party and its followers. Unlike 1917 the Catholics mainly joined with the conservative forces, but Mannix, true to conscience again, publicly declared that he would vote 'No'. Menzies campaigned with brilliant vigour yet Evatt did even better. In September 1951 a very narrow majority, (50.48 percent) of the whole electorate, voted 'No', and only Queensland, Western Australia and Tasmania voted 'Yes'. The referendum was probably lost because a majority of Australians did not think it just to place the onus of proof on the person accused of illegal communist practices rather than on the prosecution. One curious side effect was that the Communist Party lost ground but it did not mean that the problem of communism would be allowed to disappear.

In the very same month that the Australian people rejected what virtually would have been the persecution of communists at home, their government took a step designed to contain communism in the Pacific. Australia, New Zealand and the United States signed a treaty alliance called ANZUS at San Francisco, binding them to meet and consider the common danger, were a signatory attacked. For Australia the basis of the treaty was the firm conviction that only the United States would be able to come to her aid in the South Pacific in the face of any potential aggressor, although the treaty contained no assurance that it would do so. Nevertheless, the treaty was signed in the awareness that, like 1941, Churchill was alarmed at Australia's slide towards America.

The turning point for Australia was the victory of communism in China in late 1949, just as Japan's entry into the war had been in 1941. Percy Spender, Minister for Foreign Affairs, spelt out a theory in March 1950, which was based on China's becoming a communist power. Spender foresaw first Vietnam and then Laos and Cambodia falling to communism. Thailand, Burma, Malaya and finally Indonesia would then be under threat. All he needed to say to sum up Australia's position, and its consequent foreign policy for the ensuing decades, was 'No nation can escape its geography'. This was a conclusion white Australia had been groping towards since 1788.

The official public life of a nation is never as indicative of its vitality as is the growth in communal awareness that is seen in its culture, both high and popular. During and after the war, high culture developed in art, music and literature in a manner not seen since the 1890s. The development had its roots in the 1930s when the lack of abundance forced a rethinking of provincial values, and the artists, in particular, began to realize that new forms of expression had arisen in the northern hemisphere. European art had begun to reflect the agony of a society which, since the sixteenth century, had gradually moved from its Greco-Roman and Christian well-springs towards atheistic humanism and secularism. Old values could no longer be relied upon to bolster societies faced by new forms of totalitarianism of the right and the left, and art, being more universal than language, began to respond. The Melbourne *Herald* staged an exhibition of modern painting in 1939 including works by Cezanne, Matisse, Van Gogh, Chagall, Picasso and Dali. The exhibition naturally produced some negative reaction, but it was also part of the excitement and creativity that led to the founding of the Contemporary Art Society in Melbourne and Sydney. In Sydney, William Dobell painted a range of

Albert Namatjira used the artistic talent of his people to portray their land in a style
that took much from modernity but retained the haunting quality of his ancestors,
who had worked with charcoal and pigment for ages before him.

portraits which combined technique with acute insight into human
nature and culminated with his Archibald Prize winning portrait of
Joshua Smith in 1943. A court was asked to judge whether it was a portrait or a caricature and decided that it was both, which was one way of
saying that an artist had some right in what he saw. With stark realism
and understanding, Russell Drysdale painted the outback, and his

women of the bush stood upright in adversity as Lawson's women had done. Drysdale then did a series of paintings on Aborigines, which was a new field for Australian artists if one excepts those done in earlier colonial times.

In Melbourne, the days of McCubbin, Streeton and Roberts were invoked and a genuine expression of the national spirit evolved, which was no mere mimicry of the masters of the Heidelberg school. Sidney Nolan went to the flat, long plains, dotted with trees, dams and wildlife, of the Victorian Wimmera for inspiration. Later he turned to the legends of Kelly, Gallipoli, Eureka and the early explorers, while always himself exploring in an attempt to come to the heart of the continent and its people. Arthur Boyd turned from landscape to surrealism, to religious themes and then back to the bush, calling upon a long family tradition of identification with Australia, while Albert Tucker went from social realism to surrealism with his *The City in Wartime*. His strength of intellect and character marked him as a leader amongst his contemporaries, until he left Australia in 1947 as a refugee from the culture he was helping to create.

In music Peter Sculthorpe developed an aggressive but eloquent Australianism, which was first apparent in *Irkanda 1* (1955), based on Tasmanian Aboriginal lore, and most notably, in his *Sun Music* series and subsequent compositions. Sculthorpe, Richard Meale and others reflected Australia's new awareness of Asia in their use of the forms and textures of East Asian music, which would have greatly pleased Percy Grainger, perhaps Australia's best-known composer, who died in 1961.

R.D. Fitzgerald, Judith Wright, Douglas Stewart and James McAuley were poets of the national spirit, but amongst them a cause célèbre occurred which overshadowed the Archibald Prize affair and became itself a memorable cultural event. *Angry Penguins* began in 1940 as the journal of the Adelaide University Arts Association with John Reed and Max Harris as co-editors. Reed, president of the Contemporary Art Society and founder and director of the Museum of Modern Art in Melbourne, was a courageous man of large heart and spirit. With his wife, Sunday, Reed had sheltered, fed, encouraged and loved a generation of young artists and poets from whom he demanded all and received much in helping to give Australian high culture flesh and form. Both Reed and Harris used *Angry Penguins*, in Harris's words, to attack, 'the tired and mediocre nationalism which passed for poetry and the pedestrian bush whackery which gave Australia a novel of unequalled verbal dullness'. Their enthusiasm in the cause of modernism was the undoing of their journal.

In autumn 1944, *Angry Penguins* published sixteen poems written by Ern Malley, whom Harris praised as a poet of extraordinary talent. In fact Ern only existed in the fervent imaginations of James McAuley and Harold Stewart, who had compiled the poems to protest against 'the gradual decay of meaning and craftsmanship in poetry' and to debunk *Angry Penguins* as a purveyor of the absurd. They were so successful that some critics claimed that they had written excellent poetry, despite themselves. The literary world, local and international, laughed but modernism in Australian writing received a severe setback and the scoffers seemed to have won in a way never intended by McAuley and Stewart, who had taken a stand for rational modernity.

The universities began to teach Australian history and the first, full course was introduced at Melbourne University in 1946. Historians already had a small body of valuable material from which to draw including Ernest Scott's pioneering *Short History of Australia*, 1916; the four volumes by Timothy Coghlan, *Labour and Industry in Australia*, 1918; and the first and unsurpassed edition of *The Australian Encyclopaedia* in two volumes in 1925. Keith Hancock's seminal *Australia* came out in 1930, and in 1935 Stephen Roberts's *The Squatting Age in Australia* was published. It was a remarkably evocative study of the pastoral days, although it was completely insensitive to the history of the Aborigines in the period. Charles Bean's great work in twelve volumes, *The Official History of Australia in the War of 1914–1918*, was finally completed in 1942. Modern historiography in Australia began with the publication in 1937 of E.M. O'Brien's *The Foundation of Australia*, which argued from the original sources that Australia's origins as a white settlement stemmed from the need of the British to dispose of their unwanted criminals. Manning Clark was appointed to a lectureship at Melbourne in 1944, and began his life's work on Australian history with the publication of *Select Documents in Australian History* in two volumes (1950, 1955). His talent, diligence and flair saw their flowering with the publication in 1962 of the first of his six monumental volumes on Australia which take the story of his country from pre-European times to the mid 1930s.

The founding of literary journals such as *Southerly* (Sydney, 1939), which after 1944 turned its attention to Australian writing, and *Meanjin* (Brisbane, 1940) gave the new intelligentsia, who were mostly of radical bent, an outlet as contributors and readers. The *Bulletin* still retained an audience although it had become a shadow of its former self. These developments, together with the fostering of large orchestras by the A.B.C. in Sydney and Melbourne and the production of ballet and opera by the Tait brothers, helped throw up a cultural wave unnoticed by the majority of Australians. They preferred to draw their relaxation from Gwen Meredith's immensely popular radio serial 'Blue Hills' which ran from 1949 to 1976, listening to Bob and Dolly Dyer's quiz show 'Pick-a-box', reading the *Women's Weekly*, or the 'girlie' magazine *Man*, and going to the football or races. They were delighted and their national pride was bolstered in 1952 when Frank Sedgman started a twenty-year epoch in tennis by winning the first of fourteen Wimbledon Men's Singles Championships, while 1950 had seen the first of the fifteen Australian wins in the Davis Cup achieved in the next seventeen years.

War and its aftermath, with the frequently proclaimed threat of Chinese Communist expansion in the Pacific, had helped to foster a national awareness at all levels because the question of Australia's survival as a white, European outpost seemed in jeopardy. It had become essential to face the question whether there was anything distinctive enough in Australian society to make its preservation worthwhile. Most Australians thought that there was and in differing ways they attempted both to create and enjoy it. Perhaps as an expression of the differences between the two post-war generations and the increased importance given to material values, there were few monuments erected to the dead of World War II. Instead towns and municipalities throughout the land laid out parks and built swimming pools as memorials. The fact that donations to them were tax deductible was an incentive.

CHAPTER SEVENTEEN
Modern Australia

A ustralians gradually began to discover their own continent in the 1950s. Prior to that period, family holidays, honeymoons or trips away by sporting and other bodies were generally taken in the state of residence. In Victoria some people took a change of air at Mount Macedon or Daylesford, while in New South Wales the Blue Mountains and Bundanoon were popular and the other states had similar resorts. A few venturous souls in the eastern states visited the snowfields for sport and recreation, but the majority went to the beaches which surrounded the continent. Queensland's Gold Coast and the Great Barrier Reef were attracting many local and some interstate visitors by the mid-1950s.

Melburnians may have taken a journey by train across the Murray on the *Spirit of Progress* to decide for themselves whether Sydney was truly Australia's most beautiful city and to compare, fruitlessly, their bay beaches with Bondi and Manly. Some Sydneysiders came timidly south to test the rumours that it was possible to have four seasons in one day in Melbourne and that the city closed down on a weekend. Proportionally, there was more movement from the other states to New South Wales and Victoria — a journey east from Perth and Adelaide, south from Brisbane and north across Bass Strait from Tasmania was necessary in order to visit the financial, political, cultural and, in population, numerical strongholds of the country. The wealthy and adventurous still went 'overseas', which did not mean Asia but the British Isles. Some brave souls made the trip by air to arrive stupefied and exhausted at their destination. In the main, however, Australians were still state-bound.

The car was crucial to the movement of young people in the 1950s, and its use, mostly in second-hand models, spelt the end of some small country towns as centres for community life. There was more readily available petrol, and slightly improved roads, although the Hume Highway between Sydney and Melbourne remained in a scandalous condition for years, as did the Eyre Highway to Perth. Tourism was helped by the availability of money, the widespread use of bus tours and the gradual introduction of better accommodation for travellers with the first of the ever-the-same motels opening in Canberra in 1955. The war was also partially responsible for an increasing awareness of Australia, as names of places most people were scarcely aware of previously — Wyndham, Townsville, Broome, Derby — had become part of the national consciousness. People outside Australia also had become aware of it in the war as many soldiers had trained and were based in Australia or passed through it on their way to the Pacific War.

Australia, consequently, became interesting, relevant, worth taking time to see and, to the surprise of many, a place of awesome splendour, vast and lonely distances, great rolling beaches, rain forests, tropical luxuriance — in fact a microcosm of everything it was said the rest of the world could offer. It didn't seem to matter that, in the main, the meals were much the same from Cooktown to Geraldton — steak and eggs with or without tomatoes or a mixed grill — and that the regulations governing drinking hours remained uncivilized. Until 1970, when the Indian-Pacific service from Sydney to Perth was commenced, containing the world's longest stretch of straight track of 480 kilometres, trains, with few exceptions, were a recipe for boredom at the best and extreme discomfort at the worst. In any event, by the late 1950s it was apparent that Australia was there to be visited and Australians began to do so.

Conservation of the land was a preoccupation of very few, although some farmers took steps, by tree planting and contour ploughing, to repair the ravages of soil erosion, which was already affecting five percent of the country. Soil salinity showed signs of becoming a problem because of tree removal and over-irrigation in the Murray-Darling Basin. Three-quarters of the native forests were gone or endangered, seventy-six species of native flora were presumed extinct, while many others had become rare. In some places, the countryside seemed to be dying through overclearing, which had upset the ecological balance and produced serious effects on mammals and birds, some of which were extinct or close to becoming so. Little had been learnt from the Aboriginal habit of regular burning-off, so that vast areas were becoming endangered by noxious shrubs and inedible grasses. Thirty years later a clearer realization of these factors was apparent, but by that time there was little hope of turning back the clock.

Science, however, had its role and, partly through the work of a remarkable scientist, a significant change came about on farming and pastoral lands, thereby contributing to a rise in sheep numbers by sixty percent in a few years. Annie Macnamara was born in Beechworth, Victoria in 1899 and graduated in medicine with much distinction at the University of Melbourne in 1922. She devoted herself to the prevention of poliomyelitis, and her orthopaedic work for victims of the disease brought her great renown, while the first centre for spastic children was opened, in the Royal Children's Hospital, Melbourne, at her recommendation in 1940. With her rural background, she had taken an interest in attempts to eradicate the rabbit, including those made by Dr Danysz of the Pasteur Institute in France, who had conducted unsuccessful experiments with a virus but nevertheless aroused interest in such a method of rabbit control. It was not until 1950 that Dr Macnamara was able to persuade the government to resume field testing along the Murray River on the effects on rabbits of the South American virus myxomatosis.

The virus, carried by mosquitoes and later also by fleas, spread rapidly from Victoria into South Australia, through the New South Wales river system and on into Queensland. Within two years, the rabbit population was ravaged, pastures improved and sheep in ever-increasing numbers began to graze on land that had previously been the domain of the rabbit. The return from wool was augumented by £30,000,000 in three years. Dr Macnamara was rewarded by the wool-growers with a present of £800 and a clock, but at her death in 1968 she was mourned by thousands whom she had treated as victims of paralysis. Although a mortality rate amongst rabbits of over ninety percent was achieved in the early years, when myxomatosis was spread through the work of the CSIRO, the vermin increasingly developed resistance to the virus. By the mid-eighties, the pre-myxomatosis levels were returning, and some farmers were turning back to the old methods of rabbit eradication such as burrow fumigation.

Previous experiments in soldier settlement had finally taught the lesson that, instead of opening new lands, it was better to subdivide proven land for settlement. This ensured that most returned men who became soldier-settlers after World War II were successful. Nevertheless, despite the attraction of farming, many young men, who had tasted other and more attractive forms of life in wartime, chose not to return to country areas. Within a few years, many small country towns began to decline as the local population fell and better means of transport enabled country people to shop at major centres. In some areas, farmhouses were often left derelict or turned to other uses when farmers began moving

Vines for wine production were brought with the First Fleet. The industry flourished in the latter half of the nineteenth century but large scale operations were most notable from the 1960s. Much bulk production took place on irrigated areas about Griffith and Leeton in New South Wales.

into towns where there were better educational facilities, and social life and amenities, especially for women, were available. Small rural schools, especially of the one-teacher kind, began to disappear as the rural population declined and buses came into widespread use to convey children to central high schools.

The most positive aspect of farming amongst more aware members of the rural community was the realization that the days of haphazard agriculture and husbandry were over. Land management was designed scientifically to maintain fertility and increase crop yields, while flock and herd development on specialized breeding and nutritional grounds was practised more widely and successfully, thereby raising the whole standard of farming. The increasing complexity and expense of modern farm machinery led to over-capitalization in many instances resulting in debts to banks and agricultural companies. Amongst some city dwellers, especially of the more affluent kind who could write off losses as tax benefits, the old rural dream revived and gradually the land near the cities was subdivided and sold to hobby farmers. Some of them took a genuine interest in their farmlets, but it was often the case that the land was neglected, weeds and rabbits abounded, and the productivity which resulted was negligible in comparison to that achieved by the genuine farmers.

In manufacturing, further great strides were taken and from 1949 to 1959 the value of factory production rose four-fold to nearly £2,000,000,000. A trade agreement was made in 1957 with Japan, which had become Australia's second largest customer, next to Britain. Even the Labor Party and the trade unions showed little opposition to the agreement as it was plain that without it wool sales, heavily dependent on Japanese buying, were at risk. The former enemy countries agreed to give each other 'most favoured nation' treatment for imports which meant that continued wool sales were assured and there were good prospects of exporting Australian wheat to Japan. Despite the fact that Australian shops quickly began to display a wide range of quality Japanese goods, Australian industry seemed to withstand the shock easily, at least while tariffs were maintained.

A workforce for industry was readily available through the continuing immigration programme. Few immigrants were either interested in or able to go on the land, except for Italians in the cane growing areas of Queensland, on fruit blocks in the Murrumbidgee area and along irrigated sections near the Murray in Victoria. Migrants helped produce steel at Port Kembla from iron ore mined at Cockatoo Island in Western Australia, oil was refined on Cockburn Sound near Fremantle for the Anglo-Iranian Oil Company and Caltex, an American concern, began refining at Kurnell near Sydney.

Such operations required community facilities and services, as well as housing for the employees, so industrial development had its spin-off in housing and service industries of all kinds. High demand for labour, materials, machinery and buildings, coupled with the import of manufactured goods, often in the form of luxury items, caused the economy to boom. But, by 1951, a rising national trade deficit, marked increases in incomes, and inflation alarmed the government, and 1952 saw severe restrictions on imports, followed by a decision to cut that year's immigrant intake from 150,000 to 80,000. The unions demanded this decrease as unemployment, especially amongst unskilled workers, had risen, and in Victoria they wanted a complete cessation of immigration. The myth had prevailed of immigration causing unemployment, although, in fact, it boosted the economy and helped to provide further employment. As always, it was easy to seek causes for economic dislocation in factors external to the real ones affecting Australia.

On the Monte Bello Islands off Australia's western coast, Britain had begun a series of atom bomb tests, which neither the government nor the trade unions perceived as having serious implications for the future. The tests were continued at Woomera in South Australia and finally completed at Maralinga in the same state in 1957. The areas in question were said to be devoid of significant populations, although there were Aborigines living near the South Australian test sites. While Britain's actions were understandable — in that it wanted to compete with other large powers in the nuclear energy and arms race, and it could not carry out tests at home — the complaisance of the Australian government was not. It took thirty years and an official enquiry, called for in 1980, to reveal the careless planning and the long-term deleterious effects of the tests. In 1949 uranium was discovered near Rum Jungle in the Northern Territory. It was developed by Conzinc Riotinto and a ten-year agreement was made to export it to the United States. Within a few years of the destruction of Hiroshima, Australia had become both an atomic test site and a resource for an industry which few people understood and many feared.

The atmosphere of anxiety engendered by fears of Communist expansion had not abated. There were accusations that both the organizers of the Commonwealth Literary Fund, which subsidized books and periodicals of literary merit, and the staff of the Australian National University had been infiltrated by communists. On 13 April 1954, Menzies told Parliament that a Soviet diplomat, Vladimir Petrov, had asked for and been granted political asylum. Petrov stated that he had lost faith in communism and, having lived in Australia, he now wished to remain. He also said that he had been a Soviet spy and that a Russian espionage system was operating in Australia. Mrs Petrov had allegedly decided to return home to Russia, but she changed her mind and Australians were treated in the newspapers and on newsreels to her release at Darwin by Commonwealth police from the clutch of her armed Soviet escorts. That incident did more to cement the idea in the minds of Australians that Soviet communism was an ugly, repressive system than Petrov's own admissions had done, and very few were upset when the Soviet Union cut diplomatic relations with Australia. With the support of the federal caucus of the Labor Party, Menzies set up a Royal Commission to investigate Soviet espionage.

There was an election scheduled for 29 May but Menzies's prospects did not look good as all states except South Australia were under Labor governments. He managed, nevertheless, to win the election largely because of a system of electoral distribution which gave his Liberal-

Country Party coalition sixty-four out of 120 seats in the House of Representatives with 47.07 percent of the total vote while the Labor Party, led by Evatt, managed to win only forty-seven seats with 50.03 percent of the vote. It was a bitter blow to Evatt from which he never recovered and in the aftermath his Party was in disarray.

When the Royal Commission called members of Evatt's staff to appear before it concerning their possible connection with Soviet espionage, the former High Court judge rushed to defend them. The three judges of the Royal Commission listened with increasing bewilderment as Evatt alternated between sense and hysteria. On 7 September they withdrew his right to appear on the grounds that he was unable to separate his legal from his political role. In August 1955, the Commission not surprisingly reported that the Soviets did engage in espionage in Australia but refrained from asking for the prosecution of any of the alleged communist sympathizers called before it. However, the real damage was done, for which Evatt, as much as either Menzies or the Commission, was responsible. Amongst a large portion of the public, the whole affair seemed to show that the Labor Party led by Evatt was favourable to communism, and Evatt's act of asking the Soviet Foreign Minister whether documents produced by Petrov were genuine — Molotov replied that they were forgeries — was merely a symbol of his move into unreality and the ineffectiveness of the Party executive which had been unable to control him.

Within the Labor Party, the argument over communism merely hid the real struggle being enacted between right-wing and left-wing factions for control of the Party machine. The whole conflict was capable of resolution by compromise between the warring factions, as indeed happened in New South Wales, where the left wing was weak and where the first Australian-born cardinal, N.T. Gilroy, Archbishop of Sydney, worked for a peaceful settlement to the dispute. Evatt, however, was aware that his leadership was threatened in Victoria which was controlled by the right wing. He stated publicly that his Party was suffering from the behaviour of disloyal and subversive members directed by an outside body which all knew to mean Santamaria's Movement.

In the upshot, the Victorian branch was virtually destroyed as a political force, the Industrial Groups were abandoned by the official Party, and John Cain's Labor government lost office in May 1955. The Party did not return to power in Victoria until Cain's son led Labor back to government in April 1982. More importantly, the nature of the Labor Party changed radically. In the past, its most fruitful elements had been composed of idealists, many of whom were Catholics. In 1917 during the

Sir Robert Gordon Menzies always took immense pride in standing in the presence of his sovereign. He is pictured welcoming her to a reception at Parliament House, Canberra.

debacle over conscription, the Catholics remained in the Party. But in 1955, so many were expelled and so many Catholic voters repelled that the old, uneasy but fruitful alliance between idealists of the left and right was destroyed. In the long run, some of the former idealism also disappeared, and the gulf between Labor and Liberalism narrowed.

In the immediate aftermath of the 'split' in Labor ranks, a new party was formed, which eventually called itself the Democratic Labor Party. Many of its members were expelled Labor members and former Industrial Groupers. Although its stronghold was Victoria, it stood candidates in all states. Its birth helped Menzies considerably. He called a federal election in late 1955 which he won handsomely with the help of preferences from the new Party, and he relied upon it for support and electoral success for the rest of his years in office.

Whether in a conscious attempt to gain a Liberal foothold in Catholic households, or because the urgency of the case had become so apparent by 1956, Menzies decided to use Commonwealth funds to pay interest on loans raised by church bodies to build new schools in the Australian Capital Territory. After eighty years, state aid to religion re-emerged and its spread and increase throughout Australia was inevitable. The main beneficiaries were Catholics, who supported ninety percent of the private schools and whose need was pressing in parochial schools. It was anomalous though that some of the wealthiest schools, charging the highest fees in the land, also benefited. State aid inexorably meant a marked change in the texture of Catholic parochial life which had revolved around the need to raise funds for education and the need for people to join religious orders which had grown because of the demands of maintaining a separate school system. Both required great sacrifice. Time also revealed that, given the choice, many non-Catholic parents would opt for a private education system in which, they fondly hoped, and sometimes found, higher standards of teaching and discipline would prevail in comparison with the state system. The debates, acrimony and expenditure of energies of the 1860s and 1870s were repeated a century later.

In 1954 Menzies welcomed with effusive warmth the first reigning British monarch to visit Australia, Elizabeth II, and took great pride in the reception given to her throughout the country. At the same time, he presided over a period in which emotional, economic and political ties with Britain were lessening perceptibly. Asia had always been a place of little interest to him, but he encouraged Australian participation in the Colombo Plan. With nearly all South-East Asian countries participating, the Plan succeeded in serving human and social needs in Asia. Australia contributed generously with technical assistance, equipment, training of personnel, agricultural development, capital aid and in many other ways. Australia also benefited considerably in that the thousands of Colombo Plan students who came to study in its universities and schools helped to soften racist attitudes to Asians. They also became ambassadors for Australia on their return to their home countries. Furthermore, the thousands of Australians who worked for the Plan as experts and advisers in Asian countries served to educate and awaken the general community to the needs and potentialities of Asia.

Australia continued to refuse recognition to China on the grounds that her communist government was hostile to America, and there was concern about Vietnam after the fall of the French held Dien Bien Phu in 1954 and the consequent partitioning of the country into north and south. Some Australians held the view that the Vietnamese liberation movement, led from the north by Ho Chi Minh, was mainly an expression of nationalism rather than a concerted drive to make the whole country communist. John Foster Dulles, U.S. Secretary of State, and his Australian counterpart, R.G. Casey, thought otherwise. A body called the South-East Asia Treaty Organisation was consequently born with the specific purpose of combating communist aggression in the area.

With exemplary pragmatism, Menzies announced in April 1955 that Australia and New Zealand would join with Britain to help Malaya combat subversive elements operating there. In his opinion, if a battle had to be fought against communism, it was better that it take place as far away from Australia as possible. The agreement committed Australia to the deployment of naval, air and land forces in Malaya and met strong opposition from the Labor Party, where the opinion was strongly held that nationalist, anti-colonial movements in Asia had to be understood rather than be pushed into becoming communist.

If there was confusion in some Asian capitals about Australia's role in the region, Menzies's ineffective intervention in attempting to negotiate with President Nasser of Egypt over the nationalization of the Suez Canal served only to heighten the uncertainty. By his act, Menzies adopted the old stance of European colonialism and indicated that he thought that the national interests of former colonies should always remain secondary to the interests of their former masters. The old idea of Empire, power and economic advantage died slowly.

While the politicians argued and made treaties, the Australian people went about the business of living in a more affluent and relaxed manner than had been possible since the 1920s. In 1954 the voters of New South Wales, by a narrow margin, took the venturous step of extending drinking hours. After nearly forty years, it came as a surprise to see people

320

actually enjoying themselves by drinking publicly at night. South Australia followed suit. The Victorians waited until 1966 before deciding to extend hotel hours until ten o'clock at night and restrictions on Sunday trading remained in force.

Drunkenness, nevertheless, with or without six o'clock closing, remained a destructive vice. Under its influence, drinkers' health was ruined, families were broken up and road accidents caused. The problem of drink was clearly ilustrated in the case of the famous Aboriginal landscape artist, Albert Namatjira. Unlike the rest of his race, he had been granted full citizenship, which permitted him to buy liquor for his own use. In the time-honoured custom of his people he shared his possessions with them, including liquor, thus breaking the law. He was given a prison sentence of three months served 'in the open' and died soon afterwards. At the core of the problem lay the apparent inability of many Aborigines to cope with alcohol, in part or wholly because of their social situation. Despite some attempt to integrate them into white society, they remained second-class citizens. They had not become accustomed to using drink in moderation, no attempt had been made to educate them to its use and the very fact of its prohibition had tended to enhance its attraction, so that the figure of a drunken Aborigine had become one of scorn in the eyes of many whites.

By the end of the 1950s, the car had become both the symbol of prosperity and the assurance of mobility, especially amongst many young people to whom a journey by bus or train was a novelty. The cult of the teenager began, Bill Haley and the 'Comets' swept the country by storm and their record 'Rock around the Clock' was the biggest seller of all time. Boys who had previously dreamt of owning their own bat or football now wanted to buy a guitar. The 'generation gap' began to be spoken of as parents were unable to understand the new ways of musical communication and young people found them incapable of comprehending the aspirations of a generation that knew only plenty. 'Bodgies and Widgies' wore their distinctive clothing and hair styles, and parents despaired of the 'rising generation' in much the same way as others before them had done.

The preparation and choice of food gradually became more varied and people tentatively ordered European dishes. Some began to drink wine with meals, although it was often of the white, sweet kind. The housing shortage was overcome by 1960. Many new homes resembled boxes with sloping lids, while the old terrace houses of some charm and dignity in the inner cities often gave way to graceless blocks of flats which quickly became slums. By the mid-sixties, one in five new dwellings was a flat.

The first Holden was launched at Fisherman's Bend, Victoria with celebrations accompanied by a ten piece orchestra. Sir Lawrence Hartnett, the 'Father of the Holden', worked closely with Ben Chifley to make the Australian car possible. On his eightieth birthday, on 16 June 1978, he was honoured at a special commemorative luncheon.

Skyscrapers were replacing the older buildings in the cities, and because very few people now lived in the commercial areas, they became on weekends desolate, windswept places.

The suburbs expanded and drew people in hundreds of thousands who were now able to buy a block of their own on which to build. In the suburbs they could enjoy the semi-privacy of a backyard, with its Hills Hoist rotary clothes line, and a sense of achievement in getting a stake in the land, however minimal. Inevitably, the distance between work and home took up precious hours of travel, and there was either the boredom of train and tram journeys or the frustration of negotiating city traffic, which frayed nerves, consumed petrol, increased exhaust fumes and often caused chaos. Frequently the outer suburbs were still unsewered years after the construction of homes had taken place, trees were slow to grow and new lawns struggled to survive heat or rain, which either shrivelled the seeds or washed them away. At first, facilities such as schools, shops, doctors, chemists and hospitals were non-existent, municipal libraries a dream and places of recreation a rarity. Housewives endured day after day of loneliness, despite the vast range of labour saving devices which had come into the home and the now almost universal availability of the family car. Exhausted husbands returned mute from the workplace to look forward to the weekend, when they could have a bet, go to the football, drink at a local pub or club, polish the car and mow the lawn.

Few, especially among the town planners, remembered E.G. Wakefield's 'The essence of civilization is concentration' so the suburban sprawl went on and on. In European cities, people lived near their workplace, with shops, markets, theatres, churches, libraries and cafes in close proximity to their homes. As a result, a distinctive urban culture, high and low, could develop and flourish. Only a few Australians stayed in the city or came back there to find the heart of urban life. Gradually some of the older inner city suburbs came to life again. The urbanization of the continent seemed complete by 1959 as four out of every five of the estimated white population of ten million lived in the cities or in country towns. Immigration was the key to growth. Well over a million new people had arrived since the end of the war, and it was confidently forecast that by the Bicentenary in 1988 the twenty million mark would be reached. However, with increased prosperity in Europe, there were signs that the traditional sources of immigration were drying up.

Television was introduced to Australia in 1956 to coincide with the opening of the Olympic Games in Melbourne. As with radio, the A.B.C. and commercial channels operated separately and the A.B.C. offered programmes devoid of advertising. There were warnings that the new medium would be a setback to culture, make books obsolete and ruin children, whose lives would be dominated by the square box. In fact reading remained a major pastime for adults and was stimulated by television programmes as people wanted to know more about subjects the television could touch on only briefly. The sick, the old and the lonely benefited incalculably. Knowledge of Australia and the world was also enhanced, although there were grounds for believing that students spent less time doing their traditional homework and that they rarely listened to radio except for popular music. Within a few years, schools and colleges were faced with a generation of television watchers to whom reading had become almost an abnormal pastime. At all events, the television set became as much a part of the furniture of the Australian home as the radio and refrigerator. The initial sufferers at its hands were the owners of picture theatres and drive-ins, who faced declining audiences.

The excitement generated by the Olympic Games reflected a fundamental characteristic of the Australian ethos — the love of sport in a myriad of forms. Good weather, open spaces, snowfields, harbours, rivers and beaches abounded throughout the continent. They combined with an attraction to outdoor life, a propensity to match oneself physically against others, an admiration for the battler and the underdog, a tendency to gamble on practically anything that moved and an increasing degree of leisure. Participation in sport whether as players or spectators was central to the lives of the majority of Australians.

A nation singularly unencumbered by individual heroes in the military and political arenas looked to its sporting greats as the embodiment of those qualities of skill, courage and endurance most people admired. The big thing was to 'have a go', and, if a loser, to accept gracefully that to do one's best, even in defeat, was honourable. The worst disgrace was not to try, to 'turn it up' and to whinge about the result. All sports had their heroes and some had become household names: Bradman, Lindwall and Miller in cricket; Dally Messenger in Rugby League; Les Darcy in boxing; Roy Cazaly and Haydn Bunton in Australian Rules; Hubert Opperman in cycling; Peter Thompson in golf; Bill Beach and Bobby Pearce in sculling; Lindrum in billiards; Barney Kieran, Fanny Durack, 'Boy' Charlton and Frank Beaurepaire in swimming; Marjorie Jackson in sprinting; and Frank Sedgman, Lew Hoad and Ken Rosewall in tennis. The most popular of all sporting pastimes had no heroes, for fishing made everyone who caught a fish, large or small, his or her own hero. In the second largest sport, horse racing, big and small punters made temporary heroes of the horse and jockey who won. Throughout the land, hundreds of thousands of men and women went lawn bowling, every small town had a cricket pitch and golf course, and tennis was played day and night everywhere.

The Games were staged at the Melbourne Cricket Ground and Australians revelled in their success, as well as the fact that their country became the focus of international attention for a few days. Australian competitors won thirteen gold medals, broke four world records in swimming and Dawn Fraser began her long career as the world's greatest woman swimmer with her first of three successive gold medals in the 100 metres freestyle. She went on to hold twenty-seven individual world records. Betty Cuthbert was victorious in the 100 and 200 metre sprints

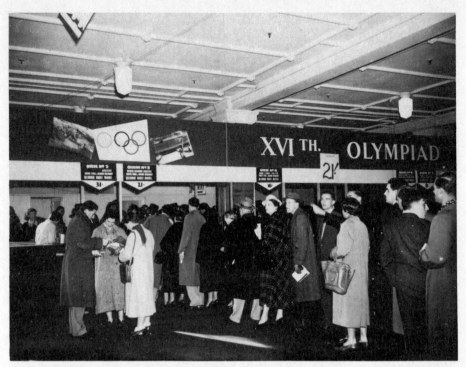

The Olympic Games in Melbourne in 1956 were an opportunity for Australians to show their prowess at, and love for, sport. Australian competitors have not since equalled the results achieved by those who represented this country in that Olympiad.

and Shirley Strickland in the eighty metre hurdles. These successes against the world's best seemed to bring to fruition all that sport had meant in Australian lives, and no one felt cheated when their great middle-distance runner, John Landy, went down to an Irishman in the 1500 metres.

The festival of athleticism was played out on a larger stage as the world watched the Games on television. The struggle for medal supremacy was won by Russia, and its victory was symbolized in the diminutive person of their supreme runner, Vladimir Kuts. A shadow hung over the Games which became reality as blood stained the Olympic Pool when Russia played Hungary in water polo. Across the other side of the world more serious matters were in progress as the Hungarian Revolution was put down by Russian tanks, and Australia gave some validity to her creed of a fair go for the underdog by promising to accept 3,000 refugees from that unhappy land.

One of the unsuccessful designs for the Sydney Opera House gives a glimpse of what could have been. The citizens of New South Wales paid for the majestic building on Bennelong Point with a lottery.

The commencement of the Sydney Opera House in both its structure and purpose was a cultural highlight because it would stand proudly in any century as one of the world's great buildings. The Opera House seemed an extension in beauty of the city and its setting on the Harbour, with its vast sail-like wings wedding land and water. Its eventual cost of over $100,000,000 was financed largely by a lottery but the project still had difficulties, due to financial stringencies, combined with the inability of Danish designer, Joern Utzon, to be more specific in his detailed planning. Despite the fact that some critics regarded it as inadequate for full-scale opera productions, the opening of the Opera House in 1973 was a seal on Australian cultural maturity and a promise that the arts would always remain precious to a people often accused of lacking refinement.

Australian literature was crowned with the work of the novelist Patrick White and the poet Alec Hope. White drew specifically on the Australian experience to write *Voss* (1957), but his more universal treatment of the larger theme of the human spirit in *The Tree of Man* and *The Eye of the Storm* helped him to win the Nobel Prize for literature in 1973. Hope's first collection of poetry, *The Wandering Islands*, appeared in 1955, and there-after he published regularly. With a high concept of the sacred role of the poet in society, Hope at times irritated, more often uplifted, and always led his readers to question the values of their generation. A more explicit Australian terminology and theme was used by the playwrights Ray Lawler and Alan Seymour. Lawler's *Summer of the Seventeenth Doll* became a classic of the Australian theatre in its exploration of the inadequate, even fragile, nature of 'mateship' while Seymour's *The One Day of the Year* further probed the weakness of the male stereotype by using Anzac Day as its theme. In the person of Barry Humphries's suburban housewife, Edna Everage, the role of the satirical humorist first appeared on the Melbourne stage in 1955. For Humphries, it began a career that has lasted over thirty years, during which he has made suburban Australians confront the realities of modern life.

Cultural immaturity was shown when the Commonwealth Govern-ment decided that there were 178 works to which the reading public was forbidden access. They included Frank Hardy's *Power without Glory*. This was a sordid tale of corruption in Victoria which would have had a res-tricted readership had not the family of John Wren, a Melbourne entre-preneur, believing that Wren's wife was libelled by the book, taken legal action, unsuccessfully, against Hardy.

More public attention could usefully have been directed to the fact that Russel Ward was denied a position as lecturer in history at the University of New South Wales in 1956 after a selection committee had unani-mously recommended his appointment. Ward had been a member of the Communist Party from 1941 until 1949 and in the opinion of the Vice-Chancellor he could not be employed in the university because of his 'character and reputation'. With the publication of his *The Australian Legend* in 1958, Ward made a memorable and significant contribution that ranks him with the foremost of historians specializing in Australian history.

There was continued concern at the state of the universities, where over forty percent of entrants failed to graduate while the results in hon-ours and post-graduate work were equally dismal. An Englishman, Keith Murray, conducted an enquiry into the matter and found over-crowded class rooms and laboratories, poor facilities, low staff salaries, too few scholarships and a general dearth of funds. The government promised to act. Although only one new university was opened in direct response to the findings of the enquiry (Monash in Melbourne in 1961), the setting up of the Universities Commission in 1959 meant that great expansion took place later in the 1960s. Menzies had always retained a reverence for learning and scholarship and his finest and most lasting legacy to his country was his genuine support of education, especially in the tertiary sector.

Apart from its sporting heroes, a few of its soldiers, especially the World War I hero General John Monash who was of Jewish origins, the author Patrick White, a handful of painters and the incomparable opera singers Nellie Melba and Joan Sutherland — Australians of note in other fields, particularly scientific ones, were not generally internationally recognized. Some English scientists were familiar with the work of Louis Brennan (1852–1932) who, although Irish-born, was educated in Melbourne as a civil engineer. Brennan invented a torpedo, and researched a mono-rail locomotive. He also invented a helicopter which was successfully tested in 1922, but further work on it was abandoned in 1926.

Only in the field of medical and related research were Australians able to make a mark, but they received little local encouragement prior to the Great War, so that some promising researchers went overseas to work. The English-born and trained medical practitioner Joseph Bancroft was an exception as he remained in Queensland. In 1876 he discovered the filaria parasite that bears his name, thus revealing the cause of a serious tropical disease. Bancroft also worked on the transmission of insect-carried infections and his son, Thomas, developed his father's work. He was the first to suggest that dengue fever was carried by the mosquito. In New South Wales, J. Ashburton Thompson and Frank Tidswell demonstrated that fleas carried bubonic plague from infected rats to man. Other important discoveries were made in Queensland on lead poisoning and in South Australia, on hydatids. Charles Martin was English, but he became the 'distinguished Master' of Australian medical research. He taught at the universities of Melbourne and Sydney in the 1890s, and, after his return to England, he often came back to Australia to encourage further work. At the Lister Institute and London University, he directed the research of many young Australians who always acknowledged his inspiration.

Eventually, research institutions and units were developed in Australia, mainly through government support, and further progress became possible. The Walter and Eliza Hall Institute was founded in Melbourne in 1916, and its major work was undertaken when Frank Macfarlane Burnet became its director in 1944. Working with Edward Derrick, he influenced Australian research, and in 1960 Burnet won the Nobel Prize for his research in immunology. Two other Australian-born Nobel Prize winners were Howard Florey and John Eccles. Florey shared the Prize in 1945 as co-developer of the first anti-biotic, penicillin, and in 1966 he became

Chancellor of the Australian National University. Eccles shared the Prize in 1963 for his work on the nervous system. In 1966 he left the John Curtin Medical School at the National University, where he was a distinguished professor, to work in Chicago, because he refused to contemplate the need to retire aged sixty-five when his powers as a research scientist were at their peak. The youngest ever Nobel Prize winner was Adelaide-born William Lawrence Bragg, who, together with his father, William Henry, received the prize for physics in 1915 at the age of twenty-five. Bragg, however, had done all of his work outside Australia.

The economic boom of the 1950s was marked with social conflict arising from the unrest within the Labor Party. That unrest and the subsequent split in the Party partially reflected the unease of a society which refused to allow a shadow cast by radical ideology to darken the path to individual and communal well-being. Elections were held in 1958, and Labor, everywhere suffering from disunity and ravaged by the loss of votes to the Democratic Labor Party, again lost ground. Evatt was by now ill and exhausted by his battles, and he resigned in 1960 to go to the Supreme Court of New South Wales as Chief Justice. He died in 1965 after a life marked by a great passion for justice. As judge, historian and international statesman, he had served his country nobly. He was driven to the edge of despair as Menzies, whom he regarded as his inferior, ruled with such ease and aplomb as Prime Minister, and he allowed himself to use the two-edged sword of sectarianism to cleanse the Labor Party of those elements which he feared would destroy it. Evatt was destroyed himself, and the labor movement shattered and rendered almost futile as a wave of bitterness over the split in the Party spread into workplaces, homes and churches. It was Evatt's great misfortune to have reacted in a way that forced so many to take up positions opposed to his which they, also, held honourably.

CHAPTER EIGHTEEN

At the Edge of Asia

S ince the war in the Pacific, any doubt as to the significance of Australia's geographical location at the base of Asia had been dispelled. It would never again be possible for Australians to ignore the proximity of Asia. In Asia, also, there was an increasing awareness of the large, thinly-populated continent to the south. This discovery of place helped to change radically the underlying assumption upon which the Australian nation had been built — that it would remain white and British in perpetuity. In the 1960s the outcome of that change was scarcely apparent. The path was open though which led inexorably to a future when Australia, in the last quarter of the twentieth century, would be scarcely recognizable to its founders at the time of federation.

Menzies summed up what he still felt was the essential link between Australia and Britain in a speech he gave in London in June 1960. To him, allegiance to the Crown was the binding element that made all the members of the Commonwealth 'brothers in a special international family'. He thought that the family would survive even such blows as 'the tragic incident of Sharpeville', when blacks died for their colour in South Africa in 1960. This had caused a shocked reaction against apartheid in Australia, as well as elsewhere in the world. It is probable that the loyalty Menzies felt towards the Crown was shared by the majority of Australians, although not to the same degree. Certainly all talk of a republic had been dead for nearly a century, and the abdication of King Edward VIII in 1936 only temporarily shook the moral basis of the throne. In the origins of its people, the Australia that lay so close to Asia was still in large measure Anglo-Saxon, and its bonds were with a world centred on London. Indeed, as Menzies quaintly put it, London was at the centre of world affairs because it is 'where the Queen is'.

There was some unease felt at the time about the prospective entry of Britain into the Common Market, especially by wool growers, Tasmanian apple growers, producers of dried fruits and dairy products, who all looked to Britain as a major market. John McEwen, leader of the Country Party and Minister for Trade in the Menzies Cabinet, visited England, Europe and America to ensure that Australia's special trading relationship with Britain was retained, but, in 1963, there was some relief when French President Charles de Gaulle temporarily blocked British entry into the Market. During the same period, Australia was rapidly moving into the orbit of Japanese and, to some extent, Chinese trade forces so that the question of the special relationship with Britain was slowly becoming of lesser moment.

In Asia, loyalties and allegiances were in the process of being destroyed, reshaped or created. The closest place to Australia affected by this was Dutch New Guinea, and the proposed new alignment had little to do with the attitudes or wishes of the people in question. When, with Australian support, the Indonesians took control of the former Dutch East Indies in 1949, the Dutch retained part of Papua New Guinea. The Indonesians always claimed that the territory, which they called West Irian, was rightfully theirs, although its inhabitants had few bonds with them. In 1960, President Sukarno demanded its cession to Indonesia, with war against the Dutch, backed by Soviet arms, offered as the alternative. The United States, fearful lest opposition to Sukarno would further increase communist strength in Indonesia, was anxious to see the question resolved, even if it meant that the people of Dutch New Guinea would have no say in their future.

Australia was concerned by the defiance of the principle of self-determination which annexation would entail and at the prospect of having Indonesia as a neighbour in New Guinea, where the Australian right to retain its control was at best shaky. Sukarno continued to talk of confrontation and war with the Dutch seemed probable, so the Americans, acting as brokers from afar, decided to let the Indonesians have their way. In January 1962, Australia had little option but to acquiesce in the annexation of almost half of New Guinea by the Indonesians. It was a bitter price to pay for peace and the future was unlikely to discount it.

Arthur Calwell warned that acceding to threats over West Irian was to invite a day when Timor, then Papua New Guinea and finally northern Australia would eventually be looked upon greedily by Indonesia. His voice was heard as little then as it was a few months later when he said that to permit the Americans to establish a communications base at North West Cape was to jeopardize Australian sovereignty and to bring the country 'a step closer to the firing line' in any future atomic conflict.

On that particular matter, Calwell and the Labor Party were out of step with the Australian people for a Gallup poll indicated that a large majority were in favour of the base on the grounds that only America was capable of defending Australia in the event of it being attacked by a hostile power.

Another source of concern to Australia was the verbal and military opposition of Sukarno to the proposed formation of the new state of Malaysia, which was intended to embrace former British colonies in South-East Asia. Sabah, or British North Borneo, had a border with the Indonesian-held part of the large island of Borneo. When the new state of Malaysia was proclaimed in 1963, the British Embassy in Djakarta was sacked. Once again Australia had to decide whether mere words were sufficient to dissuade Sukarno, whom Calwell called 'a little Hitler', from active hostility. Adroitly, if supinely, the government kept Australian troops out of direct involvement with Indonesian guerrillas in Borneo, although three Australian soldiers were killed there in 1965.

The whole sorry affair of confrontation dragged on until Suharto replaced Sukarno in 1965. Thousands then died in Indonesia itself as the army slaughtered anyone with the remotest connection with the Communist Party. Confrontation seemed to lose favour in Indonesia but it expressed itself in another form in Portuguese Timor in 1975. In that year, the Indonesian government took advantage of the civil war there to annex the territory. The United States sided with Indonesia over annexation for strategic reasons and the Australian Labor government accepted the Indonesian act without protest. Indeed, the Prime Minister, Gough Whitlam, regarded East Timor as part of the Indonesian world, and made it plain that Australia favoured eventual annexation, although American pressure probably lay at the heart of the Australian decision.

In the sixties, Menzies continued to govern with ease although he went through a rough passage when falling wool prices, inflation and a drought in 1960 caused him to impose a credit squeeze which convulsed the economy, alarmed private enterprise and brought widespread unemployment especially in the vehicle and building industries. He delayed the elections as long as possible into 1961 and had a narrow victory when one seat, hanging in the balance for a week, was finally won by the Liberals with Communist Party preferences. The Democratic Labor Party continued to support the Liberal-Country Party coalition with preferences and in 1963 Menzies called another election, for which he scarcely offered any pretext although it was a year early.

Once again, state aid loomed large in an election, with even the Labor Party softening its attitude on the issue in an attempt to woo lost Catholic

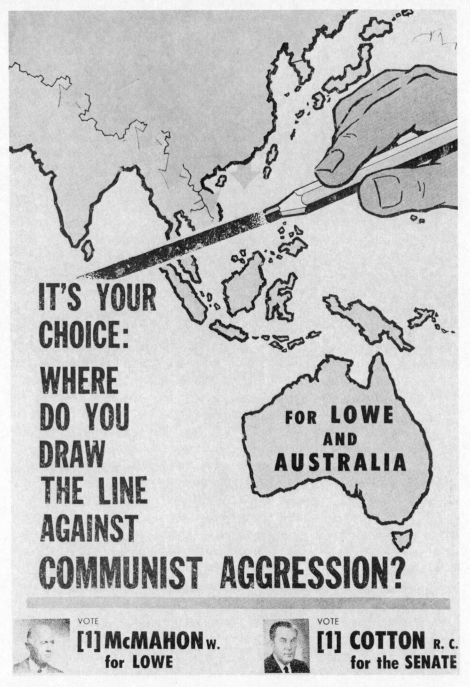

The 'domino theory' is well illustrated in this election pamphlet of 1966. Billy McMahon lost the prime ministership to Gough Whitlam in 1972.

votes. In reality, Catholics had not stopped voting for Labor because of its anti-state aid policy in the past, nor had they voted for Menzies when he handed out a crumb of assistance to private schools. The issue which had turned many of them from Labor, rightly or wrongly, was communism, and many Labor-voting Catholics returned to their traditional allegiance once it was clear that the communist threat had diminished. Other Catholics who had found security in the professions and in business never returned to the Labor Party as their economic interests were now best represented by the forces of conservatism. The Reverend Samuel Marsden's dream in the early nineteenth century of an Irish minority living in conformity with the ruling segment of Australian society had partly been fulfilled. By the 1960s the taming of the Irish in Australia was almost complete.

Menzies won the election with a twenty-one seat majority in the House of Representatives and the two Democratic Labor Party senators allowed him a majority on essential issues in the Senate. Foreign policy was the area that was most significant, especially in regard to Vietnam where the government had sent thirty military instructors in 1962 to help train South Vietnamese troops in combating the communist North. The main reason for the deployment of the instructors was to show solidarity with the Americans who needed to be able to prove that other powers, even insignificant ones, were allies in the struggle to keep Vietnam out of the communist orbit. When the number of instructors was doubled in 1963, it showed that the domino theory — which envisaged Vietnam as the next Asian country to topple, bringing down others in its train, including eventually Australia — was beginning to dominate Australian foreign policy.

At the time, there was understandable confusion about what exactly was happening in Vietnam. Clearly the communists in the North, whom some commentators thought of as nationalists, wanted to dominate the whole country. Equally, it appeared clear that the majority of the South Vietnamese people did not want to be forced to live under communist rule. The main problem seemed to be the role of China. It was alleged, indeed trumpeted, in America and Australia, by those who believed in the domino theory, that China was behind the struggle by the North to overrun the South. China assuredly wanted the Vietnamese communists to succeed, but there was never any proof that Chinese personnel went south to fight. The supporters of the domino theory in Australia kindled old phobic fires which saw China as the great Yellow Peril, threatening to pour its millions southwards to engulf Australia. That fear made a majority of Australians initially accept happily, or merely complacently, some form of military involvement by their own troops in Vietnam.

By 1965, there were 23,000 American troops in Vietnam, where they were the main obstacle to the swift overthrow of the South Vietnamese regime. Their presence assumed that, as foreigners, they had a right to be involved in a conflict in another country, but some Australians and more Americans did not accept that right existed. It was a question that did not bother Menzies who told a half-empty House of Representatives — after dinner on a Thursday night before a long weekend in April — that his government had decided to send a battalion of Australians to fight against the Viet Cong. He did not say that the troops had been readying themselves for action two months beforehand. It was a step of unusual significance, because the Australians were to engage in a military conflict without any formal declaration of war. Indeed, it was doubtful whether the troops themselves had any understanding of why they were to go to Vietnam except in the most general of terms of fighting communist aggression.

Soon there were conscripted Australian soldiers engaged in battle despite the fact that, unlike the war in the Pacific, the conflict in Vietnam involved no direct threat to Australia. The government had recognized that it was not possible to strengthen the armed forces sufficiently by voluntary means, so a system was introduced of calling up selected twenty-year olds, using a ballot involving their birthdays. It was the most ironic birthday present the nation ever gave to her young men and it was not long before Private Errol Noack became the first conscript to die in Vietnam.

The last significant act of Menzies as Prime Minister was the involvement of Australia in the Vietnam war. After sixteen years and as the longest-serving Prime Minister, he resigned in January 1966 and many were generous in their praise of his work. His most notable contribution to Australian political life was the foundation of the Liberal Party in 1944, which satisfactorily represented the aspirations of a significant and powerful minority. His other significant achievement was to work in moderate harmony with the Country Party despite the single-mindedness of its leader, John McEwen, who, however, had the ability to see beyond rural interests. Menzies's turn of phrase, powerful personality, self-assurance and dominant physique made him a formidable electoral opponent, but, like all successful politicians, he was granted good fortune. The years of his prime-ministership were notable for their overall prosperity and the split in the Labor Party gave him an unparalleled climate

An Australian soldier in Vietnam, carrying both weapons and necessities, is pictured on a jungle path. Many Australians still bear the physical and psychological scars of service in Vietnam.

for success. He sometimes came close to the people in his affection for cricket, which to him was the supreme English game. A small minority took pride in seeing him arrayed in knightly regalia standing near the Queen, but thousands were happy to join plain Bob Menzies at a cricket match.

Harold Holt, an amiable and dedicated Victorian, was elected leader of the Liberal Party and therefore Prime Minister. He had been the loyal and trusted lieutenant of Menzies and was delighted that he had risen to the position without stepping over the bodies of others in his climb to power. Holt was often unperceptive when he came to deal with the powerful of the wider world, but his association with Menzies had bred a streak of inferiority in him. Within weeks, he had agreed to triple the number of Australian servicemen in Vietnam, and, in mid-1966, he went to visit President Johnson in America, where his fulsome promise to go 'All the way with L.B.J.' dismayed even some of those closest to him.

By this time, the contrast between the government and the Labor opposition had become crystal clear on the Vietnam issue and the latter was committed to bringing home the troops. Some intellectuals joined with some churchmen, mostly Protestant, to express grave doubts and even outright opposition to the war. In October 1966, a month before the next federal election, at Holt's invitation, Johnson came to Australia. His visit was a huge success for the government despite anti-war demonstrations, and the election resulted in a landslide victory for the Liberal-Country Party coalition which spelt the end of Arthur Calwell as leader of the Labor Party. The election had been fought on the war issue, or to be more precise on what would happen to Australia were the communists to win in Vietnam, so it was now clear that the majority of electors accepted that the basis of Australian foreign policy was the domino theory. A simple application of the theory was the need to defend the nation's interests on foreign soil, which became known as 'forward defence'.

Nonetheless, Australians were now deeply divided over the question of involvement in Vietnam. Opposition to conscription had always been a matter of conscience for many but the Vietnam war exposed problems that had not previously been raised, either with the same complexity or intensity. There had been opposition to the Crimean, Sudan and Boer wars but British involvement had been decisive for most Australians. This was also true of the Great War. The Pacific War had seen Australia threatened, which led even the Labor movement to accept conscription. The difference now was that the Vietnam war forced Australians to ask questions about the morality of conscription and even of war itself as a means to resolve a conflict which did not directly threaten Australia or involve a country to which Australia had strong traditional ties. For many the issue became that of Australian involvement in an undeclared war against the people of a poor, third-world country, which had been exploited by Western colonialism for over a century.

To the thousands of Australians who attended 'Teach-ins', walked in street demonstrations or prayed at silent vigils, it was idle for the politicians to claim that to bomb, kill and maim Vietnamese, including defenceless civilians, was morally right. Those Australians were not convinced that such acts would make Australia a safer place to live in, or that they helped preserve democracy in South Vietnam. For the first time in history, the war almost literally came into homes because people were able to watch on their television screens the horrors that were being enacted in Vietnam. The big questions were whether the end, defeating the communists, justified the means, war, and whether Australians had any right to be fighting in a conflict which essentially involved another people.

For those more directly concerned, and especially the troops in Vietnam, the problem of conscience was overridden by the fact that they had become victims of the war. They were to remain its victims for long years after the end of the conflict, because, often broken in body and spirit, they returned to a country which wanted to forget it had ever sent them to Vietnam, and where they were often made to feel that they were the guilty ones. Arthur Calwell, leader of the Labor Party, also became a victim. Calwell was a Party man of the old school to whom Labor and the Catholic Church were the keystones of existence. He had pronounced the Vietnam war as both 'filthy' and 'unwinnable' and he stood by that conviction in the elections of 1966 and lost his chance to become Prime Minister. He resigned his leadership of the Party to be succeeded by Gough Whitlam, but Calwell went from politics and, in 1973, from life, secure in conscience.

Harold Holt also had a conscience, which moved him to the prosecution of war. When he augmented the Australian troops to 8,000, it was clear that he had not wavered in his conviction that it was right to do so although considerable American pressure was exterted on him to ensure that Australia continued to 'show the flag' alongside its troops in Vietnam. On 17 December 1967, Holt went for a swim in huge surf at Cheviot Beach, Portsea, Victoria and was never seen again. Some of the world's most important people, including Johnson, came to his memorial service in Melbourne. To a large number of Australians, Holt's forceful prosecution of the Vietnam war had become hateful. No one spoke harshly of him as a person, and many of his political foes, as well as his friends, mourned his passing.

The years that saw the convulsions of a remote war affect Australia also saw unprecedented prosperity. Minerals were part of that prosperity, although to what extent Australians, as well as British, Japanese and American investors, shared in the profits never became very clear. Nevertheless, the development of mineral deposits meant movements in population, absorption of immigrants, industrial expansion and the provision of transport and housing to remote places. There was an air of optimism as Australians became more aware of the enormous potential in areas of the land that had previously been regarded as barren and useless, and which, consequently, it had been considered appropriate to leave to the Aborigines.

In the Pilbara region of Western Australia, the discovery of vast deposits of high-grade iron ore in the early 1960s meant that the export of iron ore, hitherto prohibited so as not to deplete local reserves, was now possible and by 1968 fourteen million tonnes were sold, mostly to Japan. In the early and middle sixties, oil began to flow from the Moonie field, west of Brisbane, from Bass Strait and from Barrow Island, off Western Australia. Within a few years sufficient Australian oil was produced and refined to provide a considerable portion of local needs, and natural gas from Moonie was pipelined into some cities, beginning with Brisbane in 1969. Coal production developed dramatically, with Japan again taking the major share of exports, following the steep rises in oil prices, which, when low, had seriously affected coal exports.

The newspapers and television began to use the names of minerals with which most people had been unfamiliar. Bauxite, rutile, zircon, tungsten, manganese — some the product of mineral sands mined on the beaches — were added to the old familiar names of gold, silver, copper, lead and zinc all of which continued or increased in production. Gradually, members of the public with something to spare or a life's savings to invest began to look at such mysteries as share indices and to read company names as unfamiliar as the minerals they worked.

The names of the new mineral barons became prominent. Among them were Lang Hancock, discoverer of the richest iron ore deposit in the world in the Hamersley Ranges in Western Australia, which he sold to Riotinto, and Lindsay Clark, who relied on Australian capital to develop his Western Mining Corporation. Two companies, Tasminex and Poseidon, rashly claimed in 1969 that they had struck nickel in Western Australia and their share prices rose dramatically in weeks, causing a

The mineral boom from the 1960s continued with the opening of mines in remote parts of Australia. By 1976 Mt Newman in Western Australia was the world's largest producer of iron ore from an open-pit mine.

rising wave effect on other mineral shares. Both companies rapidly slumped and fortunes as well as small life savings were lost but other names such as Mt Tom Price and Mt Newman reminded Australians that their minerals were real.

Despite the mineral boom, primary products still remained the basis of the economy with wheat and wool its staple. The area sown to wheat doubled to more than ten million hectares and farmers prospered under the sensible direction of the Australian Wheat Board which sold the wheat, mostly to China in spite of that fact that Menzies blamed it for instigating the so-called 'aggression from the north' in Vietnam. Wool prices fell sharply towards the end of the decade, so the prospect of accepting a minimum reserve price was attractive to graziers. As wool contributed twenty percent of national exports, it was essential to stabilize its price and the graziers now demanded from the government the minimum price plan they had rejected in 1951 and 1965. In 1962 the first shipment of 60,000 live sheep was made to Kuwait opening a Middle East market of increasing importance.

The government was not successful with a plan to grow cotton and other crops in Western Australia under the Ord River Scheme, which was located over 1,600 kilometres from Perth in the remote Kimberley region. The concept blended with the oft-expressed desire to develop the north and keep out the Asians. The Scheme was very costly and produced little that could not be grown more efficiently and cheaply elsewhere, and Commonwealth funding was eventually withdrawn. It was also a reflection of the Western Australian faith in itself which had been fostered by the vast mineral wealth discovered in the state. Western Australia had long suffered as the forgotten outpost of Australian development but this was now at an end.

The politicians in Western Australia with such slogans as 'West is Best' were proud that their state, one third of the entire area of the continent, was 'riding the crest of a boom'. They looked increasingly to overseas investors despite concern in Canberra that it was not wise to sell too much of the national asset to foreign companies. The history of one hundred and seventy years had shown that prosperity based on production which was financed by foreign capital would hold up only as long as the resulting exports were a source of competitive profits to the investors.

A sign of prosperity, and a contributing factor to the relaxation of standards in sexual behaviour, was the contraceptive pill. After its introduction in 1961, the pill came into widespread use by married and unmarried women, including many Catholics despite its apparent prohibition by Pope Paul VI who paid a successful visit to Australia in 1970. Work was plentiful, young brides went back to work after marriage and by the end of the sixties thirty-three percent of married women were in the workforce. Much was made of the fact in 1965 that the birthrate was at its lowest since the middle of World War II, although ex-nuptial births, probably because of a sense of sexual freedom, were rising. Women comprised a quarter of the total workforce which reflected expanding industrialization rather than a feminist revolution. The expansion in the application of 'equal pay to work of equal value' which the Commonwealth Arbitration Court finally accepted in 1969, resulted in a twenty-five percent rise in women's wages and made work more attractive to them. Hire purchase on little or no deposit made many necessities and some luxuries possible, but many young couples often found themselves in difficulties with their too ambitious repayments. Several finance companies disappeared, together with their funds of over one hundred million pounds.

On 14 February 1966, pounds, shillings and pence were translated into dollars and cents when the long awaited, and sometimes dreaded, change to decimal currency took place. With the full implementation of decimalization, footballers who had stood at six feet measured 183 centi-

metres; the furlong disappeared from racing; the world's oldest professional footrace run each Easter at Stawell, Victoria, became 120 metres
instead of 130 yards; gallons of petrol became litres; there was some
argument as to the pronunciation of kilometre and housewives grappled
with the mysteries of the gram. In Western Australia, it was found that
conversion to a decimal currency cut the public debt of nearly
$700,000,000 by one cent and that there were two cents missing from the
expenditure side of $125,000,000. In most respects, the conversion
worked smoothly, and, within fifteen years, a generation of children had
grown up to whom the penny and the yard were as unfamiliar as the cent
and the metre had been to their parents.

Australians continued to read of or watch on television events which
made them realize that others were suffering while they enjoyed prosperity and that disasters, man-made or natural, could strike a discordant
note in the hymn to progress. The worst Australian long-term disaster
was the road toll with over 50,000 killed, almost twice as many as in
World War II, and countless others maimed, in car accidents from 1950
to 1970. Seat belts were made compulsory in Victoria in the latter year
and then progressively elsewhere, while newspapers drew regular attention to the death toll, and police attempted to impose speed limits. From
the 1970s the states gradually introduced random breath testing, which
had the effect of reducing drunken driving. That measure, together with
compulsory seat belts and greater public awareness of the folly of speed,
helped keep the death rate steady, despite the increasing number of
motor vehicle registrations.

In 1964, eighty-five men died when the aircraft carrier HMAS *Melbourne* sliced through the destroyer *Voyager* and the reputation of a fine
officer, Captain Robertson of the *Melbourne*, was torn to shreds in a welter
of recriminations and inconclusive investigatory commissions. An
earthquake shook parts of Western Australia from Albany to Geraldton
on 14 October 1968, and a wheatbelt town 135 kilometres east of Perth,
Meckering, was reduced to rubble but no lives were lost. Bushfires raged
throughout Tasmania and Victoria in early 1967, and eighty people perished in two fires — one on the main Melbourne to Geelong road, and the
other in and about Hobart when 650 homes were destroyed on 'Black
Tuesday' 1967. On another level, a significant step to redress the balance
of disaster was taken by the introduction of Lifeline and a Sydney doctor,
William McBride, established a link between the drug thalidomide and
deformities in babies. His discovery had much greater long-term effects
as it forced governments and drug companies everywhere to be more
scrupulous in the testing of new products.

Instances of political violence occurred: a deranged youth, who had been in Vietnam, attempted to kill Arthur Calwell as he left an anti-conscription rally in Sydney; a girl had spat at Harold Holt, and various missiles were thrown at visiting American politicians. Yet the inner core of decency in most Australians was shown when universal horror was expressed at the kidnapping and murder of an eight-year-old boy whose parents had won the Opera House lottery in Sydney in 1960. It was the first such case to be recorded. When the long-serving Premier of Victoria, Henry Bolte, decided to require the hanging of Ronald Ryan in February 1967 for the killing of a warder in an escape bid, only one of the sixteen major daily papers supported the decision. There was some support for the hanging by those citizens whose attitude to human life was selective but Ryan's execution was the last in Australia although, sporadically, there were calls for restitution of the death penalty.

Meanwhile, scientists in Britain were taking the first steps towards in vitro fertilization and at the same time more and more people in Australia, and elsewhere, were insisting that abortion was the right of a pregnant woman, although no one had proved that a foetus was not a human being. The Liberal Party in South Australia loosened the law on abortion and other states followed suit eventually, which did something to clean up the iniquity of 'backyard' operations. Under the second reforming government of Labor's Donald Dunstan, significant steps were taken in South Australia with the abolition of capital punishment, the outlawing of racial discrimination, the recognition that homosexuals had the right to human dignity and, in general, a relaxing of the rigid codes of Adelaide society.

The majority of Australians were unaware of the dreadful toll taken of livestock and the decline in agriculture during the drought in 1964–65, which struck the eastern states, especially New South Wales and Queensland, particularly badly. The wheat crop fell by seventy-five percent, sheep numbers declined by fourteen million and cattle by one and a half million. Many farmers never recovered from their losses, while others struggled for years to do so. The realization that many farms were too small to produce a consistent, worthwhile living was strengthened and, as a consequence, after the drought there began a process of consolidation into larger holdings and land prices again soared.

Drought had never much affected life in the cities, where, by the mid-1960s, increasingly, most of Australia's 11,500,000 citizens lived. Three hundred policeman were present to control a thousand fans, mostly girls, when the Beatles arrived in Sydney to a rain-drenched welcome in June 1964, but the sun shone for the highest paid model in the world, Jean

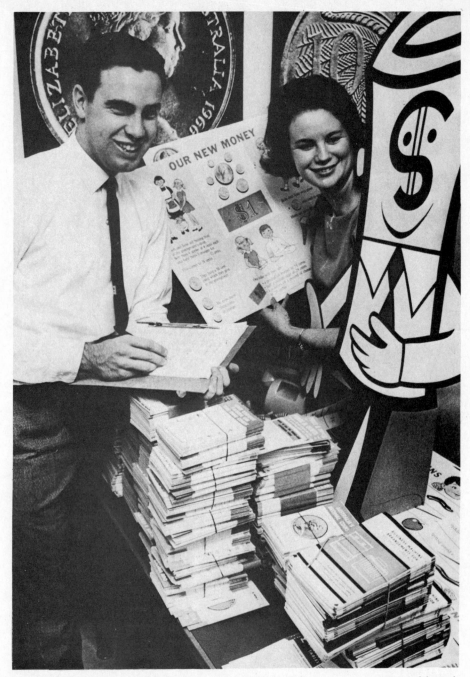

Much preparation went into the introduction of decimal currency in 1966. Although Prime Minister Menzies favoured calling the new unit a 'royal' the majority of Australians were happy with the less pretentious 'dollar'.

Shrimpton, when, dressed in a mini-skirt which exposed five inches above her knees, she caused a sensation at Flemington racecourse, Melbourne, on Derby Day in November 1965. After the initial shock many women followed suit, wearing mini-skirts as fashion dictated and continuing to do so until designers decreed otherwise. As with other things, there was always a discreet time-lag between the European mode and the Australian acceptance of it.

In other ways, rapid change was occurring and especially in 1965. Roma Mitchell became the first woman judge in Australia and women attempted to change archaic drinking customs when they organized 'sit-ins' in bars in Canberra and Brisbane. The Seekers became the most popular recording group and were Australia's first group to cut a million-copy record with 'I'll Never Find Another You' and Joan Sutherland returned home to be compared with Nellie Melba after her operatic successes overseas. In the literary world, the bans which had been imposed on D.H. Lawrence's *Lady Chatterley's Lover* and on Vladimir Nabokov's *Lolita* were withdrawn. At Siding Springs near Coonabarabran in New South Wales a huge observatory was opened; the first hydrofoil appeared on Sydney Harbour; the Ford Falcon XM car was launched; and Australia applied economic sanctions on Rhodesia for its unilateral bid towards independence.

Far-reaching change followed the awakening of consciousness brought about by involvement in the Vietnam war, or, at least, was concomitant with it. There were repeated calls for the public renunciation of the White Australia policy. Turks and Lebanese had begun to immigrate in small numbers. Some Asians had been allowed to remain in Australia on temporary permits while a selected few, judged to have useful qualifications, were permitted to enter with their families and to choose to stay on after five years. It was the first real sign of a change in racial attitudes although the New South Wales president of the Returned Services League still spoke of non-white people as 'wogs and bogs'.

The change in attitude towards foreign-born non-whites was accompanied by one embracing the Aboriginal population. In 1963 an Aboriginal leader, Charles Perkins, led a series of 'Freedom Rides' on buses to the north and west of New South Wales, which, with the aid of television, made more Australians aware of the offensive nature of discrimination against blacks in swimming pools, cinemas and hotels. With the support of all political parties, Holt put a referendum to the people in May 1967 which asked for constitutional changes that would permit Aborigines to vote, include them in the census and allow the Commonwealth to make laws for their welfare. All the states passed their powers in Aboriginal

Affairs to the Commonwealth except for Queensland where the old policy of 'protection' was continued. Less than ten percent of the electorate had voted 'No' in the referendum. In states and towns, where contact between whites and Aborigines was closest, a higher percentage voted against. The gold-field town of Kalgoorlie reinforced its history of racism, notably evident in wild riots there against foreign-born miners in 1934, when twenty-nine percent voted in the negative.

The question of land rights for Aborigines had lain hidden but it had been the nub of black-white relationships since the First Fleet sailed into Port Jackson in 1788. Australians expressed hidden guilt when they said of poor land that it might as well 'be given back to the blacks'. The matter came to the fore on a British-leased pastoral run of 15,500 square kilometres called Wave Hill in the Northern Territory. The Gurindjis had worked on the cattle station for many years, but, in 1966, they walked off rather than accept the low wages they were offered, and they set themselves up on land at Wattie Creek which they claimed was their own. William Charles Wentworth, federal Minister for Aboriginal Affairs — a direct descendant of his illustrious predecessor who had borne the same name and had regarded Aborigines as little better than brutes — saw the justice of the Gurindji claim, and persuaded the Cabinet to grant them occupancy of about twenty-six square kilometres in good country. It was not a policy decision on land rights, but it contained the seeds of dynamic change, especially as it was regarded as a just measure by the majority of white Australians.

In the 1960s the national capital started to show signs of becoming a city worthy of its title. Canberra, since the days when it was no more than a dream and then a drab reality, had always been the butt of sardonic humour or trenchant criticism. Money spent on it was considered ill-spent by many and politicians, with an eye to their electorates, had been reluctant to lose votes to the ignorant, which meant that progress in the development of the capital was painfully slow. Public servants were still unwilling to move to Canberra from interstate, and especially from Melbourne, despite the generous incentives the government gave them to do so. The business sector could not develop in an air of uncertainty about land tenure and population growth, and many Canberrans felt that they were exiles from genuine urban civilization.

With considerable courage, determination and foresight, Menzies had decided to build a capital befitting a young and prosperous nation. Canberra citizens watched with fascination in 1963–64 as, between the southern and northern portions of the city, a splendid lake slowly took shape after the damming of the Molonglo River. The lake took the name,

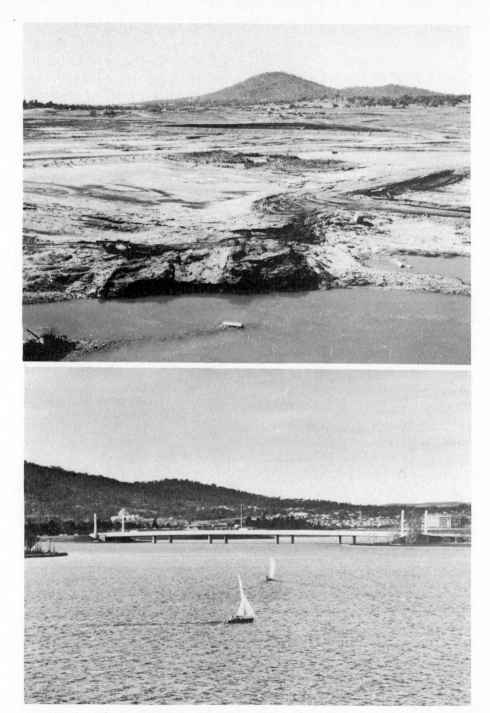

Two views of Lake Burley Griffin in Canberra, before and after it was filled in 1964.

fittingly, of Burley Griffin although its dam, more fittingly, was called Scrivener in honour of the surveyor who had selected the site for the new city. Thought was then given to the so-called parliamentary triangle and the National Library arose by the shore of the lake, looking at night like some vast Greek temple in southern Sicily. A National Gallery and a High Court were planned, new 'towns' with their centres began in the Woden and Belconnen areas. In the space of a decade Canberra came to life. Most visitors called at the War Memorial which, as a place of quiet and impressive dignity, was a fitting tribute to the men and women who had fought and died in war.

The most remarkable characteristic of Canberra was that, despite its design by an American, there was scarcely anything American about it with the exception of the American Embassy built on gracious colonial lines. The most Australian aspect of Canberra was the weekend, when, in summer, the citizens sailed on the lake, fled in thousands to the south coast, played golf, and went to the nearby bush for a swim in the Murrumbidgee or Cotter rivers and then had a barbecue on their banks. They washed down their steaks, chops and sausages with beer or flagon wines and soon were able to draw their wine from the Australian innovation of the cardboard cask with its plastic container. In winter, many Canberrans hibernated at home to watch either Australian Rules on television from Melbourne or one or both Rugby codes from Sydney, while others went to ski on the nearby Snowy Mountains. The hardy and their parents ventured forth to the innumerable ovals to participate and be cheered on in winter sports — hockey, netball, soccer, football — for in the variety of its sporting codes Canberra was emphatically cosmopolitan.

At a place called Tidbinbilla there was a nature reserve to which all the levels of Canberra society — diplomats, public servants, members of the armed forces, academics and others who made living possible such as milkmen, surgeons, chefs and garbage collectors — sometimes went to picnic and look, mostly in vain, for koalas, although emus were painfully prolific and an odd kangaroo skipped cautiously by. In 1963 the Americans decided to erect a space relay station there, but John F. Kennedy, who dreamt that the day would come when humanity would conquer the stars, did not live to see its usefulness as he was killed in November of that year. On their black and white television sets Australians watched in July 1969 as the American astronaut, Neil Armstrong, took a small step on the moon and said it was 'a giant leap for mankind'. The world was at last one because now there were other worlds to walk upon.

For Australians the end of the sixties — a decade so full of change, protest, acceptance and an awakening of consciousness, a decade perhaps without parallel in the previous history of humanity — spelt the end of the old securities and much of the life style that had reinforced the values of a white outpost at the edge of Asia. Never again would Australians look only to Britain as their economic, cultural and strategic prop, although most of them continued to enjoy British television shows, which reflected their own humour, tastes and values, while the introduction of the great bus of the airways, the Jumbo, brought London within a long day's flight of Sydney or Melbourne. America was everywhere present but especially in popular music; in the dollar, both as symbol and reality of dependence on Wall Street; in the young United States servicemen who came on recreation leave from Vietnam to Sydney and in the mediocre, or worse, serials on commercial televison. Finally there was the acceptance, even amongst the most reluctant, that American involvement in Vietnam meant Australian involvement. It was precisely that involvement which turned the Americanization of its newest province sour.

CHAPTER NINETEEN

Years of Hope

By the end of the 1960s, the bush was little more than a heritage to be treasured in art, literature and legend as the birth place of the nation. In fact, the cities always were the human and physical anvils on which the characteristics of the people were hammered out. The myth of the bush retained its vitality, but it lacked reality to the urban dwellers in the capitals, or even to the residents of the inland cities. Reality to them was home, school, family, neighbours, job, car, health, superannuation, insurance, taxes, rent, mortgages, supermarket, holidays, club and pub. They differed only in accidental ways from the citizens of London, Dublin, Chicago, New York, Berlin, Rome, and Tokyo. Over one hundred and eighty years of living on this continent had produced little that was distinctive or new. To talk about a national identity was meaningless, because Australians had become part of the industrialized world with all its values of dependence, consumerism, uncertainty, creativity, vitality and ever-surging hope. The bush remained and would always remain as a symbol of nature's hold on Australians but the cities would continue to shape them. Some of them were beginning to realize that they ought to play a greater role in that shaping.

Compulsory voting in federal and state elections always tended to inflate returns and hence obscure the reality of a lack of political interest on the part of most Australian citizens. Few people listened to the broadcasts of proceedings of Parliament, but the advent of television had brought the faces, attitudes and personalities of politicians into living rooms. As considerable political power began to move into the hands of powerful corporations, oil cartels, international banking houses and large

The anti-Vietnam war marches drew hundreds of thousands in the major capital cities, especially in Melbourne. In the main, the marchers were orderly but the demonstrations failed to make an impression on the Liberal-Country Party coalition which continued to prosecute the war.

newspapers, politicians felt bound to assert their role and importance in inverse proportion to the actual truth.

An opposition party can make an impact on an electorate only if it engages in constructive criticism of the government, spells out an alternative platform and offers attractive rewards. From the early 1970s such an impact began to be felt in Australia. With Gough Whitlam as leader of the Labor Party, it became a vital force in opposition. The contrary happened to the Liberal-Country Party coalition. Years of unchanged leadership under Menzies, the untimely death of Holt, continued affluence and sociological change, especially amongst the young, helped the coalition to falter as it tried to grapple with new values, problems and expectations. The 1970s became a decade of politics.

Changes in attitudes were reflected in a widespread collapse of traditional standards. Two children became the norm for a family; teenage promiscuity was prevalent with the highest teen pregnancy rate in fifty years, despite the contraceptive pill; the divorce rate doubled and irretrievable breakdown of a marriage became the sole ground for divorce; 'living together' was regarded as an acceptable prelude or alternative to marriage; Sydney rivalled San Francisco as a 'gay' capital and the role of religion diminished as an effective element in society, as well as in the lives of individuals.

The authority and wisdom of the Liberal and Country Parties in thrusting Australia into the Vietnam war was queried and deplored by many, as evidenced by continued street marches in the capital cities protesting Australian participation in the war. The marches clearly demonstrated that civil authority could be questioned, defied and, in part, ignored. One Melbourne moratorium march took place on 8 May 1970 when 200,000 people went to the streets to protest against Australia's continued involvement in the war. The crowd covered the Fitzroy Gardens and filled Bourke Street when they marched down it. An old veteran of both World Wars, Bill Connolly, of Plenty, Victoria, said, 'I'm proud to be here today'.

In the education field, militant teachers' unions combined with student activism to challenge traditional methods of teaching and the universities became places in which some teachers began to taste the fruits of free enquiry at first hand. In some states the voting age was reduced to eighteen, a few 'alternative' schools were set up, and there were moves to abolish external examinations in Queensland. Neville Bonner, a Queensland Aborigine, became the first of his race to enter federal Parliament when he won a seat in the Senate in 1971, and New South Wales introduced an Aboriginal Legal Service. Generally, the early 1970s was a period in which old political slogans, outmoded ways of approaching social problems, fear of facing the unknown or the risky on an international level and unwillingless to change had lost relevance and everywhere there was a feeling that the time for moderate but purposeful change had come.

When Holt died in 1967, the Country Party leader, John McEwen, briefly Prime Minister, blackballed the prospective new leader of the Liberal Party, William McMahon, by refusing to serve under him. John Gorton was elected leader and consequently Prime Minister. He possessed considerable ability, drive and vision and had in him some of the characteristics of the old Australian legend that revealed itself in a degree of recklessness and a distaste for formality which permitted criticism of his style and eventually of his personal behaviour. As a leader, he believed in keeping a firm hand over his Cabinet and using Commonwealth powers to their fullest which made some state Premiers nervous. He continued to support the war in Vietnam, although he declared he would commit no more troops there. This did not satisfy the ever-increasing number of Australians, mobilized by Jim Cairns, a Labor Member of Parliament, who had the courage to act on his conscience and protest against the war. Most of the electorate, however, ignored the war, while they enjoyed continuing affluence, high rates of employment and a general optimism about the future.

In May 1968 the Prime Minister caused much dissension, even amongst conservatives, when he told Richard Nixon at a dinner in America that Australians would 'go a-waltzing Matilda with you' — presumably to resist the spread of communism in Asia, although within weeks Nixon made it plain that henceforth Asian nations would have to attend to their own internal security. In this context, it was never clear whose security was involved when another American communications base was set up at Pine Gap, near Alice Springs. Many concerned observers thought that the very presence of such bases on its territory infringed Australian sovereignty and made it a target in any eventual war.

The crux of Gorton's problem was that he had nowhere to lead his party and many of those who supported it. He tried to replace both British and American links with his own brand of attractive, Australian, larrikin nationalism which had no genuine base amongst conservative Australians at that time, especially as a substitute for the British ties some of them still held to firmly. The coalition retained office at an election in October 1969 because of Democratic Labor Party preferences but it had gained only 43.35 percent of the vote to Labor's 46.95 percent. Gorton survived one challenge to his leadership but in March 1971 a party motion of no confidence in him was tied thirty-three to thirty-three. From the chair, he voted himself out of office to be replaced by William McMahon.

McMahon had to face a formidable Labor opponent in Gough Whitlam as well as an economy showing signs of faltering. The command Whitlam had in the Labor Party was clearly illustrated by 1970 when he broke the hold of left-wing extremists over the Victorian branch, who had been in control there since Evatt's coup in 1955. Moreover, Whitlam's image in the electorate at large was that of a vibrant, forceful, intelligent and articulate leader who had a clear set of policies, while McMahon, though a moderately successful Treasurer, seemed frequently incapable of enunciating a coherent sentence, and suffered by comparison with Whitlam despite his genuine concern for his country. On the economic level, Australia was beginning to suffer a backlash from the falling prosperity of the wealthier industrialized nations — America, Germany and Japan — but China was rapidly becoming a principal market for wool and wheat. Although, two percent unemployment and six percent inflation were far from alarming they were signals that could not be ignored, or in the event rectified.

McMahon's period in office was marked by unusually strident reactions to conservative foreign policies and by strong concern about the increasing lack of clear direction on the economic level. The Labor Party had shed its White Australia plank in 1965, and thereby moved closer to a policy of accepting immigrants irrespective of their colour. There was a general air of anti-racism in the community. When a South African Rugby Union team toured the country, widespread anti-apartheid demonstrations were mounted, especially in Sydney, Melbourne and Canberra and in Queensland where the conservative, populist Premier, Johannes Bjelke-Petersen, declared a state of emergency. Aborigines sensed for the first time that many white Australians had sympathy for their cause, and they set up an Aboriginal Embassy in a tent on the lawns in front of Parliament House, Canberra, to agitate for land rights. Anti-Vietnam demonstrators were everywhere vociferous, and there was even concern in the rural sector as farmers wondered whether it was time to recognize China, which had not renegotiated its agreement to buy a third of the Australian wheat crop. McMahon decided to do nothing about China except express outrage when Whitlam visited Peking, where he promised to recognize the communist regime which had now ruled for twenty years, were Labor elected to government.

On 2 December 1972, McMahon went to the polls with little in the way of policy but relying on the coalition's twenty-three years in office and the claim that the Labor Party was an untried and untrustworthy force. On this occasion, the Democratic Labor Party proved unable to deliver the preferences necessary for a coalition victory, and the newly-formed Australia Party gave its preferences to Labor. Despite these advantages, Labor did not have a resounding victory. Whitlam became Prime Minister with his party holding sixty-seven seats to fifty-eight in the House of Representatives, but the Democratic Labor Party, with five seats, held the balance of power in the Senate.

Whitlam had run under the slogan 'It's Time', and he proved that time was a commodity he did not propose to squander. There were still seats in the Parliament in balance and the newly-elected members had not been sworn in so Whitlam and his deputy, Lance Barnard, formed a ministry of two, and, in the next couple of weeks, Whitlam began, by regulation, to fulfil the promises he had made on the hustings. It was decided to stop all military involvement in Vietnam and to abolish conscription. All those legally in jeopardy or in prison for their non-compliance with the draft or for urging others to refuse compliance had their charges dismissed or they were restored to freedom. Plans were made to spend large amounts on education and on Aborigines whose traditional lands were to be preserved from mining leases. Formal steps were taken to recognize China. The White Australia policy was dismantled so that in law, and partly in fact, Australians could reject the label of being racists.

For a time, Australians, eighty-five percent of whom now lived in urban areas, had every reason to believe that genuine change was taking place. No government since federation had so carefully worked out its policies and then began so readily to implement them, so in the beginning only a very few said that change was going too far or too fast. An air of urgency and excitement prevailed, while Whitlam, often accompanied in public by his charming and intelligent wife, Margaret, took the helm and turned the nation around. He knew that his purpose was to create a more just, humane and civilized society in which the distribution of wealth was to be more evenly balanced.

Whitlam also knew that he could not change the bureaucracy which had been shaped at its highest level for over two decades by the conservatives. He had little control over the choice of his Cabinet colleagues, none of whom had had previous ministerial experience. Whitlam and the Cabinet were forced to rely on the advice of public servants, who, in the main, were loyal and generous to the new government. However, some ministers surrounded themselves by young and inexperienced 'experts' who proved an irritant to the long-serving public servants and, not infrequently, a source of anger and bewilderment to the wider public with which they were not in touch and to which they were not responsible.

Matters of genuine substance frequently brought no adverse public reaction while those of little moment caused unease. The American alliance remained firmly at the base of foreign policy and the government did nothing about the bases on Australian soil, but alarm was raised in conservative circles when there was outspoken criticism of the bombing of Hanoi in December 1972. 'Advance Australia Fair' was chosen as the national anthem to replace 'God save the Queen', except on special occasions, despite the inability of most Australians to sing its words; the 'British subject' on Australian passports was removed when Britain joined the European Economic Community; Lionel Murphy as Attorney-General organized a raid on the Australian Security Intelligence Organization headquarters in Melbourne in an attempt to discover documents on alleged terrorists; and Whitlam went on regular visits overseas. All these minor matters caused unease amongst conservatives, puzzled the uninformed and provided a field day for journalists.

The Prime Minister had the ill-fortune to be absent from the country in late 1974 when a disaster of unprecedented proportions occurred on Christmas Eve. Darwin, capital of the Northern Territory, was virtually destroyed by Cyclone Tracy, and, after four hours of violence, the citizens were reduced to terror and stupefaction. The government acted promptly, and an evacuation programme was organized involving the air-lifting of 26,000 citizens from the area and the Navy was sent in to help. The city was subsequently rebuilt with materials and building design more capable of resisting hurricanes, but the fact that a thousand were injured and sixty-five died was indicative of the major nature of the occurrence. Whitlam bore no responsibilty whatever for the disaster but criticism of him was strong.

There were other matters of considerable consequence for which the Labor government was given little credit. From the very beginning of its term of office, Labor pledged itself to give independence to Papua New Guinea. It acted decisively and courageously, despite the cries of those who thought that many years should pass before the local inhabitants could be judged responsible enough to direct their own affairs. The territory was given self-government by Canberra in 1973 and then independence in 1975, although it continued to rely on considerable aid from Australia to maintain its economic and social equilibrium. A decade later there had been a big decrease in aid, Papua New Guinea was forming its own independent foreign policy and there was concern in Australia that the days of mutual trust were passing.

The large scale destruction of Darwin on Christmas Eve 1974 by 'Cyclone Tracy' shocked all Australians. The damage was rapidly repaired but the devastation was a reminder of the consequences of disregarding the natural environment.

Other important steps taken by Whitlam's government were the reduction of tariffs by twenty-five percent, the abolition of tertiary education fees, a substantial increase in spending on both public and private education, the granting to public servants of wage increases and improved conditions, including twelve weeks on full pay to pregnant employees, and the reopening of the case for equal pay before the Arbitration Commission. Colleges of Advanced Education were built in every state and in the Australian Capital Territory, new universities were opened and the arts and cultural activities given support, although there was much criticism of the buying, for the future National Gallery, of Jackson Pollock's painting *Blue Poles* for $1,300,000. In rural areas none of this mattered compared to the decision that farmers would no longer receive a $50,000,000 subsidy on superphosphates.

By mid-1974, it became apparent that a concerted attempt was being made in conservative circles to get rid of Whitlam's government even though it was only half-way through its term of three years. The self-

appointed saviour of the country from the evils of what he called socialism was Queensland's Bjelke-Petersen who stomped about declaring that
he would cleanse Canberra of Whitlam and all his followers. The farmers
were by now bitterly resentful and were prepared to take any steps to
remove Labor. Segments of the business community were wringing their
hands over inflation but, at the same time, helping by their propaganda
to destroy the prospects of a referendum, subsequently lost, to control
prices as well as wages. By April 1974, the Senate had rejected ten bills
twice and nine others once, even though they bore on matters which
Labor had included in its electoral platform.

To the opposition, the electoral circumstances seemed favourable and
it proceeded to refuse passage through the Senate to three appropriation
bills unless the government promised to hold an election for both Houses.
Whitlam was forced to secure a double dissolution and his prospects did
not seem good. Inflation was running at fourteen percent, his government was under fire from intense conservative criticism and the strength
of the opposition was lined up against him. Although Labor was returned
with the loss of only one seat in the House of Representatives, the result
indicated that there was a mounting degree of unease within the electorate. Billy Snedden, leader of the coalition since McMahon's resignation after the 1972 election, was no match, in or out of Parliament,
for Whitlam. In the Senate, Labor still lacked a majority and the balance
of power was now held by two independents who could not be relied
upon to vote for the government, but the Democratic Labor Party was a
spent force.

The most significant aspects of the election were the means used to
procure an election in the first place and that the coalition was defeated
despite its confidence in winning. In the aftermath, Whitlam implemented further measures which served to enhance the animosity of
powerful elements in society. Wage indexation was introduced, a Racial
Discrimination Act came into force, and a general health scheme called
Medibank was implemented which gave free health care to Australians.
Medibank worked moderately well and brought great advantages to the
less fortunate members of the community. Despite general approval of
Medibank by the public, many medical practitioners were opposed to it,
although it served to enhance rather than diminish their economic prospects and some few were quick to use it for their own ends.

Unemployment began to climb steadily in early 1975, under the effect
of a world-wide recession, and it rose to over five percent by August.
Women in thousands were out of work, especially in the textile industry
where the lowering of tariffs had caused havoc and the building trades

were in chaos. Queues lined up at Commonwealth Employment Service offices, and some of those in them had never been unemployed, while, amongst the young, there were some also who were never to be employed. They had left school with the dole as their only expectation, and they put their names down for it much in the same way as they had done when enrolling in school subjects in the past. There was less and less chance of gaining an apprenticeship and one employer received 800 applications for the single apprenticeship he offered. Meanwhile, inflation roared along at over seventeen percent, fuelled by rising oil prices and the expenditure of the government on welfare as well as on public servants' salaries, which had been used as a pacesetter for the community.

By his tendency to 'Australianize' aspects of public life, Whitlam had caused considerable concern amongst a minority which still looked to Britain and its culture as the unique source of all things worthwhile. In July 1975, appeals to the Privy Council from the Australian High Court were abolished except in a few special cases. In February of that year, Whitlam introduced the Order of Australia. The highest award was a Companion of the Order which outstripped imperial honours. Though the Order of Australia was retained, imperial honours were reinstated by the succeeding Liberal government which mollified those Australians to whom such matters were important. The great majority of Australians remained, however, either cynical of such honours or at best indifferent, believing that

When they pin the Stars and Garters,
when they write the titles rare,
The men who earned the honours are
the men who won't be there.

The opposition had begun to show some bite when the Liberals replaced Snedden with Malcolm Fraser as leader in March 1975. Fraser was quick to promise that he would never force an election by threatening to withhold supply unless he found that the behaviour of the government was 'reprehensible'. In the circumstances, it was empty rhetoric, because to Fraser and those who supported him a Labor government was a political and social aberration which, by its very nature, lacked legitimacy. On the other hand, the coalition partners still regarded themselves as the only force capable of running the country satisfactorily and they were determined to return to the Treasury benches, which they considered to be their right. The difficulty was that Whitlam showed no signs of wanting to go back to the polls, understandably, after fighting two elections in less than two years. To force him to the polls again required 'reprehensible' circumstances, and, in some measure, they were at hand.

A miserable episode called the 'loans affair', in which the government was guilty of considerable ineptitude was used to force an election. Rex Connor, Minister for Minerals and Energy, was determined to buy back a share of the stake which foreign investors had taken out in Australian minerals and oil. The Middle East oil owners, who had thrown the international economy into chaos by their price rises for crude oil, seemed logical lenders of the vast sum of $4,000 million needed. A few simple enquiries would have revealed that loans would be forthcoming from such sources only through the normal channels of high finance rather than through intermediaries of doubtful reputation. With a flagrant disregard for propriety, the government bypassed the Loans Council when authorizing the search for a loan. When the opposition began to raise objections, the Treasury lowered the sum to $2,000 million in the vain hope that the affair would bear some semblance of proper dealing.

Whitlam's deputy Jim Cairns was dismissed from the ministry when he was found to have misled Parliament over his attempt to raise other overseas loans, and finally Connor resigned when it became public that he had continued to involve himself in loan raising activities after Whitlam had assured the Parliament that all activity in that direction had ceased. No money ever actually changed hands, but the media astounded the public with the names and faces of shady characters who were involved in the 'money deals'. The circumstances of the whole affair revealed clear imprudence and obstinancy on the part of at least Connor and Cairns, but there was nothing to suggest that anything so 'reprehensible' had occurred as to warrant the denial of supply. Fraser and his advisors did not see the matter in that light and they decided on 15 October 1975 that the Senate would use the simple device of refusing to pass the government money bills for 1975–76 when they came before it. In that way opposition Senators would not actually go as far as to block supply, they would simply make its fulfilment impossible until Whitlam met Fraser's terms with an election for the House of Representatives.

For three weeks, the whole country watched as the political game was played out. On 11 November the Governor-General, Sir John Kerr, a Whitlam appointee, called the Prime Minister to Government House, where, at Kerr's invitation, Fraser had already taken up a position in hiding, and dismissed him. During his brief interview with Kerr, Whitlam had refused to accept the ultimatum of a general election, because he wanted only a half Senate election, which, were Labor successful, would have given him control of the Senate. He remained consistent in his stand throughout the affair — unless supply were passed or rejected outright, he would not budge. In the last few days before 11 November, he came within an ace of success, as some of Fraser's senators, seized with the seriousness of the whole matter, had begun to waver. His gamble failed because he did not have in his keeping the man who could make or break him — the Governor-General.

Whitlam knew what he was doing throughout the crisis and his one unwise step was to turn, fruitlessly, to the private banks for temporary funds to finance the government. This act alarmed even some of those who were favourably disposed towards him. It was clear to him in the last week or so that if he could not obtain supply, but refused to resign or ask for a full election, he could be dismissed. On the other hand, a sympathetic Governor-General, and Whitlam was entitled to expect some sympathy from his own appointee, could have taken the view that the situation did not warrant the dismissal of a Prime Minister who held a majority in the House of Representatives, and who, for the second time in eighteen months, was being prevented from conducting the business of running the country by an opposition that used a method hitherto unheard of since the Constitution came into force, the effective negation of Supply.

One course for the Governor-General would have been to await the outcome of the blocking of supply and permit Whitlam to go to a half Senate election, which was Whitlam's advice to him. Under those circumstances, Whitlam would have faced the electorate as Prime Minister and there may have been some slim chance of success. In any case, whatever the outcome of the election, the accepted procedures of the Australian democratic process as they had been understood and applied since federation would have been followed.

In the event, Kerr chose the other course and appointed the waiting Fraser as caretaker Prime Minister pending an election. Within hours, supply was passed, as was a motion of no confidence in Fraser by the Representatives. By the late afternoon of 11 November 1975, the Parliament was dissolved amidst scenes of disbelief and dismay amongst Labor followers and to the strong resentment of many who believed that the course of Australian democracy had been perverted. Amongst conservatives, there was satisfaction, relief and rejoicing. During the previous three years, many of them had held to the view that Labor had no right to govern and that the course it had set itself of the equitable distribution of wealth was inimical to their best interests.

On 11 November 1975, after his dismissal as Prime Minister by the Governor General, Gough Whitlam appeared on the steps of Parliament House. His determination to return to office failed to impress sufficient voters but many Australians thought the Governor-General's action was a stroke against parliamentary democracy.

November 11 was a day decreed by fate to be remembered amongst Australians. On this day in 1854, the Ballarat Reform League had been started on Bakery Hill and the Eureka flag was hoisted there later as a signal to the oppressed that Australia under the Southern Cross was a land of freedom. On 11 November 1880 Ned Kelly was hanged in Melbourne Gaol, and for many his life had become a symbol of the struggle of the helpless against oppression. And 11 November 1918 saw the Armistice to end World War I in which Australians had come to realize that the sacrifice of her young manhood marked the end of innocence. To the degree that there had been political innocence in Australia prior to 11 November 1975, it too was at an end.

From the steps of Parliament House after the dissolution, Whitlam had called on his followers to maintain their 'rage' at his dismissal and their 'enthusiasm' for the return of his government. In the circumstances, 'rage' was an understandable if fruitless emotion while 'enthusiasm', so evident in the early period of Labor government, was essential for re-election and future success. In the long run, it too proved fruitless. The electorate had been led to believe by powerful sections of the media, both in newspapers and on television, that the Labor government had become bungling and inept, that it was totally responsible for the economic difficulties that Australia was encountering (which discounted the world economic situtation), and that it was socialist and therefore dangerous, which was the useful lie Labor opponents always used when desperate.

The fact was that the Whitlam government had lost its way, especially in economic matters, which was an area where Whitlam himself claimed no competence, and the appointment of the prudent and competent Bill Hayden as federal Treasurer came too late to redress the balance. Unemployment was running at a higher rate than at any time since the Great Depression; the Henderson Report on Poverty in August revealed that ten percent of the Australian adult income units were below the poverty line with another eight percent just above it; and amongst most farmers and many urban dwellers there was a fear of Whitlam and Labor that no reassuring words could allay. The media combined with the opposition to fuel that fear, so Whitlam's chance of re-election was slim.

In the elections of 13 December 1975, Fraser and his followers were rewarded with the most massive victory since federation. The coalition held ninety-one to thirty-six seats in the House of Representatives and had a majority of eight in the Senate. On the following day, Whitlam tried to stand down as leader of the Labor Party, but his deputy, Bill Hayden, was too dispirited to accept the position, and furthermore, he was still waiting to find out whether he would retain his own seat. The other person to whom Whitlam spoke about the leadership was Bob Hawke, president of the Australian Council of Trade Unions who had been for some years a prominent figure as a successful negotiator between the unions and employers. Hawke was not in Parliament so Whitlam's discussion of the leadership with him served only to create tensions amongst some powerful Labor parliamentarians despite their own frequently dismal performance when in office.

Meanwhile, Fraser became Prime Minister without any further question as to his legitimacy and Doug Anthony, who had succeeded McEwen as leader of the Country Party in 1971, became the deputy. Anthony was a tough, skilful politician, whose personally expressed principle of action was to 'kick a head' when he saw one, and the pair of them made up a formidable team. The debt owed to some rural voters for their constancy throughout the crisis and at the polls was paid almost immediately with the restoration of the superphosphate bounty.

The seven years that followed under Fraser were ones in which it was largely believed that moderation in government spending was the cure for economic ills, notably unemployment and inflation. In fact, spending was not substantially curtailed, the whole business of government grew and there was little attempt to transfer public agencies into private hands. In 1976 there were four rises in wages amounting to over fifteen percent and under wage indexation the trend continued in the following years until 1981 when the system was abandoned. As a result, ironically, a later generation of conservatives lumped Fraser with Whitlam, when they sought a long-term reason for the economic instability of the mid-eighties. Inflation did, however, drop by about five percent, but un-employment hovered at eight to nine percent. Young people, to whom unemployment was becoming a way of life rather than a temporary mis-fortune, were lumped together and branded as 'dole bludgers', although responsible coalition politicians recognized that, in the main, the unem-ployed bore no fault for their state.

In the universities, dissent largely died as a new generation of youth entered who knew that a degree was partly an insurance against un-employment, which was still rising through the late 1970s, and that work, rather than political activism, was the path to success. Some still pro-tested, often successfully, about examinations which they regarded as an unjust method of assessment, about the content of their courses in which they claimed they ought to be involved, and about their right to sit on university boards and otherwise share with academics the running of the universities. Within the wider community of youth, the widespread use of marijuana had been accepted as simply a variant on alcohol or tobacco and when the drug pushers felt the desire for greater profits they often stopped the flow of marijuana in order to entice young people onto other more injurious substances which they made readily available. By 1980 there were over 20,000 heroin addicts in the country.

The common denominators of the youth culture were dress and music. Dress was largely functional with little distinction between that worn by either sex, jeans were universal and there was an infinitude of signs, symbols or slogans appearing on T-shirts. The protest for greater indi-vidualism was suffocated in exterior conformity. In music, jazz was almost dead and the Beatles were superseded to be replaced by the preachers of a new age, who had a social message on everything ranging from love to nuclear war. Australian 'pop' culture was of the 'moonlight' kind in that it merely reflected or slavishly imitated that which prevailed amongst American youth. The Vietnam War had penetrated the consciousness of young Australians to the degree that many of them began to reflect on wider issues such as racism, the role of women in society and respect for the environment.

The Vietnam war and unemployment combined to convince many young people that all the ills of society had been foisted on them deliberately, and even maliciously, by their elders, and some parents found communication with their children well-nigh impossible. In some schools the communication of knowledge became less necessary and less formal as external examinations were replaced by internal assessment, and teacher unions expressed their militancy and drive towards higher wages and better conditions by calling strikes, which bothered mainly parents. Nevertheless, the young showed a readiness to be tolerant of each other, to share, to make sacrifices and to encourage the less fortunate in a way that no previous generation had ever done.

A change took place in the treatment of Aborigines and non-whites. Fraser, son of a grazier, came from the sort of background that had been mainly responsible for the worst atrocities committed on the Aboriginal population. Yet he was a genuine anti-racist, which he proved in his constant attempts to persuade the South African government to mitigate the grosser aspects of apartheid and in his influential support for the setting up of Zimbabwe. The tightened economic situation caused budget cuts in the area of Aboriginal welfare, but there was a general climate of greater good will towards them although their position remained deplorable in health, housing, education and employment. The Aborigines began to organize more effectively, to run their own councils and to support their own leaders, who represented their plight to governments. Land rights were granted in the Northern Territory to twenty percent of the whole area, while in Queensland leases were given on traditional lands. In South Australia, where 100,000 square kilometres of land were granted to the Aborigines, the Premier Don Dunstan appointed an Aborigine, Doug Nicholls, as state Governor. Evonne Goolagong, who was of Aboriginal descent and came from Barellan in New South Wales, became a world tennis champion and winner of two Wimbledon titles.

Although all Australian involvement in Vietnam was concluded by the end of 1972, the war itself dragged on until 1975 when a communist government was established in Saigon. People began to flee from South Vietnam, and Australia was sought as a new home by some of them. An episode that stirred the imagination of many Australians and helped to make them more receptive to Asians was the epic 8,000 kilometre voyage by the Vietnamese trawler, PK 504, from Vietnam to Darwin with fifty-six refugees aboard in late 1976. They were not the first, but their courage, endurance and the skill of the captain, who had navigated with a compass and a school map, had special appeal. The government was sympathetic to the plight of the refugees, partially as a response to a bad conscience about the Vietnam war. As camps in Thailand began to fill with thousands who had fled from Vietnam, Laos and Cambodia, selection procedures took place, and, by January 1978, 22,000 refugees had arrived with the government agreeing to take 14,000 more and another 20,000 in 1980–81.

The Asian refugees were often welcomed by members of voluntary bodies such as the Indo-China Refugee Association and helped to settle, sometimes in rural communities. By the mid-1980s, some opposition to their continued arrival was expressed by individuals and racist organizations but, in the main, the refugees continued to be accepted, although the government cut back the intake severely except in cases of family reunion, and those with special skills or financial backing. Nonetheless, to its great credit, Australia had accepted over 100,000 refugees from South-East Asia by 1987.

From the mid-1970s, some industries had a fifty percent immigrant workforce with the overall average in industry standing at forty percent. Immigrant women, many of whom lacked English, tended to be found in low-skilled jobs where they were disadvantaged and, in part, exploited. Economic survival, as had been the case in the past with the Irish and other minorities, made work of any kind acceptable. In round figures, four million immigrants settled permanently in Australia in the years following World War II with over a million from the British Isles and 350,000 from Italy being the largest groups. A.J. (Al) Grassby, former Minister for Immigration in the Whitlam government, had been appointed Commissioner for Community Relations, and he and Professor Jerzy Zubrzycki began to raise the issue of a multicultural society in Australia. They meant one in which groups, differing in their ethnicity, would all receive just and equitable treatment, share the common bond of being Australians with those who had come here before them and retain the culture they brought from their homelands. Some took this to mean much more, such as the provision of public funds for the teaching of foreign languages, the setting up of ethnic language radio stations and other measures. Widespread criticism was subsequently heard of a policy which, when correctly understood and sensibly applied, was the only practical step towards the formation of a truly human society.

Most Australians, including some newer arrivals, were happy when Australia defeated England in the 1977 Centenary Test Match played in

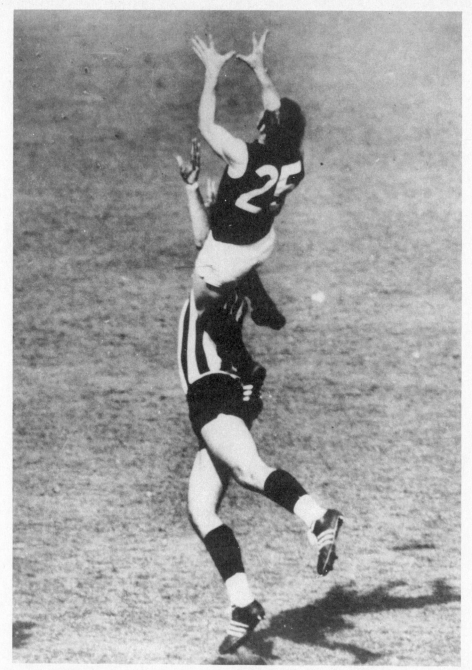

Alex Jesaulenko, an all-time great of Australian Rules Football, takes a spectacular mark in the 1970 Grand Final won by Carlton against Collingwood at the Melbourne Cricket Ground before a record crowd of 121,696 spectators.

Melbourne. The great fast bowler, Dennis Lillee, was feted by players and spectators alike for his magnificent performance. No one suspected that after the game an agent of the newspaper magnate Kerry Packer went about the dressing room handing cheques to Australian players who had consented to join Packer's World Series Cricket. The new series competed with the official version by introducing one-day and night cricket, coloured clothes, white balls and instant television replays. Crowds flocked to the new game attracted by the glamour and the certainty of a decision. The large revenue gained put the game on a firm commercial basis, but a decade later, Australian Test cricket was still struggling to recover from its virtual demolition.

Other sports followed suit and there was an epidemic of player buying led by Sydney Rugby League and, later, the Victorian Football League. Players were bought and sold like commodities and they transferred from club to club for huge sums. The whole basis of club and suburban loyalties was eroded. In a few years, some clubs were either so financially distressed, had so little success on the field, or both, that there were clear signs that the days of the Victorian Football League as the premier Australian Rules competition were finished. Supine officials, premiership hungry club members and greedy players watched the destruction of a great competition. Within a few years, a National Football League, to rival basketball, Rugby League and soccer, was in the process of development in an effort to revive the Australian game.

The decade of the 1970s suffered its share of usual natural and manmade disasters. There was the Darwin cyclone and the flooding of Brisbane, which extended right into its commercial centre, in 1974. In 1972 seventeen miners were killed in a colliery in Queensland, and another fourteen died in similar circumstances at Appin in New South Wales. During this period coal was becoming Australia's biggest export earner. In 1970 the collapse of the Westgate Bridge in Melbourne was clearly a case of negligence with thirty-five dead, and, on a summer night in January 1975, twelve people died when a ship collided with the Tasman Bridge in Hobart, thus dividing the south and north of the city. The worst rail disaster in Australian history took place on 18 January 1977 at Granville, Sydney, when a bridge collapsed on a train, killing over eighty passengers and seriously injuring many more.

On 17 August 1980 Azaria, the nine-week-old baby daughter of Seventh Day Adventist Pastor Michael Chamberlain and his wife Lindy, disappeared from a tent in the camping ground at Ayers Rock in the Northern Territory. The mother claimed that a dingo had taken Azaria, but, after two inquests and a trial she was sentenced to life imprisonment for murder and only released after spending over three years in jail. The first inquest had found that a dingo or wild dog had taken the baby. The High Court rejected Lindy's appeal in February 1984. No body or murder weapon was ever discovered and no motive was proved, and, in June 1987, a Royal Commission found that 'the evidence affords considerable support for the view that a dingo may have taken' Azaria. Lindy and her husband, who had been convicted as an accessory after the fact, were both pardoned for a ghastly crime which no one had ever proved they had committed. They were neither exonerated nor compensated. The whole bizarre and mysterious affair revealed depths of religious prejudice, ignorance, fear of the unknown and the outback, and expert incompetence, if not negligence, which caused a reaction in millions of Australians.

With appalling regularity, commercial and private small aeroplanes continued to crash killing their occupants, but the main carriers — Qantas, TAA (Australian Airlines) and Ansett — held to the highest traditions of air safety. Finally, a whiff of exotic crime and of the underworld came to Australia in 1977 when Donald Mackay, a highly respected citizen of Griffith, New South Wales, disappeared without trace. Mackay was also an anti-drug campaigner in a locality where millions of dollars were being made from marijuana plantations and drug running. His murder cast a long shadow over the police and the political administration of New South Wales which was still lengthening a decade later.

Despite its last few months, the three, short years of Whitlam had been ones of hope and excitement. The sheer volume of his government's achievements tended to be forgotten in the manner of its downfall. Despite opposition in the Senate, which had rejected ninety-three bills — fifteen more in three years than the same House had rejected in the previous seventy-one years — there were 507 pieces of legislation enacted, which was a record for any government. It was often thought later that the Fraser government undid the work of Whitlam, but in foreign affairs, especially in regard to China, which Fraser visited amicably and successfully, and in the defence area, the main thrusts were maintained. Government assistance to needy students in the tertiary sector and the abolition of fees remained, schools were funded on a needs basis, and tertiary education continued to expand, although severe cuts were made in budgets. Welfare was certainly diminished and, despite Fraser's promise to the contrary, Medibank was changed radically thereby causing the first national strike in Australia's history. Nevertheless, most of Whitlam's welfare initiatives remained in place including the indexation of pensions. Equal pay spread in the workforce, law reform was maintained with the establishment of the Federal Court, legal aid was developed, the office of Ombudsman established and family law set in place. Anti-discrimination laws on race and gender were introduced, a host of other reforms put into effect and the Fraser government passed, with modifications, the land rights bill for Aborigines in the Northern Territory formulated by the Whitlam government.

The public remained unconvinced of Whitlam's belief that it was economically more practical, and personally more just, to provide social services through the public purse than through private measures. Understandably, the business community held to the conviction that a wider and more just distribution of wealth threatened its own immediate interests, and the unions failed to perceive that an increase in social services was often more useful to the workers than a few more dollars in wage rises. Those who cried 'too much, too soon' were unable to point to important things that Whitlam did that should have been postponed, except his venture into decentralization with the failed schemes of developing Bathurst/Orange and Albury/Wodonga. Those who felt that Australia had been changed for the worse could not spell it out in any detail except in generalities that were meaningless to the millions of Australians who benefited during his government and afterwards. It was to Whitlam's credit that a new hope and a new vision were given to Australians and to Fraser's that, in considerable measure, he did not destroy either.

CHAPTER TWENTY

The End of White Australia

The changed and still changing face of Australia was everywhere obvious as the nation came close to two hundred years of white settlement. Much that was here when the first settlers came remained intact, while much too of the culture and tradition they brought with them from the British Isles had been preserved. On remote coastlines and in desolate parts of the outback little or nothing had changed since the passing of Cook on the *Endeavour* in 1770, and the landing of Phillip with his cargo of convicts in 1788. Yet those events had set the pattern of change, in which the ancient continent was to be transformed both in its physical and cultural landscapes. The cultural landscape was transformed by the introduction of a new culture that partly displaced the Aboriginal culture which had grown out of the physical landscape over 50,000 years ago. The new culture based on commerce, growth and competition altered the physical landscape. Pastoralism, agriculture, mining, deforestation and urbanization changed the landscape irrevocably.

By the 1980s the new nation was still predominantly white, spoke mainly English of the Australian variety, owed allegiance to the English Queen and observed laws derived from British sources. The structure of Parliament and the legal system was based on that which had been developed at Westminster while the education system, from the primary to the tertiary sector, owed its origins to the British Isles. Everywhere, from country court houses to railway stations, from racecourses to cricket fields, the nation's origins were apparent. With those things the majority of the people felt at ease, but they no longer spoke of England as home because Australia had become their homeland.

In the cities, there were other symbols. American chains such as Pizza Hut, McDonald's, and Kentucky Fried Chicken led the fast food outlets and in some suburbs there were streets with shops displaying signs in Italian, Greek, Arabic and Vietnamese. The cuisines of a dozen nations attracted satisfied patrons and the clothing styles of France and Italy were worn by the affluent, the cars of Germany and Sweden carried them and Japanese models were parked on every street. The religion of the British Isles, with its varied divisions of Christianity, still dominated and the Methodists, Presbyterians and Congregationalists had successfully formed the Uniting Church. The Anglican and Roman Catholic Churches, despite ecumenism, retained their separate identities and neither had the impact on society they previously enjoyed. In 1986 Pope John Paul II visited Australia and called for a return to old values, but he

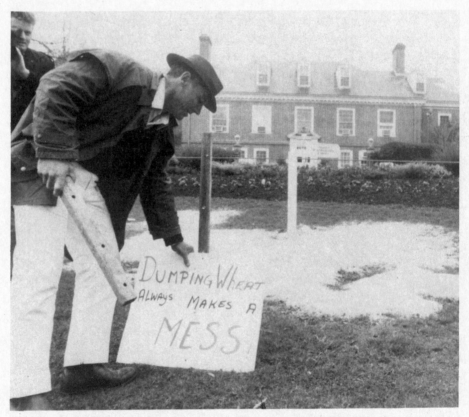

Farmers, angered by American wheat subsidies to the U.S.S.R., made their protest in Canberra near the American Embassy in August 1986, but to no avail. Prices remained low and many farmers faced ruin.

also asked for an openness to change and especially that justice be done to the Aboriginal people.

Most Australians still believed in God and in an afterlife, but some worshipped Him in the name of Allah and built mosques, some called Him Jehovah, while others followed new prophets whom they accepted as the way of truth. One or both parents of many children at city schools were born outside Australia. In their homes, such children often spoke the language of their parents who were drawn from 140 ethnic groups and in the multi-lingual society of Australia more than forty languages were in daily use. With their school friends, the children communicated in the language and accent which went back to the convict era, and favoured pies, chips and hot dogs with tomato sauce before pizzas, salamis and spring rolls.

In a population of sixteen million, one in four was an immigrant and they had immigrated from 120 different countries. Together, since World War II, they had formed one of the biggest migration waves in the world in the twentieth century. Seven out of ten of them lived in the continent's ten largest cities because Australia, the driest and flattest of all the great land masses of the earth, had vast areas inhospitable to white settlement. The decline of the Aboriginal population had stopped, although, at about 170,000, they were still less than a quarter of the number who had lived throughout the continent in 1788. About half of the Aborigines lived in the towns and cities and only a remnant followed the way of life of their ancestors.

The struggle of the Aborigines for land rights, whether in actual territory or in some form of monetary compensation for what they had lost, persisted, but, after two hundred years, they held under some kind of title only about ten percent of their original land. Most of it was in areas removed from white settlement, and little of it was of benefit to Aboriginal city and town dwellers. The opposition of pastoral and mining interests combined with other groups, whose motives rarely extended beyond racial prejudice, to persuade an initially reformist Hawke Labor government, faced with grave economic pressures, to falter and halt on the path towards genuine land rights.

Since the days of John Batman, there had been no progress in making a treaty with the Aborigines and some of them, understandably, refused to participate in preparations for the celebration of the Bicentenary. They regarded themselves as victims of a lost war that had been waged against their people for 200 years and they judged any form of celebration of its beginning as derisory. Others of a less militant frame of mind had come to accept the fact that there could be no complete return to the Dreamtime of their ancestors. They knew that they belonged now to a nation the members of which held no responsibility as individuals for the distant past and with whom they had to work towards a better future for themselves and all Australians. Amongst them even the most hopeful and fair-minded realized that their expectations would be slow in fulfilment.

In the 1970s and 1980s the most enduring and far-reaching change in society was seen in the status of women. Their involvement as equals with men in the anti-Vietnam war movement had convinced some of them that they were powerless as individuals to change the nature of the oppression to which they long regarded themselves as subject. In 1972, they founded the Women's Electoral Lobby, thereby facilitating the making of contacts between themselves and giving themselves a voice in the political process. Its foundation coincided with the coming to power of the Whitlam government, which was sympathetic to their cause. The women's movement drew some inspiration from overseas sources, concentrated on such issues as equal pay, the right to abortion, sexism in the media and advertising, and, in its extreme form, attacked the nuclear family, which was seen as pernicious because it was, allegedly, repressive.

Initially, the gains were enormous as more women began to understand, accept and demand their rights as equal to those of men, while some men began to regard such rights as fundamental justice. At the start only a few more women entered politics or attained positions of responsibility in their professions and workplaces. Three women were elected as Labor members of Parliament in 1974, the equal pay case was resolved in women's favour, statutory bodies saw women appointed to their boards, refuges and rape crisis centres were established and there were developments in child care and pre-school facilities. The government appointed women to head bodies concerned with the status of women, equal opportunity clauses were accepted by some employers, the title 'Ms' became widespread, women in the Capital Territory founded their own licensed premises, and institutions such as universities began, tentatively, to redress the balance in staff appointments and to set up women's studies programmes.

Some men began to respond positively to the women's movement although most remained unchanged. More husbands assisted at their wife's confinement, others took an active role in the home, a few accepted half-time employment. It was increasingly unacceptable to tell sexist jokes and respect for women, rather than mere male patronage, became an accepted standard of behaviour. When the newly-founded Family Court appeared to some to favour mothers, when unemployment rose and there was a suspicion that, in some areas, men were being discriminated against for jobs through a process called 'affirmative action', there was a reaction and feminism began to lose ground.

The more vocal and extreme forms of the movement, which fostered conflict as a means to overthrowing the ruling, patriarchal structure of a male-dominated society, alarmed and alienated increasing numbers of women, including Germaine Greer, who had been one of its forerunners. By the mid-1980s, the movement had lost much of its dynamism. Marriage, the home, bearing and rearing children were showing signs of revival and the worsening economic climate cut away at the advantages gained. A few Anglican women argued that there were theological reasons why they should be ordained to the priesthood and the concomitance of their discovery with the changed sociological climate was underplayed. Nevertheless, because of its essential justice and universality, the movement for women's rights was a most profound development which, in Australia, brought radical changes. That, for a time, the struggle would irritate and even infuriate those who disregarded its essential justice was understandable but regrettable.

Malcolm Fraser's government had been re-elected in 1980, but there was no turn about in the worsening economy, due to a severe and prolonged drought, an increasing national debt, a lessening demand for Australian primary products and falling overseas prices. Fraser tried, unsuccessfully, to pump the economy by attracting overseas investors to the tune of six billion dollars in 1980, with most of the profits going straight back to the investors. Large firms continued to flourish such as Broken Hill Proprietary Limited and G.J. Coles and there were takeover bids by local investment entrepreneurs. The West Australian millionaire, Alan Bond, successfully moved into the brewing business and the Bank of New South Wales bid $699,000,000 for the Commercial Bank of Australia. After the merger the new bank was called Westpac.

From the late 1970s the term used for the economic downturn was 'recession', and although, by early 1983, the rate of unemployment had risen to 10.7 percent, the highest level since the Great Depression, no one dared to use the dreaded word 'depression'. At the time, an informed estimate put one in five Australians as living below the poverty line, despite the fact that for most others there was a continued rise in living standards. An indication of the economic climate was clear in Sydney where over half of the married women were in the workforce and most of them worked for financial reasons, as both prices and taxes were rising in a way that wage increases could not match. It seemed that Australia was running down as exemplified by the decline of the once booming Broken

Hill as the enormous silver, lead and zinc mines, which had created the inland city of over 30,000 people, were nearing exhaustion. Broken Hill faced the prospect of becoming a vast ghost town as there was no prospect of creating alternative employment for the men laid off from the mines.

The normally astute Fraser made the biggest mistake of his career on 3 February 1983 by calling an early election. On that very day, a majority of Labor members in the federal Parliament convinced themselves that their party could not win an election with Bill Hayden as leader. Hayden, a highly intelligent, honest, forthright and cogent politician, had the misfortune to be confronted by Bob Hawke, who possessed, in abundance, a quality dear to the media and to the electorate which had become popularly known as charisma. The result of the election seemed to justify Labor's decision to change the leadership for Hawke led the party to its best win since World War II. Nonetheless, success in the Senate eluded it, where five senators representing the Australian Democrats, formed by the break-away Liberal Don Chipp in 1977, held the balance of power. The Democrats promised not to block supply, which was a guarantee no one had deemed necessary to give to the coalition parties in office.

Hawke and his government were determined not to repeat the mistake of bewildering the electorate with immediate and far-reaching changes. With prudent promises of reducing unemployment, cutting back the deficit and stopping inflation, a new ministry took office, some of whom had had ministerial experience under Whitlam. Possibly because of the divisions created in Australian society in the Whitlam era, Hawke was determined to govern by consensus between the major interest groups — business leaders, employers, trade unions and government. In other modern societies, consensus was only achievable in times of crisis or when a dictator ruled under the guise of consensus. At its best, consensus on economic problems could only result in the lowest common denominator being adopted, even if all concerned with it were sincere. Australia was not then in crisis and Hawke was too committed a democrat and too honest a man ever to use dictatorial methods. He could only be accused of optimism or naivety, for the chance of a lasting consensus being reached between labour and capital was slim. The 'Summit' which met in Canberra in April 1983 supported a prices and incomes accord. It lasted for nine months on wages, but there was little evidence that it ever started on prices.

Initially, there was much good will towards the government and under the direction of Paul Keating, later acclaimed by Hawke as the 'world's greatest treasurer', there was promise that the economy would recover. Even the weather and sport seemed to favour Hawke, as one of the worst droughts in the history of Australia broke in 1983 and then in September Alan Bond's *Australia II* won the America's Cup. The happy theme of sporting success was sustained when Robert de Castella, whose ancestors had come to Port Phillip in the days of Charles La Trobe, won the Rotterdam marathon and became Australian of the Year. Despite the interest of the Prime Minister in sport, and the support given to it by the previous government, which founded the Australian Institute of Sport in Canberra in 1981, the long-vaunted prowess of Australians as sportsmen and women was in decline. Apart from de Castella and the golfer Greg Norman, there was scarcely another Australian of world class, although six years after the foundation of the Institute of Sport, there was some evidence that its efforts were proving successful.

Youth and vitality were apparent in Hawke's Cabinet, which was composed of mainly young, competent, hard-working and dedicated ministers. They received the consistent backing of the public servants working for them, although the head of the Treasury, John Stone, decided that he was unhappy with a government which did not follow his own conservative fiscal policies and publicly criticized it after his retirement in 1984. A few alarmed or otherwise disconcerted conservatives joined him to form a body named after H. R. Nicholls, who, as well as achieving some notoriety at Eureka, had been tried for contempt of the Arbitration Court in 1911. Presumably, it was this later act which endeared Nicholls to Stone and those who thought that the arbitration system had been injurious to the Australian economy.

In 1982 the National Country Party had decided to break with its past and drop the word 'Country' from its title in the hope that it would have more general appeal, but it retained its conservative image. The Nationals worked harmoniously with Andrew Peacock who led the Liberals until he was replaced by John Howard in 1985. The coalition seemed to accept that the Hawke government was the legitimate representation of the will of the electorate, and, with its usual forays into invective and name calling, its tiresome and time-wasting debates, the Parliament got down to business. The government was determined to follow a moderate course and the coalition was neutralized except on some non-essential issues and it failed to regain office in an election at the end of 1984. The government did introduce a watered-down version of Medibank, now called Medicare, financed initially by a one percent levy on all incomes. Medicare commenced to provide basic health and hospital care for all

Although rich oil wells have been discovered in Australian coastal waters, without further discoveries, stocks will run low in the 1990s. Despite continued exploration no large finds have been made in recent years.

Australians in February 1984. As costs escalated, it ran a difficult course, and many medical practitioners became increasingly restless and some went on strike.

Together with the women's movement, the other popular groundswell was in the growth of conservation societies which grew to some 800 with half-a-million members by the mid-1980s. As early as 1863, Tasmania had passed laws to protect its scenic areas, and in 1879 the world's second National Park of 18,000 acres was established in New South Wales, south of Sydney. A century later, more leisure time, greater affluence, the increasing numbers who went bushwalking, urbanization, the lure of the outdoor life and the demands of the tourist industry all combined to make the conservation groups a powerful lobby.

As a political issue, conservation came to the fore with the debate over the Gordon-below-Franklin Dam in Tasmania's beautiful south-west in 1982. The Fraser government decided not to interfere with the Tasmanian government's intention to proceed with the Dam, although the whole area had been put on the World Heritage List. The Hawke government refused to allow work on the Dam to proceed when it took office, and, in July 1983, the High Court supported its right to do so. This decision threw into confusion the question of state rights, still in some measure sacrosanct since federation, and infuriated the Liberal government in Tasmania.

By 1982 five Australian locations had been put on the World Heritage List as places 'of outstanding universal value'. There was the Western Tasmanian Wilderness National Parks area which includes the Franklin and Gordon rivers. Another listing was the Great Barrier Reef, which is the largest coral reef system in the world and provides the most beautiful marine scenery on earth. The Lord Howe Island group was listed for its unique landform, intact ecosystems and evidence of independent evolutionary processes. The Willandra Lakes region in New South Wales where human beings lived 40,000 years ago and where there is evidence of the large marsupials that roamed Australia before the end of the last Ice Age is listed, as is Kakadu National Park in the Northern Territory which contains more than 1,000 known Aboriginal art sites, dating back to the Ice Age.

Despite the occasional and temporary setback, such as the Franklin Dam issue, the federal-state system had proved workable, even when governments of differing political hue held office at either level. In social welfare, education, railways and matters which crossed state boundaries the federal government had accrued more and more power since federation. One area it could not control effectively was crime, together with the associated legal structures, including the police, magistracy and judiciary, required to curb it. A Royal Commission into the Federated Ship Painters and Dockers' Union revealed in 1984 that large sections of Australian life were permeated by crime. In New South Wales, and particularly in Sydney, criminal activity had grown alarmingly during the premiership of Liberal leader, Robert Askin, from 1965 to 1975.

Askin had come into some prominence during President Johnson's visit to Sydney in 1966, when, as their official car was confronted by male and female anti-war demonstrators lying on the roadway, Askin had urged the driver to 'run over the bastards'. A national weekly paper alleged after Askin's death in 1981 that the Premier was involved in crime and corruption by the taking of huge bribes annually, that there were two corrupt police commissioners and innumerable lesser officers involved with crime, and that organized crime had become the largest industry in the state. Crime still held a prominent position in the economy of New

South Wales during the succeeding Labor government of Neville Wran, and was becoming prominent during the Bjelke-Petersen government in Queensland.

In the same period, drug peddling became widespread, and again Sydney was its centre, with the occasional prosecution of a policeman or the apprehension of a drug-ring satisfying authority that the situation was in hand. Marijuana was widely cultivated in isolated areas, Customs officials were baffled by the ingenious methods used to import drugs, young people died or were wrecked by addiction and big syndicates made fortunes out of misery. Some few, courageous people advocated the legalisation of drugs, in particular marijuana. No government was prepared to face the problem in such a radical manner, because the old forces of wowserism, which had never died, were still strong and the involvement of powerful financial interests made action difficult.

In May 1983, another face to human suffering was shown when AIDS first appeared in Sydney amongst homosexual males. It spread quickly to bisexuals, intravenous drug users, blood transfusion recipients and a few heterosexuals who had come into sexual contact with carriers. By 1987 it was clear that little could be done to stop the spread of infection except, perhaps, by the use of condoms and the distribution of free hypodermic needles to drug users both at large and in the prisons. The Federal government used the media to frighten people into having 'safe sex' by an advertisement combining the Black Death of the Middle Ages and the modern bowling alley. Any talk about moral standards, much less sin, on the part of the churches or other concerned observers was unwelcome yet, not surprisingly, there seemed to be a return to the old values of sexual behaviour and the curtain slowly came down on uninhibited promiscuity.

Lionel Murphy, reformer, Justice of the High Court and one-time Labor Attorney-General was a victim of the general corruption of some elements in New South Wales society and their long-held contempt for authority of any kind. Over his long career in politics and the law he had of necessity come into contact with shady characters and with some few of them, out of the depth of humanity which he possessed in abundance, he continued to associate when prudence indicated that to shun them was the better course for a High Court Judge to take. In the end, he was brought down because some token gesture had to be made to assure the general populace that government would not tolerate criminality and because he, as Attorney-General and judge, had earnt the deep-seated enmity of many to whom reform was a threat. Murphy had turned his back on the old conventions, and specifically on Christianity, as the reinforcer of the moral code of society and he died in 1986 when all around him it was clear that nothing had been put in its place.

In the deteriorating economic climate, the Hawke government was unable to continue the funding of education at the levels to which it had grown since the days of Menzies. Universities in particular suffered drastic budget cuts. In some areas staff numbers declined by a third causing consequent impairment to teaching and research standards. During 1986 the government decided to introduce a $250 annual fee for students in tertiary institutions under the pretext that it was not for education, but for administrative costs. The argument that education at all levels is the right of a tax-paying community was not addressed; university administrators generally accepted the decision and the student bodies, rent by their own divisions, were unable to mount an effective protest. Sixty percent of the Australian population had no post-secondary-school qualifications and thirty percent of those qualified to get into tertiary institutions were unable to gain entry despite the energy of the government in providing 30,000 more places. The imposition of the $250 fee was an unusual decision for a government which professed itself concerned both about human welfare and the future economic viability of the nation. There were calls for privately-funded universities and the financier, Alan Bond, of America's Cup fame, proceeded with plans to set one up in Queensland which may have helped console him for the loss of the Cup at Fremantle in January 1987.

The old argument about state aid to education began to show signs of a revival but in a different context. Enrolments in state schools were everywhere declining — in Victoria, by 56,000 in the five years to 1986 — while those in private schools increased — again, in Victoria, by 26,000. More than eighty percent of the children in private schools completed the final year compared to thirty percent in government schools. Social inequalities in education were even more glaringly evident in the tertiary sector because, while over half of the students in private schools went on to higher education, only fifteen percent of those in the public sector did so. Much ink was spilt and many words bandied about in parliaments on these discrepancies but the attempt to deny the existence of a malaise in public education, despite the efforts of thousands of hard-working and devoted teachers, was useless.

Generally, the arts and literature seemed to falter. Manning Clark and Patrick White continued to despair at the 'Great Australian Emptiness' in 'this country of dry bones' while calling for a new spirit to awaken its people. The playwright, David Williamson, continued to satirize Australian life in a powerful, witty and partly-crude manner in plays that drew appreciative audiences, who laughed and wondered at themselves but went away unchanged. Australia lost one of its greatest creative performers with the death in October 1986 of Robert Helpmann, pillar of the Australian ballet as well as actor, choreographer, director and producer. The death of Fred Williams deprived painting of an artist of consummate ability who brought life to the bush in a distinctive style which bordered on the abstract but remained true to the landscape. Williams was firmly in a tradition of Australian painting that always shaped its techniques on overseas trends, and, as the Heidelberg School of the 1890s and the Expressionists of the 1940s had done, Williams, Clifton Pugh, Sidney Nolan and others, when they sought to represent Australia on canvas, portrayed its landscape. They seemed to admit that the only distinctive thing to be said about Australia and its people was the land they moved in, but never conquered.

In the 1980s, three autobiographies were published, each of which gave an insight into the Australian experience from differing perspectives and they stand as a testimony to its value and endurance. A.B. Facey's *A Fortunate Life* summed up in his own experience many of the tribulations which thousands of others had been through since the depression of the 1890s. He lived as a youth on the Western Australian gold-fields, was wounded at Gallipoli, became a tram driver in Perth and had to walk off his selection in the Narragin district in 1934 when rabbits, drought, and falling prices for wheat and wool sent him broke. Despite all the hardship, Facey still entitled his book with a tribute to fortune, and in a long Australian tradition, he was always a battler, who won out over adversity. The Vasari of Australian painting, Bernard Smith, and the best loved teacher of Australian history, Kathleen Fitzpatrick, wrote of their upbringing and education in Sydney, Melbourne and Oxford in *The Boy Adeodatus* and *Solid Bluestone Foundations*. Each presents a gentle, evocative, honest and penetrating analysis of a past that marks them as Australians who gave their all to the native land.

The film industry was one area in which Australians had shown a creative flair before and after World War I, notably in the work of Raymond Longford, but American films replaced the local ones so that film making practically died out. The industry began its revival in the mid-1970s with the support of government and in the main the old, painfully brash themes of the past were avoided so that Australians could watch their own product without cringing. About 150 films were made in the decade and they dealt with mateship, women, the shearers, the landscape, the treatment of Aborigines, life in country towns and the bush. The bush was portrayed as hostile, even incomprehensible, to urban

The survival of the Australian economy was helped by high wool prices in 1987. The action of the Kelpie sheepdog was the basis of Paul Hogan's movement in the film *Crocodile Dundee*, although most Americans and many Australians failed to recognize the connection.

dwellers and throughout the films there was an underlying theme which tried to say that Australians had not come to grips with their environment.

Some of the films were of sufficient merit to be remembered. *Wake in Fright*, *Sunday Too Far Away*, *Picnic at Hanging Rock*, *Caddie*, *The Getting of Wisdom*, *My Brilliant Career*, *The Devil's Playground*, *Storm Boy*, *The Last Wave* and *Newsfront*, were followed with war topics in *Breaker Morant* and *Gallipoli*. All were successful attempts at tackling aspects of the national ethos, although the film makers kept clear of other national themes, notably Eureka, the gold-fields and the Irish, which were left to television to take up. In 1986, Paul Hogan produced and acted in *Crocodile Dundee* which was an amusing caricature of the bush and the bush hero, who, in Hogan, became a crocodile hunter rather than a drover or cattleman. The film became popular in the United States, for which audience it was made, because many Americans had begun to look at Australia as the last frontier.

By the beginning of 1986, Australians at all levels of society had become obsessed with the state of the economy. The dollar had been allowed to float, which quickly resulted in a loss of parity by thirty percent against the American dollar and there was a similar drop against other currencies such as the yen, the Deutschmark and the formerly despised Italian lira. During the course of the year, the American government subsidized wheat sales to the Soviet Union and China, which further threatened Australian wheat farmers. They had already suffered through falling prices and many of them were forced to sell up or walk off their properties as interests rates showed no sign of falling. Coal and minerals generally, with the exception of gold, were meeting overseas buyer resistance. Oil reserves were dropping at a rapid rate and further exploration was said to be hindered by high government charges on oil production.

Wool, long the staple of the economy, retained its place as a valuable export commodity, partly due to the fall in the dollar and the continued demand from Japan. However, wool could not uniquely sustain a diverse economy, especially as manufacturing industry had not kept pace with developments elsewhere, even in the Pacific region where South Korea, Taiwan, Japan and latterly China were dominant. By June 1986, the deficit was six billion dollars, $800 million more than anticipated, but few people realized that seventy percent of Australian companies were owned by foreign interests and that sixty percent of the huge overseas borrowings were by large corporations such as the newspaper groups who had begun to vie with each other for control of the Australian media.

When it became apparent that Rupert Murdoch, formerly an Australian citizen who had become an American, had a fifty-eight percent controlling interest in the Australian media the government seemed pleased. In fact, over ninety percent of Australian newspapers were in the hands of the Murdoch and Fairfax presses. In the area of television, the three major Australian networks constituted an oligopoly and that fact, together with the virtual monopoly of the press, had social implications which the government seemed unable, afraid or unwilling to address.

Throughout Australia, many small businesses were failing, the motor vehicle industry was in chaos with the lowest sales for new cars in thirty years, interest rates were slow to fall, home construction was dwindling affecting an industry that directly and indirectly employed over half a million people and the country went to second last on a list of twenty-four in trade performances for technological products. Wage levels had not risen in proportion to the cost of living, as there had been little appreciable fall in inflation, but the trade union movement, led by Simon Crean, attempted to moderate wage rises and minimize industrial unrest. Nevertheless, the Victorian nurses, in despair at their inability to receive awards commensurate with their work, struck for the first time in their history in 1986 and remained out for seven weeks. Nevertheless, the strike rate more than halved in the years 1983–85 compared with 1959–83, and Australia's rate was lower than the international norm. There seemed every reason to suppose that the accord and the Australian Conciliation and Arbitration Commission, as well as the Labor government's industrial relations policy generally, had a good deal to do with this shift in the strike rate.

The government had taken several tough and courageous decisions which, in the case of the devaluation of the dollar, the subsequent rise and fall of which Australians followed as closely as their forebears had watched the weather, ought to have resulted in a rapid decrease in imports but it was slow to occur. A capital gains tax and a fringe benefits tax did little for the economy in the immediate sense but both were regarded as outrageous measures by a minority who benefited when such taxes did not operate. In 1986, the government's desperation was shown when Treasurer Keating warned that Australia was in danger of becoming a 'banana republic', a statement which failed to amuse his Prime Minister.

Contradictions at high levels were never more evident than when the government, against its own party policy and having taken a stand against French intransigence on nuclear testing in the Pacific, decided to resume sales of uranium to that country. The decision dismayed even

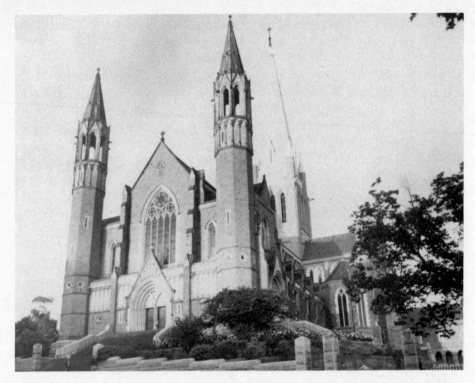

Richard Johnson's church in the infant colony was humble but many great cathedrals were later built. The Sacred Heart Cathedral, Bendigo, Victoria was a direct fruit of the goldrushes. It is probably the finest in the land.

some of the most ardent and loyal of Labor supporters and the Chernobyl disaster at a nuclear plant in the Ukraine did nothing to allay fears that the very use of nuclear energy, as well as nuclear war, threatened the future of the human race. There were falls in the level of popularity of the government and even of the Prime Minister himself, who had hitherto enjoyed unprecedented trust by the electorate. Many Labor Party branches were disturbed by charges that the Hawke government had departed from the high ideals of its Labor predecessors.

As never before in their history, Australians were bombarded with the warnings of prophets and the remedies of the wise on the state of the economy. The public was confused with the mysterious terminology of economics which engendered a feeling of helplessness and a tendency to leave everything to the politicians and financial experts in the hope that they would come up with a remedy. The leadership of farmer organizations, convinced that Australian farmers were the most technologically advanced, cost efficient and highest producers per head in the world, was not so prepared and there were demonstrations outside Parliament House, angry meetings in rural areas and big sums of money were raised to help get rid of the Hawke government.

Little attempt was made by the increasing number of critics of Hawke and Labor to understand that, with the best will in the world, no government could solve problems outside its control, such as the covert ability of international financial interests to quickly remove capital from a country where they failed to make large profits. Nonetheless, to his credit, the federal Treasurer stuck to the course he had embarked upon and lived in hope that the turn-about would come. By mid-1987 the government claimed to have created 800,000 new jobs which, while a significant step, could not help those who had been out of work for years and continued to remain unemployed, and made little difference to the overall unemployment rate.

On the international scene, a report commissioned by the federal government assured Australians that there was no direct military threat to their security, that no one wanted to invade the country and subjugate its people, and that global war was a most unlikely event amongst the superpowers. 'Forward defence' was emphasized with the earmarking of four billion dollars for six new submarines. Meanwhile, a magnificent new Parliament House was nearing completion in Canberra and there were murmurs of criticism at its proposed final cost of one billion dollars. No politician was prepared to state publicly that a building which was likely to become one of the great edifices of the world and would stand as a testimony to democracy for hundreds of years was worth as much in expenditure as a submarine, which would probably be obsolete before the end of the century.

The economic and consequent social problems that had arisen in the early 1970s and continued into the 1980s were not new in themselves. Since the 1830s Australia had always depended for its economic viability upon the caprice of overseas markets and the willingness of foreign investors to risk their capital. When, as in the 1840s, the 1890s and the 1930s, those outside factors had adversely coalesced to lessen market demand and to reduce investment, Australia and its people had suffered. In the 1980s industry had to strive hard to compete against imports and, more importantly, it had to begin to export profitably. The latter was a challenge that had never been faced and it came at a time when Asian competitors were much more advanced technologically and could rely on a cheaper workforce. Few Australians bothered to understand these problems and fewer still were prepared to take the repeated calls for belt-tightening seriously. Amongst the more affluent section of the community there were 30,000 millionaires with a total wealth of $1,000 billion. One tenth of the population owned sixty percent of the country's assets and company tax receipts totalled only ten percent of tax revenue compared with twenty percent in 1975. Small business people, wage earners, many farmers, the unemployed, those on old-age and widow's pensions wondered at a system which seemed to make the amassing of wealth possible while to them survival was a constant concern.

In February 1987 a new factor entered the national political scene in the person of the Queensland Premier Bjelke-Petersen who declared his intention of becoming the next Prime Minister. A phenomenon similar to Bjelke-Petersen had rarely been seen in Australian political life and his closest counterparts were John Dunmore Lang, Billy Hughes and King O'Malley. The difference was that in them a solid core of sanity tended to override the flamboyant or merely ridiculous. The standard bearer of old-style, Deakinite liberalism in Victoria was the Melbourne *Age* which became eloquent in its finely-phrased vitriol on the subject of Bjelke-Petersen. To the leader writer he was 'an ageing bucolic demagogue' whose crusade for the prime-ministership was 'political humbug, economic quackery and social mischief' while his 'geriatric gibberish', which consisted mainly in cries for smaller government and a flat-tax rate of twenty-five percent, provided no answer to the problems facing the country. When Hawke called an early election for 11 July, Bjelke-Petersen was in America, and, on his arrival home, he decided to forego his attempt at national leadership. The main effect of his incursion onto the federal scene was that the Liberal Party moved further to the right leaving Labor in a position to stand by its moderate policy of continued restraint.

It was not the best time for the Labor Party to go into an election unless the disarray of its conservative opponents proved a decisive factor to the electors. To most Australians, the tax system seemed out of control and the government's attempt to reform it had failed while the promise of the Liberals to drop the highest rate to thirty-eight percent had to be tested against the cost. The growth rate of the public service had doubled that of the population rate and on all levels of life, from birth to death, the involvement of government was obtrusive. The national debt was still rising, overseas pundits remarked that Australians had a first-rank standard of living based on a fourth-level economy and prices were continuing to rise. A $10 increase in wages granted in March by the Conciliation and Arbitration Commission was a mere crumb to the poor, although it had caused employer groups to cry loudly in dejection at the profligacy of the decision. Other groups were dismayed as overseas aid fell to its lowest level in twenty-five years, making Australia one of the least generous of countries in the developed world, and overseas students were asked to pay fees, which effectively restricted the intake to the children of the Asian wealthy.

Apart from a call by one Aboriginal activist for a separate Aboriginal nation and a vote to secede from Australia taken by representatives from the fourteen islands in the Torres Strait, by mid-1987 Australians generally, and their government in particular, were faced with matters of great moment which tested Australian foreign policy. Papua New Guinea appeared to enjoy stability but elsewhere in the Pacific there were causes for concern. The Russians were showing an interest in gaining a foothold on Vanuatu, the French continued their colonial administration of New Caledonia and Libya threatened to introduce its own brand of militant fanaticism wherever the opportunity showed itself, including offering support to Australian Aborigines. Finally, in May, the duly elected multiracial coalition led by the recently formed Labor Party in Fiji was toppled by an army engineered coup. The long history of Australian commerical interests in Fiji had finally come home to rest.

Colonial Sugar Refining Co. (CSR) began its century-long association with Fiji in the 1870s when, after building in Queensland an industry closely dependent on black-birding, it gained a monopoly on sugar production in Fiji. To work its mills and estates, it brought in indentured labour from India, a practice which the Indian government stopped in 1916. By then over 60,000 Indians had arrived of whom a third returned home. The rest became the basis of what now forms almost fifty percent of Fiji's population while the Melanesians who originally occupied the islands are only 45.19 percent. CSR had sold its interests to the Fijian government in 1973, when they were no longer regarded as commercially profitable.

The coup was partly a legacy of CSR's indentured labour system because the coup was directed by the Melanesians at the threat of political control by the Indians. Short of military intervention the Australian government could do little except make protestations and threaten trade embargoes. The Fiji economy, already weakened by falling world prices for sugar, stood reliant on aid rather than on embargoes but the continued presence of large Australian financial interests there, including the press, banking, insurance and television made the present reality combine with the historical past to demand a more constructive answer from Australia.

The first two weeks of July 1987 were days of winners. On Saturday night, 4 July, at an hotel in the marginal seat of Bendigo, Victoria, the Prime Minister shared the pride of millions of Australians as, on television from London, they saw Pat Cash win Wimbledon. It was the first Australian men's singles victory since 1971. A week later the electors of Bendigo returned the Labor candidate. Throughout Australia Labor won the election and Bob Hawke became the first Labor prime minister to achieve office on three occasions. The election was not easily won and in the Senate the Democrats retained the balance of power. The victory was significant because Labor had not made a weak bargain with the electorate. The levels of taxation would continue, there would be cuts in social security benefits in some areas and the public service would be pruned. Many months, even years, would pass before the deficit was reduced to acceptable proportions, interest rates were dropped significantly, inflation was slashed and unemployment levels fell. Sacrifices in wage levels would still be required, industry would have to learn to compete and subsidies would be reduced. Labor's campaign was successful because, unlike 1931 in the days of Scullin, the electors knew that the country was in the hands of a competent team. The election proved that a majority of the Australian people were capable of setting aside immediate self-interest to opt for the good of the Commonwealth. The nation had matured.

The voices of countless dead whisper from the past two hundred years of white settlement in Australia and ask that they be granted the courtesy of a hearing. The actions of the dead bear scrutiny but their motives can only be hinted at, because it is given to few to see into the human heart. White Australia, which is the work of those who laboured in the pioneering days and of those who followed them, is here for all to see. Those two hundred years are a brief moment in the course of human history but they are the indelible pattern upon which the future of this country will be traced. Because it was a human work, the making of white Australia bears the stamp of the imperfect. Yet in it there was much also that spoke of the noble, the upright, the enduring and the valiant. The white peopling of this land has ended and the old story will never be repeated. Australia, ancient but ever renewing itself, leaves its lasting legacy to all who become part of it.

Epilogue

The part of the historian is not that of the prophet. To prophets the present is the moment from which they look into the future. The historian has more the role of the psalmist. David looked back to the past of his people and he saw those thousands of years in which their history had unfolded. In that history there was much darkness but to him what mattered was their struggle towards the light. In the end he called upon Jerusalem to praise her God, 'Who hath placed peace in thy borders; and filleth thee with the fat of corn'.

Historians cannot close their eyes to the conflict between the races in Australia because it bordered on the virtual destruction of an ancient people and their precious civilization. They can only bow down in sorrow and say with gladness that, in the last fifty years, the changes have been enormous in both attitudes and progress. It is not their role to lament the slowness of change, because its implementation belongs to those who have chosen that task. They can only remind them that there can be no turning back to the ways of the past, which teaches its own lesson for those who want to read it.

There have been other conflicts in Australia. The Chinese were persecuted because China was feared, and her great traditions rejected as alien. China is no longer an adversary, and those traditions, borne by thousands who have come here, are respected. The White Australia policy, for seventy years at the heart of federation, and behind which stood the fear of China, has gone. Some of its traces remain in calls by a few to preserve the culture of the British. Relations with Japan remained strained or actively hostile for decades, but they have undergone a transformation both in trade and in cultural contacts. Asia is no longer foreign to the hundreds of thousands of Australians who visit there. The Pacific, for so long only the vast ocean that washed our shores, is now the path to the many different peoples that live on its islands and around its shores.

As in all other societies, there has been conflict between the owners of land and those who helped them work it as well as those who wanted some land of their own. There has also been conflict between those who owned capital and the workforce that helped to make it productive. Some have painted the historical past as a never-ending struggle with its only resolution lying in the elimination of ownership. Australians have asked the price of that kind of resolution and the great majority of them have rejected it. Historians look at both the suffering and the gains made in social legislation. They can recognize the grave mistakes that have been made but they know that they can only see them because there is a past. Historians know something of the past of other lands which, so often, has been painted red with the blood of civil war and territorial conquests which have resulted in the death of millions. They can weigh up the conflict that has taken place in Australia and balance it with the outcome and the commitment of many to make things better. Despite all that has been negative and destructive, there has been peace within our borders.

In the beginnings of white settlement, the sea provided its bounty until the seals and whales were reduced to a vestige of their former numbers. The settlers turned to the land and from it came the wool, the crops, minerals of all kinds and the fruits and flowers. They ravaged the land as they lived from it, cut down its forests, exhausted its pastures and polluted its waters. The land was more resilient than the people and bowed before them, but without surrendering. In time, Australians began to accept the frailty of the land and most of the ravaging ceased. Being human, they could not eliminate greed and stupidity, but their commitment to the preservation of the land had grown stronger. Many were grateful to the land because it had filled them with 'the fat of corn'.

Historians who assume the role of psalmists in Australia run the risk of not being heard, but without an act of thanksgiving the future looms sterile and bleak. Some will say that the history of Australia since 26 January 1788 is no cause for thanksgiving. They are heard and respected but they are wrong.

Bibliographical Essay

The records of white settlement in Australia over the past two hundred years are uniquely rich. The British government was in regular contact with its officials in the new penal colonies, letters and communications from both ends have been preserved and in part printed. Newspapers grew prolifically because of the scattered nature of settlement and the avid thirst for news on the part of the colonists. Private correspondence from and to the home countries, diaries, maps, photographs, business records, census counts, statistics of livestock and land under cultivation and a host of other records from myriad sources have been discovered, studied, and in some measure published. All these — together with tombstone inscriptions, folklore, songs, material remains, whether of buildings, utensils or even outback tracks — are the testimonials to the dead. From them, each historian composes his or her own image of the past. The bibliography that follows is in no sense exhaustive. Its main purpose is to act as a guide to the general reader wishing to find further material on subjects which the text of this work has touched upon briefly. In some cases, for the sake of brevity, where the first words of a title are sufficiently explanatory of the contents, the full title has not been given.

An impressive list of reference works has been published, especially in recent years, which is fundamental to fostering a knowledge of Australian history. The lives of a cross-section of the Australian community from the earliest days of white settlement are contained in chronological divisions in the ten volumes so far published of the *Australian Dictionary of Biography*, Melbourne, 1966–86. Volumes 11 and 12, completing the period 1891–1939, will be published by 1990. They are to be followed by an index volume and work will simultaneously commence to cover the period 1940–80. As an ongoing work undertaken by the Australian National University, the *Dictionary* is the single most valuable aid to Australian history and a source of immense richness for scholars and general readers.

In 1977 a group of historians met at the Australian National University to plan a set of volumes to mark 200 years of white settlement. Authors from all over Australia, historians, librarians, journalists, geographers, economists, archaeologists and others have contributed to the eleven volumes of *Australians: A Historical Library*, Sydney, 1987–88. Four volumes slice into the past by taking the years 1788, 1838, 1888 and 1938 and the fifth of that segment deals with the period from 1939. The other segments comprise *A Historical Atlas*, *A Historical Dictionary*, *Events and Places*, *Historical Statistics*, and *A Guide to Sources*. The eleventh volume will be a guide and index to the whole work. Together with the authors and editors, the publishers, Fairfax Syme & Weldon Associates, deserve recognition for the production of a set of volumes which are a monument to the publishing profession and a delight to hand and eye in their use. The volume, *Australians: A Historical Atlas*, Sydney, 1987, edited by J.C.R. Camm and John McQuilton, deserves the accolade 'noble' although it is far removed from the conventional in its contents. It needs to be supple-mented by a more pedestrian publication such as *The Reader's Digest Complete Atlas of Australia* and for an examination of the early period a useful work is E.H. and G.E. Feeken and O.H.K. Spate, *The Discovery and Exploration of Australia*, Melbourne, 1970 as well as the valuable excerpts from the explorers' journals in Kathleen Fitzpatrick, *Australian Explorers*, London, 1958.

Manning Clark's *A History of Australia*, commenced publication by Melbourne University Press in 1962 and the sixth and final volume was published in 1987. His *History* is immense in its scope and vital in its language and its completion marks the maturity of Australian historical writing. Clark's two volumes of *Select Documents*, Sydney, 1950, 1955 and his *Sources of Australian History*, London, 1957 stand with F.K. Crowley's five volumes, *A Documentary History of Australia*, three volumes, Melbourne, 1980, and *Modern Australia in Documents*, two volumes, Melbourne, 1973, and the three volumes by Russel Ward and John Robertson, *Such Was Life: Select Documents in Australian Social History*, Sydney, 1969, 1980, 1986 as sources for students of the periods covered and of interest to those who want to develop their knowledge and familiarity with the past. Another useful and constantly readable source is Stephen Murray-Smith (ed.) *The Dictionary of Australian Quotations*, Richmond, 1984.

The *Australian Enyclopaedia*, Sydney, two volumes, 1925; ten volumes, 1958; six volumes, 1977 has been a massive undertaking in each of its three editions and all other work on Australian history and biography owes it a debt. Given the complexity and vast range of subjects, reserve is advisable on some entries, but, generally, the standard and reliabilty of each entry is high. On the nine-teenth century the first edition remains a singularly valuable work, and it treats in detail some subjects which later editions tended to underplay. Brian Murphy, *Dictionary of Australian History*, Sydney, 1982 and Jan Bassett, *The Concise Oxford Dictionary of Australian History*, Melbourne, 1986 put little treas-ures into the hands of students, writers and general readers while the volume in the *Australians* series entitled *Events and Places*, Sydney, 1987, and *Collins*

Milestones in Australian History: 1788 to the Present, Sydney, 1986 have done the same in greater detail. Macquarie University continues to delight and educate a wide readership with *The Macquarie Dictionary*, Sydney, 1981 and in 1988 under the authorship of the Australian National University and the editorship of W.S. Ramson, Oxford University Press, Australia will publish *The Australian National Dictionary: A Dictionary of Australianisms on Historical Principles*. Upon its publication, Australians, and others, will no longer have to puzzle over the meaning, derivation and first usage of the language they have created since 1788.

The general histories of Australia are too numerous to mention individually and those referred to in the text of this work will not be listed. In the 1950s it seems that only professors of history had the courage to undertake the task, and works by A.G.L. Shaw, *The Story of Australia*, London, 1955, R.M. Crawford, *Australia*, London, 1955 and Gordon Greenwood, (ed.) *Australia: A Social and Political History*, Sydney, 1955 appeared. Because the latter was written by a group of younger historians who were experts in their respective fields it stood the test of time as a valuable teaching aid until the publication of a work edited by Frank Crowley, *A New History of Australia*, Melbourne, 1974 which was also a composite work written by twelve authors and contained an excellent bibliography. The 1960s produced a splendid understatement, devoid of all flamboyance, by the first great editor of the *Australian Dictionary of Biography*, Douglas Pike, who fittingly entitled his work *Australia: The Quiet Continent*, Cambridge, 1962, as if to imply that nothing much had happened here. In that decade F. Alexander's 'narrative and critical analysis' of the twentieth century, *Australia Since Federation*, Melbourne, 1966 also appeared. At the same time, Donald Horne published *The Lucky Country*, Melbourne, 1964 and the title was used in diverse ways in both good and bad times afterwards.

In the 1970s the industry began to boom and many histories were published amongst which the following deserve recognition: John Ritchie, *Australia as once we were*, Melbourne, 1975 with many excellent and original illustrations; S. Mellor, (ed.), *Australian History The Occupation of a Continent*, Melbourne, 1978; H. McQueen, *Social Sketches of Australia, 1888–1975*, Ringwood, 1975 which broke new gound in social history; W.F. Mandle's *Going it Alone*, Ringwood, 1978 was a series of ten vignettes on twentieth century Australia ranging from Gallipoli to Menzies; Russel Ward, *Australia: A Short History*, Sydney, 1979 was revised in 1982 and retitled *Australia Since the Coming of Man*; Gavin Souter, *Lion and Kangaroo: The Initiation of Australia 1901–19*, Sydney, 1976, and M. Cannon, *Australia in the Victorian Age*, volumes 1, 2 and 3, Melbourne, 1971–5. Apart from a spate of heavily illustrated works of varying worth the 1980s have already seen a recent reprint of Russel Ward's excellent *A Nation for a Continent: The History of Australia, 1901–1975*, Richmond, 1985 as well as his *Finding Australia: the History of Australia to 1821*, Richmond, 1987; the two volumes edited by Tim Gurry, *The European Occupation* and *An Emerging Identity*, Richmond, 1981. Geoffrey Blainey's *A Land Half Won*, Melbourne, 1980 is studded with the insights the author has displayed in his other publications and Stuart McIntyre with *The Succeeding Age*, Melbourne, 1986, which deals with Australia 1901–42, has given us the first volume so far published of *The Oxford History of Australia* and has received much acclaim. For a detailed analysis of one decade see Frank Crowley, *Tough Times: Australia in the Seventies*, Richmond, 1986 and to complement it Robert Pullan (ed.), *The Way We Are — A National Portrait* by the National Times, Sydney, 1985.

Works on particular colonies and states abound. The thirty-three volumes of *Historical Records of Australia* stand alongside the eight books of the *Historical Records of New South Wales*, all of which were published between 1892 and 1925, as a mine of information on Australia before 1850. Two early accounts of New South Wales are David Collins, *An Account of the English Colony in New South Wales*, two volumes, London, 1798, reprinted Adelaide, 1971 and W. Tench, *A Complete Account of the Settlement at Port Jackson*, London, 1793 and reprinted, L.F. Fitzhardinge (ed.), as *Sydney's First Four Years*, Sydney, 1961. Since then there have been the five excellent volumes by J. Cobley, *Sydney Cove*, London, 1962 and Sydney, 1963–86, which deal with the years of settlement from 1788 to 1800. Other works worth reading are Allan Frost, *Arthur Phillip*, Melbourne, 1987 and H.V. Evatt, *Rum Rebellion*, Sydney, 1938 and reprinted Sydney, 1980. For the early legal system see C.H. Currey, *The Brothers Bent*, Sydney, 1968 and John Molony, *An Architect of Freedom: John Hubert Plunkett in New South Wales 1832–1869*, Canberra, 1973 and for a splendid study of the legal and constitutional system A.C.V. Melbourne, *Early Constitutional Development in Australia*, second edition, St Lucia, 1963.

Apart from many early works, much has been written more recently on Victoria beginning with G. Serle, *The Rush to be Rich*, Melbourne, 1971 and followed by several works in 1984, the sesquicentenary year of the settlement of the state, during which a three volume series of an 'official' history called *The Victorians* was published. The volumes were Richard Broome, *Arriving*; Tony Dingle, *Settling*, and Susan Priestley, *Making Their Mark*, all published Melbourne, 1984. In that same year Geoffrey Blainey published *Our Side of the Country* and Donald Garden, *Victoria: A History*, Melbourne, 1984. Michael Cannon (ed.) commenced the multi-volume *Historical Records of Victoria*, Melbourne, in 1981 of which three volumes have so far appeared. The best modern work on Tasmania is Lloyd Robson, *A Short History of Tasmania*, Melbourne, 1985 but John West's two volume work, *The History of Tasmania*, Launceston, 1852, still stands as a monument to a great pioneer. South Australia now has its own sesquicentenary history series, Eric Richards (ed.), *Flinders History of South Australia*, three volumes, Cowandilla, 1986 as well as the monumental work of Douglas Pike, *Paradise of Dissent*, Melbourne, 1957. Queensland has Ross Fitzgerald, *A History of Queensland From the Dreaming to 1915*, and *From 1915 to the Early 1980s*, St Lucia, 1982, 1984. F.K. Crowley, *Australia's Western Third*, Melbourne, 1960 stands well with C.T. Stannage (ed.) *A New History of Western Australia*, Nedlands, 1981 for the West of the continent, although the pioneering work which remains valuable is J.S. Battye, *Western Australia*, Oxford, 1924. J.H. Kelly, *Struggle for the North*, Sydney, 1966 is now joined by Alan Powell, *Far Country*, Melbourne, 1982, for the history of the Northern Territory. For those interested in the history of Papua New Guinea there is no better reference than the article and critical bibliography in the chapter by Hank Nelson, 'Looking North' in G. Osborne and W.F. Mandle, *New History*, Sydney, 1982.

So far no general account of the Aboriginal people has been written by an Aborigine so that accounts written by whites have to suffice. Since the 1970s there has been a conscious attempt by historians, prehistorians, archaeologists and anthropologists to redress the 'Great Australian Silence' that ignored the existence of the Aborigines. The list of works is now far too long for other than selective mention. The most influential work was the trilogy by C.D. Rowley, *Aboriginal Policy and Practice*, of which the first volume, *The Destruction of Aboriginal Society*, Canberra, 1970 was the most important and dealt a severe blow to the heroic, pioneering myth. Rowley's last work was again full of a moral theme — *Recovery. The Politics of Aboriginal Reform*, Ringwood, 1986. D.J. Mulvaney led the field in prehistory with *The Prehistory of Australia*, Melbourne, 1969 and the most recent and best of all work is D.J. Mulvaney and J. Peter White, *Australians to 1788*, Sydney, 1987. Others since Rowley which deserve reading are G. Blainey, *The Triumph of the Nomads*, South Melbourne, 1975; Peter Biskup, *Not Slaves Not Citizens*, Brisbane, 1973; Josephine Flood, *The Moth Hunters: Aboriginal Prehistory of the Australian Alps*, Canberra, 1980; and by the same author *Archaeology of the Dreamtime*, Sydney, 1983; L. Ryan, *The Aboriginal Tasmanians*, St Lucia, 1981; Henry Reynolds, *The Other Side of the Frontier*, Ringwood, 1982; R. Broome, *Aboriginal Australians*, Sydney, 1982, and R.H.W. Reece, *Aborigines and Colonists*, Sydney, 1974 while Keith Willey's *When the Sky Fell Down*, Sydney, 1975 details the destruction of the Aboriginal people in the Sydney region. A full bibliography and critical essay on writings on the Aborigines is Peter Biskup's chapter 'Aboriginal History' in Osborne and Mandle, *New History*.

The other segment of Australian society whose historical role was rarely mentioned are women. Starting in the 1970s with Anne Summers, *Damned Whores and God's Police*, Ringwood, 1975; Beverley Kingston, *My Wife, My Daughter and Poor Mary Ann*, Melbourne, 1975; Edna Ryan and Anne Conlan, *Gentle Invaders: Australia's Women at Work*, Melbourne, 1975; Miriam Dixson, *The Real Matilda*, revised edition, Ringwood, 1984, followed by Ruth Teale, (ed.), *Colonial Eve: Sources on Women in Australia, 1788–1914*, Melbourne, 1978 and in the 1980s the output became impressive. Some titles are Kay Daniels and Mary Murnane, *Uphill all the Way. A Documentary History of Women in Australia*, St Lucia, 1980; Jill Matthews, *Good and Mad Women: The Historical Construction of Femininity in Twentieth-Century Australia*, Sydney, 1984; and K.M. Reiger, *The Disenchantment of the Home: Modernizing the Australian Family, 1880–1940*, Melbourne, 1985. For an enchanting insight into the lives of a few colonial women, there are no better sources than Lucy Frost's *No Place For a Nervous Lady*, Fitzroy, 1984 and Eve Pownall, *Mary of Maranoa, Tales of Australian Pioneer Women*, Melbourne, 1959.

One set of Australians who have received treatment proportionate to their importance are the convicts who, together with the reasons for the original settlement, figure prominently in our historical research and writing. Writers on the reasons for settlement have tended to bore both themselves and their readers; and the whole argument as to why the British decided on Botany Bay is summed up in Ged Martin, *The Founding of Australia*, Sydney, 1978. Two other titles are worth reading and one of them, Geoffrey Blainey, *The Tyranny of Distance*, South Melbourne, 1966, gave a phrase to Australian English. The other is K.M. Dallas, *Trading Posts or Penal Colonies*, Hobart, 1969. On the convicts A.G.L. Shaw, *Convicts and the Colonies*, London, 1966 remains an important book still as do C. Bateson, *The Convict Ships, 1788–1868*, Glasgow, 1959 and L.L. Robson, *The Convicts Settler of Australia*, Melbourne, 1965. Since J.B. Hirst's important contribution, *Convict Society and Its Enemies. A History of Early New South Wales*, Sydney, 1983, we have had the publication of Robert Hughes, *The Fatal Shore*, London, 1987. Notwithstanding some of the criticism levelled at it for a lack of originality and a concentration on the worst aspects of the penal period, Hughes's work has to be recognized as the single most important contribution to our knowledge of the convict days so far published. It is a veritable *tour de force*, sweeping in its themes, startling in its language and thorough in its research.

Because all white Australians were immigrants or the descendents of immigrants, whether free or in bondage, this great phenomenon, which has shaped our history from the earliest years, tended to be taken for granted. The new wave of immigration since World War II and the development of sociology as a discipline in the universities have combined to cause a good deal of study and writing on immigration and such related matters as racism. Geoffrey Sherington, *Australia's Immigrants 1788–1978*, Sydney, 1980, as well as being useful itself, contains a full bibliography of works published before 1980 and Andrew Markus has made an important contribution with his analysis of the field in Osborne and Mandle, *New History*. Amongst early works were R.B. Madgwick, *Immigration into Eastern Australia*, London, 1937; M. Kiddle, *Caroline Chisholm*, Melbourne, 1957; C.A. Price, *Southern Europeans in Australia*, Melbourne, 1963; J. Zubrzycki, *Settlers of the La Trobe Valley*, Canberra, 1964; James Jupp, *Arrivals and Departures*, Melbourne, 1966; R.T. Appleyard, *British Emigration to Australia*, Canberra, 1964; and A.T. Yarwood, *Asian Migration to Australia*, Melbourne, 1964. Three most important works by the sociologist, Jean Martin, are *Refugee Settlers*, Canberra, 1965, *Community and Identity*, Canberra, 1972 and *The Migrant Presence*, Sydney, 1978. For a very readable account of the experience of a small group of Italian immigrants see M. Loh, *With Courage in their Cases*, Melbourne, 1975 and for a gripping story of the voyage of the migrants there is Don Charlwood, *The Long Farewell*, Ringwood, 1981.

War and depression are recurrent themes in history, literature and life and both have received considerable attention, although of the depressions only the Depression of the 1930s has been studied in any detail. The literature on war is vast, especially World War I. Apart from C.E.W. Bean's great work in twelve volumes there is his more usable condensation into one volume, *Anzac to Amiens*, Canberra, 1946. The other best titles are L.L. Robson, *Australia and the Great War*, Melbourne, 1969; L.C. Jauncey, *The Story of Conscription in Australia*, London, 1935 and Melbourne, 1968; F.B. Smith, *The Conscription Plebiscites in Australia, 1916–1917*, Melbourne, 1965; Michael McKernan, *The Australian People and the Great War*, Sydney, 1984; Patsy Adam-Smith, *The Anzacs*, Melbourne, 1978 and the story told from diaries and letters, Bill Gammage, *The Broken Years*, Ringwood, 1975. World War II has been written on more extensively in recent years and one well illustrated story of a single year is Brian McKinlay, *Australia 1942: End of Innocence*, Sydney, 1985. More detailed studies are Michael McKernan, *All In!: Australia during the Second World War*, Melbourne, 1983; John Robertson, *Australia Goes to War 1939–1945*, Sydney, 1984; John Hammond More, *Americans in Australia, 1941–1945*, St Lucia, 1981 and Patsy Adam-Smith, *Australian Women at War*, Melbourne, 1984.

There have been both general and regional studies of the Great Depression. The regional include G.C. Bolton, *A Fine Country to Starve In*, Perth, 1972; L. Richardson, *The Bitter Years: Wollongong During the Great Depression*, Sydney, 1984 and R. Broomhill, *Unemployed Workers: A Social History of the Great Depression in Adelaide*, St Lucia, 1978. More general studies are L.J. Louis and Ian Turner, *The Depression of the 1930s*, Melbourne, 1968; Wendy Lowenstein, *Weevils in the Flour*, Melbourne, 1978; Judy Mackinolty, *The Wasted Years?*, Sydney, 1981 and R. Cooksey, (ed.), *The Great Depression in Australia*, Canberra, 1970. The economics of the Depression are well explored in C.B. Schedvin, *Australia and the Great Depression*, Sydney, 1970 and the best account in literature is George Johnston, *My Brother Jack*, Sydney, 1964 although, because it was such a deeply personal experience, probably some years will pass before the best individual accounts of the Depression will be compiled from diaries and oral history.

Australia and her relations with the wider world are increasingly studied, although the number and quality of the publications is insignificant as compared to social and political history which indicates the long continued reliance of Australians on Britain for the formulation and even implementation of their foreign policies. A. Watt had published *The Evolution of Australian Foreign Policy, 1938–1965*, Cambridge, 1967 and C. Hartley Grattan's *The South West Pacific since 1900*, Ann Arbor, 1963 was another forerunner. In the 1970s and 1980s some impressive studies have come out including T.B. Millar, *Australia in Peace and War: External Relations, 1788 –1977*, Canberra, 1978; W.J. Hudson (ed.), *Australia in World Affairs 1971–75*, Sydney, 1980; and E.M. Andrews, *The Writing on the Wall*, Sydney, 1987 which deals with the years 1931-35. The most useful work done so far is Neville Meaney's *Australia And*

The World: A Documentary History from the 1870s to the 1970s, Melbourne, 1985. It is thorough, scholarly and readable throughout which is a quality not often found in books on such subjects.

Given the role of education in the shaping of Australian society its treatment in monograph form has been sketchy. R. Fogarty, *Catholic Education in Australia 1806–1950*, two volumes, Melbourne, 1959 has remained unsurpassed as also has A. Barcan, *A History of Australian Education*, Melbourne, 1980; J.S. Gregory, *Church and State*, Melbourne, 1973 and G.M. Dow, *George Higinbotham: Church and State*, Melbourne, 1964 have dealt with some aspects of the problem of education in a society in transition. Social welfare has fared better than educa-tion, although few titles are of interest to a general public. Some which deserve listing are K.S. Inglis, *Hospital and Community*, Melbourne, 1958; Bryan Gandevia, *Tears Often Shed*, Sydney, 1978; F.B. Smith, *The People's Health*, London, 1979; Joan C. Brown, *Poverty is not a Crime: The Development of Social Services in Tasmania, 1803–1900*, Hobart, 1972; Brian Dickey, *No Charity There*, Melbourne, 1980; Sue Fabian and Morag Loh, *Children in Australia*, Melbourne, 1980; Richard Kennedy, (ed.), *Australian Welfare History: Critical Essays*, Melbourne, 1982; T.H. Kewley, *Social Security in Australia, 1900–72*, Sydney, 1973 and Jill Roe, (ed.), *Social Policy in Australia; Some Perspectives*, Stanmore, 1975.

Bushrangers have been a social phenomenon whose lives and activities have been extensively worked on in such books as T. Prior, B. Wannon and H. Nunn, *Plundering Sons*, Melbourne, 1966 and Charles White, *History of Australian Bushranging*, two volumes, Melbourne, reprinted 1970. Ned Kelly has a rich and varied bibliography which seems to increase almost annually. Max Brown, the first to publish Ned's 'Jerilderie Letter', wrote a creditable account in *Australian Son: The Story of Ned Kelly*, Melbourne, 1956 while Douglas Stewart's play, *Ned Kelly*, Sydney, 1943 will long stand as a vivid and powerful portrayal of Ned and his mates. Two other works are John Molony, *I am Ned Kelly*, Ringwood, 1980 and John McQuilton, *The Kelly Outbreak*, Melbourne, 1979 which is a thorough study of the Kellys in their geographical setting. The Kellys are also part of the Irish ethos in Australia and two books in particular on the early Irish that deserve mention are Patsy Adam-Smith, *Heart of Exile*, Melbourne, 1986 which deals with the seven exiled patriots of 1848 and Patrick O'Farrell, *The Irish in Australia*, Kensington, 1986.

Australian literature has been well served by the two volumes by H.M. Green, *A History of Australian Literature*, Sydney, 1961 and by Leonie Kramer who edited *The Oxford History of Australian Literature*, Melbourne, 1981, and then, with Adrian Mitchell, *The Oxford Anthology of Australian Literature*, Melbourne, 1984. These were followed by the masterly *The Oxford Companion to Australian Literature*, Melbourne, 1985, edited by William H. Wilde, Joy Hooton and Barry Andrews. *The Oxford Literary Guide to Australia*, Melbourne, 1987, edited by Peter Pierce, reveals the literary connections of many otherwise humble Australian towns and localities. Some female authors have been studied by Drusilla Modjeska in *Exiles at Home: Australian Women Writers, 1925–1945*, Sydney, 1981.

There have been numerous editions of the Australian classics and they are held in every major and municipal library. Details of all Australian publications of merit and otherwise are found in the monumental guide by J.A. Ferguson, *Bibliography of Australia*, seven volumes, Sydney 1941–69. Geoffrey Dutton made a valiant attempt at understanding the nation through its books in *The Australian Collection: Australia's Greatest Books*, Sydney, 1985 ranging from the entrancing *Letters of Rachel Henning* to the ravages by pests imported into Australia in *They All Ran Wild* by Eric Rolls. For a sensitive, well-planned and enriching introduction to literature the reader can turn to Leonie Kramer's selection *My Country: Australian Poetry and Short Stories: Two Hundred Years*, Sydney, 1985.

All aspects of Australian culture, as befits their origins and uncertain development, have received prudent and careful treatment. J.W.C. Cumes, *Their Chastity was not too Rigid*, Melbourne, 1979, is a fine study of the use of leisure in early Australia and there are at least two books worth reading on Australian cooking — Anne Gollan, *The Tradition of Australian Cooking*, Canberra, 1978 and Richard Beckett, *Convicted Tastes: Food In Australia*, Sydney, 1984. Studies on general trends in culture and on authors and their works include A.R. Chisholm, (ed.) *The Poems*, Sydney, 1965 dealing with Neilson; Susan Dermody et al. (eds) *Nellie Melba, Ginger Meggs and Friends: Essays in Australian Cultural History*, Malmsbury, 1982; A.L. McLeod, (ed.) *The Pattern of Australian Culture*, Melbourne, 1963; A.A. Phillips, *The Australian Tradition*, Melbourne, 1958; John Barnes, *The Writer in Australia: A Collection of Literary Documents, 1856 to 1964*, Melbourne, 1969; G. Serle, *From Deserts the Prophets Come. The Creative Spirit in Australia, 1788–1960*, Melbourne, 1973 which has now been revised, well illustrated and entitled *The Creative Spirit in Australia, 1788–1972*, Richmond, 1987 and Peter Spearitt and David Walker, (eds) *Australian Popular Culture*, Sydney, 1979. G. Nadel, *Australia's Colonial Culture*, Melbourne, 1957; David Walker, *Dream and Disillusion: A Search for the Australian Cultural Identity*, Canberra, 1976; Richard White, *Inventing Australia: Images and Identity, 1788–1980*, Sydney, 1981; and John Carroll (ed.), *Intruders in the Bush: The Australian Quest for Identity*, Melbourne, 1982 are of a more critical genre and the latter in particular seeks to destroy the legend so creatively evoked in Russel Ward's classic, *The Australian Legend*, Melbourne, 1976. For an excellent work on the *Bulletin* and its great editor, see Sylvia Lawson, *The Archibald Paradox*, Melbourne, 1983.

High and popular culture of all kinds have their histories and analysts. Bernard Smith has made the most significant contribution to art criticism and art history in his *Australian Painting,1788–1970*; *Taste and Tradition: A Study in Australian Art since 1788*; and *European Vision and the South Pacific, 1768–1850*, Melbourne, 1971, 1945, 1960 respectively. Other valuable works are Robert Hughes, *The Art of Australia*, Melbourne, 1966; R. Haese, *Rebels and Precursors:*

The Revolutionary Years of Australian Art, Ringwood, 1981; Humphrey McQueen, *The Black Swan of Trespass*, Sydney, 1979; Tim Bonyday's delightfully illustrated *The Colonial Image: Australian Painting 1800–1880*, Sydney, 1987 and G. Sturgeon, *Australian Sculpture, 1788–1975*, London, 1978. Architecture in all its forms has been well served. J.M. Freeland wrote *Architecture in Australia*, Melbourne, 1968 as well as *The Australian Pub*, Melbourne, 1966; and Robin Boyd moved from his serious study *Australia's Home: Its Origins, Builders and Occupiers*, Melbourne, 1952 to his critical assessment *The Australian Ugliness*, Melbourne, 1960. See also R.J. Unstead and W.F. Henderson, *Homes in Australia*, London, 1969 and the well-illustrated *Australia's National Trusts' Historic Homes*, new edition, Melbourne, 1982. Leslie Rees, *A History of Australian Drama*, two volumes, Sydney, 1973 and 1978 is the standard history, but there is also Peter Fitzpatrick, *After 'The Doll'. Australian Drama since 1955*, Melbourne, 1979. The film industry is treated by J. Baxter, *The Australian Cinema*, Sydney, 1970, and A. Pike and R. Cooper, *Australian Film 1900–1977*. The press is well served by R.B. Walker, *The Newspaper Press in New South Wales 1803–1920*, Sydney, 1976 and in H. Mayer, *The Press in Australia*, Melbourne, 1968 while Ross Haig has given short and interesting cuttings from the *West Australian* and Perth *Daily News* in *The Years of News*, Perth, 1984 and 1985.

Despite the widespread interest in sport, its history was not deemed an appropriate study for respectable historians until W.F. Mandle began to write of it in the 1970s in both an academic and highly competent way. Since then Richard Cashman and Michael McKernan have edited *Sport in History*, St Lucia, 1979 and *Sport, Money, Morality and Media*, Kensington, 1981 although the field is still generally left to sporting journalists. Since 1968 there have been six editions of the thorough and comprehensive John Blanch (ed.) *Australian Sporting Records*, Sydney, 1968–81. Cricket has fared the best of all sports at the hands of its writers and two books will stand the test of time, A.G. (Johnnie) Moyes, *Bradman*, Sydney, 1948 and R. Hart-Davis, *Cardus on Cricket*, London, 1949, 1977 but Jack Pollard's *Australian Cricket: The Game and the Players*, Sydney, 1982 is a thoroughly comprehensive account. Keith Dunstan's *The Paddock That Grew*, Melbourne, 1974 is an interesting story of the Melbourne Cricket Club and its magnificent ground while the best academic and thoroughly enjoyable work on an individual sport is Richard Stremski's *Kill For Collingwood*, Melbourne, 1986. It is a history of the Australian Rules club based on the suburb of Collingwood and loses nothing by the fact that its author is an American nor that the reader may not share his enthusiasm for the club in question.

Religion, like sport, was left in the hands of its devotees until K.S. Inglis pointed to the gap with a seminal article, 'Catholic Historiography in Australia', *Historical Studies*, volume 8, number 31, 1958, although in 1946 J.G. Murtagh's *Australia: The Catholic Chapter* had been published in New York. Since Inglis wrote his article, there have been many published works, mostly by academic historians and often in the form of a doctoral or master's thesis redone for publication, which has not made them attractive to the general reader. As a result, the history of religion continues to be a field of which the vast majority of Australians remain in undisturbed ignorance, despite its influence on the shaping of their society. Most of the early work was done under the guidance of Manning Clark at the Australian National University and the 1960s saw four books come from there: M. Roe, *Quest for Authority in Eastern Australia, 1833–1851*, Melbourne 1965; T.L. Suttor, *Hierarchy and Democracy in Australia 1788–1870*, Melbourne 1965; John Barrett, *That Better Country: The Religious Aspect of Life in Eastern Australia, 1835–1850*, Melbourne, 1966 and J.N. Molony, *The Roman Mould of the Australian Catholic Church*, Melbourne, 1969. In that same decade the foremost historian of the Catholic Church and of the Irish in Australia, P.J. O'Farrell began his work with *The Catholic Church in Australia: A Short History: 1788–1967*, Melbourne, 1968. His *The Catholic Church and Community* came out in a revised edition in 1985 but previously he had published *Documents in Australian Catholic History*, two volumes, London, 1969.

Other denominations and Protestant Christianity in general were studied in J.D. Bollen, *Protestantism and Social Reform in New South Wales, 1890–1910*, Melbourne, 1972; Richard Broome, *Treasure in Earthern Vessels: Protestant Christianity in New South Wales, 1900–1914*, St Lucia, 1980 and W. Phillips, *Defending a Christian Country: Churchmen and Society in New South Wales in the 1880s and after*, St Lucia, 1981. There have been very few biographies of Australian churchmen and, so far, no one has written anything of lasting value on Daniel Mannix, despite several attempts. The exception in biography is D.W.A. Baker's *Days of Wrath: A Life of John Dunmore Lang*, Melbourne, 1985 which gives a rare insight into the complex and turbulent character of a man whose whole life helped shaped the history of white Australia and also makes the times in which he lived intelligible. Sociological studies of religion in Australia are rare but Hans Mol's *The Faith of Australians*, Sydney, 1985 is a valuable attempt to argue the case that the Christian religion has been fundamental to our history.

Politics and political economy have generated an immense literature, perhaps indicating the extent to which Australians generally leave to others the control of their destiny and a mere list of the works written on political movements, trades unions, political parties and personalities would themselves fill a volume. Out of that vast morass, some important works have emerged and, whether because of the role of the labour movement in Australian history or the flamboyance of some of its characters, writings on it have led the field. William Spence's *Australia's Awakening*, Sydney, 1909 was an early study of the trade union movement as was L. Ross, *Trade Unions in Australia*, Sydney, 1959. Ian Turner, *In Union is Strength*, Melbourne, 1978 was quickly followed by Jim Hagan's thorough *The History of the A.C.T.U.*, Melbourne, 1981 and then by John Merritt's *The Making of the A.W.U.*, Melbourne, 1986 which is the best study so far of an individual union. Other works are A. Davidson, *The Communist Party of Australia*, Stanford, 1969; Frank

Farrell, *International Socialism and Australian Labour*, Sydney, 1981 and Bill Ford and David Plowman, *Australian Unions*, Melbourne, 1983. For a full bibliography and an enlightened judgement of the field, the reader can turn to John Merritt's chapter 'Labour History' in Osborne & Mandle, *New History*.

Political biographies relieve the general tedium of writings on politics and from them most of the material that is contained on both government and politics can be gleaned by an interested reader. The best are L.F. Fitzhardinge, *William Morris Hughes*, two volumes, Sydney 1964 and 1979; L.F. Crisp, *Ben Chifley*, Sydney, 1961; J.A. La Nauze, *Alfred Deakin*, two volumes, Melbourne, 1965; Bede Nairn, *The 'Big Fella' Jack Lang and the Australian Labor Party 1891–1949*, Melbourne, 1986; A.W. Martin, *Henry Parkes*, Melbourne, 1980; Cecil Edwards, *Bruce of Melbourne: Man of Two Worlds*, London, 1965 and John Robertson, *J.H. Scullin*, Nedlands, 1974. Gough Whitlam wrote *The Whitlam Government*, Melbourne, 1985, but no one has yet managed to tackle successfully his most eminent predecessor since World War II, R.G. Menzies, whose personal accounts of his stewardship pass without comment. The best of recent biographies deals with the first great autocrat in Australian history and for its economy, language and judgement it is outstanding — John Ritchie, *Lachlan Macquarie: A Biography*, Melbourne, 1986.

Other useful studies on politics and government are L.F. Crisp, *Australian National Government*, Melbourne, 1965 which is a general and careful study while Bede Nairn's *Civilising Capitalism*, Canberra, 1973 is the best account of the early Labor movement and Party in New South Wales and R.A. Gollan's *Radical and Working Class Politics: A Study of Eastern Australia, 1850–1910*, Melbourne, 1963, remains a milestone as an analysis of the forces that shaped organized Labor. Others of merit are T.R. Reece, *Australia in the Twentieth Century: A Political History*, Melbourne, 1964; P. Loveday et al. (eds) *The Emergence of the Australian Party System*, Sydney, 1977; Tim Rouse, *Australian Liberalism and National Character*, Malmsbury, 1978; and C. Hazlehurst (ed.) *Australian Conservatism: Essays on Twentieth Century Political History*, Canberra, 1979.

Studies on the Australian economy are also abundant and selectivity remains problematic. Brian Fitzpatrick's works, for their clarity and incisiveness, remain valuable — *British Imperialism and Australia 1783–1833*, London, 1939 and *The British Empire in Australia*, Melbourne, 1941. T.A. Coghlan's *Labor and Industry in Australia*, four volumes, London, 1918 is still a useful reference on the colonial period while the years up to the end of Macquarie's reign are done in G.J. Abbott and N.B. Nairn, *Economic Growth of Australia, 1788–1821*, Melbourne, 1969. Other detailed studies are S.J. Butlin, *Foundations of the Australian Monetary System, 1788–1851*, Melbourne, 1953 and N.G. Butlin, *Australian Domestic Product, Investment and Foreign Borrowing, 1861–1938/9*, Cambridge, 1962 and *Investment in Australian Economic Development, 1861–1900*, Cambridge, 1964 by the same author. Other, general works are W.A. Sinclair, *The Process of Economic Development in Australia*, Melbourne, 1976; A.G.L. Shaw, *Economic Development of Australia*, Melbourne, 1966; C. Forster, (ed.), *Australian*

Economic Development in the Twentieth Century, Sydney, 1970 and E. Shann, *An Economic History of Australia*, Cambridge, 1930 and Melbourne, 1948, 1963.

The pastoral industry, agriculture and mining have their copious histories. C.E.W. Bean's *On the Wool Track*, Sydney, 1945 and S.H. Roberts's two works *History of Australian Land Settlement 1788–1920*, Melbourne, 1924 and 1968 and *The Squatting Age in Australia, 1835–1847*, Melbourne, 1935 and 1964 are still outstanding. Two works on colonial Australia which put the economy in a social setting are David Denholm, *The Colonial Australians*, Ringwood, 1979 and K.S. Inglis *The Australian Colonists*, Melbourne, 1974. The best study of the links between the parent economy and colonial development, including an analysis of Wakefield's influence, is P. Burrough's *Britain and Australia, 1831–1855*, Oxford, 1976 while a revisionist study of the predominant role of the Macarthur family is J.C. Garran and L. White, *Merinos, Myths and Macarthurs; Australian Graziers and Their Sheep, 1788–1900*, Canberra, 1985. S.M. Wadham, *Australian Farming, 1788–1965*, Melbourne, 1967; Frances Wheelhouse, *Digging Stick to Rotary Hoe*, Melbourne, 1966; J.M. Powell, *The Public Lands of Australia Felix*, Melbourne, 1970, and Robin Bromby, *The Farming of Australia*, Sydney, 1986 are all valuable and the latter is illustrated profusely with wonderful photographs. Two accounts by squatters themselves are still worth reading — W.A. Brodribb, *Recollections of an Australian Squatter*, Sydney, 1883 and E.M. Curr, *Recollections of Squatting in Victoria*, Melbourne, 1883. For an excellent account of how Australians have shaped the land there is Geoffrey Bolton, *Spoils and Spoilers: Australians make their environment 1788–1980*, Sydney, 1981. Another work of particular value to the novice in geography is R.L. Heathcote, *Australia*, Essex, 1975 which also deals well with the environment.

Mining generally and the golden years are splendidly done by G. Blainey, *The Rush that Never Ended: A History of Australian Mining*, Melbourne, 1963 and G. Serle, *The Golden Age: A History of the Colony of Victoria, 1851–1861*, Melbourne, 1963. Weston Bate's *Lucky City. The First Generation at Ballarat, 1851–1901*, Melbourne, 1978 is a remarkable study of the city and its people while on Eureka there is the first-hand account by Raffaello Carboni, *The Eureka Stockade*, Melbourne, 1855 and reprinted frequently since, the composite study in *Historical Studies, Eureka Centenary Supplement*, Melbourne, 1954, revised and enlarged in 1965 and John Molony, *Eureka*, Ringwood, 1984.

In recent years, some attention has been paid to urban life in an attempt to focus more attention on the cities rather than the bush as the centres of Australian civilization. Melbourne has fared better than Sydney and both of them are ahead of other capitals in their treatment so far. General themes are explored in M. Neutze, *Urbanization in Australia*, Sydney, 1977; H. Streeton, *Ideas for Australian Cities*, Adelaide, 1970; J.W. McCarty and C.B. Schedvin (eds) *Australian Capital Cities*, Sydney, 1978; S. Glynn *Urbanization in Australian History, 1788–1900*, Melbourne, 1970; 'Urbanization in Australia', a special issue of *Australian Economic History Review* volume 10, number two, 1970; M. Cannon, *Life in the Cities*, Melbourne, 1975 and R.E.N. Twopeny, *Town Life in Australia*,

London, 1883 and Melbourne, 1976 which deals with life in Sydney, Melbourne and Adelaide in the nineteenth century and has been extensively used by historians since.

For Sydney, see P. Spearritt, *Sydney Since the Twenties*, Sydney, 1978, and A. Birch and D.S. Macmillan, *The Sydney Scene 1788–1960*, Melbourne, 1962. The best work on Melbourne is G. Davison, *The Rise and Fall of Marvellous Melbourne*, Melbourne, 1978 which is complemented by a splendid study of a Melbourne suburb by Janet McCalman, *Struggletown: Public and Private Life in Richmond, 1900–1965*, Melbourne, 1984. Life in Melbourne during the boom of the late 1880s has been well portrayed by M. Cannon in *The Land Boomers*, Melbourne, 1966 while there is a broader treatment in J. Grant and G. Serle, (eds) *The Melbourne Scene, 1803–1956*, Sydney, 1978. For other cities: C.T. Stannage, *The People of Perth*, Perth, 1979; Peter Bolger, *Hobart Town*, 1973; Ronald Lawson, *Brisbane in the 1890's*, St Lucia, 1973, the last chapter of which is a pointless attack on Ward's *Legend*. Michael Williams *The Making of the South Australian Landscape*, London, 1974 deals in part with Adelaide as does J.B. Hirst, *Adelaide and the Country: 1870–1917*, Melbourne, 1973.

An abundance of regional and country town histories exist but many of them are of uneven quality, although all give an insight into the times they treat. The most outstanding are M. Kiddle, *Men of Yesterday; A Social History of the Western District of Victoria, 1834–1890*, Melbourne, 1961; D.B. Waterson, *Squatter, Selector and Storekeeper: The Darling Downs 1859–1893*, Sydney, 1968; G.L. Buxton, *The Riverina 1861–1891: An Australian Regional Study*, Melbourne, 1967; W.K. Hancock, *Discovering Monaro*, Cambridge, 1972 and Bill Gammage, *Narrandera Shire*, Narrandera, 1986. Further on rural environment there are D.W. Meinig, *On the Margins of the Good Earth: the South Australian Wheat Frontier 1869–1884*, Adelaide, 1962 and J.M. Powell and M. Williams, *Australian Space, Australian Time*, Melbourne, 1975.

Anyone who enters a bookshop in Australia today will be struck by the quantity of new material, a great deal of it of high standard, being written and published almost weekly. The academic historians have been joined by writers from the general public to the benefit of both and it is likely that the forth-coming Bicentenary will augment the flow of books. More and more Australians will come to know something of the history of their own country and its people and from that knowledge they will derive both wisdom and hope.

Pictorial Acknowledgements

The author and publisher wish to express their gratitude to the librarians, archivists and private individuals who gave permission for the reproduction of works from their collections. Special thanks go to James Gibbney for his efforts in carrying out the picture research for this book and to the staff of the National Library of Australia which provided so many of the illustrations. Individual sources are listed together with the numbers of pages upon which works from each collection appear. An asterisk accompanying a page number refers the reader to the additional details of art works given in the second part of these acknowledgements.

Australian War Memorial 223*; 284*; 286*; 336*
Herald & Weekly Times 367
La Trobe Collection, State Library of Victoria 288
Mitchell Library, State Library of New South Wales 12*
Museum of Applied Arts and Sciences 57*
National Film and Sound Archive 30; 252
National Library of Australia 4; 8*; 15; 18; 23*; 34*; 36*; 43*; 46*; 49*; 55; 62*; 66*; 70; 74*; 78*; 81*; 85*; 89; 91*; 95; 98; 102*; 106*; 111; 115*; 127; 129; 137; 142; 148; 152; 154; 161; 164; 167; 169; 173; 176; 181; 184; 186; 188; 192; 195; 198; 201; 205; 210; 213; 215; 221; 227; 229; 233; 245; 246; 250; 254; 259; 267; 273; 278; 280; 291; 296; 301; 307; 314; 318; 325; 326; 333; 340; 344; 347; 351; 357; 362; 372; 378; 383; 386
New South Wales Parliamentary Archives 117*
Tattersall's Club, Sydney 266
University of Melbourne Archives 240; 261; 322

NLA, p. 8, Sherwin, W. *engraver*, Wheatley, F. *artist*, Arthur Phillip Esq. Captain general and Commander in Chief in and over the Territory of New South Wales, 1789, copper engraving: 23 × 14 cm: NK 3799, in *The*

Voyage of Governor Phillip to Botany Bay . . ., in the Rex Nan Kivell Collection.

NLA and Mitchell, p. 12, William Bradley, Sydney Cove, Port Jackson, 1788, reproduced from his *A Voyage to New South Wales Sydney*, Trustees of the Public Library of New South Wales, 1969, original MS in the Mitchell Library.

NLA, p. 23, Dayes, Edward *artist*, 1763–1804, Jukes, Francis *engraver*, 1746–1812, A view of Sydney Cove, New South Wales (from a drawing after Thomas Watling), hand-coloured aquatint: 44 × 62 cm: NK 270, in the Rex Nan Kivell Collection.

NLA, pp. 34, 36, Dennis Dogherty *convict*, Thomas Kelly *convict*, carte de visite, in T.J. Nevin Collection.

NLA, p. 43, Evans, George William, 1778–1852, This south-west view of Hobart Town, Van Dieman's [sic] Land . . . 1820, hand-coloured aquatint: 36 × 55 cm: NK 4867, in the Rex Nan Kivell Collection.

NLA, p. 46, Wilson, William Hardy, 1881–1955, Old Government House, Parramatta, N.S.W., pencil drawing: 46 × 36 cm.

NLA, p. 49, Wilson, William Hardy, 1881–1955, St Matthew's Church, Windsor, N.S.W., 1919, pencil and French crayon drawing: 30 × 40 cm.

Mus. Arts and Sciences, p. 57, long case clock, 1882, cedar case, pine stringing: silvered brass dial, James Oatley, Sydney, height 259 cm, width 55.9 cm, depth 16 cm, purchased 1957.

NLA, p. 62, Bickley, Wallace, View of Fremantle, Western Australia, from the Canning Road, 1832, hand-coloured aquatint: 16.5 × 27.9 cm: NK 10354, in the Rex Nan Kivell Collection.

NLA, p. 66, Angas, George French, 1822–86, Bethany, a village of German settlers at the foot of the Barossa hills [1846], hand-coloured lithograph: 24.2 × 34 cm: NK 54/60, in his *South Australia Illustrated*, in the Rex Nan Kivell Collection.

NLA, p. 74, Mackie, Frederic, Port Arthur, Tasman's Peninsula, V.D.L. [c.1849], planographic print: 12 × 20 cm: NK 2092/10, in his *Sketches in the Australian Colonies, Van Diemen's Land, New Zealand and South Africa, 1849–56*, in the Rex Nan Kivell Collection.

NLA, p. 78, Carmichael, John, 1791–1869, Sydney from Woolloomooloo Hill, copper engraving: 14.7 × 22.7 cm, in his *Select views of Sydney, New South Wales*.

NLA, p. 81, Royston and Brown lithographers, Malahide, Van Dieman's [sic] Land, sepia lithograph: 28 × 41 cm: NK 426, in the Rex Nan Kivell Collection.

NLA, p. 85, Staniland, C.J., Emigrants going to Australia [c.1850], hand-coloured wood engraving: 31.5 × 46 cm.

NLA, p. 91, Angas, George French, 1822–86, The Kapunda copper mine, hand-coloured lithograph: 21.5 × 32.4 cm, in his *South Australia Illustrated*: NK 4742, in the Rex Nan Kivell Collection.

NLA, p. 102, Gill, Samuel Thomas, 1818–80, Rundle Street looking east, lithograph: 14.1 × 22.3 cm: NK 3544/c, from *Views in Adelaide*, in the Rex Nan Kivell Collection.

NLA, p. 106, Gill, Samuel Thomas, 1818–80, Diggers licensing — Forrest [sic] Creek 1852, coloured litograph: 16 × 21 cm: NK 586/14, in his *Victoria: gold diggings and diggers as they are*, in the Rex Nan Kivell Collection.

NLA, p. 115, Gill, Samuel Thomas 1818–80, Port Adelaide [South Australia, 1845], wash drawing: 12 × 20 cm.

NSW Parl. Arch., p. 117, Legislative Council 1, Proceedings in the Committee of the Whole — Constitution Bill, Session 1853, Part 1: Chairman's Copy of the Bill, p. 4 (LC Box CA 26).

Reference numbers for works in the Australian War Memorial are: p. 223: G392; p. 284: 127971; p. 286: 9509; p. 336: 70/26/VN.

Index

Numbers in *italics* refer to illustrations.